Stocks, Bonds, Bills,
and Inflation

SBBI

Valuation Edition
2003 Yearbook

IbbotsonAssociates

Stocks, Bonds, Bills, and Inflation® Valuation Edition 2003 Yearbook.

Stocks, Bonds, Bills, and Inflation® and SBBI® are registered trademarks of Ibbotson Associates.

Published by:

Ibbotson Associates
225 North Michigan Avenue, Suite 700
Chicago, Illinois 60601-7676
Telephone (312) 616-1620
Fax (312) 616-0404
www.ibbotson.com

ISBN 1-882864-17-4
ISSN 1523-343X

Additional copies of this Yearbook may be obtained for $110, plus shipping and handling, by calling or writing to the address above. Additional product information can be found at the end of this publication or at our Cost of Capital Center, http://valuation.ibbotson.com. Order forms are provided inside the back cover. Information about volume discounts, companion publication and consulting services may also be obtained.

Table of Contents

Chapters

List of Tables

List of Graphs

Acknowledgements

As anyone who has ever written a book knows, it takes the input of a lot of people to produce. This publication was no exception. In this book, we have tried to build from the previous work in the *Stocks, Bonds, Bills, and Inflation (SBBI) Yearbook* series produced by Ibbotson Associates for over 25 years.

The *SBBI Yearbook* is based on the original work of Roger Ibbotson and Rex Sinquefield, but many others have contributed to the evolution of that book over the years. Most relevant to the *Valuation Edition* are the contributions of Paul Kaplan and Michael Mattson, who wrote portions of the original SBBI that have been carried forward to the *Valuation Edition*.

Michael Annin and Dominic Falaschetti were the primary authors of the original *Valuation Edition* published in 1999. Each year since then the *Valuation Edition* has been updated and improved upon thanks to the contributions of many. Michael Barad of Ibbotson Associates authored the chapter on business valuation and contributed to the chapter on size premium. Roger Ibbotson of Ibbotson Associates and Paul Kaplan, formerly of Ibbotson Associates, also provided valuable insights.

Listed below are some of the Ibbotson Associates personnel that played a significant role in the timely completion of this publication. Many others within Ibbotson Associates provided valuable feedback or other contributions that helped in the formulation of this product.

Senior Editor

Michael Barad

Contributing Editors/Production

Tara McDowell, Contributing Editor
James Licato, Contributing Editor
Devoki Dasgupta, Contributing Editor
Anne Jablo, Contributing Editor
Edward Lopez, Contributing Editor
Scott Moore, Design Manager
Jim Hampton, Graphic Design

Introduction

Ibbotson Associates, established by Professor Roger Ibbotson in 1977, offers consulting and training services, software, data, and presentation materials to the investment and business community. In 1976, Professor Ibbotson co-published a seminal study analyzing the long-term returns of the principal asset classes in the U.S. economy. His findings documented the relationship between risk and return and quantified the ability to reduce risk through diversification. These concepts were expanded upon through the work of Ibbotson Associates, which helped develop the modern science of asset allocation by building on the work of Nobel Prize-winning economists William F. Sharpe and Harry Markowitz.

The study of long-term returns on asset classes also led to the development of such relevant cost of capital concepts as the equity risk premium and the size premium. The original 1976 study was extended into Stocks, Bonds, Bills, and Inflation (SBBI), which has been revised and updated annually for over 25 years. SBBI has become a standard reference publication in both the investment and business valuation communities. As the field of finance has progressed, the demands have also increased for SBBI to serve a diverse audience.

In an effort to better serve the different markets for SBBI, we decided to produce a separate version of the publication targeted to people involved in the valuation of businesses. This will allow us to provide a greater variety of information relative to those individuals and companies involved in business valuation.

The model for creating a new version of SBBI came primarily from our workshops. Over the course of a year, we receive literally hundreds of inquiries regarding how to use the data and statistics we provide in our publications. In an effort to address these questions, we developed a series of workshops on the cost of capital.

The success of these topic-specific workshops led us to modify the existing SBBI to a more refined target market. In this sense, we have come full circle—the publications led to the formation of a workshop, which in turn led to the development of a new publication. We do not expect the evolutionary process to stop. In fact, we view this newest version of SBBI as a work in progress that will address new and different topics as they arise in the field of business valuation.

We have selected for this book topics that we feel are relevant for people performing discounted cash flow analysis. Wherever possible, we support our conclusions with real data and provide examples for clarification. It is our hope that our readers will continue to drive the content of this book. For example, there have been many requests from our readers to provide more details on the industry premium calculations we present. This led to the creation of the *Industry Premia Company List Report* available to all purchasers of the *Yearbook*. While we will always devote some space to industry premium issues, there will undoubtedly be other issues regarding business valuation and cost of capital analysis that will arise in the future and demand our attention. It is our intention that this publication will address those issues in a timely and informative fashion.

If you have issues that you would like to address, please contact us at the address listed in the front of this book.

Recent Changes and Additions

Now in its fifth year of production, the *Valuation Edition* has had a strong impact in the world of business valuation. To build upon this success, we have improved this year's book in many ways to help add value as a resource to valuation professionals.

Since Ibbotson first started publishing industry risk premia for use in the buildup model, we have been making advances each year in response to client needs. The *2000 Yearbook* first presented industry premia for more than 60 industries. The *2001 Yearbook* presented premia on more than 300 industries as we expanded coverage. As usage of the industry premia data increased each year, we got more and more requests for additional information on the construction of the data. This year, Ibbotson is excited to offer the *Industry Premia Company List Report* as a supplement to the *2003 Yearbook*. The report provides the list of companies used to construct each industry premium estimate presented in Table 3-5 of this book. Download your copy of the report for free at www.ibbotson.com/irp.

The most popular exhibit in the *Yearbook* is the Key Variables in Estimating the Cost of Capital table printed in Appendix C and again on the inside back cover of the book. This table may be the most frequently referenced source in valuation reports nationwide. This year we have redesigned and reformatted the Key Variables in Estimating the Cost of Capital table to include more size premium data. In the past, only size premia for mid-, low-, and micro-cap companies were presented. The new design presents data for all ten deciles, along with a breakout of the tenth decile into two smaller divisions. While this size premium data and methodology has and will continue to reside in the Firm Size and Return chapter of the *Valuation Edition*, our hope is that a reformatted Key Variables table will put the most relevant cost of capital data in one spot for easy reference.

As always, we appreciate any feedback our readers provide regarding the contents of this book or any of our other products.

References

1. Amihud, Yakov, and Haim Mendelson

   "Asset Pricing and the Bid-Ask Spread,"

   Journal of Financial Economics, Vol. 17, 1986, pp. 223–249.

2. Banz, Rolf W.

   "The Relationship Between Return and Market Value of Common Stocks,"

   Journal of Financial Economics, Vol. 9, 1981, pp. 3–18.

3. Black, Fischer

   "Beta and Return,"

   Journal of Portfolio Management, Fall 1993, pp. 8–18.

4. Blume, M. E.

   "On the Assessment of Risk,"

   Journal of Finance, Vol. 26, 1971, pp. 1–10.

5. Chan, Louis K.C., and Josef Lakonishok

   "Are Reports of Beta's Death Premature?"

   Journal of Portfolio Management, Summer 1993, pp. 51–61.

6. Chen, Nai-fu

   "Some Empirical Tests of Arbitrage Pricing,"

   Journal of Finance, Vol. 18, no. 5, December 1983, pp. 1393–1414.

7. Chen, Nai-fu, Richard Roll, and Stephen A. Ross

   "Economic Forces and the Stock Market: Testing the APT and Alternative Pricing Theories,"

   Journal of Business, Vol. 59, July 1986, pp. 383–403.

8. Clare, Andrew D., and Paul Kaplan

   "A Globally Nested Capital Asset Pricing Model,"

   Ibbotson Associates' Working Paper, July 1998.

9. Clare, Andrew D., and Paul Kaplan

   "A Macroeconomic Model of the Equity Risk Premium,"

   Ibbotson Associates' Working Paper, November 1998.

10. Coleman, Thomas S., Lawrence Fisher, and Roger G. Ibbotson

    U.S. Treasury Yield Curves 1926–1988,

    Moody's Investment Service, New York, 1990.

11. Coleman, Thomas S., Lawrence Fisher, and Roger G. Ibbotson

    Historical U.S. Treasury Yield Curves 1926–1992 with 1994 update,

    Ibbotson Associates, Chicago, 1994.

12. Courdes, Joseph, and Steven Sheffrin

    "Estimating the Tax Advantage of Corporate Debt,"

    Journal of Finance, Vol. 38, 1983, pp. 95–105.

13. Erb, Claude, Campbell R. Harvey, and Tadas Viskanta

    "Country Credit Risk and Global Portfolio Selection,"

    Journal of Portfolio Management, Winter 1995, pp. 74–83.

14. **Fama, Eugene F., and Kenneth French**

    "Industry Costs of Equity,"

    Working Paper 396, University of Chicago, July 1994.

15. **Fama, Eugene F., and Kenneth R. French**

    "Permanent and Temporary Components of Stock Prices,"

    Journal of Political Economy, April 1988, pp. 246–273.

16. **Fama, Eugene F., and Kenneth R. French**

    "The Cross-Section of Expected Stock Returns,"

    Journal of Finance, Vol. 47, 1992a, pp. 427–465.

17. **Finnerty, John D., and Dean Leistikow**

    "The Behavior of Equity and Debt Risk Premiums: Are They Mean Reverting and Downward-Trending?"

    The Journal of Portfolio Management, Summer 1993, pp. 73–84.

18. **Finnerty, John D., and Dean Leistikow**

    "The Behavior of Equity and Debt Risk Premiums: Reply to Comment,"

    The Journal of Portfolio Management, Summer 1994, pp. 101–102.

19. **Goetzmann, William, and Philippe Jorion**

    "A Century of Global Stock Markets,"

    Working Paper 5901, National Bureau of Economic Research, 1997.

20. **Gordon, Myron J., and Eli Shapiro**

    "Capital Equipment Analysis: The Required Rate of Profit,"

    Management Science, Vol. 3, October 1956, pp. 102–110.

21. **Grabowski, Roger and David W. King**

    "New Evidence on Size Effects and Rates of Return,"

    Business Valuation Review, September 1996, p. 103.

22. **Graham, John**

    "Debt and the Marginal Tax Rate,"

    Journal of Financial Economics, Vol. 41, 1996a, pp. 41–73.

23. **Graham, John**

    "Proxies for the Corporate Marginal Tax Rate,"

    Journal of Financial Economics, Vol. 42, 1996, pp. 187–221.

24. **Graham, John, Michael Lemon, and James Schallheim**

    "Debt, Leases, Taxes and the Endogeneity of Corporate Tax Status,"

    Journal of Finance, Vol. 53, 1998.

25. **Ibbotson, Roger G., and Scott L. Lummer**

    "The Behavior of Equity and Debt Risk Premiums: Comment,"

    The Journal of Portfolio Management, Summer 1994, pp. 98–100.

26. **Ibbotson, Roger G., and Gary P. Brinson**

    Global Investing: The Professional's Guide to the World of Capital Markets,

    McGraw-Hill, New York, 1991.

27. **Ibbotson, Roger G., and Rex A. Sinquefield**

    Stocks, Bonds, Bills, and Inflation: Historical Returns (1926–1987), 1989 ed.,

    Dow-Jones Irwin, Homewood, IL, 1989.

28. Ibbotson, Roger G., and Rex A. Sinquefield (foreword by Laurence B. Siegel)

Stocks, Bonds, Bills, and Inflation: The Past and the Future, 1982 ed.,

Institute of Chartered Financial Analysts, Charlottesville, VA, 1982.

29. Ibbotson, Roger G., and Rex A. Sinquefield

Stocks, Bonds, Bills, and Inflation: Historical Returns (1926–1978),

Institute of Chartered Financial Analysts, Charlottesville, VA, 1979.

30. Ibbotson, Roger G., and Rex A. Sinquefield (foreword by Jack L. Treynor)

Stocks, Bonds, Bills, and Inflation: the Past (1926–1976) and the Future (1977–2000), 1977 ed.,

Institute of Chartered Financial Analysts, Charlottesville, VA, 1977.

31. Ibbotson, Roger G., and Rex A. Sinquefield

"Stocks, Bonds, Bills, and Inflation: Simulations of the Future (1926–2000),"

The Journal of Business, 49, No. 3 (July 1976), pp. 313–338.

32. Ibbotson, Roger G., and Rex A. Sinquefield

"Stocks, Bonds, Bills, and Inflation: Year-By-Year Historical Returns (1926–1974),"

The Journal of Business, 49, No. 1 (January 1976), pp. 11–47.

33. Kaplan, Paul D., and James D. Peterson

"Full-Information Industry Betas,"

Financial Management, Vol. 27, No. 2, Summer 1998.

34. Kothari, S.P., Jay Shanken, and Richard G. Sloan

"Another Look at the Cross-Section of Expected Stock Returns,"

Working Paper, December 1992.

35. Lo, Andrew W., and A. Craig MacKinlay

"Stock Market Prices Do Not Follow Random Walks: Evidence from a Simple Specification Test,"

The Review of Financial Studies, Spring 1988, pp. 41–66.

36. Lo, Andrew W., and A. Craig MacKinlay

"When are Contrarian Profits Due to Stock Market Overreaction?"

Review of Financial Studies, Vol. 3, No. 2, 1990.

37. McQueen, Grant, Michael Pinegar, and Steven Thorley

"Delayed Reaction to Good News and the Cross-autocorrelation of Portfolio Returns,"

Journal of Finance, July 1996.

38. Mehra, Rajnish, and Edward Prescott

"The Equity Premium: A Puzzle,"

Journal of Monetary Economics, vol. 15, 1985, pp. 145–161.

39. Peterson, James D., and Gary C. Sanger

"Cross-autocorrelations, Systematic Risk and the Period of Listing,"

Working Paper, University of Notre Dame, 1995.

40. **Poterba, James M., and Lawrence H. Summers**

    "Mean Reversion in Stock Prices,"

    Journal of Financial Economics, October 1988, pp. 27–59.

41. **Roll, Richard, and Stephen A. Ross**

    "An Empirical Investigation of the Arbitrage Pricing Theory,"

    Journal of Finance, Vol. 35, no. 5, December 1980, pp. 1073–1103.

42. **Shumway, Tyler**

    "The Delisting Bias in CRSP Data,"

    Journal of Finance, Vol. 52, 1997, pp. 327–340.

43. **Stocks, Bonds, Bills, and Inflation Yearbook**

    annual. 1983, 1984, 1985, 1986, 1987, 1988, 1989, 1990, 1991, 1992, 1993, 1994, 1995, 1996, 1997, 1998, 1999, 2000, 2001.

    Ibbotson Associates, Chicago.

44. **Williams, John Burr**

    The Theory of Investment Value,

    Harvard University Press, Cambridge, Mass., 1938.

Stocks, Bonds, Bills, and Inflation

Valuation Edition

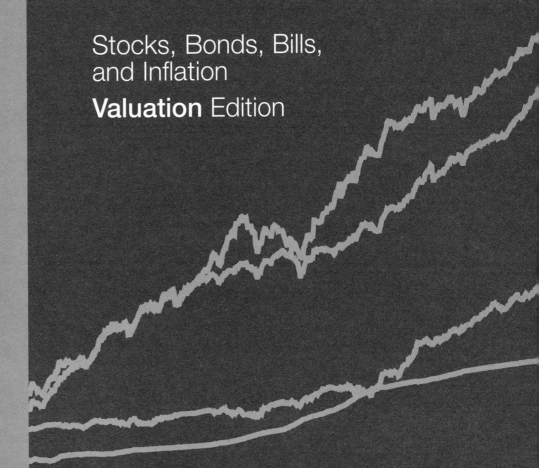

Chapters

IbbotsonAssociates

Chapter 1
Business Valuation

Valuation, at its purest, is the act of placing a value or worth on an asset. Stock analysts determine an equity's value based on its earnings outlook, market value, and other economic variables. Public companies are typically easier to value than private ones due to availability of data. The practice of assigning value, considered a combination of science and art, can be more difficult for non-public companies. Ibbotson Associates provides empirical data for many areas of valuation and is constantly expanding the body of knowledge that serves as the basis for the scientific approach to assigning value. Although this chapter focuses on the specifics of business valuation, the data presented throughout the entire book can be applied to many other areas of valuation, such as corporate treasury, capital budgeting, and security analysis.

The three most commonly used approaches to valuing a business are the income, market, and asset-based approaches. In the income approach, a company's cash flows are projected into the future and discounted at an appropriate cost of capital rate to determine present value. The cost of capital, or discount rate, used in the denominator can have a dramatic effect on the ultimate value of a business and is the topic of discussion throughout much of this book. The market approach to valuation uses financial ratio analysis from comparable guideline companies to determine value. Finally, the asset-based approach requires a comprehensive revaluation of all of a company's assets and liabilities, both tangible and intangible. This chapter discusses all three approaches to valuation, focusing mainly on the income approach and other areas where Ibbotson Associates has contributed.

Preparation

Determining a business entity's worth is a complicated process, where preparation demands as much attention as the actual analysis. Prior to examining financial statements and assessing company risk factors, ample time and care must be taken to lay out the valuation process road map. Before discussing the three approaches to business valuation, we will first discuss some of the decision process that provides direction to the valuation process. The following guidelines and definitions are meant to serve as an outline, the details and procedures of which may vary across different organizations that certify valuation practitioners.

Standard of Value

While the obvious driving force behind business valuation is determining the value of a business, defining "value" is not so straightforward. Value can mean many things. So for the purpose of valuing a business, certain standards of value have been formulated. One of the first choices to make when mapping out a business valuation is to determine the standard of value appropriate for the situation at hand.

Definitions and Guidelines

Fair market value is defined by IRS Revenue Ruling 59-60 as "...the price at which the property would change hands between a willing buyer and a willing seller when the former is not under any compulsion to buy and the latter is not under any compulsion to sell, both parties having reasonable knowledge of relevant facts."

Fair value is the amount that will compensate an owner involuntarily deprived of property. Commonly there is a willing buyer but not a willing seller, and the buyer may have more knowledge than the seller. Fair value is a legal term left to judicial interpretation. Many consider fair value to be fair market value without discounts.

Investment value is the value to a particular investor based on individual investment requirements and expectations.[1]

Book value with respect to a business enterprise is the difference between total assets (net of accumulated depreciation, depletion, and amortization) and total liabilities as they appear on the balance sheet (synonymous with "shareholder's equity"). With respect to a specific asset, book value is the capitalized cost less accumulated amortization or depreciation as it appears on the books of account of the business enterprise.[1]

Intrinsic value is the value that an investor considers, on the basis of an evaluation or available facts, to be the "true" or "real" value that will become the market value when other investors reach the same conclusion.[1]

Going concern value is the value of a business enterprise that is expected to continue to operate into the future. The intangible elements of going concern value result from factors such as having a trained work force, an operational plant, and the necessary licenses, systems, and procedures in place.[1]

Liquidation value is the net amount that would be realized if the business is terminated and the assets are sold piecemeal. Liquidation can be either "orderly" or "forced."[1]

Fair market value is the standard most often used in business valuation; hence, much of the analysis throughout this book is based on this assumption. Most of the data presented in this book also assumes that the company being valued is a going concern. Going concern and liquidation value are concepts that extend beyond the "standards of value" and into the "premise of value." The premise of value is a choice between valuing a company as an ongoing entity or one facing liquidation. At times a firm may be valued assuming that the company is a going concern only to find that the business is worth more if liquidated. This information should be stated in the valuation report, and is the reason why it is necessary to exhaust all reasonable possibilities when performing analysis on a company.

Ownership Interest

To accurately apply the correct data and formulas in the approach to valuation, the practitioner must have knowledge of the ownership interest to be valued. The two terms commonly used to describe ownership interest are "control" and "minority." Someone with a controlling interest in a company has the ability to direct the firm's management and policies. An interest in a business of more than 50 percent is considered to be a controlling interest. Typically, an owner with a controlling interest can affect both the equity and debt of the company. Ownership of less than 50 percent in a company is considered a minority interest and typically does not have the ability to direct management.

1 *International Glossary of Business Valuation Terms.*

Valuation Date

IRS Revenue Ruling 59-60 changed the way business is valued and is the cornerstone of the valuation process. Among other things, Ruling 59-60 states that valuation is a forward-looking process but must be based on facts available as of the required date of appraisal. Some carry this out to the letter of the law and assume that only data available as of the relevant valuation date should be used. Others claim that events happening after the valuation date can be considered relevant if they were reasonably foreseeable as of the valuation date.

Ibbotson Associates provides data critical to the valuation process as far back as 1926, such as the equity risk premia and size premia presented in Appendix A of this book. Appendix A can be used to develop a cost of equity as of a previous date. Assuming that the historical data presented in Appendix A was available to the public as of the date of valuation, then many people would argue that the data from the current book can be used in valuations. Others would argue that only yearbooks published as of the valuation date are appropriate. Ibbotson Associates has been calculating and publishing data since 1976. While our method for calculating equity risk premia has remained constant, methodologies for calculating size premia have vastly improved over the years. It is up to the valuation practitioner to decide whether to use a current book with data from prior years or whether a book published as of the valuation date is the only resource appropriate.[2]

Fundamental Factors

A number of relevant factors should be considered carefully when appraising a business to fair market value—especially when valuing a closely held corporation whose owners have a controlling interest and whose stock quotations are sparse or lacking. According to IRS Revenue Ruling 59-60, there are eight such factors:

1. The nature of the business and the history of the enterprise from its inception.
2. The economic outlook in general and the condition and outlook of the specific industry in particular.
3. The book value of the stock and the financial condition of the business.
4. The earning capacity of the company.
5. The dividend-paying capacity of the company.
6. Whether or not the enterprise has goodwill or other intangible value.
7. Sales of the stock and the size of the block of stock to be valued.
8. The market price of stocks of corporations engaged in the same or a similar line of business having their stocks actively traded in a free and open market, either on an exchange or over-the-counter.

2 Contact the Ibbotson Associates Sales department at 800-758-3557 for information on obtaining prior editions of the *Stocks, Bonds, Bills, and Inflation Yearbook* (Classic and Valuation Editions).

Ibbotson Associates publishes information that can help in many of these areas. The *Stocks, Bonds, Bills, and Inflation Classic Edition Yearbook* begins with a chapter on highlights of the past year and decade, describing the economic climate for the given year by outlining major economic events as well as headlining mergers and acquisitions. Market performance is also presented to complete the picture on short- and intermediate-term economic performance. The *Cost of Capital Yearbook* and the related online data available on the Cost of Capital Center at www.ibbotson.com provide analyses that expose the strengths and weaknesses across industries. Included in this data are five-year earnings growth rate forecasts and one- and five-year financial ratios. See Graph 1-2 for a sample *Cost of Capital Yearbook* page.

Once all of the preparation has been completed—the standard of value selected and the ownership interest, valuation date, and fundamental factors addressed—the approach to valuation must be decided. For each approach, the appropriate calculation method must also be applied.

Income Approach to Valuation

One of the more common business valuation methodologies is the income approach. Under the income approach, the analyst must first identify future cash flows to be generated by the asset being valued. Second is the identification of the appropriate rate to use in discounting the cash flows to present value. The discount rate or cost of capital should reflect the level of risk inherent in the cash flows being valued.

The income approach can be expressed in the following formula:

$$PV_s = \frac{CF_1}{(1+k_s)^1} + \frac{CF_2}{(1+k_s)^2} + ... + \frac{CF_i}{(1+k_s)^i}$$

where:

PV_s = the present value of the expected cash flows for company s;

CF_i = the cash flow (or dividend) expected to be received at the end of year i; and

k_s = the cost of capital for company s.

While the basic concept of the income approach to valuation is fairly straightforward, implementing it can be quite arduous. The two most commonly used methods for applying the income approach are the discounted cash flow (DCF) and capitalization of earnings methods. The DCF method is used when future returns are expected to be substantially different from current operations. In this case, the cost of capital with which to discount is the total expected return that a buyer would demand on the purchase price of an ownership interest in the company, given the risk of that interest. The capitalization of earnings method takes the same discount rate the DCF uses, but subtracts the company's expected annual growth rate. This is most appropriate when a company's current operations are indicative of its future operations. Chapter 4 discusses estimated growth rates in detail.

Free Cash Flow

In the field of business valuation, the appropriate cash flows used in the equation are the free cash flows generated by the entity that is being valued. Free cash flow represents a company's after-tax cash once adjustment is made for non-cash accounting entries and capital expenditures required to maintain the company as a going concern. Free cash flow for the entire invested capital of a firm is most often determined by the following formulas:

Cash Flow Formula	*Alternate Cash Flow Formula*
EBIT x (1 – t)	Net Income
+ Depreciation and Amortization	+ Depreciation and Amortization
+ Deferred Taxes	+ Deferred Taxes
- Capital Expenditures	- Capital Expenditures
- Changes in Working Capital	- Changes in Working Capital
	+ Interest Expense x (1 – t)
= Free Cash Flow	*= Free Cash Flow*

Free cash flow represents the total amount of cash that can potentially flow to the shareholders and long term interest bearing debt holders of the company; it is thus the free cash flow that drives the value for all equity and debt holders of the entity.

Several things can be noted about free cash flow. First, it is an after-tax concept. While the equation starts with earnings before interest and taxes (EBIT), this number is tax adjusted to get to an after-tax value. The equation starts with tax-adjusted EBIT because we want to focus on cash flows independently of capital structure. We must therefore start with earnings before interest expenses and then tax adjust those earnings. Secondly, pure accounting adjustments need to be added back into the analysis. It is for this reason that depreciation expense and deferred tax expense are added back into the after-tax EBIT. Finally, cash flows necessary to keep the company going forward must be subtracted from the equation. These cash flows represent necessary capital expenditures to maintain plant, property, and equipment or other capital expenditures that arise out of the ordinary course of business. Another common subtraction is reflected in changes in working capital. The assumption in most business valuation settings is that the entity in question will remain a long-term going concern that will grow over time. As companies grow, they accumulate additional accounts receivable and other working capital elements that require additional cash to support.

Free cash flow is the relevant cash flow stream because it represents the broadest level of earnings that can be generated by the asset. With free cash flow as a starting point, the owners of a firm can decide how much of the cash flow stream should be diverted toward new ventures, capital expenditures, interest payments, and dividend payments. It is incorrect to focus on earnings as the cash flow stream to be valued because earnings contain a number of accounting adjustments and already include the impact of capital structure.

Weighted Average Cost of Capital

Since free cash flow represents the cash flow stream flowing from the entire entity, the appropriate discount rate to use in the income approach model is the weighted average cost of capital (WACC). The WACC is represented by the following equation:

$$WACC = W_D k_D (1-t) + W_E k_E$$

where:

W_D = weight of debt in the capital structure;
k_D = cost of debt capital;
t = effective tax rate for the company;
W_E = weight of equity in the capital structure; and
k_E = cost of equity capital.

Ideally, a firm's target or optimal capital structure should be used in weighting the cost of equity and cost of debt. Unfortunately, many companies are either not able to obtain their target capital structure, or information to support the target capital structure is not available (as may be the case for a minority-interest shareholder). In the absence of a reliable target capital structure, the capital structure weights should be market value weighted. While it is typically a straightforward process to measure the market value of equity capital for a public company, it usually is not so simple for debt capital because so little debt is publicly traded. Therefore, in most cases the market value of debt in the capital structure is assumed to be the book value of debt. The weights are calculated from the market values as follows:

$$W_D = \frac{D}{D+E}, \quad W_E = \frac{E}{D+E}$$

where:

W_D = weight of debt in the capital structure;
W_E = weight of equity in the capital structure;
D = the market value of debt outstanding; and
E = the market value of equity outstanding.

Together the weights should add up to 100 percent. An excellent source for industry average capital structure weights is the Ibbotson *Cost of Capital Yearbook*.

The WACC formula above is primarily applicable to a controlling interest valuation. For a minority interest, adjustments may be made to both the numerator and the denominator of the present value formula. The free cash flow in the numerator should be adjusted to remove the effect of debt, as a minority owner does not have the power to influence capital structure and the issuance of debt. For this reason, net changes in long-term debt should be added (add new debt principal in and subtract debt principal out). If tax-effected interest expense has been added to the formula, make sure to subtract it back out. Once free cash flow has been recalculated to remove the effect of debt, the cost of capital must be calculated independent of debt as well. One way to do this is to simply discount using the cost of equity in the denominator. This is the same as using a capital structure of 100 percent equity and 0 percent debt in the WACC formula.

There may also be times when the WACC formula will apply to a minority interest valuation. In these cases, the actual capital structure of the company should be used, as opposed to an industry average or target structure, since minority shareholders will not have the power to change it.

Another adjustment may need to be made when valuing an S corporation, a form of corporation with less than 75 shareholders that enjoys the benefits of incorporation but is taxed like a partnership. For S corporations the taxes are passed through to the individual level (no corporate taxes). There has been much controversy over whether or not to tax effect data derived from publicly traded companies for application in discounting an S corporation. At this time, Ibbotson Associates makes no recommendation as to whether the data should be tax effected.

Tax Rate Assumptions

In calculating the WACC, one important element that is often overlooked is the tax rate. While it has been known for quite some time that companies do not necessarily pay the statutory rate, it has been common practice to use the marginal statutory rate in cost of capital calculations.[3] One reason the use of the marginal tax rate has persisted is the difficulty in accurately measuring what the firm's expected tax rate will be.

The tax rate is an important determinant of the WACC. Its significance is demonstrated in the following simple example:

Assume a company is financed with 50 percent debt and 50 percent equity. The cost of equity (k_E) is 15 percent, and the cost of debt (k_D) is 10 percent. Calculating the WACC using a tax rate (t) of 35 percent results in a value of 10.8 percent:

$$WACC = W_D k_D (1-t) + W_E k_E = [0.5 \times 0.1(1-0.35)] + (0.5 \times 0.15) = 10.8 \text{ percent}$$

However, if the company does not expect to pay the statutory rate and instead has a tax rate of 10 percent, the WACC increases to 12.0 percent—a change of 120 basis points:

$$WACC = W_D k_D (1-t) + W_E k_E = [0.5 \times 0.1(1-0.1)] + (0.5 \times 0.15) = 12.0 \text{ percent}$$

Recent research by John Graham provides a way for practitioners to determine more accurate estimates of expected future tax rates.[4] Under Graham's methodology, expected future earnings are simulated using current tax code provisions. The Graham methodology shows that a majority of firms can expect to pay less than the marginal rate. Under the current tax code, 56 percent of firms can expect to pay substantially less than the marginal rate (tax rates under 10 percent).

---

3 Courdes, Joseph and Steven Sheffrin. "Estimating the Tax Advantage of Corporate Debt," *Journal of Finance*, Vol. 38, 1983, 95–105.

4 Graham, John. "Debt and the Marginal Tax Rate," *Journal of Financial Economics*, Vol. 41, 1996a, 41–73.
   Graham, John. "Proxies for the Corporate Marginal Tax Rate," *Journal of Financial Economics*, Vol. 42, 1996, 187–221.
   Graham, John, Michael Lemon, and James Schallheim. "Debt, Leases, Taxes and the Endogeneity of Corporate Tax Status," *Journal of Finance*, Vol. 53, 1998.

Graph 1-1 shows the distribution of tax rates for over 10,000 companies.

Graph 1-1

Effective Tax Rate Distribution
Fiscal Year 2001

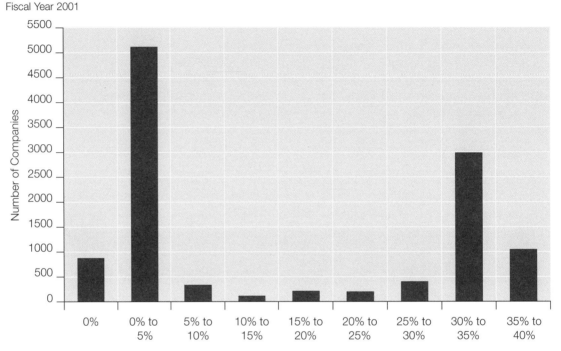

Range of Effective Tax Rate

Other Income Approach Considerations

One important aspect of the income approach model is that the discount rate and the cash flows need to be estimated on the same basis. For instance, if pre-tax cash flows are projected in the model, they must be discounted to present using a pre-tax cost of capital (as opposed to an after-tax cost of capital). If nominal cash flows are projected in the model, then a nominal cost of capital should be used in the discount rate. Failure to properly match the discount rate with the cash flows will produce an inaccurate value.

Another common mistake in the income approach is the use of a "most likely"—as opposed to an expected—cash flow. The calculation of an expected cash flow requires the estimation of future cash flows under different scenarios, to which probabilities are then attached. For instance, suppose there are only two possible scenarios affecting the expected cash flow, economic boom and recession. The likelihood of each of these economic scenarios is 75 percent and 25 percent, respectively. Also suppose that under an economic boom, the projected cash flow is $100, while in a recession the projected cash flow is $50. The expected cash flow is calculated by multiplying the projected cash flow under each economic scenario by its corresponding probability, then summing these products ($100 × 0.75) + ($50 × 0.25) = $87.50. The result is a probability-weighted projection of cash flow, rather than a "most likely" cash flow.

Market Approach to Valuation

The market approach to valuation uses data from comparable guideline companies to develop a measure of value for a particular subject company. Two types of data are used to implement the market approach. The first is data from guideline publicly traded companies. A wealth of data exists for the publicly traded equity market, including the type of financial ratios applied when determining value using the market approach. Transaction data for private and public companies can also be used in computing value using the market approach. In this case, a database of bought and sold companies is used to base transaction prices and financial fundamentals on companies similar to the subject company. Data derived from guideline public companies should be used when determining a minority interest value because the shareholders of publicly traded companies usually have a minority stake in the company. Merger and acquisition data is typically used to derive a controlling interest value because data concerns the sale of an entire company, equity and debt.

Guideline Public Companies

Implementation of the market approach using publicly traded companies typically relies on the use of financial ratios that compare the stock price of a company to its various accounting measures of fundamental data. Many ratios contain stock price or market value of equity and work well in the market approach to determining value:
- Price to Earnings
- Price to Cash Flow
- Price to Shareholder's Equity

The above ratios can be used to determine a value of equity, but sometimes it may be desirable to determine the entire market value of invested capital (MVIC). Market value of invested capital is the combination of both equity and debt of a given company. Some common ratios used to determine market value of invested capital are:
- MVIC to Sales
- MVIC to EBIT (earnings before interest and taxes)
- MVIC to EBITDA (earnings before interest, taxes, depreciation, and amortization)

Gathering Data

Publicly traded companies offer many options for obtaining relevant data. Determining value using a price/earnings multiple requires obtaining the current market price of the guideline company's equity as well as the company's earnings. Stock price data is rather easy to find, but earnings data can be more difficult. Moody's and Standard & Poor's both provide this type of data in a variety of products. Standard & Poor's Compustat database contains comprehensive financial data on more than 10,000 companies traded on U.S. exchanges.

Once data has been gathered, determining the appropriate financials to use requires some analysis. For example, earnings are needed to compute a price/earnings ratio, but what exactly should be used to represent earnings? In Ibbotson's *Cost of Capital Yearbook*, income before extraordinary items is used to represent earnings because this is the item that focuses on the reoccurring income stream. Income that includes one-time charges can be misleading on a forward-looking basis.

Time periods for both the numerator and the denominator of any ratio must match as closely as possible. Mismatching time periods from which data is gathered can result in drastic distortion of results, especially when market conditions have changed significantly. While values for stock price can be obtained as of the valuation date, values from a company's financial statements are often from the latest fiscal year-end or latest four quarters. While some analysts use only the most recent financials, others prefer to use an average from a number of years (commonly five years). The decision on an appropriate time frame from which to gather fundamental data depends heavily on the quality and availability of the data and the stability of market conditions.

Example Using the P/E Ratio

In this hypothetical example, assume that the subject company is a privately held commercial printer with $2 million in earnings. Using a page from Ibbotson Associates' *Cost of Capital Yearbook*, an appropriate peer group represented by SIC 275 (Commercial Printing) is identified, as seen in Graph 1-2. The median price/earnings ratio for the group is 36.03. To solve for the implied market value of equity of the subject company, solve for the price of the subject company as follows:

$$\frac{Price_{Subject\ Company}}{Earnings_{Subject\ Company}} \quad \frac{Price_{Peer\ Group}}{Earnings_{Peer\ Group}}$$

Since the P/E for the peer group is obtained from the *Cost of Capital Yearbook* (36.03), all we need is the earnings for the subject company and the terms can be rearranged to solve for the implied value of equity for the subject company.

$$\frac{Price_{Subject\ Company}}{\$2,000,000} \approx 36.03 \qquad so;$$

The market value of equity for the subject company is approximated at $72,060,000. The importance of choosing an appropriate group of guideline companies is evident.

Graph 1-2

SIC 275 from *Cost of Capital 2002 Yearbook*

STATISTICS FOR SIC CODE 275

Commercial Printing
This Industry Comprises 10 Companies

Industry Description

Establishments primarily engaged in commercial printing by the lithographic process and in gravure printing.

Sales (million$)

Total	7,580
Average	758.0

Three Largest Companies

DONNELLEY (R R) & SONS CO	5,297.8
BOWNE & CO INC	1,113.5
CONSOLIDATED GRAPHICS INC	683.4

Three Smallest Companies

SUCCESSORIES INC	53.7
GEOGRAPHICS INC	36.6
DIMENSIONAL VISIONS GRP LTD	0.2

Total Capital (million$)

Total	5,854
Average	585.4

Three Largest Companies

DONNELLEY (R R) & SONS CO	4,562.5
BOWNE & CO INC	553.2
CONSOLIDATED GRAPHICS INC	527.6

Three Smallest Companies

GEOGRAPHICS INC	14.9
SUCCESSORIES INC	11.6
DIMENSIONAL VISIONS GRP LTD	0.6

SIC vs. S&P 500 for Last 10 Years (%)

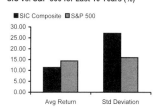

Number of Companies & Total Capital (billion$)

S&P Debt Rating	Large Cap	Mid Cap	Low Cap	Micro Cap	Totals	
AAA, AA, A	0	1	0	0	1	(companies)
	0.0	4.6	0.0	0.0	4.6	(capital)
BBB	0	0	0	0	0	
	0.0	0.0	0.0	0.0	0.0	
BB, B, CCC, CC, D	0	0	0	0	0	
	0.0	0.0	0.0	0.0	0.0	
Not Rated	0	0	1	8	9	
	0.0	0.0	0.6	0.7	1.3	
Totals	0	1	1	8	10	
	0.0	4.6	0.6	0.7	5.9	

Annualized Statistics for Last 10 Years (%)

	Avg Return	Std Deviation
S&P 500	14.36	15.93
SIC Composite	11.37	27.14
Large Composite	10.82	27.90
Small Composite	0.10	73.36

Compound Annual Equity Return (%)

	5 Years	10 Years
75th Percentile	-0.15	7.43
Median	-7.63	5.65
25th Percentile	-32.02	0.61
SIC Composite	5.25	6.20
Large Composite	4.11	6.03
Small Composite	-14.66	NMF

Sales, Income & Market Capitalization (billion$)

	Sales	Operating Income	Net Income	Equity Capital	Debt Capital
Current Yr.	7.6	0.9	0.1	4.4	1.5
Last Yr.	7.9	1.1	0.4	3.8	1.4
2 Yrs. Ago	6.9	1.1	0.4	3.4	1.5
3 Yrs. Ago	6.4	1.1	0.4	5.8	1.2
4 Yrs. Ago	5.9	0.9	0.3	7.8	1.3

Growth Over Last 5 Years (%)

	Net Sales	Operating Income	Net Income
Median	6.94	10.79	6.12
SIC Composite	0.40	0.30	NMF
Large Composite	0.05	-0.60	NMF
Small Composite	5.05	NMF	-1.22

Capital Structure Ratios (%)

	Debt/Total Capital Latest	Debt/Total Capital 5-Year Avg	Debt/MV Equity Latest	Debt/MV Equity 5-Year Avg
Median	23.20	27.42	30.21	38.13
SIC Composite	19.40	20.12	24.08	25.19
Large Composite	19.84	20.18	24.75	25.28
Small Composite	3.84	35.27	3.99	54.49

Distribution of Sales & Total Capital (million$)

	Distribution of Sales Latest	Distribution of Sales 5-Year Avg	Total Capital Latest	Total Capital 5-Year Avg
90th Percentile	1,532.0	1276.5	954.1	1,064.3
75th Percentile	545.6	348.3	415.8	432.4
Median	97.9	87.4	41.2	62.9
25th Percentile	56.9	53.7	16.3	26.5
10th Percentile	33.0	23.8	10.5	18.2

Margins (%)

	Operating Margin Latest	Operating Margin 5-Year Avg	Net Margin Latest	Net Margin 5-Year Avg	Asset Turnover Latest	Asset Turnover 5-Year Avg	Return on Inv. Cap. Latest	Return on Inv. Cap. 5-Year Avg	Return on Assets Latest	Return on Assets 5-Year Avg	Return on Equity Latest	Return on Equity 5-Year Avg
Median	9.19	9.82	0.72	2.42	151.34	143.48	1.73	5.01	1.26	4.11	2.78	5.89
SIC Composite	11.95	14.60	0.79	4.16	142.94	134.01	0.71	8.09	1.13	5.58	1.43	5.35
Large Composite	12.08	14.89	0.76	4.32	141.82	132.69	0.88	8.37	1.08	5.73	1.34	5.45
Small Composite	1.97	-0.20	6.23	-9.86	165.61	140.01	3.82	-20.11	-10.31	-13.81	-28.80	-18.11

Equity Valuation Ratios (Multiples)

	Price/Earnings Latest	Price/Earnings 5-Year Avg	Market/Book Latest	Market/Book 5-Year Avg	Price/Sales Latest	Price/Sales 5-Year Avg	Price/Cash Flow Latest	Price/Cash Flow 5-Year Avg	Price/Operating Income Latest	Price/Operating Income 5-Year Avg	Dividend Yield (% of Price) Latest	Dividend Yield (% of Price) 5-Year Avg
Median	36.03	16.98	0.74	1.54	0.33	0.53	22.51	18.64	3.51	4.72	0.00	0.00
SIC Composite	69.86	61.28	2.21	2.44	0.55	0.78	47.23	15.67	4.63	5.33	2.87	2.25
Large Composite	74.67	61.07	2.36	2.51	0.57	0.79	50.63	15.21	4.72	5.32	2.93	2.32
Small Composite	NMF	NMF	0.40	1.46	0.22	0.54	NMF	NMF	10.97	NMF	0.00	0.00

Growth Rates (%) / Cost of Equity Capital (%) / Weighted Average Cost of Capital (%) / Betas

	Analysts' Estimate	CAPM + Size Prem	CAPM Fama-French	3-Factor 1-Stage	Discounted Cash Flow 3-Stage	CAPM + Size Prem	CAPM Fama-French	3-Factor 1-Stage	Discounted Cash Flow 3-Stage	Levered Betas Raw Beta	Levered Betas Adjusted Beta	Unlevered Betas Adjusted Beta
Median	6.28	10.50	13.10	16.01	6.28	13.05	10.51	11.93	13.37	9.09	12.63
SIC Composite	6.28	10.92	12.34	17.10	6.39	14.10	10.77	11.86	15.48	7.32	13.20
Large Composite	6.28	10.97	11.69	17.35	6.41	14.30	10.78	11.33	15.64	7.31	13.32
Small Composite	6.28	10.25	13.55	11.02	6.28	6.50	10.50	12.33	10.93	8.30	8.43

	Raw Beta	Adjusted Beta	Unlevered Adjusted Beta
Median	0.63	0.60	0.31
SIC Composite	0.72	0.66	0.54
Large Composite	0.74	0.66	0.55
Small Composite	0.72	0.57	0.29

Guideline Transaction Data

In addition to publicly traded company data, transaction or sales data can be used to determine value with the market approach. Mergers and acquisitions provide much of the comparable sales data necessary to implement this approach. This type of data is not as readily available as public stock data. Table 1-1 is a partial list of providers. The implementation of the market approach is the same whether using data on publicly traded companies or merger and acquisition transactions. Multiples used to derive value with transaction data ordinarily use the market value of invested capital (MVIC) in the numerator, since the entire capital structure of the company is typically being sold and reported in the merger and acquisition data. Instead of using market prices, the transaction or deal price is used to represent invested capital. When the entire invested capital is sold, the value derived is typically that for a majority ownership with a controlling interest.

Table 1-1

Mergers and Acquisitions

Name of Publication/Database	Vendors
BIZCOMPS	BIZCOMPS
IBA Market Database	Institute of Business Appraisers
Mergerstat Review	Applied Financial Information LP
Merger & Acquisition Sourcebook	NVST.com
Merger Yearbook	Securities Data Publishing
Mergers & Acquisitions Magazine	Securities Data Publishing
Pratt's Stats	Business Valuation Resources
Done Deal	NVST.com
SDC Platinum	Securities Data Company
Mergerstat/Shannon Pratt-Control Premium Study	Business Valuation Resources

Asset-Based Approach to Valuation

With this approach, the value of a business is determined by valuing each component of the business separately. Taking the sum of the asset values, both tangible and intangible, and subtracting the value of liabilities derives the ultimate value of the business. The asset-based approach to valuation is primarily used when appraising a holding company, family limited partnership, or in bankruptcy proceedings.

The asset-based approach revaluation is organized into a balance sheet where each asset is revalued at fair market value. The presentation of results in this format is one of the benefits of the asset approach. Many potential purchasers of a business are familiar with the balance sheet format, making it easy to demonstrate where some of the value of a business is coming from. While all three major valuation approaches should arrive at the same or similar value for a company, the asset-based approach is the only one that allows identification of the areas producing the greatest value. For example, the fair market value of a business may be 50 percent greater than its historical cost value according to its balance sheet. A direct comparison of historical costs and fair market value using the asset-based approach will show where that 50 percent is located.

The greatest disadvantage of the asset-based approach is that it can be time-consuming and expensive. It also may require more involvement from the subject company's management team. Of course, the analyst will also need extensive training in accounting and may require the aid of outside experts to help value certain types of assets and liabilities that may be outside of his/her expertise. Also, the asset-based approach is the least desirable approach for minority-interest valuations because minority shareholders rarely have access to the necessary level of information and cooperation from management. Valuing intangible assets, such as goodwill, is very difficult and the resulting value may not actually explain much. Unrecorded intangible assets will not show up in the asset-based approach, but may be captured in the cash flows of the income approach. For this reason, when a substantial portion of the assets cannot be valued with accuracy, the asset-based approach is not ideal.

Chapter 2
Introduction to the Cost of Capital

Defining the Cost of Capital

The *Stocks, Bonds, Bills, and Inflation* historical data can be used, along with other inputs, to make forecasts of the future, including estimates of the cost of capital. A cost of capital estimate seeks to discern the expected return, or forecast mean return, on an investment in a security, firm, project, or division.

The cost of capital (sometimes called the expected or required rate of return or the discount rate) can be viewed from three different perspectives. On the asset side of a firm's balance sheet, it is the rate that should be used to discount to a present value the future expected cash flows. On the liability side, it is the economic cost to the firm of attracting and retaining capital in a competitive environment, in which investors (capital providers) carefully analyze and compare all return-generating opportunities. On the investor's side, it is the return one expects and requires from an investment in a firm's debt or equity. While each of these perspectives might view the cost of capital differently, they are all dealing with the same number.

The cost of capital is always an expectational or forward-looking concept. While the past performance of an investment and other historical information can be good guides and are often used to estimate the required rate of return on capital, the expectations of future events are the only factors that actually determine the cost of capital. An investor contributes capital to a firm with the expectation that the business' future performance will provide a fair return on the investment. If past performance were the criterion most important to investors, no one would invest in start-up ventures. It should also be noted that the cost of capital is a function of the investment, not the investor.

The cost of capital is an opportunity cost. Some people consider the phrase "opportunity cost of capital" to be more correct. The opportunity cost of an investment is the expected return that would be earned on the next best investment. In a competitive world with many investment choices, a given investment and the next best alternative have practically identical expected returns.

A Look at Historical Returns

Keeping in mind that the cost of capital is a forward-looking concept, historical returns can reveal important information about the return behavior of different investments. It is the relationship between these historic returns that can be exploited. Graph 2-1 depicts the growth of $1.00 invested in large company stocks, small company stocks, long-term government bonds, Treasury bills, and a hypothetical asset returning the inflation rate from the end of 1925 to the end of 2002. All results assume the reinvestment of dividends on stocks or coupons on bonds and no taxes. Transaction costs are not included, except in the small stock index starting in 1982.

The graph vividly illustrates that large and small company stocks were the big winners over the entire 77-year period: by year-end 2002 investments of $1.00 in these assets would have grown to $1,775.34 and $6,816.41, respectively. This phenomenal growth was earned by taking substantial risk. In contrast, long-term government bonds (with an approximate 20-year maturity) exposed the holder to much less risk and grew to only $59.70. The lowest-risk strategy over the past 77 years was to buy U.S. Treasury bills. Since Treasury bills tended to track inflation, the resulting real (inflation-adjusted) returns were just above zero for the entire 1926–2002 period.

It is also clear from Graph 2-1 that the higher returns of stocks over bonds and Treasury bills comes at a cost. There is considerably more volatility in the returns of stocks compared to the other investments. The large peaks and valleys in return index lines for both large and small company stocks are an indication of their higher risk or volatility. As will be discussed throughout this publication, the relationship between risk and return can be used to estimate expected returns or the cost of capital.

Graph 2-1

Wealth Indices of Investments in the U.S. Capital Markets
Year-end 1925 = $1.00

From 1925 to 2002

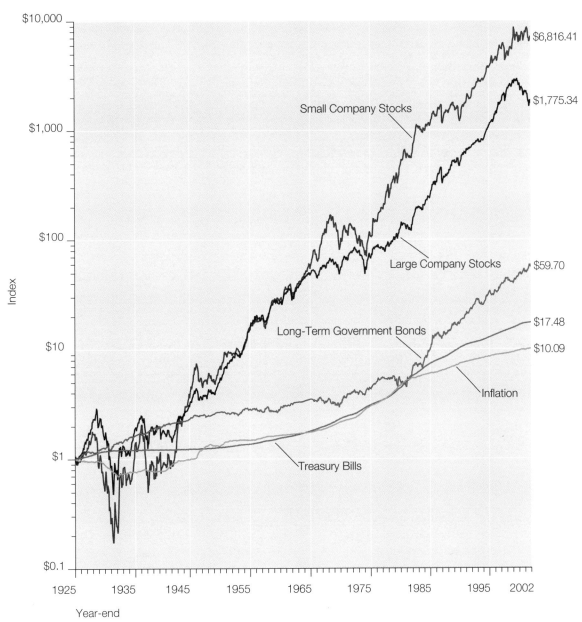

Description of SBBI Data Series

The series presented here are total returns and, where applicable or available, capital appreciation returns and income returns. A description of the Center for Research in Security Prices small stock data is found in Chapter 7, Firm Size and Return.

SBBI Data Series	Series Construction	Index Components	Approximate Maturity
1. Large Company Stocks	S&P 500 Composite with dividends reinvested. (S&P 500, 1957–Present; S&P 90, 1926–1956)	Total Return Income Return Capital Appreciation Return	n/a
2. Ibbotson Small Company Stocks	Fifth capitalization quintile of stocks on the NYSE for 1926–1981. Performance of the Dimensional Fund Advisors (DFA) Small Company Fund 1982–March 2002. Performance of DFA Micro Cap Fund April 2002-Present.	Total Return	n/a
3. Long-Term Corporate Bonds	Salomon Brothers Long-Term High Grade Corporate Bond Index	Total Return	20 Years
4. Long-Term Government Bonds	A One-Bond Portfolio	Total Return Income Return Capital Appreciation Return Yield	20 Years
5. Intermediate-Term Government Bonds	A One-Bond Portfolio	Total Return Income Return Capital Appreciation Return Yield	5 Years
6. U.S. Treasury Bills	A One-Bill Portfolio	Total Return	30 Days
7. Consumer Price Index	CPI—All Urban Consumers, not seasonally adjusted	Inflation Rate	n/a

Summary Statistics for Basic Series

Table 2-1 presents summary statistics of annual returns, and where applicable, income and capital appreciation, for each asset class. The summary statistics presented here are arithmetic mean, geometric mean, standard deviation, and serial correlation. Again it is clear the higher returns of the stock series compared to fixed income are also accompanied by higher risk (as measured by standard deviation). Small stocks had the highest return over the period 1926–2002. Other asset classes are progressively less risky and have correspondingly lower average returns. Treasury bills were nearly riskless and had the lowest return. In general, risk is rewarded by a higher return over the long term.

Table 2-1

Total Returns, Income Returns, and Capital Appreciation of the Basic Asset Classes
Summary Statistics of Annual Returns

from 1926 to 2002

Series	Geometric Mean	Arithmetic Mean	Standard Deviation	Serial Correlation
Large Company Stocks				
Total Returns	10.2%	12.2%	20.5%	0.05
Income	4.3	4.3	1.5	0.88
Capital Appreciation	5.7	7.6	19.8	0.05
Ibbotson Small Company Stocks				
Total Returns	12.1	16.9	33.2	0.07
Mid-Cap Stocks*				
Total Returns	11.0	13.8	25.1	−0.01
Income	4.2	4.2	1.6	0.87
Capital Appreciation	6.6	9.4	24.3	−0.01
Low-Cap Stocks*				
Total Returns	11.2	15.2	29.9	0.05
Income	3.8	3.8	1.9	0.88
Capital Appreciation	7.3	11.2	29.1	0.04
Micro-Cap Stocks*				
Total Returns	12.1	18.2	39.3	0.10
Income	2.7	2.7	1.8	0.90
Capital Appreciation	9.4	15.4	38.7	0.10
Long-Term Corporate Bonds				
Total Returns	5.9	6.2	8.7	0.08
Long-Term Government Bonds				
Total Returns	5.5	5.8	9.4	−0.07
Income	5.2	5.2	2.8	0.96
Capital Appreciation	0.1	0.4	8.2	−0.22
Intermediate-Term Government Bonds				
Total Returns	5.4	5.6	5.8	0.15
Income	4.8	4.8	3.0	0.96
Capital Appreciation	0.5	0.6	4.5	−0.20
Treasury Bills				
Total Returns	3.8	3.8	3.2	0.91
Inflation	3.0	3.1	4.4	0.65

Total return is equal to the sum of three component returns; income return, capital appreciation return, and reinvestment return.

*Source: Center for Research in Security Prices, University of Chicago. See Chapter 7 for details on decile construction.

Annual Total Returns

Table 2-2 shows the annual total returns for seven basic asset classes for the full 77-year time period. This table can be used to compare the performance of each asset class for the same annual period. Monthly total returns for large company stocks, small company stocks, long-term corporate bonds, long-term government bonds, intermediate-term government bonds, Treasury bills, and inflation rates are presented in Appendix B.

Table 2-2

Basic Series
Annual Total Returns (in percent)

from 1926 to 1970

Year	Large Company Stocks	Ibbotson Small Company Stocks	Long-Term Corporate Bonds	Long-Term Government Bonds	Intermediate-Term Government Bonds	U.S. Treasury Bills	Inflation
1926	11.62	0.28	7.37	7.77	5.38	3.27	−1.49
1927	37.49	22.10	7.44	8.93	4.52	3.12	−2.08
1928	43.61	39.69	2.84	0.10	0.92	3.56	−0.97
1929	−8.42	−51.36	3.27	3.42	6.01	4.75	0.20
1930	−24.90	−38.15	7.98	4.66	6.72	2.41	−6.03
1931	43.34	49.75	−1.85	−5.31	−2.32	1.07	−9.52
1932	−8.19	−5.39	10.82	16.84	8.81	0.96	−10.30
1933	53.99	142.87	10.38	−0.07	1.83	0.30	0.51
1934	−1.44	24.22	13.84	10.03	9.00	0.16	2.03
1935	47.67	40.19	9.61	4.98	7.01	0.17	2.99
1936	33.92	64.80	6.74	7.52	3.06	0.18	1.21
1937	−35.03	−58.01	2.75	0.23	1.56	0.31	3.10
1938	31.12	32.80	6.13	5.53	6.23	−0.02	−2.78
1939	−0.41	0.35	3.97	5.94	4.52	0.02	−0.48
1940	−9.78	−5.16	3.39	6.09	2.96	0.00	0.96
1941	−11.59	−9.00	2.73	0.93	0.50	0.06	9.72
1942	20.34	44.51	2.60	3.22	1.94	0.27	9.29
1943	25.90	88.37	2.83	2.08	2.81	0.35	3.16
1944	19.75	53.72	4.73	2.81	1.80	0.33	2.11
1945	36.44	73.61	4.08	10.73	2.22	0.33	2.25
1946	−8.07	−11.63	1.72	−0.10	1.00	0.35	18.16
1947	5.71	0.92	−2.34	−2.62	0.91	0.50	9.01
1948	5.50	−2.11	4.14	3.40	1.85	0.81	2.71
1949	18.79	19.75	3.31	6.45	2.32	1.10	−1.80
1950	31.71	38.75	2.12	0.06	0.70	1.20	5.79
1951	24.02	7.80	−2.69	−3.93	0.36	1.49	5.87
1952	18.37	3.03	3.52	1.16	1.63	1.66	0.88
1953	−0.99	−6.49	3.41	3.64	3.23	1.82	0.62
1954	52.62	60.58	5.39	7.19	2.68	0.86	−0.50
1955	31.56	20.44	0.48	−1.29	−0.65	1.57	0.37
1956	6.56	4.28	−6.81	−5.59	−0.42	2.46	2.86
1957	−10.78	−14.57	8.71	7.46	7.84	3.14	3.02
1958	43.36	64.89	−2.22	−6.09	−1.29	1.54	1.76
1959	11.96	16.40	−0.97	−2.26	−0.39	2.95	1.50
1960	0.47	−3.29	9.07	13.78	11.76	2.66	1.48
1961	26.89	32.09	4.82	0.97	1.85	2.13	0.67
1962	−8.73	−11.90	7.95	6.89	5.56	2.73	1.22
1963	22.80	23.57	2.19	1.21	1.64	3.12	1.65
1964	16.48	23.52	4.77	3.51	4.04	3.54	1.19
1965	12.45	41.75	−0.46	0.71	1.02	3.93	1.92
1966	−10.06	−7.01	0.20	3.65	4.69	4.76	3.35
1967	23.98	83.57	−4.95	−9.18	1.01	4.21	3.04
1968	11.06	35.97	2.57	−0.26	4.54	5.21	4.72
1969	−8.50	−25.05	−8.09	−5.07	−0.74	6.58	6.11
1970	4.01	−17.43	18.37	12.11	16.86	6.52	5.49

Table 2-2 (continued)

Basic Series
Annual Total Returns (in percent)

from 1971 to 2002

Year	Large Company Stocks	Ibbotson Small Company Stocks	Long-Term Corporate Bonds	Long-Term Government Bonds	Intermediate-Term Government Bonds	U.S. Treasury Bills	Inflation
1971	14.31	16.50	11.01	13.23	8.72	4.39	3.36
1972	18.98	4.43	7.26	5.69	5.16	3.84	3.41
1973	−14.66	−30.90	1.14	−1.11	4.61	6.93	8.80
1974	−26.47	−19.95	−3.06	4.35	5.69	8.00	12.20
1975	37.20	52.82	14.64	9.20	7.83	5.80	7.01
1976	23.84	57.38	18.65	16.75	12.87	5.08	4.81
1977	−7.18	25.38	1.71	−0.69	1.41	5.12	6.77
1978	6.56	23.46	−0.07	−1.18	3.49	7.18	9.03
1979	18.44	43.46	−4.18	−1.23	4.09	10.38	13.31
1980	32.42	39.88	−2.76	−3.95	3.91	11.24	12.40
1981	−4.91	13.88	−1.24	1.86	9.45	14.71	8.94
1982	21.41	28.01	42.56	40.36	29.10	10.54	3.87
1983	22.51	39.67	6.26	0.65	7.41	8.80	3.80
1984	6.27	−6.67	16.86	15.48	14.02	9.85	3.95
1985	32.16	24.66	30.09	30.97	20.33	7.72	3.77
1986	18.47	6.85	19.85	24.53	15.14	6.16	1.13
1987	5.23	−9.30	−0.27	−2.71	2.90	5.47	4.41
1988	16.81	22.87	10.70	9.67	6.10	6.35	4.42
1989	31.49	10.18	16.23	18.11	13.29	8.37	4.65
1990	−3.17	−21.56	6.78	6.18	9.73	7.81	6.11
1991	30.55	44.63	19.89	19.30	15.46	5.60	3.06
1992	7.67	23.35	9.39	8.05	7.19	3.51	2.90
1993	9.99	20.98	13.19	18.24	11.24	2.90	2.75
1994	1.31	3.11	−5.76	−7.77	−5.14	3.90	2.67
1995	37.43	34.46	27.20	31.67	16.80	5.60	2.54
1996	23.07	17.62	1.40	−0.93	2.10	5.21	3.32
1997	33.36	22.78	12.95	15.85	8.38	5.26	1.70
1998	28.58	−7.31	10.76	13.06	10.21	4.86	1.61
1999	21.04	29.79	−7.45	−8.96	−1.77	4.68	2.68
2000	−9.11	−3.59	12.87	21.28	12.59	5.89	3.39
2001	−11.88	22.77	10.65	3.70	7.62	3.83	1.55
2002	−22.10	−13.28	16.33	17.84	12.93	1.65	2.38

Real Rates versus Nominal Rates

The cost of capital embodies a number of different concepts or elements of risk. Two of the most basic concepts in finance are real and nominal returns. The nominal return includes both the real return and the impact of inflation.

The real rate of interest represents the exchange rate between current and future purchasing power. An increase in the real rate indicates that the cost of current consumption has risen in terms of future goods. It is the real rate of interest that measures the opportunity cost of foregoing consumption.

The relationship between real rates and nominal rates can be expressed in the following equation:

$$Real = \left[\frac{1+Nominal}{1+Inflation}\right] - 1$$

$$Nominal = [(1+Real) \times (1+Inflation)] - 1$$

It is important to note that the conversion of nominal and real rates is not an additive process; rather, it is a geometric calculation. The arithmetic sum or difference is calculated by adding or subtracting one number from the other. As illustrated in the above equation, the real rate of return involves taking the geometric difference of the nominal rate of return and the rate of inflation. Conversely, the nominal rate of return can be determined by taking the geometric sum of the real rate of return and the rate of inflation. Thus, if the real rate is 2.5 percent and the inflation rate is 5.0 percent, the nominal rate of interest is not 7.5 percent (2.5 + 5.0) but 7.625 percent, or [(1.025)(1.05) − 1]. Similarly, if the nominal rate is 7.625 percent and the inflation rate is 2.5 percent, the real rate is not 5.125 percent (7.625 − 2.5) but 5.0 percent, [(1.07625/1.025) − 1].

Discount rates are most often expressed in nominal terms. That is, they usually have an inflation estimate included in them. Unless stated otherwise, the cost of capital data presented in this book are expressed in nominal terms.

Real Rates as a Component of the Cost of Capital

In terms of cost of capital analysis, the distinction between real and nominal is only the beginning. It is possible to identify other premiums to add to the real rate and inflation forecast to determine the ultimate cost of capital. Each premium represents the reward required for an investor to take on additional risk. The idea of adding a premium to account for the required reward associated with taking on specific risks is referred to as the buildup method. Some of these premiums are identified below:

Investment Instrument	Components
Treasury Bill	Real Rate + Inflation Forecast
Treasury Notes	Real Rate + Inflation Forecast + Intermediate Horizon Premium
Treasury Bonds	Real Rate + Inflation Forecast + Long Horizon Premium
Corporate Bonds	Real Rate + Inflation Forecast + Long Horizon Premium + Default Premium
Large Capitalization Stocks	Real Rate + Inflation Forecast + Equity Risk Premium
Small Capitalization Stocks	Real Rate + Inflation Forecast + Equity Risk Premium + Size Premium

Cost of Debt

Like the cost of equity, cost of debt is a forward-looking concept. Yet, unlike the cost of equity, the required return on debt can be directly observed in the market. The current yield-to-maturity (or yield) on the applicable debt best approximates the cost of debt. The yield embodies the market's expectation of future returns on debt. If these expectations are different from those implicit in the price, the market price of the debt is bid up or down until the market's expectations are again reflected.

For debt instruments that are subject to default risk, such as corporate bonds, this approximation of expected return contains an upward bias. The yield-to-maturity is a promised yield. That is, it contains compensation for the expected loss from default. Because of this default risk, the debt cost of capital is actually the yield-to-maturity minus the expected default loss.

This upward bias is not constant over time and may be negligible in some cases. Two main factors influence the probability of default and therefore the size of the upward bias: 1) the strength of the economy and 2) the quality of the debt. A healthy (poor) economy results in a lower (higher) probability of default on all qualities of debt. A higher (lower) quality debt results in a lower (higher) probability of default. The upward bias in the estimation of the cost of debt is greatest for lower-quality issues but is usually negligible for higher-quality issues.

In addition, the spread between the yields of different-quality debt issues is not constant over time. The quality spread tends to shrink when the economy is healthy and widen when the economy is weak. Though the economic environment affects the probability of default on all qualities of debt, companies with higher-quality debt are better able to withstand weak economic periods without much risk of default. On the other hand, companies with lower-quality debt are less able to withstand poor economic conditions and therefore have a higher probability of default. This causes the quality spread to widen during weak economic periods.

For companies whose debt instruments are regularly traded, the yield-to-maturity is readily available. For companies whose debt instruments are not regularly traded, the cost of debt needs to be approximated. The average yield-to-maturity on corporate debt with similar maturity and quality can be used as a proxy. Both Moody's and Standard and Poor's provide average yields for varying qualities of debt over different horizons.

Application of the Cost of Capital

The cost of capital has many different applications in investment management, corporate finance, and regulatory and tax proceedings. Some applications that merit special mention are the valuation of business entities, regulatory proceedings, and shareholder value added (SVA) analysis.

Business Valuation

One required element of the income approach to company valuation is the discount rate. Under the income approach, cash flows are projected into the future and discounted back to present value using a discount rate reflective of the risk inherent in those cash flows. The income approach is expressed in the following formula:

$$PV_s = \frac{CF_1}{(1+k_s)^1} + \frac{CF_2}{(1+k_s)^2} + ... + \frac{CF_i}{(1+k_s)^i}$$

where:

PV_s = the present value of the expected cash flows for company s;

CF_i = the dividend or cash flow expected to be received at the end of period i; and

k_s = the cost of capital for company s.

The discount rate is synonymous with the cost of capital.

While determining the appropriate future cash flow stream is an essential element of the income approach, determining the appropriate discount rate is equally important. Under the income approach, small changes in the discount rate can have a large impact on the ultimate value that is derived.

Table 2-3 is a simple valuation example that illustrates the impact of small changes in the discount rate. In the example, the entity being valued produces cash flows of $1,000 each year and has a perpetuity value in year five of $10,000. The lower portion of the table shows the values derived from this cash flow stream using different discount rates.

Table 2-3

Valuing Future Cash Flows with Different Discount Rates

Projected	Year 1	Year 2	Year 3	Year 4	Year 5	
Cash Flows	$1,000	$1,000	$1,000	$1,000	$10,000	

Discount			Present Value of Cash Flows			
Rate	Year 1	Year 2	Year 3	Year 4	Year 5	Total
10 percent	$909	$826	$751	$683	$6,209	$9,379
11 percent	$901	$812	$731	$659	$5,935	$9,037
12 percent	$893	$797	$712	$636	$5,674	$8,712
13 percent	$885	$783	$693	$613	$5,428	$8,402
14 percent	$877	$769	$675	$592	$5,194	$8,107
15 percent	$870	$756	$658	$572	$4,972	$7,827

Whether this entity is worth $9,037 using a discount rate of 11 percent or $8,107 using a discount rate of 14 percent may seem trivial. If these values were in thousands or millions of dollars, however, the differences would be significant.

The example in the preceding paragraph focused on values produced from discount rates that are 300 basis points apart. While this may seem extreme, basic assumptions in the determination of the cost of capital can lead to discount rates that are widely divergent. Understanding the assumptions that underlie the discount rate is as important as understanding the assumptions that underlie the cash flows.

Regulatory Proceedings

Even in this era of deregulation, most utilities are regulated to some extent by local government bodies. An appointed commission ensures that the utility, because of its alleged monopolistic power, does not take advantage of its customers and that its investors receive a fair rate of return on their invested capital. One of the most important functions of the commission is to determine an appropriate (often called the "allowed") rate of return. The procedures for setting rates of return for regulated utilities often specify or suggest that the required rate is that which would allow the firm to attract and retain debt and equity capital over the long term.

Although the cost of capital estimation techniques set forth later in this book are applicable to rate setting, certain adjustments may be necessary. One such adjustment is for flotation costs (amounts that must be paid to underwriters by the issuer to attract and retain capital). In addition, certain regulatory environments may require that shareholders not earn more than the allowed rate of return. If a shareholder does earn more, future rates for the utilities services may be reduced by the regulating body. If the allowed rate of return falls below the cost of capital, regulators may allow a rate increase in order to compensate the investor so that they will on average over time earn the market-required rate of return. Yet other regulatory conditions may require that the allowed rate of return be different from the cost of capital.

One cost of capital estimation technique, the full information approach, is especially useful for utilities entering into deregulated markets. The full information approach allows for the splitting of an entity into separate pieces to identify the risk associated with different lines of business. Even under deregulation, elements of utilities often remain regulated. One example is the differentiation between generating assets and transmission and distribution assets of electric utilities. The generation of electric power is being deregulated, but the transmission and distribution assets currently remain regulated. This technique will be discussed further in Chapter 6.

Project Selection

In a situation where there is no significant budget constraint (capital rationing), a firm should accept every project that has a positive net present value (NPV). The NPV of a project is calculated by discounting all of the cash flows to and from the project—including the initial and subsequent investment amounts—at the project's cost of capital. The cost of capital for a project is typically estimated by studying capital costs (including debt and equity) for existing projects deemed to be comparable in risk. It is related to the risk of the project, not to the risk or credit-worthiness of the firm that is contemplating undertaking the project. Thus, if different firms have the same expectations about the cash flows and risks of a project, they will each perceive the project as having the same NPV. This illustrates the point made earlier that cost of capital is specific to the investment, not the investor.

Shareholder Value Added

The concept of economic or shareholder value added is an idea that the consulting firm of Stern Stewart & Co. has brought to the forefront of both the business management and investment management communities. The principle of shareholder value added is simple—as long as a business is earning returns higher than its cost of capital, it is adding shareholder value. Under shareholder value added, managers are rewarded when returns exceed the cost of capital.

Obviously, cost of capital is a key element of the shareholder value added management process. As more companies tie their executive compensation packages to shareholder value added, the measurement of cost of capital within businesses has taken on increased emphasis.

There are some key concepts to consider in evaluating the cost of capital for different lines of business within a given organization. The first concept is that different lines of business have different levels of risk associated with them. Therefore, the cost of equity will probably vary by business line. The second is that different industries often retain different capital structures. The capital structure of the overall company may not apply to individual business units. For instance, financial services companies tend to have a different capital structure than retail merchandisers, though many retail merchandisers have captive finance subsidiaries. How the issue of capital structure is addressed in the implementation of a shareholder value added management program can have a significant impact on how well the program will work.

Chapter 3
The Buildup Method

Estimating the equity cost of capital is a difficult task, to which much of modern financial theory is devoted. The equity cost of capital is equal to the expected rate of return for a firm's equity; this return includes all dividends plus any capital gains or losses. A properly specified cost of equity must include, if appropriate, provisions for flotation costs and certain market inefficiencies that might not be captured by standard methods for estimating equity rates of return.

There are several widely used and effective methods to estimate the equity cost of capital. The most common of these are: 1) the buildup method, 2) the capital asset pricing model (CAPM), 3) the discounted cash flow (DCF) method, 4) arbitrage pricing theory (APT), and 5) the Fama-French three factor model. This chapter will focus on the buildup method, while Chapter 4 will cover all other cost of equity models.

The Buildup Method for Cost of Equity Capital

The buildup method is an additive model in which the return on an asset is estimated as the sum of a risk-free rate and one or more risk premia. Each premium represents the reward an investor receives for taking on a specific risk. The building blocks are summed arithmetically to form an estimate of the cost of capital.

	Risk-Free Rate
+	Equity Risk Premium
+	Firm Size Premium
+	?
=	Cost of Equity

Risk-Free Rate

Since any risky investment should return at least as much as the riskless asset, the risk-free rate is the starting point of the buildup method. The buildup method, the capital asset pricing model, and the Fama-French three factor model all implicitly assume the presence of a single riskless asset, that is, an asset perceived by all investors as having no risk. Selecting the appropriate risk-free rate is discussed in detail in the CAPM section of Chapter 4.

Risk Premia

There are several risk premia that can be used with the buildup method. Some are widely accepted, while others are more controversial. The equity risk premium is the most common; like the risk-free rate, it is a component of the capital asset pricing model and the Fama-French three factor model. The same equity risk premium can be used in each of these models. For additional information on the equity risk premium, see Chapter 5, which has been devoted exclusively to this subject.

Small Stock or Size Premia

A small stock or size premium may also be added in the buildup method to account for the additional risk inherent in small company stocks. (For additional information regarding size premia, see Chapter 7, which is devoted to this subject.) It is important to note, however, that the size premia presented elsewhere in this publication have been adjusted for beta. In other words, the portion of the excess return on small stocks that can be explained by their higher betas is not included in the size premia. Some assert that a small stock premium that has not been adjusted for beta would be more appropriate for use in the buildup method. This non-beta-adjusted small stock premium can be calculated by subtracting the arithmetic mean of the large company stock return from the arithmetic mean of the small company stock return. Table 3-1 shows the various size premia on both a beta-adjusted and a non-beta-adjusted basis. Table 3-2 shows how the non-beta-adjusted small stock premia are calculated using the arithmetic mean returns from Table 2-1. Calculation of the beta-adjusted size premia is explained in detail in Chapter 7.

Table 3-1

Size Premia on a Beta-Adjusted versus Non-Beta-Adjusted Basis
1926–2002

	Beta-Adjusted Size Premia	Non-Beta-Adjusted Small Stock Premia
Mid-Cap	0.8%	1.6%
Low-Cap	1.5%	3.0%
Micro-Cap	3.5%	6.0%
Ibbotson Small Company Stocks	2.9%	4.7%

Table 3-2

Derivation of Non-Beta Adjusted Small Stock Premia
1926–2002

	Small Company Stock Arithmetic Mean Return		Large Company Stock Arithmetic Mean Return		Non-Beta-Adjusted Small Stock Premia
Mid-Cap	13.8%	–	12.2%	=	1.6%
Low-Cap	15.2%	–	12.2%	=	3.0%
Micro-Cap	18.2%	–	12.2%	=	6.0%
Ibbotson Small Company Stocks	16.9%	–	12.2%	=	4.7%

The problem with using a non-beta-adjusted small stock premium is that in doing so one assumes that the company being valued has the same systematic risk (or beta) as the portfolio of small stocks used in the calculation of the size premium. This ignores much of the information that we have regarding market returns. Primarily, different industries tend to have different levels of systematic risk. For example, companies within health services industries tend to have less systematic risk than the market as a whole. Since the beta-adjusted size premium isolates the excess return due to size, it can be applied to a company without making any assumptions regarding the company's systematic risk.

Suppose we wish to calculate the cost of equity for a small electric utility company falling within the micro-cap size group by using the buildup method. Based on our industry knowledge, we know that the electric utility industry tends to exhibit less risk than the market as a whole. We can calculate the cost of equity with either a beta-adjusted size premium or a non-beta-adjusted size premium as follows:

$$k_s = r_f + ERP + SP_s = 4.8\% + 7.0\% + 3.5\% = 15.3\% \text{ or}$$

$$k_s = r_f + ERP + SSP_s = 4.8\% + 7.0\% + 6.0\% = 17.8\%$$

where:

k_s = the cost of equity for company s;

r_f = the expected return of the riskless asset;

ERP = the expected equity risk premium, or the amount by which investors expect the future return on equities to exceed that on the riskless asset;

SP_s = the expected beta-adjusted size premium for company s based on the firm's equity market capitalization; and

SSP_s = the expected non-beta-adjusted small stock premium for company s based on the firm's equity market capitalization.

The first calculation assumes that the company is neither more nor less risky than the market as a whole. The second calculation, however, assumes that the risk of the company is the same as the micro-cap portfolio as a whole. This poses a problem. The micro-cap portfolio is riskier than the market, but the electric utility industry is less risky than the market as a whole. Therefore, in this example, using the non-beta-adjusted size premium may overstate the cost of equity. Since the beta-adjusted size premium assumes that beta is equal to one, the buildup method may still overstate the cost of equity. We know that the electric utility industry exhibits less risk than the market and should therefore exhibit a lower return. Further adjustments for industry risk are necessary.

Industry Premia

One common element appraisers often add to the buildup approach is an industry risk premium. Traditionally, the appraiser looks at aspects and characteristics of the industry in which the subject company participates to determine the magnitude of the industry risk premium. The major problem with this process is the qualitative nature of the analysis. The magnitude of the industry premium is left to the professional opinion of the appraiser instead of a more quantitative methodology.

We have developed an industry premium methodology that appraisers can now reference and cite in their appraisal reports. This methodology relies on the full information beta estimation process outlined in Chapter 6. The full information beta methodology uses data from companies participating in an industry to evaluate the risk characteristics of that industry. To learn more about the full information approach, please refer to Chapter 6.

The full information approach provides a risk index for each industry. This risk index compares the risk level of the industry with the market as a whole. In calculating the industry risk premia presented at the end of this chapter, we only considered industries that had a full information beta between 0 and 3, and had at least five companies participating in them. Our industry risk premium estimation methodology uses the following equation:

$$IRP_i = (RI_i \times ERP) - ERP$$

where:

IRP_i = the expected industry risk premium for industry i, or the amount by which investors expect the future return of the industry to exceed that of the market as a whole;

RI_i = the risk index for industry i; and

ERP = the expected equity risk premium.

The equity risk premium figure used in this estimation process is the long-horizon expected equity risk premium outlined in Appendix C. For an industry with a risk index of 1, the expected industry risk premium will be 0, for those with a risk index less than one, the expected industry risk premium is negative, and for those with a risk index greater than 1, the expected industry risk premium is positive.

The industry risk premium estimates can be found in Table 3-5 at the end of this chapter and should be added to the risk-free rate, equity risk premium, and size premium as follows to determine a cost of equity estimate:

$$k_s = r_f + ERP + IRP_s + SP_s$$

where all of the variables are as given above and IRP_s is the appropriate expected industry risk premium for company s. Table 3-5 also presents the number of companies included in each estimate. For a full list of companies, visit www.ibbotson.com/irp and download the Industry Premia Company List Report.

Please note that the size premium to use should be the beta-adjusted size premium found in Appendix C or Table 7-5, not the simple difference in returns of large and small company stocks. Using the later in conjunction with the industry risk premium will most likely overestimate the cost of equity. As stated earlier, the simple difference between large and small company returns makes the assumption that the systematic risk of the company is the same as the risk of the small company portfolio. The industry risk premium presented here is a better measure of the appropriate systematic risk to apply.

Other Building Blocks

Other building blocks that have been used with this approach are minority discounts, control premia, and a key person discount. Use of these discounts and premia is more controversial, primarily because it is difficult to quantify their size; generally, the magnitude of the premia or discount is set subjectively. In addition, these premia do not necessarily represent rewards an investor receives for taking on a specific risk. For instance, does having a majority owner increase or decrease the risk of the business? Most would agree that the risk of a business does not change with ownership.

In some cases, however, a controlling owner may have influence on decisions that affect the risk of a business. Quantifying the effect of this controlling party in terms of a premium is not easily accomplished. Unlike other risk premia, a control premium is not readily measurable. An additional complication is that it is possible for some of these additional factors to already be present as part of the size premia.

In attempting to account for controlling interests or key people, it may be preferable to include these items when projecting cash flows, rather than making arbitrary adjustments to the discount rate. A probability weight can be assigned to the expected future cash flows based on the influence of these factors under various scenarios. From this probability distribution, the expected cash flow can be determined. By discounting these expected cash flows at a pure discount rate, one can achieve a cleaner analysis.

Estimating the Cost of Equity Using the Data Presented in this Book: Buildup Method

Due to the vast amount of data presented in this publication, the need for a reference that makes it easy to find all of the relevant data to estimate the cost of equity arose. Through the following examples, you will see how to use this book to estimate the cost of equity with the current data set as well as for any prior year using the buildup method. For similar examples using the CAPM method, refer to Chapter 4. Table numbers and alternatives are also provided to make your search easy.

Example Using Current Data

Develop a cost of equity estimate for a company operating in SIC Code 36, the Electronic and Other Electrical Equipment industry, with a market capitalization of $400 million.

Table 3-3

Buildup Method Cost of Equity Example Estimate: Current Data
Year-end 2002

	Components		Current Estimates	Table Reference
	Riskless Rate		4.8	Appendix C
+	Equity Risk Premium	+	7.0	Appendix C
+	Industry Risk Premium	+	6.5	Table 3-5
+	Size Premium	+	1.5	Appendix C
	Cost of Equity Estimate		19.8	

Table 3-3 illustrates the estimation of the cost of equity using current data and the buildup method. From Appendix C, select the yield on the riskless asset. This is the current yield on a government security or the market's current forecast of the riskless rate for the term on the security. Since we are looking to estimate the cost of equity for the entire firm, and the firm is a going concern; we should choose the long-term U.S. Treasury coupon bond yield of 4.8 percent. This current yield can also be found in Table 4-1.

Again, from Appendix C, the long horizon equity risk premium of 7.0 percent should be used.

The industry premium of 6.54 percent can be found in Table 3-5 for the Electronic and Other Electrical Equipment industry.

The company falls within the low-cap category based on the figures in Appendix C or Table 7-2, so the appropriate size premia is 1.5 percent. Alternatively, one could use the decile analysis found in Appendix C and Chapter 7, Table 7-5, to determine the appropriate size premium. In addition to size premia estimates for mid-, low-, and micro-cap companies, Appendix C and Table 7-5 contain estimates by decile. Due to the magnitude of difference between deciles, especially in the smallest deciles, it may be appropriate to use the size premium for the corresponding decile. In this example, the company we are analyzing falls within decile 8 based on the figures found in Appendix C and Table 7-2. Therefore, an alternative size premium would be 2.1 percent, the size premium for decile 8.

Example Estimating the Cost of Equity for a Prior Year

Develop a cost of equity estimate for the same company as of 1996. The company operates in SIC Code 36, the Electronic and Other Electrical Equipment industry, with a market capitalization of $186 million as of December 30, 1996.

Table 3-4

Buildup Method Cost of Equity Example Estimate: Prior Year Data
Year-end 1996

	Components		1996 Estimates	Table Reference
	Riskless Rate		6.7	Appendix B-9
+	Equity Risk Premium	+	7.5	Appendix A-1
	Industry Risk Premium	+	NA	
+	Size Premium	+	3.4	Appendix A-6
	Cost of Equity Estimate		17.6	

Table 3-4 illustrates the estimation of the cost of equity using data from 1996 and the buildup method. From Table B-9, select the yield on the riskless asset, the long-term U.S. Treasury coupon bond yield, for year-end 1996 of 6.7 percent.

From Table A-1, select the long horizon equity risk premium with starting date 1926 and ending date 1996, 7.5 percent. To find a value from Appendix A, select a beginning date across the top of the page. These tables span six pages each, so you will have to find the appropriate page. Once you find the beginning date, scroll down the first column to find the appropriate ending date. The number contained at the intersection of the beginning date 1926 and the ending date 1996, is the average value over that period.

Since Ibbotson did not calculate industry premia in 1996, this estimate is not available. In 1996, the company fell within the micro-cap category based on the figures in Table 7-3. From Table A-6, select the micro-cap size premium with starting date 1926 and ending date 1996, 3.4 percent. Please note that the omission of the industry premium results in an estimate that is lower than that of the CAPM model. An adjustment, either positive or negative, to account for industry risk may be applied. However, as stated above, Ibbotson does not provide a statistically based estimate for prior years.

Table 3-5

Industry Premia Estimates

Through Year-end 2002

SIC Code	Short Descriptions	Number of Companies*	Industry Premia
	Agriculture, Forestry, and Fishing		
01	Agricultural Production-Crops	18	-5.16%
018	Horticultural Specialties	7	-5.23%
02	Agricultural Production-Livestock and Animal Specialties	9	-0.09%
	Mining		
10	Metal Mining	15	-3.72%
104	Gold and Silver Ores	8	-4.29%
12	Coal Mining	14	-6.74%
122	Bituminous Coal and Lignite Mining	14	-6.57%
13	Oil and Gas Extraction	192	-0.83%
131	Crude Petroleum and Natural Gas	156	-1.94%
132	Natural Gas Liquids	7	-5.72%
138	Oil and Gas Field Services	46	2.90%
14	Mining and Quarrying of Nonmetallic Minerals, Except Fuels	17	-3.19%
	Construction		
15	Building Construction--General Contractors and Operative Builders	40	-1.27%
152	General Building Contractors-Residential Buildings	7	2.14%
153	Operative Builders	28	-1.22%
154	General Building Contractors-Nonresidential Buildings	7	-2.87%
16	Heavy Construction Other than Building Construction--Contractors	29	0.04%
162	Heavy Construction, Except Highway and Street Construction	26	-0.69%
17	Construction-Special Trade Contractors	28	-1.56%
173	Electrical Work	9	1.36%
179	Miscellaneous Special Trade Contractors	12	-1.77%
	Manufacturing		
20	Food and Kindred Products	126	-4.46%
201	Meat Products	14	-3.79%
203	Canned, Frozen, and Preserved Fruits, Vegetables, and Food Specialties	17	-4.90%
204	Grain Mill Products	16	-6.38%
205	Bakery Products	9	-3.82%
206	Sugar and Confectionery Products	13	-6.06%
208	Beverages	36	-4.58%
209	Miscellaneous Food Preparations and Kindred Products	21	-0.98%
21	Tobacco Products	6	-5.90%
22	Textile Mill Products	34	-4.10%
221	Broadwoven Fabric Mills, Cotton	11	-6.83%
225	Knitting Mills	6	-6.67%
227	Carpets and Rugs	6	-2.29%
23	Apparel and Other Finished Products Made from Fabrics	53	0.58%
230	Apparel and other Finished Products	7	-0.13%
232	Men's and Boys' Furnishings, Work Clothing, and Allied Garments	19	0.85%
233	Women's, Misses', and Juniors' Blouses and Shirts	19	2.47%
239	Miscellaneous Fabricated Textile Products	6	-3.15%
24	Lumber and Wood Products, Except Furniture	44	1.54%
241	Logging	10	-5.14%
242	Sawmills and Planing Mills	15	0.80%
243	Millwork, Veneer, Plywood, and Structural Wood Members	8	2.87%

*To view the full list of companies, download the Industry Premia Company List Report at www.ibbotson.com/irp.

Table 3-5 (continued)

Industry Premia Estimates

Through Year-end 2002

SIC Code	Short Descriptions	Number of Companies*	Industry Premia
	Manufacturing (continued)		
245	Wood Buildings and Mobile Homes	15	1.17%
25	Furniture and Fixtures	34	-1.33%
251	Household Furniture	14	-1.45%
252	Office Furniture	9	-0.98%
253	Public Building and Related Furniture	5	-1.97%
254	Partitions, Shelving, Lockers, and Office and Store Fixtures	5	5.69%
259	Miscellaneous Furniture and Fixtures	5	-6.33%
26	Paper and Allied Products	58	-4.54%
261	Pulp Mills	5	-2.25%
262	Paper Mills	15	-0.22%
263	Paperboard Mills	12	0.52%
265	Paperboard Containers and Boxes	9	-0.99%
267	Converted Paper and Paperboard	31	-5.91%
27	Printing, Publishing, and Allied Industries	87	-3.02%
271	Newspapers: Publishing, or Publishing and Printing	18	-3.68%
275	Commercial Printing	18	-3.67%
276	Manifold Business Forms	5	-4.76%
28	Chemicals and Allied Products	459	-2.95%
281	Industrial Inorganic Chemicals	45	-1.15%
282	Plastics Materials and Synthetic Resins	34	-2.32%
283	Drugs	288	-2.87%
284	Soap, Detergents, and Cleaning Preparation; Cosmetics, Perfumes	45	-4.59%
285	Paints, Varnishes, Lacquers, Enamels, and Allied Products	15	-2.04%
286	Industrial Organic Chemicals	29	-2.06%
287	Agricultural Chemicals	20	0.12%
289	Miscellaneous Chemical Products	29	0.17%
29	Petroleum Refining and Related Industries	24	-3.99%
291	Petroleum Refining	18	-3.83%
30	Rubber and Miscellaneous Plastics Products	95	-1.99%
301	Tires and Inner Tubes	5	-0.55%
302	Rubber and Plastics Footwear	6	-1.32%
305	Gaskets, Packing, and Sealing Devices and Rubber and Plastics Hose and Belting	5	7.54%
306	Fabricated Rubber Products, Not Elsewhere Classified	16	-6.01%
308	Miscellaneous Plastics Products	68	-1.33%
31	Leather and Leather Products	28	1.12%
314	Footwear, Except Rubber	19	0.81%
317	Handbags and Other Personal Leather Goods	5	-2.55%
32	Stone, Clay, Glass, and Concrete Products	52	-0.11%
322	Glass and Glassware, Pressed or Blown	9	6.71%
324	Cement, Hydraulic	6	-1.35%
326	Pottery and Related Products	7	5.90%
327	Concrete, Gypsum, and Plaster Products	11	-5.23%
329	Abrasive, Asbestos, and Miscellaneous Nonmetallic Mineral Products	19	4.65%
33	Primarily Metal Industries	99	3.11%
331	Steel Works, Blast Furnaces, and Rolling and Finishing Mills	42	0.96%
333	Primary Smelting and Refining of Nonferrous Metals	9	0.59%

*To view the full list of companies, download the Industry Premia Company List Report at www.ibbotson.com/irp.

Table 3-5 (continued)

Industry Premia Estimates

Through Year-end 2002

SIC Code	Short Descriptions	Number of Companies*	Industry Premia
	Manufacturing (continued)		
335	Rolling, Drawing, and Extruding of Nonferrous Metals	39	4.88%
34	Fabricated Metal Products, Except Machinery and Transportation Equipment	129	-4.93%
341	Metal Cans and Shipping Containers	7	-3.74%
342	Cutlery, Handtools, and General Hardware	20	-4.20%
343	Heating Equipment, Except Electric and Warm Air; and Plumbing Fixtures	11	-2.90%
344	Fabricated Structural Metal Products	34	-4.06%
345	Screw Machine Products, and Bolts, Nuts, Screws, Rivets, and Washers	9	-2.34%
346	Metal Forgings and Stampings	12	-1.70%
347	Coating, Engraving, and Allied Services-Con.	10	-0.02%
349	Miscellaneous Fabricated Metal Products	33	-0.19%
35	Industrial and Commercial Machinery and Computer Equipment	428	4.92%
351	Engines and Turbines	10	2.49%
352	Farm and Garden Machinery and Equipment	9	-4.05%
353	Construction, Mining, and Materials Handling Machinery and Equipment	39	0.33%
354	Metalworking Machinery and Equipment	27	-0.32%
355	Special Industry Machinery, Except Metalworking Machinery	70	9.09%
356	General Industrial Machinery and Equipment	66	-1.97%
357	Computer and Office Equipment	182	5.96%
358	Refrigeration and Service Industry Machinery	45	-2.03%
359	Miscellaneous Industrial And Commercial Machinery And Equipment	16	-1.74%
36	Electronic and Other Electrical Equipment	483	6.54%
361	Electric Transmission and Distribution Equipment	12	-4.81%
362	Electrical Industrial Apparatus	40	-0.94%
363	Household Appliances	13	0.46%
364	Electrical Lighting and Wiring Equipment	29	-1.14%
365	Household Audio and Video Equipment	21	0.35%
366	Communications Equipment	157	6.52%
367	Electronic Components and Accessories	218	8.00%
369	Miscellaneous Electrical Machinery, Equipment, and Supplies	33	-1.62%
37	Transportation Equipment	137	-2.43%
371	Motor Vehicles and Motor Vehicle Equipment	75	-0.17%
372	Aircraft Parts	39	0.02%
379	Miscellaneous Transportation Equipment	8	-3.41%
38	Measuring, Analyzing, and Controlling Equipment	390	-2.24%
382	Laboratory Apparatus and Analytical, Optical, Measuring Instruments	145	3.90%
384	Surgical, Medical, and Dental Instruments and Supplies	201	-3.24%
385	Ophthalmic Goods	7	-0.63%
386	Photographic Equipment and Supplies	17	-1.71%
39	Miscellaneous Manufacturing Industries	71	-4.62%
394	Dolls, Toys, Games and Sporting and Athletic Goods	40	-3.63%
399	Miscellaneous Manufacturing Industries	21	-3.10%
	Transportation, Communications, Electric, Gas, and Sanitary Services		
40	Railroad Transportation	12	-3.84%
401	Railroads	12	-3.84%
42	Motor Freight Transportation and Warehousing	48	-3.75%

*To view the full list of companies, download the Industry Premia Company List Report at www.ibbotson.com/irp.

Table 3-5 (continued)

Industry Premia Estimates

Through Year-end 2002

SIC Code	Short Descriptions	Number of Companies*	Industry Premia
	Transportation, Communications, Electric, Gas, and Sanitary Services (continued)		
421	Trucking and Courier Services, Except Air	42	-3.61%
422	Public Warehousing and Storage	6	-3.68%
44	Water Transportation	17	-0.40%
441	Deep Sea Foreign Transportation of Freight	7	-0.97%
45	Transportation by Air	35	0.37%
451	Air Transportation, Scheduled, and Air Courier Services	25	0.64%
452	Air Transportation, Nonscheduled	9	-3.83%
458	Airports, Flying Fields, and Airport Terminal Services	5	-2.53%
46	Pipelines, Except Natural Gas	12	-5.79%
461	Pipelines, Except Natural Gas	12	-5.41%
47	Transportation Services	33	-0.07%
472	Arrangement of Passenger Transportation	7	8.17%
473	Arrangement of Transportation of Freight and Cargo	20	-1.79%
48	Communications	178	0.73%
481	Telephone Communications	85	1.10%
483	Radio and Television Broadcasting Stations	46	4.67%
484	Cable and Other Pay Television Services	24	-0.46%
489	Communications Services, Not Elsewhere Classified	41	3.00%
49	Electric, Gas, and Sanitary Services	172	-6.62%
492	Gas Production and Distribution	67	-5.67%
493	Combination Electric and Gas, and Other Utility Services	8	-6.53%
495	Sanitary Services	42	-2.81%
499	Cogeneration Power Producers	20	-0.21%
	Wholesale Trade		
50	Wholesale Trade-Durable Goods	207	-1.75%
501	Motor Vehicles and Motor Vehicle Parts and Supplies-Wholesale	15	-5.98%
503	Lumber and Other Construction Materials	8	-5.56%
504	Professional and Commercial Equipment and Supplies	65	-2.44%
505	Metals and Minerals, Except Petroleum	14	-3.34%
506	Electrical Goods	46	2.86%
507	Hardware, and Plumbing and Heating Equipment and Supplies	16	-0.29%
508	Machinery, Equipment, and Supplies	33	-1.82%
509	Miscellaneous Durable Goods	20	-0.96%
51	Wholesale Trade-Nondurable Goods	151	-4.01%
511	Paper and Paper Products	13	0.20%
512	Drugs, Drug Proprietaries, and Druggists' Sundries	26	-5.56%
513	Apparel , Piece Goods, and Notions	7	-4.04%
514	Groceries and Related Products	25	-3.29%
516	Chemicals and Allied Products	9	-4.59%
517	Petroleum and Petroleum Products	49	-2.09%
518	Beer, Wine, and Distilled Alcoholic Beverages	5	-2.18%
519	Miscellaneous Nondurable Goods	17	-5.03%
	Retail Trade		
52	Building Materials, Hardware, Garden Supply, and Mobile Home Dealers	14	1.40%
521	Lumber and Other Building Materials Dealers	7	1.53%
53	General Merchandise Stores	31	-0.25%

*To view the full list of companies, download the Industry Premia Company List Report at www.ibbotson.com/irp.

Table 3-5 (continued)

Industry Premia Estimates

Through Year-end 2002

SIC Code	Short Descriptions	Number of Companies*	Industry Premia
	Retail Trade (continued)		
531	Department Stores	12	-0.64%
533	Variety Stores	16	-0.16%
539	Miscellaneous General Merchandise Stores	5	-0.52%
54	Food Stores	29	-3.38%
541	Grocery Stores	28	-3.40%
55	Automotive Dealers and Gasoline Service Stations	27	-1.41%
551	Motor Vehicle Dealers (New and Used)	8	-1.33%
553	Auto and Home Supply Stores	5	-2.89%
56	Apparel and Accessory Stores	67	2.18%
561	Men's and Boys' Clothing ad Accessory Stores	5	3.21%
562	Women's Clothing Stores	19	3.10%
565	Family Clothing Stores	23	2.19%
566	Shoe Stores	12	-0.44%
569	Miscellaneous Apparel and Accessory Stores	5	3.57%
57	Home Furniture, Furnishings, and Equipment Stores	36	3.22%
571	Home Furniture and Furnishings Stores	17	0.62%
573	Radio, Television, Consumer Electronics, and Music Stores	17	6.05%
58	Eating and Drinking Places	92	-2.75%
581	Eating and Drinking Places	92	-2.74%
59	Miscellaneous Retail	160	0.03%
591	Drug Stores and Proprietary Stores	15	-3.06%
593	Used Merchandise Stores	6	-3.12%
594	Miscellaneous Shopping Goods Stores	39	1.58%
596	Nonstore Retailers	79	5.49%
598	Fuel Dealers	12	-6.55%
599	Retail Stores, Not Elsewhere Classified	18	1.53%
	Finance, Insurance, and Real Estate		
60	Depository Institutions	675	-1.50%
602	Commercial Banks	412	-1.30%
603	Savings Institutions	249	-3.85%
609	Functions Related to Depository Banking	14	0.31%
61	Nondepository Credit Institutions	135	-2.71%
611	Federal and Federally-Sponsored Credit Agencies	6	-4.61%
614	Personal Credit Institutions	36	2.75%
615	Business Credit Institutions	44	0.27%
616	Mortgage Bankers and Brokers	41	-5.80%
62	Security and Commodity Brokers, Dealers, Exchanges, and Services	91	6.21%
621	Security Brokers, Dealers, and Floatation Companies	47	6.69%
628	Services Allied With the Exchange of Securities or Commodities	54	2.91%
63	Insurance Carriers	151	-2.98%
631	Life Insurance	50	-1.05%
632	Accident and Health Insurance and Medical Service Plans	35	-2.82%
633	Fire, Marine, and Casualty Insurance	70	-3.90%
635	Surety Insurance	30	-2.23%
636	Title Insurance	8	-4.62%
637	Pension, Health, and Welfare Funds	6	-1.17%

*To view the full list of companies, download the Industry Premia Company List Report at www.ibbotson.com/irp.

Table 3-5 (continued)

Industry Premia Estimates

Through Year-end 2002

SIC Code	Short Descriptions	Number of Companies*	Industry Premia
	Finance, Insurance, and Real Estate (continued)		
64	Insurance Agents, Brokers, and Service	53	-3.42%
641	Insurance Agents, Brokers, and Service	53	-2.96%
65	Real Estate	127	-5.28%
651	Real Estate Operators and Lessors	64	-4.84%
653	Real Estate Agents and Managers	22	-4.16%
655	Land Subdividers and Developers	47	-5.76%
67	Holding and Other Investment Offices	351	-5.29%
679	Miscellaneous Investing	349	-5.32%
	Services		
70	Hotels, Rooming Houses, and Other Lodging Places	35	-1.12%
701	Hotels and Motels	32	-1.09%
72	Personal Services	18	-5.05%
721	Laundry, Cleaning, and Garment Services	6	-4.52%
726	Funeral Service and Crematories	5	-0.21%
73	Business Services	986	4.97%
731	Advertising	26	0.98%
732	Consumer Credit Reporting Agencies, Mercantile Reporting Agencies, and Adjustment and Collection Agencies	9	-1.85%
733	Mailing, Reproduction, Commercial Art, and Stenographic Services	10	4.82%
734	Services to Dwellings and Other Buildings	8	-4.93%
735	Miscellaneous Equipment Rental and Leasing	41	1.81%
736	Personnel Supply Services	50	-0.33%
737	Computer Programming, Data Processing, and Other Computer Services	769	5.35%
738	Miscellaneous Business Services	116	0.31%
75	Automotive Repair, Services, and Parking	21	10.24%
751	Automotive Rental and Leasing, Without Drivers	10	13.92%
753	Automotive Repair Shops	6	-5.89%
76	Miscellaneous Repair Services	11	-5.08%
78	Motion Pictures	44	9.20%
781	Motion Picture Production and Allied Services	29	6.47%
782	Motion Picture Distribution and Allied Services	6	3.71%
783	Motion Picture Theatres	7	-3.84%
79	Amusement and Recreation Services	89	0.15%
792	Theatrical Producers (Except Motion Picture), Bands, Orchestras, and Entertainers	9	6.16%
794	Commercial Sports	18	-1.88%
799	Miscellaneous Amusement and Recreation Services	64	-2.42%
80	Health Services	98	-4.17%
801	Offices and Clinics of Doctors of Medicine	7	-5.98%
802	Offices and Clinics of Dentists	5	0.91%
805	Nursing and Personal Care Facilities	6	-0.73%
806	Hospitals	17	-5.09%
807	Medical and Dental Laboratories	20	-3.09%
808	Home Health Care Services	15	-2.80%

*To view the full list of companies, download the Industry Premia Company List Report at www.ibbotson.com/irp.

Table 3-5 (continued)

Industry Premia Estimates

Through Year-end 2002

SIC Code	Short Descriptions	Number of Companies*	Industry Premia
	Services (continued)		
809	Miscellaneous Health and Allied Services, Not Elsewhere Classified	31	-2.28%
82	Educational Services	32	-5.14%
822	Colleges, Universities, Professional Schools, and Junior Colleges	10	-4.54%
824	Vocational Schools	10	-6.23%
83	Social Services	18	-3.06%
836	Residential Care	11	-1.32%
87	Engineering, Accounting, Research, Management, and Related Services	213	-2.11%
871	Engineering, Architectural, and Surveying Services	42	-1.29%
872	Accounting, Auditing, and Bookkeeping Services	15	-1.85%
873	Research, Development, and Testing Services	87	-1.22%
874	Management and Public Relations Services	83	-1.79%

*To view the full list of companies, download the Industry Premia Company List Report at www.ibbotson.com/irp.

Chapter 4
Overview of Cost of Equity Capital Models

There are many methods for calculating the equity cost of capital. Chapter 3 discusses the buildup method for estimating the equity cost of capital. Other popular methods of calculation include the capital asset pricing model (CAPM), the discounted cash flow (DCF) method, arbitrage pricing theory (APT), and the Fama-French three factor model.

The Capital Asset Pricing Model

The capital asset pricing model (CAPM) is a simple and elegant model that describes the expected (future) rate of return on any security or portfolio of securities. It is among the most widely used techniques to estimate the cost of equity. The CAPM resulted from the efforts of three recipients of the Nobel Memorial Prize in Economic Science: Harry M. Markowitz, James Tobin, and William F. Sharpe. The Nobel committee cited the contributions to the CAPM of Tobin and Markowitz when awarding the prizes to both men. Sharpe's work on the model was the primary reason for which he won the Nobel Prize.

Systematic Risk

The principal insight of the CAPM is that the expected return on an asset is related to its risk; that is, risk-taking is rewarded. The model assumes that there is a riskless rate of return that can be earned on a hypothetical investment with returns that do not vary. A risky investment (one with returns that vary from one period to the next) will provide the investor with a reward in the form of a risk premium—an expected return higher than the riskless rate. For a particular risky investment, the CAPM indicates that the size of the risk premium is proportionate, in a linear fashion, to the amount of systematic risk taken.

The CAPM breaks up the total risk (the variability of returns) of an investment into two parts: systematic risk and unsystematic risk. Systematic risk is unavoidable and pervades (to a greater or lesser degree) every asset in the real economy and every claim (such as a stock) on those assets. Systematic risk generally springs from external, macroeconomic factors that affect all companies in a particular fashion, albeit with different magnitudes. The CAPM concludes that taking systematic risk is rewarded with a risk premium. The size of the risk premium is proportionate to the degree of co-movement of the security or portfolio (called beta) with the market portfolio consisting of all risky assets.

In contrast, unsystematic risk is that portion of total risk that can be avoided through diversification. The CAPM concludes that unsystematic risk is not rewarded with a risk premium. For example, the possibility that a firm will lose market share to a competitor is a source of unsystematic risk for its stock. (See Chapter 6 for additional information on beta and systematic risk.)

The security market line represents the relationship between expected return and systematic risk. This linear relationship forms the security market line, which is depicted in Graph 4-1.

Graph 4-1

The Security Market Line

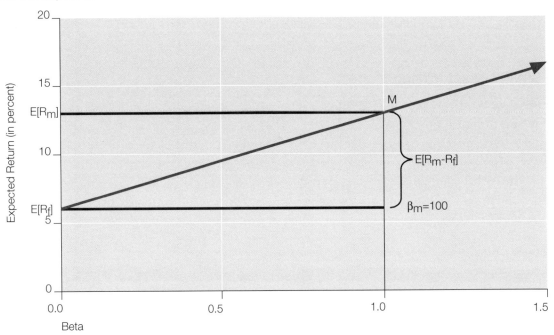

The riskless asset forms the y-intercept of the security market line and represents the expected return on the asset with no systematic risk (beta equal to zero). The market portfolio by definition has a beta of one. Drawing a line that passes through the riskless asset and the market portfolio forms the security market line. Theoretically, to be fairly priced, every stock or portfolio of stocks should fall on the line.[1]

The relationship between systematic risk and expected return can also be expressed mathematically. The CAPM describes the cost of equity for any company's stock as equal to the riskless rate plus an amount proportionate to the systematic risk an investor assumes.

$$k_s = r_f + (\beta_s \times ERP)$$

where:

k_s = the cost of equity for company s;

r_f = the expected return of the riskless asset;

β_s = the beta of the stock of company s; and

ERP = the expected equity risk premium, or the amount by which investors expect the future return on equities to exceed that on the riskless asset.

Since the CAPM has only three variables—the expected return on the riskless asset, the beta of the stock, and the expected equity risk premium—it is one of the easiest models to implement in practice.

---

1 This relationship does not seem to hold empirically with small company stocks. This size effect is discussed in Chapter 7.

However, an estimate of each of the above three variables must be formed. Like all components of the cost of capital, these variables should be measured on a forward-looking basis. Chapters 5 and 6 are devoted to estimating the equity risk premium and beta, respectively. Factors to consider in estimating the riskless rate are covered below.

Risk-Free Rate

The CAPM implicitly assumes the presence of a single riskless asset, that is, an asset perceived by all investors as having no risk. A common choice for the nominal riskless rate is the yield on a U.S. Treasury security. The ability of the U.S. government to create money to fulfill its debt obligations under virtually any scenario makes U.S. Treasury securities practically default-free. While interest rate changes cause government obligations to fluctuate in price, investors face essentially no default risk as to either coupon payment or return of principal.

The horizon of the chosen Treasury security should match the horizon of whatever is being valued. When valuing a business that is being treated as a going concern, the appropriate Treasury yield should be that of a long-term Treasury bond. Note that the horizon is a function of the investment, not the investor. If an investor plans to hold stock in a company for only five years, the yield on a five-year Treasury note would not be appropriate since the company will continue to exist beyond those five years.

In February of 1977 the Treasury began to issue 30-year Treasury securities. Prior to this date, the longest-term Treasury security was 20 years. To remain consistent with Ibbotson's historical data series, the *Stocks, Bonds, Bills, and Inflation Yearbook* continues to base the yield for its long-term government bond on one with close to 20 years to maturity. In recent years the Treasury ceased offering 30-year securities, however. As long as there are bonds being traded with at least 20 years to maturity, there will be a proxy for the yield on 20 year Treasury securities. It would not be for a number of years from now that lack of data may become an issue. Currently, the longest term security offered by the Treasury is 10 years. Differences in the yields of these long-term instruments tend to be very small. Therefore, it would be appropriate to use either maturity bond to represent a long-term riskless rate. Table 4-1 shows the current yields for several different horizons.

Table 4-1

Current Yields or Expected Riskless Rates
December 31, 2002

	Yield (Riskless Rate)*
Long-Term (20-year) U.S. Treasury Coupon Bond Yield	4.8%
Long-Term (10-year) U.S. Treasury Coupon Bond Yield	3.8%
Intermediate-Term (5-year) U.S. Treasury Coupon Note Yield	2.6%
Short-term (30-day) U.S. Treasury Bill Yield	1.2%

*Maturities are approximate.

Should the yield on a Treasury bond or a Treasury strip be used to represent the riskless rate? In most cases the yield on a Treasury coupon bond is most appropriate. If the asset being measured spins off cash periodically, the Treasury bond most closely replicates this characteristic. On the other hand, if the asset being measured provides a single payoff at the end of a specified term, the yield on a Treasury Strip would be more appropriate.

CAPM Modified for Firm Size

One of the important characteristics not necessarily captured by the Capital Asset Pricing Model is what is known as the size effect. This is discussed in detail in Chapter 7. The need for this premium when using the CAPM arises because, even after adjusting for the systematic (beta) risk of small stocks, they outperform large stocks. The betas for small companies tend to be greater than those for large companies; however, these higher betas do not account for all of the risks faced by those who invest in small companies.[2] This premium can be added directly to the results obtained using the CAPM:

$$k_s = r_f + (\beta_s \times ERP) + SP_s$$

where all of the variables are as given in the previous section on the CAPM and SP_s is the appropriate size premium based on the firm's equity market capitalization. The market capitalization of company s will determine the relevant size premium: mid-cap, low-cap, or micro-cap.

Suppose we wish to calculate the cost of equity for a small electric utility company. To better account for both the industry risk and the firm size, we wish to use the modified CAPM approach. The company has a market capitalization of \$135 million and falls within the micro-cap size group. Assume that the beta of the company is 0.53. The key variables for calculating the cost of equity using this size-premium-adjusted CAPM are:

Risk-free rate	= 4.8 percent
Expected equity risk premium	= 7.0 percent
The appropriate size premium	= 3.5 percent

Using the modified CAPM equation, the cost of equity for the electric utility company is:

$$k_s = r_f + (\beta_s \times ERP) + SP_s = 4.8\% + (0.53 \times 7.0\%) + 3.5\% = 12.0\%$$

The beta-adjusted size premium is the most appropriate for use with this model. Please note that the size premia commonly referred to in this publication are the beta-adjusted size premia, unless stated otherwise. The non-beta-adjusted size premia already account for the added return generally attributed to the higher betas of small companies. The non-beta-adjusted size premium makes the assumption that the beta of the company is the same as that of the small stock portfolio. If the non-beta-adjusted size premium is used in the context of the modified CAPM equation above, the effect of beta on return will essentially be counted double. Multiplying the equity risk premium by another measure of beta (either the company beta or industry beta) introduces to the same equation a duplicate, though possibly different, measure of systematic risk.[3]

2 In general, small company betas are expected to be higher than large company betas. This, however, does not hold for all time periods. Chapter 6 discusses in more detail the measurement of beta for small stocks.

3 The beta-adjusted size premia are different from the small stock premia (or non-beta-adjusted size premia) shown in previous editions of the *Stocks, Bonds, Bills, and Inflation Yearbook* (prior to the *1995 Yearbook*). The small stock premium reported in older editions of *Stocks, Bonds, Bills, and Inflation* is the difference in long-term average returns between the large company stock total return series (currently represented by the S&P 500) and the small company stock total return series (currently represented by the Dimensional Fund Advisors U.S. Micro Cap Portfolio). The size premia given here are based on slightly different baskets of stocks from the CRSP (Center for Research in Security Prices) data set and, more importantly, they are adjusted for beta. That is, small stocks do have higher betas than large stocks; the return, above what might be expected because of the higher betas, is the size premium. These size premia increase as the capitalization of the company decreases. Chapter 7 describes the development of these premia in more detail.

Estimating the Cost of Equity Using the Data Presented in this Book: Modified CAPM Method

Due to the vast amount of data presented in this publication, the need for a reference that makes it easy to find all the relevant data to estimate the cost of equity arose. Through the following examples, you will see how to use this book to estimate the cost of equity with the current data set as well as for any prior year using the modified CAPM method. For similar examples using the buildup method, refer to Chapter 3. Table numbers and alternatives are also provided to make your search easy.

Example Using Current Data

Develop a cost of equity estimate for a company operating in SIC Code 36, the Electronic and Other Electrical Equipment industry, with a market capitalization of $400 million. The beta for this industry is estimated to be 1.94.[4]

Table 4-2

Modified CAPM Cost of Equity Example Estimate: Current Data
Year-end 2002

	Components		Current Estimates		Table Reference
	Riskless Rate		4.8		Appendix C
+	Industry Beta ×	+	1.94	×	Beta Book
	Equity Risk Premium		7.0		Appendix C
+	Size Premium	+	1.5		Appendix C
	Cost of Equity Estimate		19.9		

Table 4-2 illustrates the estimation of the cost of equity using current data and the CAPM modified for size. From Appendix C, select the yield on the riskless asset. This is the current yield on a government security or the market's current forecast of the riskless rate for the term on the security. Since we are looking to estimate the cost of equity for the entire firm, and the firm is a going concern; we should choose the long-term U.S. Treasury coupon bond yield of 4.8 percent. This current yield can also be found in Table 4-1.

Again, from Appendix C, the long horizon equity risk premium of 7.0 percent is the appropriate horizon equity risk premium.

The company falls within the low-cap category based on the figures in Appendix C or Table 7-2, so the appropriate size premium is 1.5 percent. Alternatively, one could use the decile analysis found in Chapter 7, Table 7-5, to determine the appropriate size premium. In addition to size premia estimates for mid-, low-, and micro-cap companies, Table 7-5 contains estimates by decile. Due to the magnitude of difference between deciles, especially in the smallest deciles, it may be appropriate to use the size premium for the corresponding decile from Table 7-5. In this example, the company

---

4 Beta estimate is based on the full information beta for SIC code 36 from the *Ibbotson Associates' Beta Book* as of December 31, 2002. This beta estimation methodology is described in detail in Chapter 6.

we are analyzing falls within decile 8 based on the figures found in Table 7-2. Therefore, an alternative size premium would be 2.1 percent, the size premium for decile 8 from Table 7-5.

Example Estimating the Cost of Equity for a Prior Year

Develop a cost of equity estimate for the same company as of 1996. The company operates in SIC Code 36, the Electronic and Other Electrical Equipment industry, with a market capitalization of $186 million as of December 30, 1996. The beta for this industry was estimated at 1.29 as of 1996.

Table 4-3

Modified CAPM Cost of Equity Example Estimate: Prior Year Data
Year-end 1996

	Components			1996 Estimates		Table Reference
	Riskless Rate			6.7		Appendix B-9
+	Industry Beta	×	+	1.29	×	Beta Book
	Equity Risk Premium			7.5		Appendix A-1
+	Size Premium		+	3.4		Appendix A-6
	Cost of Equity Estimate			19.8		

Table 4-3 illustrates the estimation of the cost of equity using data from 1996 and the modified CAPM. From Table B-9, select the yield on the riskless asset, the long-term U.S. Treasury coupon bond yield, for year-end 1996 of 6.7 percent.

The industry beta for SIC 36 was estimated using the full information approach. It was taken from the December 31, 1996 edition of the *Ibbotson Beta Book*. Alternative industry betas can also be found in Ibbotson's *Cost of Capital Yearbook*.

From Table A-1, select the long horizon equity risk premium with starting date 1926 and ending date 1996, 7.5 percent. To find a value from Appendix A, select a beginning date across the top of the page. These tables span five pages each, so you will have to find the appropriate page. Once you find the beginning date, scroll down the first column to find the appropriate ending date. The number contained at the intersection of the beginning date 1926 and the ending date 1996, is the average value over that period.

In 1996, the company fell within the micro-cap category based on the figures in Table 7-3. From Table A-6, select the micro-cap size premium with starting date 1926 and ending date 1996, 3.4 percent. Unlike the above example using current data, a further breakout of this analysis by decile is not available on a historic basis.

Arbitrage Pricing Theory

The arbitrage pricing theory (APT) is a model of the expected return of a security. It was developed by Stephen A. Ross and elaborated by Richard Roll.[5] APT treats the expected return on a security (i.e., its cost of capital) as the sum of the payoffs for an indeterminate number of risk factors; the

5 Roll, Richard, and Stephen A. Ross. "An Empirical Investigation of the Arbitrage Pricing Theory," *Journal of Finance*, Vol. 35, no. 5, December 1980, pp. 1073–1103.

exposure to each risk factor inherent in a given security is estimated. The measures of exposure are called the factor loadings of the security. Like the CAPM, APT is a model that is consistent with equilibrium and does not attempt to outguess the market.

Nai-fu Chen, with Roll and Ross, conducted an empirical investigation of APT relating stock returns to macroeconomic factors.[6] They found five factors to be important: 1) changes in industrial production, 2) changes in anticipated inflation, 3) unanticipated inflation, 4) the return differential between low-grade corporate bonds and government bonds (both with long maturities), and 5) the return differential between long-term government bonds and short-term Treasury bills. APT risk premia are additive, as in the CAPM; therefore, differences of arithmetic means should be used as estimates of future risk premia.

The cost of capital for a stock, bond, or company can be estimated using APT. This is generally accomplished by estimating the size of the payoffs for each risk factor and the amount of each risk factor inherent in the given security.

A standard APT formulation is:

$$k_s = r_f + \beta_{s1}RP_1 + \beta_{s2}RP_2 + \ldots + \beta_{sn}RP_n$$

where:

k_s	= the cost of equity for company s;
r_f	= the riskless rate;
$RP_1, RP_2, \ldots RP_n$	= the various risk premia; and
$\beta_{s1}, \beta_{s2}, \ldots \beta_{sn}$	= the factor loadings (or exposure of the security to each of the risks).

Fama-French Three Factor Model

Other models for computing the cost of equity capital rely on "anomalies"—or apparent violations of the CAPM or other equilibrium models—such as the size effect, described above. Professors Eugene Fama and Kenneth French developed one such model. They found that returns on stocks are better explained as a function of a company's size (capturing the size effect) and its book-to-market ratio (capturing the financial distress of a firm) in addition to the single market factor of the CAPM.[7] Specifically, they found that the return on a firm's cost of equity is negatively related to its size and positively related to its book-to-market ratio. In other words, firms with smaller equity capitalization have higher expected cost of equity, and firms with higher book value relative to market value also have higher expected cost of equity. This finding suggests a predictive model in which these variables—size and book-to-market ratio—are used (in conjunction with beta) to estimate the expected return or cost of equity capital. Chapter 8 covers this model in detail.

---

6 Chen, Nai-fu. "Some Empirical Tests of Arbitrage Pricing," *Journal of Finance*, Vol. 18, no. 5, December 1983, pp. 1393–1414.
  Chen, Nai-fu, Richard Roll, and Stephen A. Ross. "Economic Forces and the Stock Market: Testing the APT and Alternative Pricing Theories," *Journal of Business*, Vol. 59, July 1986, pp. 383–403.
7 Fama, Eugene, and Kenneth French. "The Cross-Section of Expected Stock Returns," *Journal of Finance*, Vol. 47, 1992a, pp. 427–465.

The Discounted Cash Flow Model

The discounted cash flow model, or income method, was developed by John Burr Williams and elaborated by Myron J. Gordon and Eli Shapiro.[8] The model uses the cost of capital to discount the expected cash flows to the present value. There are several different forms of the discounted cash flow model. The most general form of the model can be written as follows:

$$PV_s = \frac{CF_1}{\left(1+k_s\right)^1} + \frac{CF_2}{\left(1+k_s\right)^2} + ... + \frac{CF_i}{\left(1+k_s\right)^i}$$

where:
PV_s = the present value of the expected cash flows for company s;
CF_i = the dividend or cash flow expected to be received at the end of period i; and
k_s = the cost of capital for company s.

In order to solve for the cost of capital, one must forecast each of the future cash flows, and the present value of the company must be known. Solving for the cost of capital, k, is an iterative process that generally requires the use of a computer program. The model in the long form is difficult to work with since each and every future cash flow must be forecasted. A simplification of the long form of the model is required to make it more useful. This can be accomplished by assuming that the cash flows grow at a constant rate.

The Single-Stage Growth Model (Gordon Growth Model)

In its simplest form, this model describes the cost of equity capital for a dividend-paying stock that has a constant expected dividend growth rate in perpetuity. This form of the discounted cash flow approach is known as the single-stage growth model or the Gordon Growth Model. We can simplify the equation by replacing the cash flows of the long-form discounted cash flow model with the following:

$$CF_i = CF_1\left(1+g_s\right)^{(i-1)}$$

where:
CF_i = the dividend or cash flow expected to be received at the end of period i; and
g_s = the expected dividend or cash flow growth rate into perpetuity.

That is, each cash flow is now assumed to grow at a constant rate, g_s. The discounted cash flow equation simplifies to the following:

$$PV_s = \frac{CF_1}{\left(k_s - g_s\right)}$$

8 Williams, John Burr. *The Theory of Investment Value*, Harvard University Press, Cambridge, Mass., 1938.
Gordon, Myron J., and Eli Shapiro. "Capital Equipment Analysis: The Required Rate of Profit," *Management Science*, Vol. 3, October 1956, pp. 102–110.

Rearranging the terms to solve for the equity cost of capital results in:

$$k_s = \frac{CF_1}{PV_s} + g_s$$

where:

$$CF_1 = CF_0(1 + g_s)$$

k_s = the cost of equity for company s;

CF_0 = the current period dividend or cash flow earned by shareholders in company s;

CF_1 = the expected dividend or cash flow to be earned in the next period by shareholders in company s;

PV_s = the current market value of company s; and

g_s = the expected dividend or cash flow growth rate into perpetuity.

The discounted cash flow model in this form is simple to use. The value of a stock is directly observable as its price in the market. One difficulty with this model, however, is obtaining an accurate perpetual dividend or cash flow growth forecast because dividends and cash flows do not in fact grow at stable rates forever. It is typically easier to forecast a company-specific or project-specific growth rate over the short run than over the long run. One way of obtaining such a forecast is to use a consensus of security analysts' estimates, which generally cover a short period of time.

For example, assume that a company has a current market price of $50 and a recent annual dividend of $2, and that the consensus of the security analysts' growth estimates is 8 percent. The estimated cost of capital would be:

$$CF_1 = CF_0(1 + g_s) = \$2(1 + 0.08) = \$2.16$$

$$k_s = \frac{CF_1}{PV_s} + g_s = \frac{\$2.16}{\$50} + 0.08 = 0.0432 + 0.08 = 12.32 \text{ percent}$$

In this example, we made the assumption that the analysts' growth rate is constant.

Another difficulty with implementing the single-stage growth model is that it does not allow the growth rate to exceed the cost of equity. Recall that in the original equation, the term $(k_s - g_s)$ was in the denominator. If g_s exceeds k_s, the result is a negative present value. Growth can exceed the cost of equity for some rapidly growing firms. A model that allows the growth rate to change over time and to exceed the cost of equity can produce a better estimate of the equity cost of capital.

The Two-Stage Growth Model

To produce a better estimate of the equity cost of capital, one can use a multi-stage discounted cash flow model. All multi-stage discounted cash flow models allow for the growth rate to exceed the cost of equity in all but the last stage. The two-stage growth model can be expressed as follows:

$$PV_s = \sum_{i=1}^{n} \frac{CF_0(1+g_1)^i}{(1+k_s)^i} + \frac{\dfrac{CF_n(1+g_2)}{(k_s-g_2)}}{(1+k_s)^n}$$

where:

k_s	=	the cost of equity for company s;
PV_s	=	the current market value of company s;
i	=	a measure of time (in this example the unit of measure is a year);
n	=	the number of years in the first stage of growth;
CF_0	=	the dividend or cash flow amount (in $) in year 0;
CF_n	=	the expected dividend or cash flow amount (in $) in year n;
g_1	=	the expected dividend or cash flow growth rate from year 1 to year n; and
g_2	=	the expected perpetual dividend or cash flow growth rate starting in year (n + 1).

The equity cost of capital is given by the value of k_s, which makes the right-hand side of the above equation equal to the current stock price (PV_s). The first summation term denotes the present value of dividends expected over the first n years, and the second summation term denotes the present value of dividends expected over all the years thereafter. For the resulting cost of capital estimate to be useful, the growth rate over the latter period should be sustainable indefinitely. An example of an indefinitely sustainable growth rate is the expected long-run growth rate of the economy.

To illustrate the two-stage growth model, we can alter the growth assumptions of the example found under the single-stage model. Assume that the analysts' growth rate of 8 percent applies only to years one through five. For years 6 and onwards, assume a growth rate of 5 percent.

Year	Growth Rate	Annual Dividend	Present Value Factor @ 9.78 Percent	Present Value of Dividend
0		$2.00	1.00	
1	8.0%	$2.16	0.91	$1.97
2	8.0%	$2.33	0.83	$1.94
3	8.0%	$2.52	0.76	$1.90
4	8.0%	$2.72	0.69	$1.87
5	8.0%	$2.94	0.62	$1.84
6–forever	5.0%	$3.09	13.12	$40.48
			Total	$50.00

We arrive at the current stock price of $50 by discounting this stream of cash flows at an estimated rate of 9.78 percent. This is a considerably different estimate compared to the 12.32 percent we arrive at using a constant growth rate of 8 percent. Therefore, the growth rate assumptions can have a significant impact on the cost of equity estimate.

The Three-Stage Growth Model

Additional growth stages can be used but, in practice, only one-, two-, or three-stage discounted cash flow models are usually employed. The three-stage model is denoted as follows:

$$PV_s = \sum_{i=1}^{n1} \frac{CF_0(1+g_1)^i}{(1+k_s)^i} + \sum_{i=n1+1}^{n2} \frac{CF_{n1}(1+g_2)^i}{(1+k_s)^i} + \frac{\frac{CF_{n2}(1+g_3)}{(k_s-g_3)}}{(1+k_s)^{n2}}$$

where:

k_s	=	the cost of equity for company s;
PV_s	=	the current market value of company s;
i	=	a measure of time (in this example the unit of measure is a year);
n_1	=	the number of years in the first stage of growth;
n_2	=	the number of years in the second stage of growth;
CF_0	=	the dividend or cash flow amount (in $) in year 0;
CF_{n1}	=	the expected dividend or cash flow amount (in $) in year n_1;
CF_{n2}	=	the expected dividend or cash flow amount (in $) in year n_2;
g_1	=	the expected dividend or cash flow growth rate from year 1 to year n_1;
g_2	=	the expected dividend or cash flow growth rate from year (n_1 + 1) to year n_2; and
g_3	=	the expected perpetual dividend or cash flow growth rate starting in year (n_2 + 1).

To illustrate the three-stage growth model, we alter the growth assumptions of the two-stage model example. Again we assume that the analysts' growth rate of eight percent applies only to years one through five. For years 6 through 10, we assume a growth rate of 6.5 percent. In the last stage, from year 11 and beyond, we assume a perpetual growth rate of 5 percent.

Year	Growth Rate	Annual Dividend	Present Value Factor @ 10.03 Percent	Present Value of Dividend
0		$2.00	1.00	
1	8.0%	$2.16	0.91	$1.96
2	8.0%	$2.33	0.83	$1.93
3	8.0%	$2.52	0.76	$1.89
4	8.0%	$2.72	0.69	$1.86
5	8.0%	$2.94	0.62	$1.82
6	6.5%	$3.13	0.56	$1.76
7	6.5%	$3.33	0.51	$1.71
8	6.5%	$3.55	0.47	$1.65
9	6.5%	$3.78	0.42	$1.60
10	6.5%	$4.03	0.38	$1.55
11–forever	5.0%	$4.23	7.63	$32.26
			Total	$50.00

By discounting this stream of cash flows at a rate of 10.03 percent, we arrive at the current stock price of $50.

Quarterly Dividend Adjustment

When valuing a stock, one should remember that even though dividends grow and are declared annually, they are usually paid in equal quarterly installments. In order to account for this in the discounted cash flow model, each cash flow can be replaced by the following term:

$$CF_i \times \frac{1 + (1+k)^{\frac{1}{4}} + (1+k)^{\frac{1}{2}} + (1+k)^{\frac{3}{4}}}{4}$$

If we look at the same example that was used for the two-stage discounted cash flow model but use the quarterly dividend adjustment, the cost of equity estimate becomes 9.95 percent instead of 9.78 percent. The higher discount rate reflects the difference in timing of the cash flows.

Year	Growth Rate	Annual Dividend	Periodic Dividend	Reinvestment	Total Dividend	Present Value Factor @ 9.95 Percent	Present Value of Dividend
0		$2.00				1.00	
1	8.0%	$2.16	$0.54	$0.08	$2.24	0.91	$2.04
2	8.0%	$2.33	$0.58	$0.09	$2.42	0.83	$2.00
3	8.0%	$2.52	$0.63	$0.09	$2.61	0.75	$1.96
4	8.0%	$2.72	$0.68	$0.10	$2.82	0.68	$1.93
5	8.0%	$2.94	$0.73	$0.10	$3.05	0.62	$1.90
6–forever	5.0%	$3.09	$0.77	$0.11	$3.20	12.56	$40.17

Total $50.00

Estimating Growth Rates

One of the advantages of a three-stage discounted cash flow model is that it fits with life cycle theories in regards to company growth. In these theories, companies are assumed to have a life cycle with varying growth characteristics. Typically, the potential for extraordinary growth in the near term eases over time and eventually growth slows to a more stable level.

In Ibbotson's *Cost of Capital Yearbook* publication the three-stage growth model is used. In the first stage (the first five years), analysts' consensus estimates of earnings growth are used. These should reflect any extraordinary near-term growth potential. Over years 6 through 10, an average of the analysts' consensus estimates of growth for the entire industry is used. (We assume that over a middle horizon, growth of any particular company will lie more in line with the industry as a whole.) Finally, in years 11 and beyond, a growth rate estimate for the entire economy is used, reflecting the belief that even in a rapidly growing industry there will come a time when growth slows to be more in line with the overall economy.

Short-term growth rates are generally available from security analysts who follow a particular company or industry. Long-term growth rates can be estimated in a number of ways. One rudimentary estimate of long-term growth is the sustainable-growth model. This model relies on two accounting concepts: return on equity and the plow-back ratio.

Sustainable growth is then given by:

$$g_s = b_s \times ROE$$

where:

g_s =   the sustainable growth rate for company s;

b_s =   the plow-back ratio of company s calculated as follows:

$$\frac{\text{Annual Earnings} - \text{Annual Dividends}}{\text{Annual Earnings}} \text{; and}$$

ROE_s =   the return on book equity of company s calculated as follows:

$$\frac{\text{Annual Earnings}}{\text{Book Value of Equity}}$$

This model relies on a number of assumptions that may or may not hold. The first of these assumptions is that ROE and the plow-back of earnings are constant over time. That is, there exists a forecast of these two accounting ratios that is sustainable in the long term. Though the model appears simple to implement at first glance, finding a forecast of the ratios that is sustainable indefinitely is extremely difficult. Dividend policy and potential investment opportunities change over time and have a direct impact on these ratios.

The model assumes that the only possible source of corporate earnings growth is the reinvestment of earnings into the existing business and that any investment of funds in the firm will earn the same rate of return as existing projects. However, firms generally seek projects that have a higher return than existing projects. The sustainable growth model may therefore underestimate a firm's future growth. Other problems may arise because the model relies on accounting practices that can distort earnings.

In addition, other sources of growth may exist that do not require the plow-back of earnings. Changes in technology can advance growth with little capital expenditure by a firm. For instance, efficiency in the transfer of information has improved tremendously over the years as a result of internet technology. Many companies benefit from this increased efficiency with little directly investing in the Internet. A company may also grow at the rate of inflation without retaining any earnings. The growth rate that the model estimates is a nominal growth rate, not a real growth rate. If retained earnings are zero, the model predicts zero growth; however, a firm could still grow at the general rate of inflation.

Another approach to estimating long-term growth rates is to focus on estimating the overall economic growth rate. Again, this is the approach used in Ibbotson's *Cost of Capital Yearbook* publication. To obtain the economic growth rate, a forecast is made of the growth rate's component parts. Expected growth can be broken into two main parts: expected inflation and expected real growth. By analyzing these components separately, it is easier to see the factors that drive growth.

There are numerous approaches to estimate expected inflation. Surveys tend to focus on the short term and therefore are not representative of long-term expectations. Inflation-indexed bonds are a relatively new investment vehicle. In theory, the yield on these bonds is equal to the real default-free rate of return. In addition, the face value of these bonds is marked to the consumer price index (CPI). Since this investment vehicle is so new, however, its predictive ability has not been sufficiently tested. One can also obtain a market consensus long-term inflation estimate from analyzing the conventional bond market.

The market consensus forecast of inflation is embedded into the long-term yields of Treasury bonds. The yield on a Treasury bond can be broken down into three components:

Yield = Expected Inflation Rate + Expected Real Riskless Rate of Return + Horizon Premium

None of the three components are observable. Estimates of the expected real riskless rate and the horizon premium are formed from statistical relationships evident in forward rates and historical data. These estimates are then subtracted from the observed market yield to obtain the expected inflation rate. For example, if the long-term government bond has a yield of 4.8 percent, the expected real rate of return is 0.6 percent and the expected horizon premia is 1.4 percent, then the long-term inflation estimate would be 2.8 percent (4.8 percent less 0.6 percent less 1.4 percent).

Once the long-term expected inflation rate is estimated, the real growth rate must be determined. The growth rate in real Gross Domestic Product (GDP) for the period 1929 to 2002 was approximately 3.5 percent. Growth in real GDP (with only a few exceptions) has been reasonably stable over time; therefore, its historical performance is a good estimate of expected long-term (future) performance.

By combining the inflation estimate with the real growth rate estimate, a long-term estimate of nominal growth is formed:

2.8 percent + 3.5 percent = 6.3 percent.

Chapter 5
The Equity Risk Premium

The expected equity risk premium can be defined as the additional return an investor expects to receive to compensate for the additional risk associated with investing in equities as opposed to investing in riskless assets. It is an essential component in several cost of equity estimation models, including the buildup method, the capital asset pricing model (CAPM), and the Fama-French three factor model. It is important to note that the expected equity risk premium, as it is used in discount rates and cost of capital analysis, is a forward-looking concept. That is, the equity risk premium that is used in the discount rate should be reflective of what investors think the risk premium will be going forward.

Unfortunately, the expected equity risk premium is unobservable in the market and therefore must be estimated. Typically, this estimation is arrived at through the use of historical data. The historical equity risk premium can be calculated by subtracting the long-term average of the income return on the riskless asset (Treasuries) from the long-term average stock market return (measured over the same period as that of the riskless asset).

In using a historical measure of the equity risk premium, one assumes that what has happened in the past is representative of what might be expected in the future. In other words, the assumption one makes when using historical data to measure the expected equity risk premium is that the relationship between the returns of the risky asset (equities) and the riskless asset (Treasuries) is stable. The stability of this relationship will be examined later in this chapter.

Since the expected equity risk premium must be estimated, there is much controversy regarding how the estimation should be conducted. The range of equity risk premium estimates used in practice is surprisingly large. Using a low equity risk premium estimate as opposed to a high estimate can have a significant impact on the estimated value of a stream of cash flows. This chapter addresses many of the controversies surrounding estimation of the equity risk premium.

Calculating the Historical Equity Risk Premium

In measuring the historical equity risk premium one must make a number of decisions that can impact the resulting figure; some decisions have a greater impact than others. These decisions include selecting the stock market benchmark, the risk-free asset, either an arithmetic or a geometric average, and the time period for measurement. Each of these factors has an impact on the resulting equity risk premium estimate.

The Stock Market Benchmark

The stock market benchmark chosen should be a broad index that reflects the behavior of the market as a whole. Two examples of commonly used indexes are the S&P 500® and the New York Stock Exchange Composite Index. Although the Dow Jones Industrial Average is a popular index, it would be inappropriate for calculating the equity risk premium because it is too narrow.

Ibbotson Associates uses the total return of its large company stock index (currently represented by the S&P 500) as its market benchmark when calculating the equity risk premium. The S&P 500 was selected as the appropriate market benchmark because it is representative of a large sample of companies across a large number of industries. As of December 31, 1993, 88 separate industry groups were included in the index, and the industry composition of the index has not changed since. The S&P 500 is also one of the most widely accepted market benchmarks. In short, the S&P 500 is a good measure of the equity market as a whole. Table 5-1 illustrates the equity risk premium calculation using several different market indices and the income return on three government bonds of different horizons.

Table 5-1

Equity Risk Premium with Different Market Indices
1926–2002

	Equity Risk Premia		
	Long-Horizon	Intermediate-Horizon	Short-Horizon
S&P 500	6.97%	7.40%	8.37%
Total Value-Weighted NYSE	6.67	7.10	8.07
NYSE Deciles 1–2	6.23	6.66	7.63

The equity risk premium is calculated by subtracting the arithmetic mean of the government bond income return from the arithmetic mean of the stock market total return. Table 5-2 demonstrates this calculation for the long-horizon equity risk premium.

Table 5-2

Long-Horizon Equity Risk Premium Calculation
1926–2002*

	Arithmetic Mean				
	Market Total Return		Risk-Free Rate		Long-Horizon Equity Risk Premium
S&P 500	12.20%	–	5.23%	=	6.97%
Total Value-Weighted NYSE	11.91	–	5.23	=	6.68
NYSE Deciles 1–2	11.47	–	5.23	=	6.24

Data for the New York Stock Exchange is obtained from the Center for Research in Security Prices (CRSP) at the University of Chicago's Graduate School of Business. The "Total" series is a capitalization-weighted index and includes all stocks traded on the New York Stock Exchange except closed-end mutual funds, real estate investment trusts, foreign stocks, and Americus Trusts. Capitalization-weighted means that the weight of each stock in the index, for a given month, is proportionate to its market capitalization (price times number of shares outstanding) at the beginning of that month. The "Decile 1-2" series includes all stocks with capitalizations that rank within the upper 20 percent of companies traded on the New York Stock Exchange, and it is therefore a large-capitalization index. For more information on the Center for Research in Security Pricing data methodology, see Chapter 7.

The resulting equity risk premia vary somewhat depending on the market index chosen. It is expected that using the "Total" series will result in a higher equity risk premium than using the "Decile 1–2" series, since the "Decile 1-2" series is a large-capitalization series. As of September 30, 2002, deciles 1–2 of the New York Stock Exchange contained the largest 350 companies traded on the exchange. The "Total" series includes smaller companies that have had historically higher returns, resulting in a higher equity risk premium.

The higher equity risk premium arrived at by using the S&P 500 as a market benchmark is more difficult to explain. One possible explanation is that the S&P 500 is not restricted to the largest 500 companies; other considerations such as industry composition are taken into account when determining if a company should be included in the index. Some smaller stocks are thus included, which may result in the higher equity risk premium of the index.

Another possible explanation would be what is termed the "S&P inclusion effect." It is thought that simply being included among the stocks listed on the S&P 500 augments a company's returns. This is due to the large quantity of institutional funds that flow into companies that are listed in the index.

Comparing the S&P 500 total returns to those of another large-capitalization stock index may help evaluate the potential impact of the "S&P inclusion effect." Graph 5-1 shows that, excluding the years 1999 and 2000, the difference in returns on the S&P 500 and the NYSE deciles 1–2 has been decreasing; from the middle of the 1950s to the present, the two benchmarks appear to track each other more closely. This result is the opposite of what one would expect with an increase in institutional monies invested in S&P 500 companies, yet it does correspond to a change in the way the S&P large company index is measured.

Graph 5-1

Annual Excess Returns of the S&P 500 Over the NYSE Deciles 1–2

1926–2002

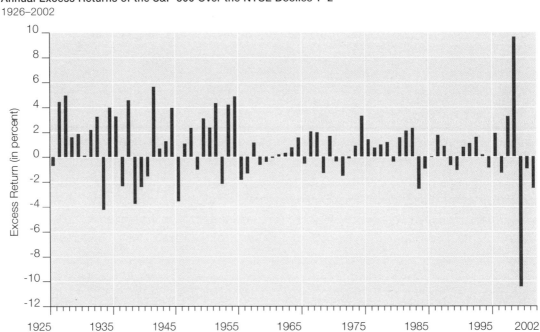

Year-end

Prior to March 1957, the S&P index that is used throughout this publication consisted of 90 of the largest stocks. The index composition was then changed to include 500 large-capitalization stocks that, as stated earlier, are not necessarily the 500 largest. Deciles 1–2 of the NYSE contained just over 200 of the largest companies, ranked by market capitalization, in March of 1957. The number of companies included in the deciles of the NYSE fluctuates from quarter to quarter, and by September of 2002, deciles 1–2 contained 350 companies. Though one cannot draw a causal relationship between the change in construction and the correlation of these two indices, this analysis does indicate that the "S&P inclusion effect" does not appear to be very significant in recent periods.

Another possible explanation could be differences in how survivorship is treated when calculating returns. The Center for Research in Security Prices includes the return for a company in the average decile return for the period following the company's removal from the decile, whether caused by a shift to a different decile portfolio, bankruptcy, or other such reason. On the other hand, the S&P 500 does not make this adjustment. Once a company is no longer included among the S&P 500, its return is dropped from the index. However, this effect may be lessened by the advance announcement of companies being dropped from or added to the S&P 500. In many instances throughout this publication we will present equity risk premia using both the S&P 500 and the NYSE "Deciles 1–2" portfolio to provide a comparison between these large-capitalization benchmarks.

The Market Benchmark and Firm Size

Although not restricted to include only the 500 largest companies, the S&P 500 is considered a large company index. The returns of the S&P 500 are capitalization weighted, which means that the weight of each stock in the index, for a given month, is proportionate to its market capitalization (price times number of shares outstanding) at the beginning of that month. The larger companies in the index therefore receive the majority of the weight. The use of the NYSE "Deciles 1–2" series results in an even purer large company index. Yet many valuation professionals are faced with valuing small companies, which historically have had different risk and return characteristics than large companies. If using a large stock index to calculate the equity risk premium, an adjustment is usually needed to account for the different risk and return characteristics of small stocks. This will be discussed further in Chapter 7 on the size premium.

The Risk-Free Asset

The equity risk premium can be calculated for a variety of time horizons when given the choice of risk-free asset to be used in the calculation. The *Stocks, Bonds, Bills, and Inflation Yearbook* provides equity risk premia calculations for short-, intermediate-, and long-term horizons. The short-, intermediate-, and long-horizon equity risk premia are calculated using the income return from a 30-day Treasury bill, a 5-year Treasury bond, and a 20-year Treasury bond, respectively.

Although the equity risk premia of several horizons are available, the long-horizon equity risk premium is preferable for use in most business-valuation settings, even if an investor has a shorter time horizon. Companies are entities that generally have no defined life span; when determining a company's value, it is important to use a long-term discount rate because the life of the company is assumed to be infinite. For this reason, it is appropriate in most cases to use the long-horizon equity risk premium for business valuation.

20-Year versus 30-Year Treasuries

Our methodology for estimating the long-horizon equity risk premium makes use of the income return on a 20-year Treasury bond; however, the Treasury currently does not issue a 20-year bond. The 30-year bond that the Treasury issued until recently is theoretically more correct due to the long-term nature of business valuation, yet Ibbotson Associates instead creates a series of returns using bonds on the market with approximately 20 years to maturity. The reason for the use of a 20-year maturity bond is that 30-year Treasury securities have only been issued over the relatively recent past, starting in February of 1977, and have since been discontinued by the Treasury.

Currently, the longest term security offered by the Treasury is 10 years. The same reason exists for why Ibbotson does not use the 10-year Treasury bond; that is, a long enough history of market data is not available for 10 year bonds. Ibbotson Associates has persisted in using a 20-year bond to keep the basis of the time series consistent.

Income Return

Another point to keep in mind when calculating the equity risk premium is that the income return on the appropriate-horizon Treasury security, rather than the total return, is used in the calculation. The total return is comprised of three return components: the income return, the capital appreciation return, and the reinvestment return. The income return is defined as the portion of the total return that results from a periodic cash flow or, in this case, the bond coupon payment. The capital appreciation return results from the price change of a bond over a specific period. Bond prices generally change in reaction to unexpected fluctuations in yields. Reinvestment return is the return on a given month's investment income when reinvested into the same asset class in the subsequent months of the year. The income return is thus used in the estimation of the equity risk premium because it represents the truly riskless portion of the return.[1]

Yields have generally risen on the long-term bond over the 1926–2002 period, so it has experienced negative capital appreciation in the time series presented in this book. Graph 5-2 illustrates the yields on the long-term government bond series compared to an index of the long-term government bond capital appreciation. In general, as yields rose, the capital appreciation index fell, and vice versa. Had an investor held the long-term bond to maturity, he would have realized the yield on the bond as the total return. However, in a constant maturity portfolio, such as those used to measure bond returns in this publication, bonds are sold before maturity (at a capital loss if the market yield has risen since the time of purchase). This negative return is associated with the risk of unanticipated yield changes.

Graph 5-2

Long-term Government Bond Yields versus Capital Appreciation Index
1925–2002

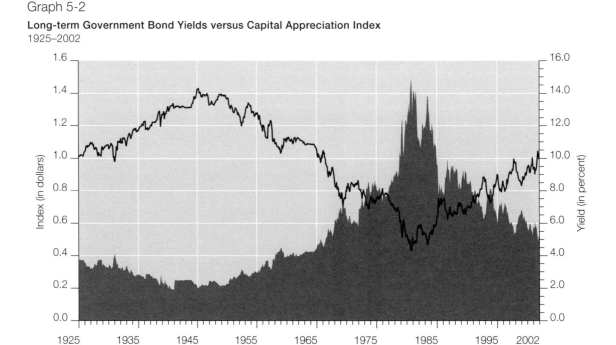

Year-end

1 Please note that the appropriate forward-looking measure of the riskless rate is the yield to maturity on the appropriate-horizon government bond. This differs from the riskless rate used to measure the realized equity risk premium historically. Chapter 1 includes a thorough discussion of riskless rate selection in this context.

For example, if bond yields rise unexpectedly, investors can receive a higher coupon payment from a newly issued bond than from the purchase of an outstanding bond with the former lower-coupon payment. The outstanding lower-coupon bond will thus fail to attract buyers, and its price will decrease, causing its yield to increase correspondingly, as its coupon payment remains the same. The newly priced outstanding bond will subsequently attract purchasers who will benefit from the shift in price and yield; however, those investors who already held the bond will suffer a capital loss due to the fall in price.

Anticipated changes in yields are assessed by the market and figured into the price of a bond. Future changes in yields that are not anticipated will cause the price of the bond to adjust accordingly. Price changes in bonds due to unanticipated changes in yields introduce price risk into the total return. Therefore, the total return on the bond series does not represent the riskless rate of return. There is no evidence that investors expect the historical trend of bond capital losses to be repeated in the future (otherwise, bond prices would be adjusted accordingly). Therefore, historical total returns are biased downward as indicators of future expectations. The income return better represents the unbiased estimate of the purely riskless rate of return, since an investor can hold a bond to maturity and be entitled to the income return with no capital loss.

Arithmetic versus Geometric Means

The equity risk premium data presented in this book are arithmetic average risk premia as opposed to geometric average risk premia. The arithmetic average equity risk premium can be demonstrated to be most appropriate when discounting future cash flows. For use as the expected equity risk premium in either the CAPM or the building block approach, the arithmetic mean or the simple difference of the arithmetic means of stock market returns and riskless rates is the relevant number. This is because both the CAPM and the building block approach are additive models, in which the cost of capital is the sum of its parts. The geometric average is more appropriate for reporting past performance, since it represents the compound average return.

The argument for using the arithmetic average is quite straightforward. In looking at projected cash flows, the equity risk premium that should be employed is the equity risk premium that is expected to actually be incurred over the future time periods. Graph 5-3 shows the realized equity risk premium for each year based on the returns of the S&P 500 and the income return on long-term government bonds. (The actual, observed difference between the return on the stock market and the riskless rate is known as the realized equity risk premium.) There is considerable volatility in the year-by-year statistics. At times the realized equity risk premium is even negative.

Graph 5-3

Realized Equity Risk Premium Per Year

1926–2002

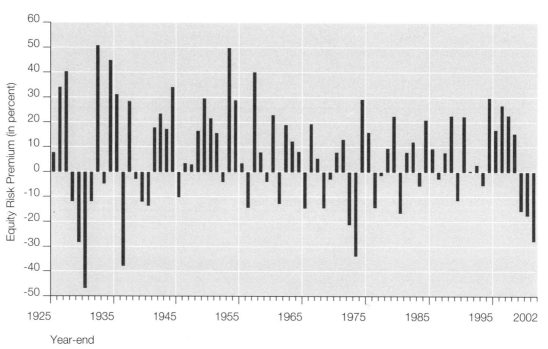

Year-end

To illustrate how the arithmetic mean is more appropriate than the geometric mean in discounting cash flows, suppose the expected return on a stock is 10 percent per year with a standard deviation of 20 percent. Also assume that only two outcomes are possible each year— +30 percent and –10 percent (i.e., the mean plus or minus one standard deviation). The probability of occurrence for each outcome is equal. The growth of wealth over a two-year period is illustrated in Graph 5-4.

Graph 5-4

Growth of Wealth Example

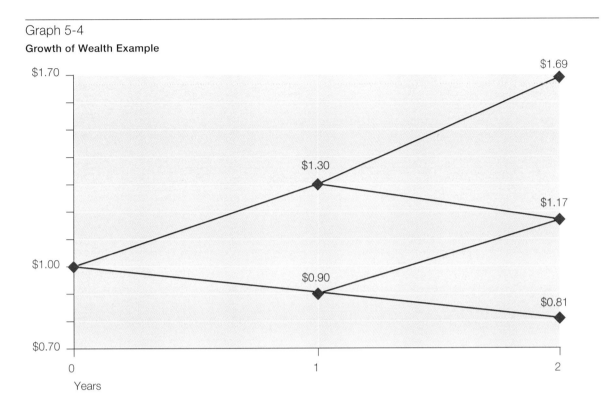

The most common outcome of $1.17 is given by the geometric mean of 8.2 percent. Compounding the possible outcomes as follows derives the geometric mean:

$$[(1+0.30)\times(1-0.10)]^{1/2} - 1 = 0.082$$

However, the expected value is predicted by compounding the arithmetic, not the geometric, mean. To illustrate this, we need to look at the probability-weighted average of all possible outcomes:

$$(0.25 \times \$1.69) = \$0.4225$$
$$+ (0.50 \times \$1.17) = \$0.5850$$
$$+ (0.25 \times \$0.81) = \underline{\$0.2025}$$
$$\text{Total} \qquad \overline{\$1.2100}$$

Therefore, $1.21 is the probability-weighted expected value. The rate that must be compounded to achieve the terminal value of $1.21 after 2 years is 10 percent, the arithmetic mean:

$$\$1\times(1+0.10)^2 = \$1.21$$

The geometric mean, when compounded, results in the median of the distribution:

$$\$1\times(1+0.082)^2 = \$1.17$$

The arithmetic mean equates the expected future value with the present value; it is therefore the appropriate discount rate.

Appropriate Historical Time Period

The equity risk premium can be estimated using any historical time period. For the U.S., market data exists at least as far back as the late 1800s. Therefore, it is possible to estimate the equity risk premium using data that covers roughly the past 100 years.

The Ibbotson Associates equity risk premium covers the time period from 1926 to the present. The original data source for the time series comprising the equity risk premium is the Center for Research in Security Prices. CRSP chose to begin their analysis of market returns with 1926 for two main reasons. CRSP determined that the time period around 1926 was approximately when quality financial data became available. They also made a conscious effort to include the period of extreme market volatility from the late twenties and early thirties; 1926 was chosen because it includes one full business cycle of data before the market crash of 1929. These are the most basic reasons why Ibbotson Associates' equity risk premium calculation window starts in 1926.

Implicit in using history to forecast the future is the assumption that investors' expectations for future outcomes conform to past results. This method assumes that the price of taking on risk changes only slowly, if at all, over time. This "future equals the past" assumption is most applicable to a random time-series variable. A time-series variable is random if its value in one period is independent of its value in other periods.

Does the Equity Risk Premium Revert to Its Mean over Time?

Some have argued that the estimate of the equity risk premium is upwardly biased since the stock market is currently priced high. In other words, since there have been several years with extraordinarily high market returns and realized equity risk premia, the expectation is that returns and realized equity risk premia will be lower in the future, bringing the average back to a normalized level. This argument relies on several studies that have tried to determine whether reversion to the mean exists in stock market prices and the equity risk premium.[2] Several academics contradict each other on this topic; moreover, the evidence supporting this argument is neither conclusive nor compelling enough to make such a strong assumption.

Our own empirical evidence suggests that the yearly difference between the stock market total return and the U.S. Treasury bond income return in any particular year is random. Graph 5-3, presented earlier, illustrates the randomness of the realized equity risk premium.

2 Fama, Eugene F., and Kenneth R. French. "Permanent and Temporary Components of Stock Prices," *Journal of Political Economy*, April 1988, pp. 246–273. Poterba, James M., and Lawrence H. Summers. "Mean Reversion in Stock Prices," *Journal of Financial Economics*, October 1988, pp. 27–59. Lo, Andrew W., and A. Craig MacKinlay. "Stock Market Prices Do Not Follow Random Walks: Evidence from a Simple Specification Test," *The Review of Financial Studies*, Spring 1988, pp. 41–66. Finnerty, John D., and Dean Leistikow. "The Behavior of Equity and Debt Risk Premiums: Are They Mean Reverting and Downward-Trending?" *The Journal of Portfolio Management*, Summer 1993, pp. 73–84. Ibbotson, Roger G., and Scott L. Lummer. "The Behavior of Equity and Debt Risk Premiums: Comment," *The Journal of Portfolio Management*, Summer 1994, pp. 98–100. Finnerty, John D., and Dean Leistikow. "The Behavior of Equity and Debt Risk Premiums: Reply to Comment," *The Journal of Portfolio Management*, Summer 1994, pp. 101–102.

A statistical measure of the randomness of a return series is its serial correlation. Serial correlation (or autocorrelation) is defined as the degree to which the return of a given series is related from period to period. A serial correlation near positive one indicates that returns are predictable from one period to the next period and are positively related. That is, the returns of one period are a good predictor of the returns in the next period. Conversely, a serial correlation near negative one indicates that the returns in one period are inversely related to those of the next period. A serial correlation near zero indicates that the returns are random or unpredictable from one period to the next. Table 5-3 contains the serial correlation of the market total returns, the realized long-horizon equity risk premium, and inflation.

Table 5-3
Interpretation of Annual Serial Correlations
1926–2002

Series	Serial Correlation	Interpretation
Large Company Stock Total Returns	0.05	Random
Equity Risk Premium	0.06	Random
Inflation Rates	0.65	Trend

The significance of this evidence is that the realized equity risk premium next year will not be dependent on the realized equity risk premium from this year. That is, there is no discernable pattern in the realized equity risk premium—it is virtually impossible to forecast next year's realized risk premium based on the premium of the previous year. For example, if this year's difference between the riskless rate and the return on the stock market is higher than last year's, that does not imply that next year's will be higher than this year's. It is as likely to be higher as it is lower. The best estimate of the expected value of a variable that has behaved randomly in the past is the average (or arithmetic mean) of its past values.

Table 5-4 also indicates that the equity risk premium varies considerably by decade, from a high of 17.9 percent in the 1950s to a low of 0.3 percent in the 1970s. This look at the historical equity risk premium reveals no observable pattern.

Table 5-4
Long-Horizon Equity Risk Premium by Decade
1926–2002

1920s*	1930s	1940s	1950s	1960s	1970s	1980s	1990s	2000s**	1993-2002
17.6%	2.3%	8.0%	17.9%	4.2%	0.3%	7.9%	12.1%	−20.2%	4.8%

*Based on the period 1926–1929.

**Based on the period 2000–2002.

Finnerty and Leistikow perform more econometrically sophisticated tests of mean reversion in the equity risk premium. Their tests demonstrate that—as we suspected from our simpler tests—the equity risk premium that was realized over 1926 to the present was almost perfectly free of mean reversion and had no statistically identifiable time trends.[3] Lo and MacKinlay conclude, "the rejection of the random walk for weekly returns does not support a mean-reverting model of asset prices."

Choosing an Appropriate Historical Period

The estimate of the equity risk premium depends on the length of the data series studied. A proper estimate of the equity risk premium requires a data series long enough to give a reliable average without being unduly influenced by very good and very poor short-term returns. When calculated using a long data series, the historical equity risk premium is relatively stable.[4] Furthermore, because an average of the realized equity risk premium is quite volatile when calculated using a short history, using a long series makes it less likely that the analyst can justify any number he or she wants. The magnitude of how shorter periods can affect the result will be explored later in this chapter.

Some analysts estimate the expected equity risk premium using a shorter, more recent time period on the basis that recent events are more likely to be repeated in the near future; furthermore, they believe that the 1920s, 1930s, and 1940s contain too many unusual events. This view is suspect because all periods contain "unusual" events. Some of the most unusual events of this century took place quite recently, including the inflation of the late 1970s and early 1980s, the October 1987 stock market crash, the collapse of the high-yield bond market, the major contraction and consolidation of the thrift industry, the collapse of the Soviet Union, and the development of the European Economic Community—all of these happened in the last 20 years.

It is even difficult for economists to predict the economic environment of the future. For example, if one were analyzing the stock market in 1987 before the crash, it would be statistically improbable to predict the impending short-term volatility without considering the stock market crash and market volatility of the 1929–1931 period.

Without an appreciation of the 1920s and 1930s, no one would believe that such events could happen. The 77-year period starting with 1926 is representative of what can happen: it includes high and low returns, volatile and quiet markets, war and peace, inflation and deflation, and prosperity and depression. Restricting attention to a shorter historical period underestimates the amount of change that could occur in a long future period. Finally, because historical event-types (not specific

---

3 Though the study performed by Finnerty and Leistikow demonstrates that the traditional equity risk premium exhibits no mean reversion or drift, they conclude that, "the processes generating these risk premiums are generally mean-reverting." This conclusion is completely unrelated to their statistical findings and has received some criticism. In addition to examining the traditional equity risk premia, Finnerty and Leistikow include analyses on "real" risk premia as well as separate risk premia for income and capital gains. In their comments on the study, Ibbotson and Lummer show that these "real" risk premia adjust for inflation twice, "creating variables with no economic content." In addition, separating income and capital gains does not shed light on the behavior of the risk premia as a whole.

4 This assertion is further corroborated by data presented in *Global Investing: The Professional's Guide to the World of Capital Markets* (by Roger G. Ibbotson and Gary P. Brinson and published by McGraw-Hill, New York). Ibbotson and Brinson constructed a stock market total return series back to 1790. Even with some uncertainty about the accuracy of the data before the mid-nineteenth century, the results are remarkable. The real (adjusted for inflation) returns that investors received during the three 50-year periods and one 51-year period between 1790 and 1990 did not differ greatly from one another (that is, in a statistically significant amount). Nor did the real returns differ greatly from the overall 201-year average. This finding implies that because real stock-market returns have been reasonably consistent over time, investors can use these past returns as reasonable bases for forming their expectations of future returns.

events) tend to repeat themselves, long-run capital market return studies can reveal a great deal about the future. Investors probably expect "unusual" events to occur from time to time, and their return expectations reflect this.

A Look at the Historical Results

It is interesting to take a look at the realized returns and realized equity risk premium in the context of the above discussion. Table 5-5 shows the average stock market return and the average (arithmetic mean) realized long-horizon equity risk premium over various historical time periods. Similarly, Graph 5-5 shows the average (arithmetic mean) realized equity risk premium calculated through 2002 for different starting dates. The table and the graph both show that using a longer historical period provides a more stable estimate of the equity risk premium. The reason is that any unique period will not be weighted heavily in an average covering a longer historical period. It better represents the probability of these unique events occurring over a long period of time.

Table 5-5

Stock Market Return and Equity Risk Premium Over Time
1926–2002

Period Length	Period Dates	Large Company Stock Arithmetic Mean Total Return	Long-Horizon Equity Risk Premium
77 years	1926–2002	12.2%	7.0%
70 years	1933–2002	13.3%	7.9%
60 years	1943–2002	13.4%	7.5%
50 years	1953–2002	12.5%	5.9%
40 years	1963–2002	11.8%	4.4%
30 years	1973–2002	12.2%	4.1%
20 years	1983–2002	14.0%	6.2%
15 years	1988–2002	13.0%	6.0%
10 years	1993–2002	11.2%	4.8%
5 years	1998–2002	1.3%	−4.5%

Looking carefully at Graph 5-5 will clarify this point. The graph shows the realized equity risk premium for a series of time periods through 2002, starting with 1926. In other words, the first value on the graph represents the average realized equity risk premium over the period 1926–2002. The next value on the graph represents the average realized equity risk premium over the period 1927–2002, and so on, with the last value representing the average over the most recent five years, 1998–2002. Concentrating on the left side of Graph 5-5, one notices that the realized equity risk premium, when measured over long periods of time, is relatively stable. In viewing the graph from left to right, moving from longer to shorter historical periods, one sees that the value of the realized equity risk premium begins to decline significantly. Why does this occur? The reason is that the severe bear market of 1973–1974 is receiving proportionately more weight in the shorter, more recent average. If you continue to follow the line to the right, however, you will also notice that when 1973 and 1974 fall out of the recent average, the realized equity risk premium jumps up by nearly 1.5 percent.

Graph 5-5

Equity Risk Premium Using Different Starting Dates

1926–2002

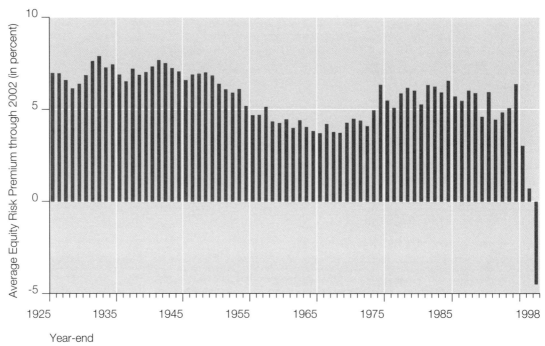

Year-end

Additionally, use of recent historical periods for estimation purposes can lead to illogical conclusions. As seen in Table 5-5, the recent bear market has caused the realized equity risk premium in the shorter historical periods to be much lower than the long-term average.

The impact of adding one additional year of data to a historical average is lessened the greater the initial time period of measurement. Short-term averages can be affected considerably by one or more unique observations. On the other hand, long-term averages produce more stable results. A series of graphs looking at the realized equity risk premium will illustrate this effect. Graph 5-6 shows the average (arithmetic mean) realized long-horizon equity risk premium starting in 1926. Each additional point on the graph represents the addition of another year to the average. Although the graph is extremely volatile in the beginning periods, the stability of the long-term average is quite remarkable. Again, the "unique" periods of time will not be weighted heavily in a long-term average, resulting in a more stable estimate.

Graph 5-6

Equity Risk Premium Using Different End Dates

1926–2002

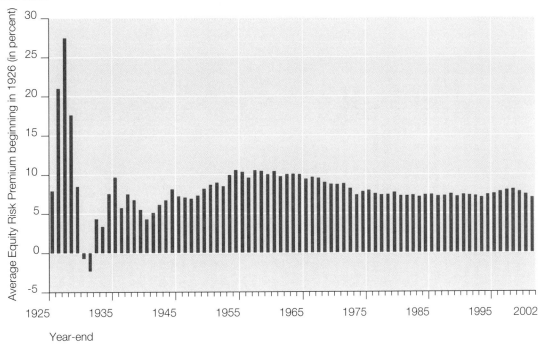

Some practitioners argue for a shorter historical time period, such as 30 years, as a basis for the equity risk premium estimation. The logic for the use of a shorter period is that historical events and economic scenarios present before this time are unlikely to be repeated. Graph 5-7 shows the equity risk premium measured over 30-year periods, and it appears from the graph that the premium has been trending downwards. The 30-year equity risk premium remained close to 4 percent for several years in the 1980s and 1990s but started to increase in the late 1990s before dropping again in the most recent 30-year periods.

Graph 5-7

Equity Risk Premium Over 30-Year Periods
1926–2002

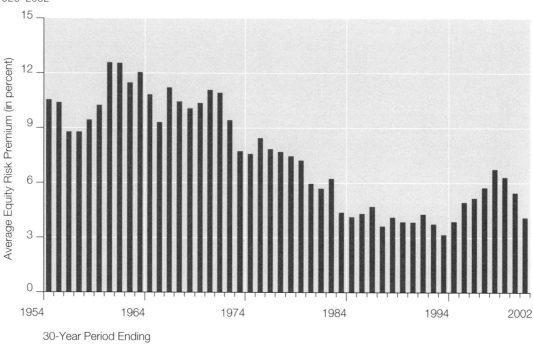

30-Year Period Ending

The key to understanding this result lies again in the years 1973 and 1974. The oil embargo during this period had a tremendous effect on the market. The equity risk premium for these years alone was –21 and –34 percent, respectively. If we look at the last 30 years excluding 1973 and 1974, the 28-year period results in an equity risk premium of 6.3 percent, as opposed to 4.1 percent with these years included. The early 2000s have also had an enormous effect on the equity risk premium.

The effect of the 1973–1974 period is even more pronounced when looking at the equity risk premium over 20-year periods, as seen in Graph 5-8. Using the 20-year historical average equity risk premium results in a very unstable estimate. Periods that include the years 1973 and 1974 result in an average equity risk premium as low as 1.4 percent. In the more recent 20-year periods that exclude 1973 and 1974, the average rises dramatically to over 8.0 percent. It is difficult to justify such a large divergence in estimates of return over such a short period of time. This does not suggest, however, that the years 1973 and 1974 should be excluded from any estimate of the equity risk premium; rather, it emphasizes the importance of using a long historical period when measuring the equity risk premium in order to obtain a reliable average that is not overly influenced by short-term returns. The same holds true when analyzing the poor performance of the early 2000s.

Graph 5-8

Equity Risk Premium Over 20-Year Periods
1926–2002

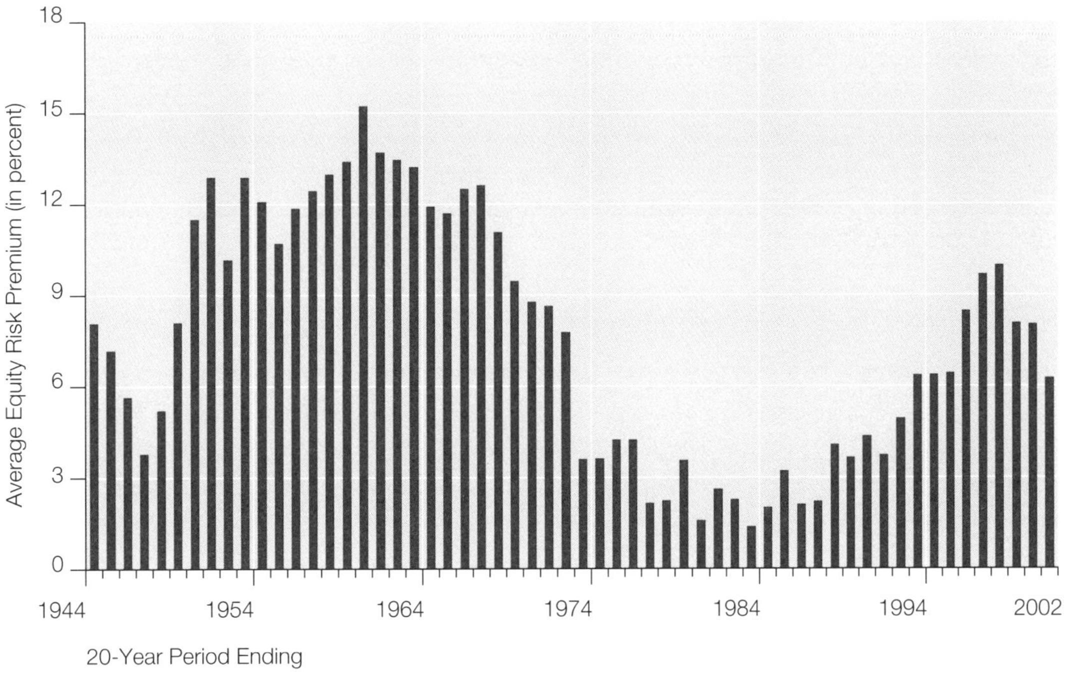

20-Year Period Ending

Does the Equity Risk Premium Represent Minority or Controlling Interest?

There is quite a bit of confusion among valuation practitioners regarding the use of publicly traded company data to derive the equity risk premium. Is a minority discount implicit in this data? Recall that the equity risk premium is typically derived from the returns of a market index: the S&P 500, the New York Stock Exchange (NYSE), or the NYSE Deciles 1-2. (The Ibbotson Associates' size premia that are covered in Chapter 7 are derived from the returns of companies traded on the NYSE, in addition to those on the AMEX and NASDAQ). Both the S&P 500 and the NYSE include a preponderance of companies that are minority held. Does this imply that an equity risk premium (or size premium) derived from these data represents a minority interest premium? This is a critical issue that must be addressed by the valuation professional, since applying a minority discount or a control premium can have a material impact on the ultimate value derived in an appraisal.

Since most companies in the S&P 500 and the NYSE are minority held, some assume that the risk premia derived from these return data represent minority returns and therefore have a minority discount implicit within them. However, this assumption is not correct. The returns that are generated by the S&P 500 and the NYSE represent returns to equity holders. While most of these companies are minority held, there is no evidence that higher rates of return could be earned if these companies were suddenly acquired by majority shareholders. The equity risk premium represents expected premiums that holders of securities of a similar nature can expect to achieve on average into the future. There is no distinction between minority owners and controlling owners.

The discount rate is meant to represent the underlying risk of being in a particular industry or line of business. There are instances when a majority shareholder can acquire a company and improve the cash flows generated by that company. However, this does not necessarily have an impact on the general risk level of the cash flows generated by the company.

When performing discounted cash flow analysis, adjustments for minority or controlling interest value may be more suitably made to the projected cash flows than to the discount rate. Adjusting the expected future cash flows better measures the potential impact a controlling party may have while not overstating or understating the actual risk associated with a particular line of business.

Appraisers need to note the distinction between a publicly traded value and a minority interest value. Most public companies have no majority or controlling owner. There is thus no distinction between owners in this setting. One cannot assume that publicly held companies with no controlling owner have the same characteristics as privately held companies with both a controlling interest owner and a minority interest owner.

Other Equity Risk Premium Issues

There are a number of other issues that are commonly brought up regarding the equity risk premium that, if correct, would reduce its size. These issues include:

1. Survivorship bias in the measurement of the equity risk premium
2. Utility theory models of estimating the equity risk premium
3. Reconciling the discounted cash flow approach to the equity risk premium
4. Over-valuation effects of the market
5. Changes in investor attitudes toward market conditions

In this section, we will examine each of these issues.

Survivorship

One common problem in working with financial data is properly accounting for survivorship. In working with company-specific historical data, it is important for researchers to include data from companies that failed as well as companies that succeeded before drawing conclusions from elements of that data.

The same argument can be made regarding markets as a whole. The equity risk premium data outlined in this book represent data on the United States stock market. The United States has arguably been the most successful stock market of the twentieth century. That being the case, might equity risk premium statistics based only on U.S. data overstate the returns of equities as a whole because they only focus on one successful market?

In a recent paper, Goetzmann and Jorion study this question by looking at returns from a number of world equity markets over the past century.[5] The Goetzmann-Jorion paper looks at the survivorship bias from several different perspectives. They conclude that once survivorship is taken into consideration the U.S. equity risk premium is overstated by approximately 60 basis points.[6] The non-U.S. equity risk premium was found to contain significantly more survivorship bias.

While the survivorship bias evidence may be compelling on a worldwide basis, one can question its relevance to a purely U.S. analysis. If the entity being valued is a U.S. company, then the relevant data set should be the performance of equities in the U.S. market.

Equity Risk Premium Puzzle

In 1985, Mehra and Prescott published a paper that discussed the equity risk premium from a utility theory perspective.[7] The point that Mehra and Prescott make is that under existing economic theory, economists cannot justify the magnitude of the equity risk premium. The utility theory model employed was incapable of obtaining values consistent with those observed in the market.

This is an interesting point and may be worthy of further study, but it does not do anything to prove that the equity risk premium is too high. It may, on the other hand, indicate that theoretical economic models require further refinement to adequately explain market behavior.

Discounted Cash Flow versus Capital Asset Pricing Model

Two of the most commonly used cost of equity models are the discounted cash flow model and the capital asset pricing model. We should be able to reconcile the two models. In its basic form, the discounted cash flow model states that the expected return on equities is the dividend yield plus the expected long-term growth rate. The capital asset pricing model states that the expected return on equities is the risk-free rate plus the equity risk premium.[8]

For the discounted cash flow model we can obtain an estimate of the long-term growth rate for the entire economy by looking at its component parts. Real Gross Domestic Product growth has averaged approximately three percent over long periods of time. Long-term expected inflation is currently in the range of three percent. Combining these two numbers produces an expected long-term growth rate of about six percent. Dividend yields have been between two percent and three percent historically. The discounted cash flow expected equity return is thus between eight percent and nine percent using these assumptions.

If we try to reconcile this expected equity return with that found using the capital asset pricing model, we find a significant discrepancy. The yield on government bonds has been about five percent. If

5 Goetzmann, William, and Philippe Jorion. "A Century of Global Stock Markets," Working Paper 5901, National Bureau of Economic Research, 1997.

6 Note that the equity risk premium referred to in the Goetzmann and Jorion paper is not the same as the equity risk premium covered in this publication. Among other differences, their equity risk premium is based on a longer history of data and does not take dividend income or reinvestment into account.

7 Mehra, Rajnish, and Edward Prescott. "The Equity Premium: A Puzzle," *Journal of Monetary Economics*, vol. 15, 1985, p. 145–161.

8 The discounted cash flow model is a modification of the Gordon Growth model, which states that: where P_0 is the price of the security today, D_1 is the dividend from next period, k is the cost of equity, and g is the expected growth rate in dividends. The capital asset pricing model is stated as $k_i = b_i (ERP) + r_f$ where k_i is the cost of equity for company i, β_i is the beta for company i, ERP is the equity risk premium, and r_f is the risk-free rate. For the market as a whole, the capital asset pricing model can be written as $k = ERP + r_f$ because the market beta, by definition, is one. For more information on these models, see Chapter 4.

the two models are to reconcile, the equity risk premium must be in the two to three percent range instead of the seven to eight percent range we have observed historically.

It is not easy to explain why these two models are so difficult to reconcile. While it is possible to modify the assumptions slightly, doing so still does not produce the desired results. One explanation might be that one or both of the models are too simplistic and therefore lack the ability to resolve this inconsistency.

Market Bubbles

Another criticism of using the historical equity risk premium is that the market is overvalued. This argument is often offered after stock prices have seen a sustained increase. The logic of the argument is that abnormally high market returns drive the historical equity risk premium higher while at the same time driving the expected equity risk premium lower. As evidence of the market being over-valued, one can look at the price/earnings multiple of the market. Graph 5-9 attempts to demonstrate the relationship between the price/earnings multiple and the subsequent period's equity risk premium. If the above argument held, one would expect to find a low equity risk premium associated with a high price/earnings multiple from the prior period. One would also expect a high equity risk premium to be associated with a low price/earnings multiple in the prior period. From the graph there does not seem to be a clear indication of the market being overvalued or undervalued with respect to the next period's realized equity risk premium.

Graph 5-9

Price-Earnings Multiple versus Subsequent Year's Realized Equity Risk Premium
1926–2002

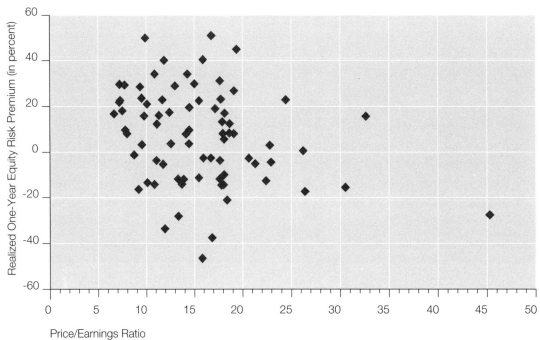

Price/Earnings Ratio

Source: Historical price/earnings ratios from Standard & Poor's Security Price Index Record and Compustat database.

There are yet other problems with this theory. First, the equity risk premium is measured over a long historical time period. Several years of strong market returns have a relatively small impact on the ultimate equity risk premium estimate. Second, we are attempting to forecast a long-term equity risk premium. Even if the market were to underperform over several consecutive time periods, this should not have a significant impact on expected long-term returns. Finally, one ratio does not necessarily tell the whole story. The price/earnings ratio shows the current stock price divided by the historical earnings per share. Stock prices should, on the other hand, incorporate expectations of future earnings growth. A high market price/earnings ratio may indicate that investors expect significant future earnings growth.

Change in Investor Attitudes

There is no law that states that investor attitudes must remain constant over time. With the advent of 401(k) investing and the increase in education of the investing public, the market may have changed. In fact, stock returns have become less volatile over time. From Graph 5-10, one can see that the fluctuations in monthly returns have lessened in more recent periods. In addition, Graph 5-11 demonstrates a steady decline in the rolling 60-month standard deviation of both large and small stocks. (Standard deviation is a measure of the returns' volatility or risk.) This may suggest that we have moved into a new market regime in which stocks are less volatile and therefore require a lower risk premium than in the past.[9]

Graph 5-10

Monthly Returns of Large Company Stocks
January 1926–December 2002

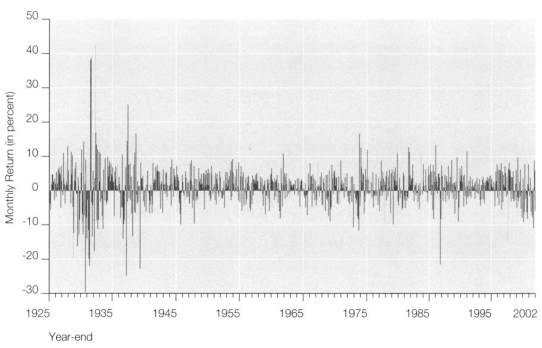

Year-end

[9] Note that the recent increase in market volatility, particularly in 1998, may also place into question the validity of this argument.

Graph 5-11

Rolling 60-Month Standard Deviation for Large and Small Stocks
January 1926–December 2002

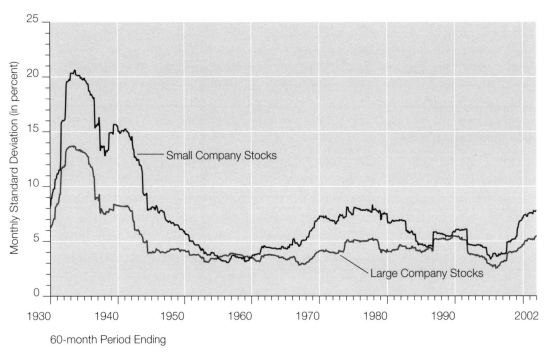

60-month Period Ending

There are two arguments against this rationale. First, it could easily be argued that we have moved through a series of market regimes during the 77-year history of the equity risk premium calculation window used in this book. Given that markets and investor attitudes have changed over time and the equity risk premium has remained relatively constant, there is no reason to believe that a new market regime will have any greater or lesser impact than any other time period.

A second argument relates to the demand for investments. If investors are more comfortable with the market and with stock investing, they will probably place more money into the market. This influx of funds will increase the demand for stocks, which will ultimately increase, not decrease, the equity risk premium.

This section has briefly reviewed some of the more common arguments that seek to reduce the equity risk premium. While some of these theories are compelling in an academic framework, they do little to prove that the equity risk premium is too high. When examining these theories, it is important to remember that the equity risk premium data outlined in this book are from actual market statistics over a long historical time period.

Taxes and Equity Risk Premium Calculations

All of the risk premium statistics included in this publication are derived from market returns earned by an investor. The investor receives dividends and realizes price appreciation after the corporation has paid its taxes. Therefore, it is implicit that the market return data represents returns after corporate taxes but before personal taxes.

When performing a discounted cash flow analysis, both the discount rate and the cash flows should be on the same tax basis. Most valuation settings rely on after-tax cash flows; the use of an after-tax discount rate would thus be appropriate in most cases. However, there are some instances (usually because of regulatory or legal statute reasons) in which it is necessary to calculate a pre-tax value. In these cases, a pre-tax cost of capital or discount rate should be employed. There is no easy way, however, to accurately modify the return on a market index to a pre-tax basis. This modification would require estimating pre-tax returns for all of the publicly traded companies that comprise the market benchmark.

This presents a problem when a pre-tax discounted cash flow analysis is required. Although not completely correct, the easiest way to convert an after-tax discount rate to a pre-tax discount rate is to divide the after-tax rate by (1 minus the tax rate). This adjustment should be made to the entire discount rate and not to its component parts (i.e., the equity risk premium). Take note that this is a "quick and dirty" way to approximate pre-tax discount rates.

The tax rate to use in this "quick and dirty" method presents yet another problem. As seen in the discussion of the weighted average cost of capital in Chapter 1, companies do not always pay the top marginal tax rate. New research has shown some progress in quantifying the expected future tax rates. See Chapter 1 for more detail.

Chapter 6

Beta Estimation Methodologies

The capital asset pricing model (CAPM) states that where a security falls on the security market line is dependent on its beta. Beta represents the systematic risk of a security as estimated by regressing the security's excess returns against the market portfolio's excess returns. The slope of the regression equation is the beta.

Graph 6-1

International Business Machines Corp. Excess Returns versus S&P 500 Excess Returns
October 1997 through September 2002

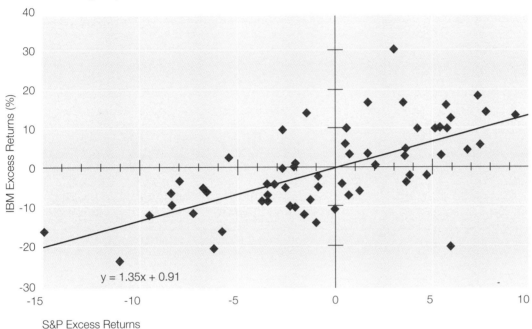

IBM Excess Returns (%)

y = 1.35x + 0.91

S&P Excess Returns

Graph 6-1 shows a typical beta plot, in which the beta of the company is the slope of the fitted line. In this case the company is IBM Corp. and the resulting beta is 1.35. This historical beta uses monthly data over a five-year time period with the S&P 500® as the market benchmark. As we will discuss throughout this chapter, there are a number of assumptions and choices, such as market benchmark and historical time period, that go into the calculation of beta and can impact its result.

Beta measures a security's sensitivity to the market, which is otherwise known as its systematic risk. According to the CAPM, systematic risk is unavoidable and is common to all risky securities; it cannot be eliminated through diversification. The amount of an asset's systematic risk is measured by its beta.

A company whose stock has a beta of 1.0 has the same systematic risk as the overall stock market and, therefore, will provide expected returns to investors equal to those of the market. The return on a stock with a beta of 2.0 will, on average, rise approximately twice as much as the overall stock market during periods of rising stock prices. Stocks with betas less than 1.0 have risk levels and, consequently, expected returns that are lower than that of the overall stock market.

For example, an unexpected increase in interest rates will generally result in a decline in prices across the entire equity market; however, this does not mean that all securities decline by the same amount. The CAPM states that, in general, the higher the beta, the greater the reaction (both positive and negative) to changes in the overall market.

Measuring Beta via Equation

Beta can be estimated by using an equation or by performing a regression. The equation for beta can be stated as follows:

$$\beta_s = \frac{Cov(r_s, r_m)}{Var(r_m)}$$

where:

$$Cov(r_s, r_m) = \frac{1}{n-1}\sum_{t=1}^{n}(r_{s,t} - r_{s,A})(r_{m,t} - r_{m,A})$$

$$Var(r_m) = \frac{1}{n-1}\sum_{t=1}^{n}(r_{m,t} - r_{m,A})^2$$

β_s	=	the beta of the portfolio or security s;
$Cov_{(rs,rm)}$	=	the expected covariance between the return on portfolio or security s and the market return;
$r_{s,t}$	=	the return on portfolio or security s in period t;
$r_{m,t}$	=	the market return in period t;
$r_{s,A}$	=	the arithmetic mean return for portfolio or security s;
$r_{m,A}$	=	the arithmetic mean of the market return;
n	=	the number of periods; and
$Var(r_m)$	=	the expected variance of the return on the overall stock market.

The formula states that the beta of a security is equal to its covariance with the market divided by the variance of the market. The covariance between a security and the market measures the degree to which the security's return and the market's return move together. A positive covariance indicates that these variables tend to move in the same direction, whereas a negative covariance indicates that they move in opposite directions. The variance measures the extent to which the return in each period differs from the average return.

Measuring Beta via Regression

Beta is typically measured via regression. The excess returns of an asset across time are regressed against the excess returns of the market across time. Excess return is equal to the total return on the asset or market less the risk-free rate for the period in question.

$$\text{Excess return} = \left[\frac{(P_t + D)}{P_{t-1}} - 1 \right] - r_f$$

where:

P_t = the price of the stock at time t;
P_{t-1} = the price of the stock at time t–1;
D_t = the dividends at time t; and
r_f = the 30-day Treasury bill for that period.

For example, assume that a stock has a month-end price of $25.50, a dividend payment of $0.25, and a prior month-end price of $25.00 and that the 30-day Treasury bill return for the month was 0.4 percent. The excess return would be calculated as follows:

$$\text{Excess return} = \left[\frac{(25.50 + 0.25)}{25.00} - 1 \right] - 0.004 = 0.030 - 0.004 = 0.026$$

or a monthly excess return of 2.6 percent.

Excess returns are used because, in the context of the CAPM, what we are truly interested in measuring is the excess return. Recall that the CAPM equates the expected return with the following:

$$k_s = r_f + \beta_s \times (r_m - r_f)$$

However, regressing the total return of the asset against the total return of the market provides similar results. Table 6-1 compares betas calculated using monthly excess returns to betas calculated using monthly total returns.

Table 6-1

Betas Calculated Using Excess Returns versus Total Returns
October 1997 through September 2002*

		Excess Return Betas	Total Return Betas
ABT	Abbott Laboratories	0.32	0.33
ONE	Bank One Corp.	1.18	1.17
BLS	BellSouth Corp.	0.58	0.59
BP	BP PLC -ADS	0.67	0.67
EK	Eastman Kodak Co.	0.57	0.57
GE	General Electric Co.	1.09	1.09
GM	General Motors Corp.	1.26	1.25
INTC	Intel Corp.	1.75	1.75
IBM	International Business Machines Corp.	1.35	1.35
MCD	McDonalds Corp.	0.84	0.84

*Betas calculated using five years of monthly data.

The beta regression equation is as follows:

$$\left(r_s - r_f\right) = \alpha_s + \beta_s \times \left(r_m - r_f\right) + \varepsilon_s$$

where:

r_s = the return on portfolio or security s;

r_f = the expected return of the riskless asset;

α_s = regression constant term;

β_s = the beta of portfolio or security s;

r_m = the return on the market; and

ε_s = regression error term.

In order to perform a regression, you must first make the following three choices:

1. The appropriate market proxy (e.g., S&P 500, New York Stock Exchange [NYSE])
2. The amount of history over which returns should be measured (e.g., two years, five years, six years)
3. The incremental time period for returns (e.g., daily, weekly, monthly)

Market Proxy

The CAPM tells us that the appropriate market measure to use in the regression equation is the entire market of all risky assets measured in a value-weighted index. Unfortunately, such a measure is unobtainable, so a proxy must be chosen instead.

There are several obvious choices, including the S&P 500, the NYSE index, or the NYSE/AMEX/ NASDAQ index. The S&P 500 index is a value-weighted index that includes most of the largest U.S. companies in a number of different industries. The NYSE index is a value-weighted index that measures the performance of all New York Stock Exchange companies. The NYSE/AMEX/NASDAQ index is a value-weighted index that measures the performance of New York Stock Exchange and American Stock Exchange companies in addition to those companies traded on the NASDAQ system.

Theoretically, the broader the index, the more accurate the data measure. Therefore, the logical choice from the above list would be the NYSE/AMEX/NASDAQ index. However, few commercial beta services actually utilize this market proxy. The market measure is in fact not as critical as one might think because the correlation across the various indexes listed above is quite high.

Table 6-2

Correlation of Monthly Market Proxy Returns
October 1997 through September 2002

	S&P 500	NYSE	NYSE/ AMEX	NYSE/ AMEX/ NASDAQ
S&P 500	1.00			
NYSE	0.95	1.00		
NYSE/AMEX	0.95	1.00	1.00	
NYSE/AMEX/NASDAQ	0.97	0.90	0.91	1.00

Because of this high correlation, the ultimate market proxy chosen has only a minor impact on the beta calculation. Table 6-3 shows the betas of several companies measured using excess returns for four separate market indices: the S&P 500 total return index, the NYSE total return index, the NYSE/AMEX total return index, and the NYSE/AMEX/NASDAQ total return index. Graph 6-2 illustrates the similar distribution of betas for over 5,600 companies included in Ibbotson's *Beta Book* using the S&P 500 and the New York Stock Exchange as the market proxy.

Table 6-3

Company Betas Using Different Market Proxies
October 1997 through September 2002*

		S&P 500	NYSE	NYSE/AMEX	NYSE/AMEX/ NASDAQ
ABT	Abbott Laboratories	0.32	0.45	0.44	0.23
ONE	Bank One Corp.	1.18	1.58	1.58	0.97
BLS	BellSouth Corp.	0.58	0.76	0.75	0.41
BP	BP PLC-ADS	0.67	0.83	0.83	0.59
EK	Eastman Kodak Co.	0.57	0.57	0.57	0.50
GE	General Electric Co.	1.09	1.16	1.16	0.98
GM	General Motors Corp.	1.26	1.39	1.39	1.17
INTC	Intel Corp.	1.75	1.42	1.43	1.66
IBM	Intl. Business Machines Corp.	1.35	1.34	1.34	1.24
MCD	McDonalds Corp.	0.84	1.11	1.11	0.65

*Betas calculated using five years of monthly excess return data.

Graph 6-2

Beta Distribution Using Different Market Proxies

October 1997 through September 2002

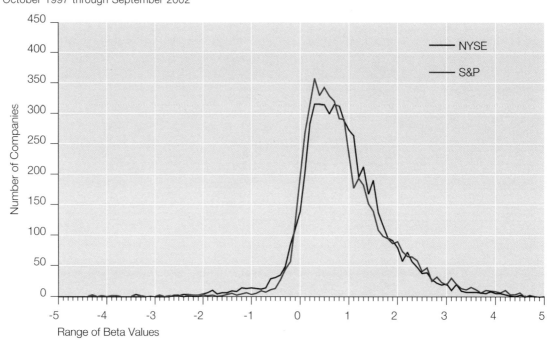

What is important to note is that the indexes used above are value weighted and include dividend reinvestment. Equally weighted indexes would provide much different regression results. Some indexes also fail to include dividend reinvestment, a crucial element in measuring the total return for some securities.

Historical Time Period

Ideally, beta should be measured over the longest time period possible. With a large number of data points, the statistical precision of the regression equation should be high. Unfortunately, as more history is included in the regression equation, the possibility for irrelevant information to be included in the analysis increases. Companies change over time, so their systematic risk can change over time as well. Including older data may bias the regression results.

The amount of history included in beta calculations done by commercial beta services is fairly consistent at five years. Using five years of data is a rather arbitrary decision that attempts to use as much data as possible without including irrelevant historical data. Using five years of data would ideally cover a number of different economic scenarios such as expansion and contraction in the economy.

There may be instances, however, when using five years of data is too much. If company- or industry-specific events can be identified, a shorter historical time interval may be appropriate. An example of a company-specific event is a change in industry focus, as was the case with Westinghouse Electric. Through a series of acquisitions and divestitures, Westinghouse transformed itself from a consumer and defense electronics firm to a broadcast communications firm and changed its name to CBS Corp. Measuring the beta of CBS Corp. using a longer time period may not be appropriate due to differences in the risk characteristics of those industries that the company concentrated in five or six years ago compared with its recent industry focus. The beta of CBS Corp. was 1.12 when using five years of monthly data, and 0.90 when using only three years of monthly data—both through September 1999. While CBS Corp has since been acquired by Viacom, Inc., it still serves as an excellent example of a company changing focus and the relevance of measuring beta over a shorter time period.

An example of an industry-specific event that may cause one to focus on a shorter period of time is the deregulation of the electric utility industry, which has created the opportunity for companies to concentrate on specific sectors of the industry such as electric production, transmission, or distribution. For example, a company may choose to purchase its electricity from another provider rather than generate the electricity itself. In the past, most electric utilities companies had transmission, distribution, and generation capabilities. Though deregulation is not complete, it will be interesting to see its impact on the systematic risk of the electric utility industry.

Deregulation within the telecommunications industry is more complete. Table 6-4 shows the betas of several telecommunications firms calculated using two years of weekly data. The overall trend was for betas to rise as the industry became more deregulated.

Table 6-4
Changes in Beta of Telecommunications Companies

Ticker	Company	1992	1993	1994	1995	1996
ALNT	Aliant Communications	0.76	0.89	0.98	0.73	0.43
AIT	Ameritech	0.71	0.75	0.91	1.05	1.26
BEL	Bell Atlantic	0.83	0.92	0.92	1.01	1.17
BLS	BellSouth Corp.	0.76	0.84	0.78	0.88	1.21
FRO	Frontier Corp.	0.62	0.77	0.94	1.03	0.66
GTE	GTE	0.75	0.67	0.67	0.78	1.08
NYN	NYNEX	0.77	0.69	0.76	0.91	1.06
PAC	Pacific Telesis Group	0.79	1.06	0.97	0.98	1.10
SBC	SBC Communications	0.94	0.95	0.80	0.74	1.00
SNG	Southern New England Telecom	0.46	0.63	0.96	0.92	0.80
USW	US West Communications	0.73	0.71	0.56	0.79	0.99
AT	AllTel	0.80	0.78	0.85	0.76	0.98
CTL	Century Telephone	0.85	0.88	0.91	0.88	0.76
	Average	0.75	0.81	0.85	0.88	0.96

*Betas calculated using two years of weekly data ending in the period specified.
Source: Direct testimony of Roger G. Ibbotson for Ameritech Illinois, Illinois Commerce Commission Docket No. 96-0178.

The overall increase in beta cannot be attributed to increases in the leverage of firms in the telecommunications industry. A rise in leverage causes more financial risk to be shouldered by a firm's equity holders and results in a higher levered beta. (Levered beta is the most commonly referred to measure of beta. It measures both business and financial risks.)[1]

Table 6-5 demonstrates a slight fall in the debt-to-total-capital ratios of the same telecommunications firms. The lower debt-to-total-capital ratios indicate that there is less leverage and therefore less financial risk. All else held constant, one would expect the levered beta to fall, given a reduction in leverage. However, we observed the opposite for the telecommunications industry in the 1990's.

Table 6-5

Changes in Leverage of Telecommunication Companies

		Debt to Debt Plus Market Equity				
Ticker	Company	1992	1993	1994	1995	1996
ALNT	Aliant Communications	17.95%	12.29%	10.86%	14.43%	14.79%
AIT	Ameritech	25.83	24.19	22.18	16.94	18.55
BEL	Bell Atlantic	31.13	27.67	29.07	22.17	23.32
BLS	BellSouth Corp.	26.17	24.27	26.03	20.10	20.33
FRO	Frontier Corp.	33.99	25.21	28.07	12.12	15.15
GTE	GTE	34.43	30.84	32.77	25.83	25.01
NYN	NYNEX	32.72	37.83	38.91	29.65	31.67
PAC	Pacific Telesis Group	26.44	19.96	29.85	30.39	26.13
SBC	SBC Communications	23.97	21.56	23.41	17.41	18.55
SNG	Southern New England Telecom	33.46	35.59	32.20	35.34	35.46
USW	US West Communications	35.78	26.24	26.81	28.59	28.23
AT	AllTel	19.58	23.07	25.27	24.53	25.30
CTL	Century Telephone	23.59	29.21	30.44	25.86	25.31
	Average	28.08	25.99	27.37	23.33	23.68

Source: Direct testimony of Roger G. Ibbotson for Ameritech Illinois, Illinois Commerce Commission Docket No. 96-0178.

Time Interval

The final element to select in the calculation of beta is the time interval over which excess returns are calculated. The choices are daily, weekly, monthly, quarterly, or annually.

In the previous section, we identified five years as the appropriate time period over which beta should be calculated in most cases. With such a short time period, annual or quarterly data produce too few data points; furthermore, a great deal can happen to a company during these time intervals that makes them inappropriate. Daily data, in addition to being cumbersome to work with, is also most likely to add noise to the regression equation. This is especially true for small companies whose securities may not trade everyday. The addition of noise reduces the statistical quality of the regression.

---

1 Sometimes referred to as the equity beta, levered beta is measured from observable returns of a company and takes into account the financial risk or financial structure of the firm. The analysis contained in this chapter to this point has been with respect to the levered beta. For more information on levered and unlevered betas, see the sections titled Levered and Unlevered Beta later in this chapter.

This leaves weekly and monthly data as the logical alternatives. Most beta services have settled on using monthly interval data. If shorter time periods are used for the beta calculation (in cases such as a change in a company or an industry) then shorter interval data (i.e., weekly data) may be preferred to increase the number of observations. However, using weekly data may also add noise to the regression calculation.

Regression Statistics and Beta

While it is possible to calculate a beta statistic for any company having 60 months of data, not all betas are equal from a statistical standpoint. Because the beta is arrived at by regression, it may be necessary to examine, or at least consider, some common regression statistics when evaluating the statistical significance of any beta calculation.

t-Statistic

The first statistic that bears consideration is the t-statistic. The t-statistic indicates whether the beta coefficient is statistically different than zero at a certain confidence level. It is an important measure of the statistical significance of the beta that the regression produces. It is important to note, however, that the t-statistic does not measure the statistical accuracy of the numerical value found for the beta itself. The t-statistic only indicates if the beta coefficient is statistically different from zero. Other statistical tests can help determine the accuracy of the numerical value and will be discussed later in this chapter.

An illustration would help demonstrate the significance of the t-statistic with regard to beta. If a regression produces a beta of 0.90 for Company A and has a t-statistic of 3.05, then we can say that the beta coefficient is statistically different than zero. If a regression produces a beta of 0.90 for Company B with a t-statistic of 0.50, then we cannot say that the beta coefficient is statistically different than zero.

How do we know this? If the regression we are performing has 60 months of data, this gives us 59 degrees of freedom. The degrees of freedom provide a guide as to what the appropriate t-statistic should be. For a regression statistic with 59 degrees of freedom at an 90 percent confidence level, the critical t-statistic is approximately 1.67. What does this mean? Any regression statistic whose t-statistic is greater than 1.67 in absolute value would be considered statistically different from zero at the 90 percent confidence level. T-statistic critical values can be found in tables in most statistics textbooks. The appropriate critical value is that for the two-tailed test, as we are concerned with both the upper and lower extremes of the distribution. An abbreviated t-statistic distribution table for a two-tailed test is presented in Table 6-6.

Table 6-6

Critical Values for the t-Statistic

Degrees of Freedom	Confidence Interval				
	90%	95%	97.5%	99%	99.5%
1	6.314	12.706	25.452	63.656	127.321
2	2.920	4.303	6.205	9.925	14.089
3	2.353	3.182	4.177	5.841	7.453
4	2.132	2.776	3.495	4.604	5.598
5	2.015	2.571	3.163	4.032	4.773
6	1.943	2.447	2.969	3.707	4.317
7	1.895	2.365	2.841	3.499	4.029
8	1.860	2.306	2.752	3.355	3.833
9	1.833	2.262	2.685	3.250	3.690
10	1.812	2.228	2.634	3.169	3.581
11	1.796	2.201	2.593	3.106	3.497
12	1.782	2.179	2.560	3.055	3.428
13	1.771	2.160	2.533	3.012	3.372
14	1.761	2.145	2.510	2.977	3.326
15	1.753	2.131	2.490	2.947	3.286
16	1.746	2.120	2.473	2.921	3.252
17	1.740	2.110	2.458	2.898	3.222
18	1.734	2.101	2.445	2.878	3.197
19	1.729	2.093	2.433	2.861	3.174
20	1.725	2.086	2.423	2.845	3.153
21	1.721	2.080	2.414	2.831	3.135
22	1.717	2.074	2.405	2.819	3.119
23	1.714	2.069	2.398	2.807	3.104
24	1.711	2.064	2.391	2.797	3.091
25	1.708	2.060	2.385	2.787	3.078
26	1.706	2.056	2.379	2.779	3.067
27	1.703	2.052	2.373	2.771	3.057
28	1.701	2.048	2.368	2.763	3.047
29	1.699	2.045	2.364	2.756	3.038
30	1.697	2.042	2.360	2.750	3.030
40	1.684	2.021	2.329	2.704	2.971
50	1.676	2.009	2.311	2.678	2.937
60	1.671	2.000	2.299	2.660	2.915
70	1.667	1.994	2.291	2.648	2.899
80	1.664	1.990	2.284	2.639	2.887
90	1.662	1.987	2.280	2.632	2.878
100	1.660	1.984	2.276	2.626	2.871
110	1.659	1.982	2.272	2.621	2.865
120	1.658	1.980	2.270	2.617	2.860

Recalling the prior example, the beta regression for Company A produced a t-statistic of 3.05, which is greater than 1.67. Therefore, the beta of Company A is statistically different than zero at an 90 percent confidence level. The t-statistic for the beta regression of Company B is 0.50, which is less than 1.67;

thus, the beta of Company B is not statistically different than zero at that confidence level. If the regression provides a beta of 0.90 but is not statistically different than zero, then other measures of beta may need to be consulted (such as the company's peer betas or industry average betas).

To better illustrate the typical range of a beta's t-statistic, Graph 6-3 depicts the distribution of all t-statistics calculated with respect to the betas of over 5,600 companies included in Ibbotson's *Beta Book*. Since these beta calculations use 60 months of data, the critical value for the t-statistic is again 1.67 at the 90 percent confidence level. Recall that the absolute value is what is compared to the critical value; t-statistics above 1.67 or below –1.67 would therefore be considered statistically significant.

Graph 6-3

t-Statistic Distribution

October 1997 through September 2002

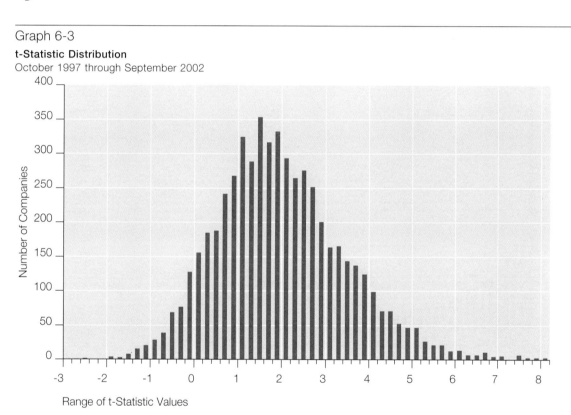

Range of t-Statistic Values

R-Squared

Another valuable regression statistic is the coefficient of determination, or R-squared. The R-squared is a statistic that measures the "goodness of fit" of the regression line and describes the percentage of variation in the dependent variable that is explained by the independent variable. The R-squared measure may vary from zero to one. An R-squared of 1.00 means that the independent variable explains 100 percent of the variation of the dependent variable. An R-squared of 0 indicates that the independent variable does not explain any of the variation of the dependent variable.

In terms of measuring beta via regression, a high R-squared means that the movements of the returns of the security are explained largely by the movements of the returns of the market. The R-squared for security betas are usually quite low. Graphs 6-4 and 6-5 show a distribution of R-squared statistics from Ibbotson Associates' *Beta Book*. The first graph shows the distribution of R-squared for all 5,600 plus companies included in the publication. The second graph shows the distribution of R-squared for the largest 100 companies, in terms of equity capitalization, that are included in the book.

Graph 6-4

R-Squared Distribution for Entire Population
October 1997 through September 2002

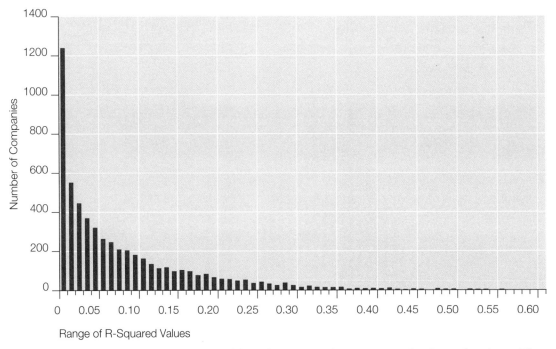

Note that most betas have an R-squared less than 0.3. What can we infer from this data? There may be other company- or industry-specific factors that drive security prices. While the CAPM includes only one factor in determining expected returns, it does not disallow the existence of others.

Graph 6-5

R-Squared Distribution for Largest 100 Companies
October 1997 through September 2002

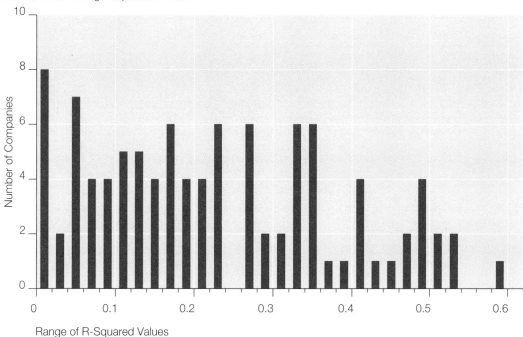

Standard Error

A third common regression statistic is the standard error of the regression coefficient. The standard error measures the extent to which each individual observation in a sample differs from the value predicted by the regression. In other words, the standard error attempts to measure sampling error. The standard error can be interpreted in a fashion similar to the standard deviation of a return. For example, suppose a beta regression results in a standard error of 0.2. There is therefore a 68 percent likelihood that the true measure of this company's beta lies within 0.2 of the estimated beta coefficient. Likewise, there is a 96 percent likelihood that the true beta measure lies within two standard errors of the estimate, or plus or minus 0.4.

Stability of beta is a key issue under the CAPM. While we expect betas to change over time as companies increase or decrease their systematic risk, we do not expect a huge fluctuation in beta from one period to the next. One would expect the beta of a company with a low standard error to be more stable over time than the beta of a company with a high standard error. An example of two companies is presented in Graph 6-6. The current beta of 1.06 for Boise Cascade has a low standard error of 0.16. On the other hand, Rymer Foods has a current beta of 2.74 with a high standard error of 2.45. The chart shows the beta of each company on a rolling 60-month basis, meaning that the beta is calculated over the 60-month period October 31, 1992 through September 30, 1997, then the calculation is carried forward for each consecutive 60-month period through September 30, 2002. The company with the small standard error, Boise Cascade, exhibits remarkable stability in its beta when calculated over different time periods. On the other hand, the company with the high standard error, Rymer Foods, displays considerable variation depending on the period of the regression.

Graph 6-6

60-Month Rolling Betas with High versus Low Standard Error

September 1997 through September 2002

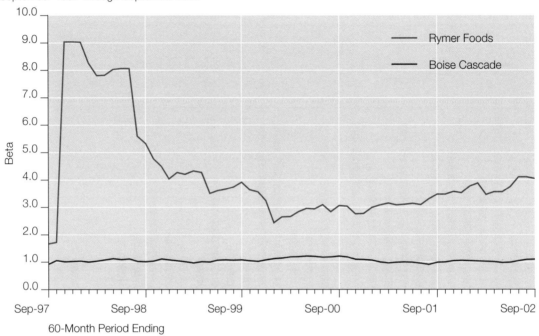

The standard error provides another statistical clue to help determine the reliability of the beta produced by the regression. To better illustrate the typical range of standard errors with respect to beta estimation, Graph 6-7 shows the distribution of standard error statistics across the Ibbotson Associates' *Beta Book* population of companies.

Graph 6-7

Standard Error Distribution

October 1997 through September 2002

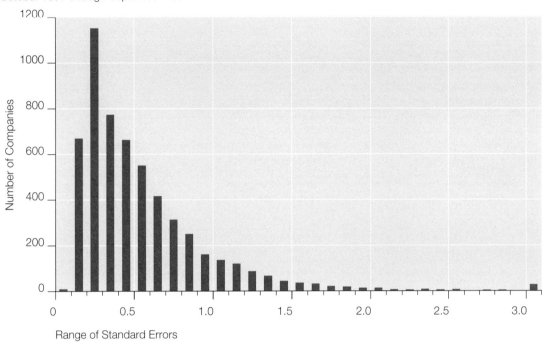

Range of Standard Errors

Beta Adjustment Methodologies

In calculating beta estimates for cost of capital projections, we are seeking a forward-looking or prospective beta. What we have measured using historical data in the beta regression is a historical beta. In this section we will examine two of the most common techniques used to adjust betas from historical to prospective or forward-looking.

Blume

One of the first academics to study whether historical betas are reliable estimates of future systematic risk was Marshall Blume.[2] What Blume found is that betas tend to revert toward their mean value, or the market beta of one. This means that high historical betas (those in excess of one) tend to overestimate betas in future time periods, and low historical betas (those under one) tend to underestimate betas in future time periods.

2 Blume, M. E. "On the Assessment of Risk," *Journal of Finance*, vol. 26, 1971, pp. 1–10.

Blume's analysis regressed estimates of beta in one period against estimates in the previous period. By performing this analysis over different time periods, Blume was able to develop a convergence tendency that could be measured by the following formula:

$$\beta_1 = 0.371 + 0.635\beta_0$$

where:

β_1 = prospective beta; and

β_0 = historical beta.

The formula tells us that the forecast of next year's beta is equal to 0.635 times this year's historical beta plus 0.371. Stated another way, betas will trend toward the market average of one (the market beta) times 0.371 plus 0.635 times the historical beta.

What are the practical implications of Blume's analysis? The Blume equation has the impact of lowering high historical betas and increasing low historical betas. A historical beta of 1.40 becomes an adjusted beta of 1.26 under the Blume methodology. Similarly, a historical beta of 0.80 becomes an adjusted beta of 0.88.

In short, Blume suggests that all betas using historical regression techniques should be adjusted in this fashion. The closer a historical beta is to 1.0, the less the magnitude of the adjustment. The Blume equation is often referred to as the 1/3 + 2/3 adjustment. When simplified, the adjustment procedure takes 1/3 plus 2/3(β_0). Use of this type of adjustment procedure is common and will be discussed further in the commercial beta section.

Vasicek

Vasicek has proposed another beta adjustment technique that considers the statistical accuracy of the beta calculation.[3] The Vasicek adjustment seeks to overcome one weakness of the Blume model by not applying the same adjustment to every security; rather, a security-specific adjustment is made depending on the statistical quality of the regression.

The Vasicek adjustment process focuses on the standard error of the beta estimate—the higher the standard error, the lower the statistical significance of the beta estimate. Therefore, a company beta with a high standard error should have a greater adjustment than a company beta with a low standard error. The Vasicek formula is as follows:

$$\beta_{s1} = \frac{\sigma_{\beta s0}^2}{\sigma_{\beta 0}^2 + \sigma_{\beta s0}^2}\beta_0 + \frac{\sigma_{\beta 0}^2}{\sigma_{\beta 0}^2 + \sigma_{\beta s0}^2}\beta_{s0}$$

3 Vasicek, O.A. "A Note on Using Cross-Sectional Information in Bayesian Estimation of Security Betas," *Journal of Finance*, vol. 28, 1973, pp. 1233–1239.

where:

β_{s1} = the Vasicek adjusted beta for security s;

β_{s0} = the historical beta for security s;

β_0 = the beta of the market, industry, or peer group;

$\sigma^2_{\beta 0}$ = the variance of betas in the market, industry, or peer group; and

$\sigma^2_{\beta s0}$ = the square of the standard error of the historical beta for security s.

While the Vasicek formula looks intimidating, it is really quite simple. The adjusted beta for a company is a weighted average of the company's historical beta and the beta of the market, industry, or peer group. How much weight is given to the company historical beta depends on the statistical significance of the company beta statistic. If a company beta has a low standard error, then it will have higher weighting in the Vasicek formula. If a company beta has a high standard error, then it will have lower weighting in the Vasicek formula. In all cases, the Vasicek weights will sum to one.

An advantage of this adjustment methodology is that it does not force an adjustment to the market as a whole. Instead, the adjustment can be toward an industry or some other peer group. This is most useful in looking at companies in industries that on average have high or low betas. If evaluating the beta for a company in the petroleum refining industry, which traditionally has had betas below one, it may be more desirable to adjust the beta of that company toward the industry average rather than toward the market average of one.

Because this method varies by company and allows for adjustment toward industry averages, Ibbotson Associates has selected the Vasicek adjustment technique for our beta calculations.

Sum Beta (Including Lag)

Motivation

In calculating betas for our *Stocks, Bonds, Bills, and Inflation Yearbook*, we began to notice that the betas of the small company portfolios, though higher than the betas of the large company portfolios, were not high enough to explain all of the excess returns historically found in small stocks.[4] In addition, while calculating betas for Ibbotson's first *Cost of Capital Quarterly (CCQ)* and *Beta Book* publications, we found that the betas of individual small companies tend to be lower than those of large companies. For the beta population from the *CCQ* and *Beta Book*, it appears that the standard ordinary least squares (OLS) regression technique is calculating betas that are too low for smaller companies. Graph 6-8 illustrates the capitalization-weighted average OLS betas for 25 size portfolios containing every company listed in Ibbotson's *Beta Book*. The portfolios were derived by dividing the entire population of companies into 25 equally populated portfolios, of which portfolio 1 contains the largest companies and portfolio 25 contains the smallest.

4   The size effect and an alternative method of correcting for it are examined in more detail in Chapter 7.

Graph 6-8

Ordinary Least Squares Betas by Company Size

October 1997 through September 2002*

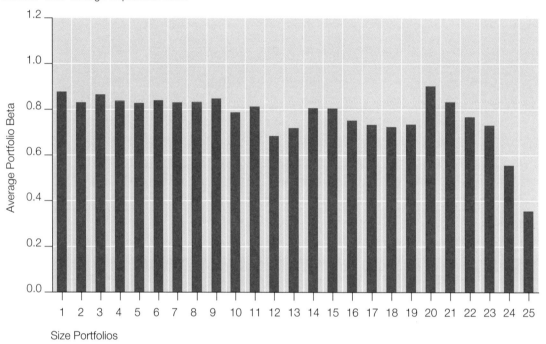

Size Portfolios

*Each bar represents the capitalization-weighted average of the betas for each company in the portfolio. Individual company betas were calculated using 60 months of excess return data.

Possible Measurement Error in Small Company Betas

As will be discussed in Chapter 7, there is a relationship between risk and return. Small companies are generally considered riskier investments than large companies. Therefore, we should expect small company betas to be, on average, higher than large company betas.

Table 6-7 shows the ordinary least squares betas for each of the size portfolios over the most recent 60-month period and over the entire history of data available. Decile 1 contains the largest companies, ranked by market capitalization, and decile 10 contains the smallest companies. (For additional information on how these deciles are constructed, see Chapter 7.) Based on these statistics, it is clear that there is a relationship between risk and return. Unfortunately, the relationship that we see in the most recent period is counter to what we would expect, since the low-capitalization stocks appear to have less systematic risk than large-capitalization stocks. Though the expected relationship between the betas of the large and small portfolios exists over the long period, the small portfolio betas are still not large enough to account for all of the excess return exhibited by these small stocks. There are several possible explanations for these results.

Table 6-7

**Ordinary Least Squares Betas for the
NYSE Size Portfolios**
1926–2002

	January 1998–December 2002	1926–2002
Decile 1	0.86	0.90
Decile 2	0.74	1.02
Decile 3	0.86	1.07
Decile 4	0.79	1.11
Decile 5	0.78	1.14
Decile 6	0.73	1.16
Decile 7	0.66	1.20
Decile 8	0.72	1.24
Decile 9	0.72	1.31
Decile 10	0.66	1.40

By looking at the same analysis over a number of 60-month periods, the relationship between the betas of large and small companies becomes more clear. Graph 6-9 shows rolling 60-month betas for selected NYSE deciles. The beta of each decile is calculated over the 60-month period January 1, 1926 through December 31, 1930, then the calculation is carried forward for each consecutive 60-month period through December 31, 2002. While the portfolio containing the largest companies has a very stable beta, the portfolio containing the smallest companies has periods where the beta is high and periods where it is low. Referring back to Table 6-7, the most recent 60-month period is one in which small company betas are low. There does not appear to be the consistency in the beta measure of smaller companies as there is with larger companies.

Graph 6-9

60-Month Rolling Ordinary Least Squares Betas by NYSE Size Decile

January 1926 through December 2002

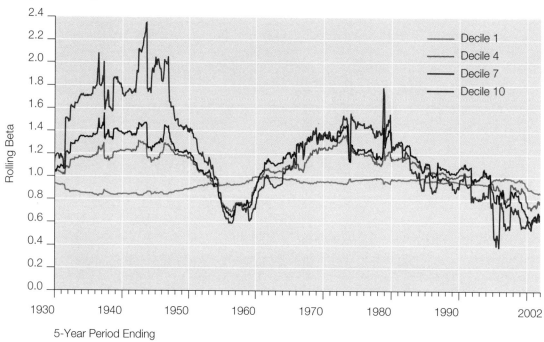

5-Year Period Ending

The lower-capitalization decile betas from both the most recent and long-term time periods tend to be lower than expected. For all but the largest companies, the prices of individual stocks tend to react in part with a lag to movements in the overall market; the smaller the company, the greater the lagged price reaction. The lagged price reaction of small company stocks has been documented by a number of researchers.[5]

There are a number of explanations for the low betas exhibited by small stocks. One common explanation is the infrequent trading that often accompanies small company stocks. Many securities do not trade everyday. The market for some securities is so thin that they may not trade for several days. If a stock is not trading, its stock price is not reflecting the movement of the market, which drives down the covariance with the market, creating an artificially low beta.

Note that this is only the apparent covariance. Because the security is not actively trading, the posted price is that of the last trade or some combination of the bid and ask prices. Inactive trading makes calculating accurate betas for these companies quite difficult.

One way to lessen the impact of lagged price reaction and infrequent trading in small stocks is to modify the beta calculation to include a term for the lagged reaction of small company prices to market movements. The remainder of this section will focus on the correction for this lagged reaction to market movements.

5 Lo, Andrew W., and A. Craig MacKinlay. "When are Contrarian Profits Due to Stock Market Overreaction?," *Review of Financial Studies*, Vol. 3, No. 2, 1990.
McQueen, Grant, Michael Pinegar, and Steven Thorley. "Delayed Reaction to Good News and the Cross-autocorrelation of Portfolio Returns," *Journal of Finance*, July 1996.
Peterson, James D., and Gary C. Sanger. "Cross-autocorrelations, Systematic Risk and the Period of Listing," Working Paper, University of Notre Dame, 1995.

Possible Solution

The traditional beta regression assumes that the beta of a company is related to current market movements. This is why the regression formula compares returns of the security for a given period to the returns of the market for that same period.

What if the company is thinly traded? The fact that a company is thinly traded would mean that changes in the price of the stock might lag the market. Therefore, in calculating beta for thinly traded companies, it may be useful to compare the returns of the security against the returns of the market in the current period as well as the returns of the market in the prior period by performing a multiple regression. The security returns at time zero could be regressed with both the market returns at time zero and the market returns for the prior period.

Methods for calculating betas for the lagged price effect were first proposed by Scholes, Williams, and Dimson.[6] Ibbotson Associates' methodology, developed by Ibbotson, Kaplan, and Peterson, calculates a current and lagged beta coefficient in a multiple regression.[7] We then sum the two coefficients to arrive at the beta estimate that we call sum beta.

The sum beta equation is expressed as:

$$(r_s - r_f) = \alpha_s + \beta_{s0} \times (r_{m0} - r_{f0}) + \beta_{s-1} \times (r_{m-1} - r_{f-1}) + \varepsilon_t$$

where:

$(r_s - r_f)$	= excess return on security s;
α_s	= regression constant;
β_{s0}	= beta coefficient for realized market excess returns;
$(r_{m0} - r_{f0})$	= realized market excess return;
β_{s-1}	= beta coefficient for lagged realized market excess returns;
$(r_{m-1} - r_{f-1})$	= lagged realized market excess return; and
ε_t	= the error term of the regression.

$$\text{SumBeta} = \beta_{s0} + \beta_{s-1}$$

The distribution of over 5,600 betas included in Ibbotson's *Beta Book*, using both OLS and sum beta methods of estimation, is shown in Graph 6-10. The sum betas are more widely dispersed and have a higher median than the OLS betas. We need to examine this further to determine if the sum beta method is properly correcting for the lagged reaction of stock prices.

6 Scholes, Myron, and Joseph Williams. "Estimating Betas from Nonsynchronous Data," *Journal of Financial Economics*, vol. 14, 1977, pp. 327–348.
Dimson, Elroy. "The Stability of U.K. Risk Measures and the Problem of Thin Trading," *Journal of Finance*, vol. 38, 1983, pp. 753–783.
7 Ibbotson, Roger G., Paul D. Kaplan, and James D. Peterson. "Estimates of Small-Stock Betas Are Much Too Low," *Journal of Portfolio Management*, Summer 1997.

Graph 6-10

Beta Distribution Using OLS versus Sum Beta Estimation

October 1997 through September 2002

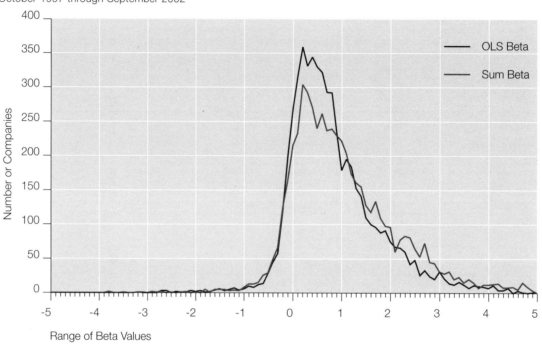

Table 6-8 compares beta estimates for the 10 size decile portfolios of the NYSE calculated using the ordinary least squares (OLS) method and the sum beta method described above. (For more information on the construction of the NYSE size decile portfolios, see Chapter 7.) Using the sum beta method results in a significant increase in the beta estimates for the smallest of the deciles for both the recent and long-term periods. The sum beta method seems to work well in accounting for the lag in the stock price reaction of small stocks.[8]

---

8 As will be discussed further in Chapter 7, when using sum beta in calculating the cost of equity, there must be a corresponding adjustment to the size premium.

Table 6-8

Ordinary Least Squares Betas versus Sum Betas for the NYSE Size Portfolios

| | January 1998–December 2002 | | 1926–2002 | |
	OLS Beta	Sum Beta	OLS Beta	Sum Beta
Decile 1	0.86	0.88	0.90	0.90
Decile 2	0.74	0.82	1.02	1.05
Decile 3	0.86	0.92	1.07	1.11
Decile 4	0.79	0.85	1.11	1.18
Decile 5	0.78	0.88	1.14	1.22
Decile 6	0.73	0.86	1.16	1.28
Decile 7	0.66	0.84	1.20	1.35
Decile 8	0.72	0.92	1.24	1.45
Decile 9	0.72	1.06	1.31	1.52
Decile 10	0.66	1.09	1.40	1.71

Full Information Beta

Because betas for individual companies can be unreliable, many analysts seek to calculate industry or peer group average betas to determine the systematic risk inherent in a given industry. In addition, industry or peer group averages are commonly used when the beta of a company or division cannot be determined. A beta is either difficult to determine or unattainable for companies that lack sufficient price history (i.e., non-publicly traded companies, divisions of companies, and companies with short price histories). Typically, this type of analysis involves the determination of companies competing in a given industry and the calculation of some sort of industry average beta.

Unfortunately, this type of analysis includes only the "pure play" companies in the calculation of beta. Many of the largest companies in the United States are conglomerates, making it difficult or impossible to include these large companies in the industry average. In some cases, divisions from conglomerates represent some of the largest players in a given industry. Therefore, one weakness of the conventional pure play approach is the failure to include information from all industry participants.

For a company to be considered a pure play company in an industry, the revenue that the company generates from that industry should constitute a vast majority of the company's total revenue. The Ibbotson Associates rule of thumb is that a minimum of 75 percent of revenues must come from a single SIC code for a company to be considered a pure play company. Unfortunately, there are instances when this rule eliminates some of the largest participants in an industry from the analysis. Table 6-9 illustrates an example of how this may occur when analyzing SIC Code 352, Farm and Garden Machinery and Equipment. The largest participant in the industry, Deere & Co., derives only 68.1 percent of its total revenue from this particular industry; it would therefore be excluded from a pure play analysis of this industry.

Table 6-9

Industry Sales by Company for SIC 352
as of September 30, 2002*

Ticker	Company Name	Industry Sales by Company as a Percent of: Total Company Sales	Total Industry Sales	Company Beta
TTC	Toro Co.	100.0%	9.7%	0.51
AG	Agco Corp.	100.0%	18.1%	0.54
ARTW	Arts Way Mfg. Inc.	100.0%	0.1%	-0.34
CTBC	CTB International Corp.	100.0%	1.7%	0.01
LNN	Lindsay Manufacturing Co.	84.4%	0.8%	0.33
DE	Deere & Co.	68.1%	63.6%	0.55
ALG	Alamo Group Inc.	56.1%	1.0%	0.10
MMG	Metromedia International Grp.	55.8%	1.2%	1.40
GEHL	Gehl Co.	50.2%	0.9%	0.60
VMI	Valmont Industries	27.3%	1.7%	0.28
OTTR	Otter Tail Corp.	18.9%	0.9%	0.04

Total 100.0%

*Betas calculated using five years of monthly excess return data, October 1997 through September 2002.

Only five companies meet the criteria to be included in a pure play analysis of this industry. However, six additional participants account for almost 70 percent of the total industry sales.

One solution to the conglomerate problem is called the full information approach developed by Kaplan and Peterson.[9] The full information approach seeks to include in the calculation of the industry beta data from all companies participating in a given industry. The full information approach is a cross-sectional regression that solves for betas for a variety of industries based on the exposure a given company has to that industry.

To perform the full information analysis for a set of companies, you must first calculate a beta for each company in the population being analyzed. In addition, you must also calculate the exposure each company has to the industries in which it competes. This exposure or weighting scheme can be sales based, asset based, or based on any other weighting that makes sense and for which data is available. The Ibbotson Associates methodology uses a sales-based weighting scheme.

Once the company betas and industry exposure levels have been determined, the cross-sectional regression is performed with the company-specific betas as the dependent variable and the industry exposures as the independent variables. A final element to the regression analysis is the market capitalization weighting of the observations for each company. The results of the regression produce a coefficient for each industry that forms the estimates of pure play industry betas for which data from every participant in the industry has been considered.

Using the same example as above, Table 6-10 compares the beta of a pure play analysis of SIC 352 with the full information approach. The full information approach utilizes the data available of all eleven participants in the industry, whereas the pure play approach only includes the five companies with industry participation above 75 percent.

9 Kaplan, Paul D., and James D. Peterson. "Full-Information Industry Betas," *Financial Management,* Summer 1998.

Table 6-10

Full Information versus Pure Play Beta Analysis for SIC 352
October 1997 through September 2002

Pure Play Beta	0.44
Full Information Beta	0.37

Levered Beta

A levered beta measures the systematic risk for the equity shareholders of a company and is therefore commonly referred to as the equity beta. It is measured directly from the company's returns with no adjustment made for the debt financing undertaken by the company. Therefore, a levered equity beta incorporates the business and financing risks undertaken by the company and borne by the equity shareholders.

The levered beta is the measure that should be used in calculating the cost of equity. It is also a helpful tool in examining the effects of changes in financing or leverage on a company's cost of equity. This will be examined further in the following section.

Unlevered Beta

The unlevered beta (also known as asset beta) removes a company's financing decisions from the beta calculation. In other words, the unlevered beta represents the risk of the firm excluding the risks implicit in the financial structure of the company. The calculation of the unlevered beta therefore attempts to isolate the business risk of a firm. The unlevered beta is a weighted average of the debt and equity beta, and it is therefore appropriately used in the calculation of the overall cost of capital.

Understanding the relationship between levered and unlevered beta can be a powerful tool in evaluating financing decisions. Debt generally has a beta equal to or close to zero. Assuming that the beta of debt is zero allows for some simplification in the calculation. The unlevered beta is equal to the levered beta divided by the tax-adjusted debt shield, computed as follows:

$$\beta_{Ui} = \frac{\beta_{Li}}{1+\frac{D_i}{E_i}(1-t_i)}$$

where:
b_{Ui} = the unlevered beta for company i;
b_{Li} = the levered beta for company i;
D_i = total debt for company i;
E_i = total equity capitalization for company i; and
t_i = marginal tax rate for company i.

Consequently, this equation can be rearranged to solve for the levered equity beta. These two equations can be used to first unlever the observable levered equity beta, then relever the beta using a different capital structure. Solving for the levered equity beta results in the following:

$$\beta_{Li} = \beta_{Ui}\left[1 + \frac{D_i}{E_i}(1 - t_i)\right]$$

Take, for example, a company that has much higher leverage than that of its peers. The equity holders of the firm would shoulder comparatively more risk, as the bondholders' claim to the company's cash flows is larger. Suppose you compare this company to another firm or peer group. For example, as of September 30, 2002, Delta Airlines Inc. had a debt-to-equity ratio of 821 percent, about 2.5 times the industry average. As a whole, the air transportation industry had a capitalization-weighted debt-to-equity ratio of 323.3 percent and an average levered beta of 1.19. The levered beta for Delta Airlines Inc. was 1.42.

Does Delta Airlines Inc. exhibit more or less business risk than the industry as a whole? It would be difficult to determine simply by comparing the levered betas of the company with the industry since the levered beta also includes the effect of financial risk. To compare the betas on a level basis we can unlever the beta of Delta Airlines Inc. and relever the beta using the same debt structure as the industry. This is accomplished using the two beta equations presented so far. First we unlever the beta of Delta Airlines Inc. to arrive at the unlevered asset beta:

$$\beta_{Ui} = \frac{\beta_{Li}}{1 + \frac{D_i}{E_i}(1 - t_i)} = \frac{1.42}{1 + 8.21(1 - 0.21^*)} = \frac{1.42}{7.49} = 0.19$$

* Company-specific tax rates are available through the Cost of Capital Center at www.ibbotson.com.

Once the unlevered asset beta is obtained, we can relever the beta at the industry average debt-to-equity ratio of 323.3 percent.

$$\beta_{Li} = \beta_{Ui}\left[1 + \frac{D_i}{E_i}(1 - t_i)\right] = 0.19\left[1 + 3.233(1 - 0.21)\right] = 0.19 \times 3.554 = 0.675$$

Delta Airlines Inc.'s relevered beta of 0.675 is actually much lower than the industry average levered beta of 1.19. This result contrasts with the firm's actual levered beta, which was slightly higher than the industry average. This implies that Delta Airlines Inc. carries more financial risk than the industry but at the same time exhibits less business risk.

Commercial Beta Sources

There are a number of different sources for company betas that analysts can utilize in developing cost of equity estimates. Every analyst should have an understanding of how betas are calculated and how these methodologies differ by beta source. As we have outlined in this chapter, the assumptions underlying the beta calculation have an impact on the ultimate statistic produced.

Table 6-11 lists the beta calculation methodology for four different commercial beta services. Bloomberg offers the most flexible beta calculation system, allowing users of their service to specify market proxy, historical time period, and whether daily, weekly, monthly, or annual data is used. The other beta services utilize either the S&P 500 or NYSE as their market proxy. Most services utilize five years of monthly data; however, Value Line uses weekly data. The most important difference of these services is the adjustment method used in the calculation of beta. Most services utilize the Blume methodology outlined earlier in this chapter. Ibbotson Associates utilizes the Vasicek methodology.

The far right column of the table shows the actual beta statistic for a sample company, Deere & Co. We have tried to select betas from similar time periods for comparison purposes. Although the calculation methodologies are similar across beta calculation services, there is some disparity in the results obtained.

Table 6-11

Commercial Beta Sources

	Market Proxy	Time Period	Frequency of Data	Adjustment Factors	Deere & Co.
Bloomberg	Over 20 domestic series	Adjustable	Daily, weekly, monthly, or annually	(0.67 x unadjusted beta) + (0.33 x 1.0)	0.69†
Compustat	S&P 500	5 years	Monthly (24-month minimum)	None	0.54
Ibbotson	S&P 500	5 years	Monthly (36 month minimum)	Adjusted toward peer group beta weighted by statistical significance	0.59
Value Line	NYSE Composite Series	5 years	Weekly	0.35 + 0.67 x (unadjusted beta)*	1.05

*Rounded to nearest 0.05

†Using 60 months of monthly data and the S&P 500

Chapter 7

Firm Size and Return

The Firm Size Phenomenon

One of the most remarkable discoveries of modern finance is that of a relationship between firm size and return. The relationship cuts across the entire size spectrum but is most evident among smaller companies, which have higher returns on average than larger ones. Many studies have looked at the effect of firm size on return.[1] In this chapter, the returns across the entire range of firm size are examined.

Construction of the Decile Portfolios

The portfolios used in this chapter are those created by the Center for Research in Security Prices (CRSP) at the University of Chicago's Graduate School of Business. CRSP has refined the methodology of creating size-based portfolios and has applied this methodology to the entire universe of NYSE/AMEX/NASDAQ-listed securities going back to 1926.

The New York Stock Exchange universe excludes closed-end mutual funds, preferred stocks, real estate investment trusts, foreign stocks, American Depository Receipts, unit investment trusts, and Americus Trusts. All companies on the NYSE are ranked by the combined market capitalization of their eligible equity securities. The companies are then split into 10 equally populated groups, or deciles. Eligible companies traded on the American Stock Exchange (AMEX) and the Nasdaq National Market (NASDAQ) are then assigned to the appropriate deciles according to their capitalization in relation to the NYSE breakpoints. The portfolios are rebalanced, using closing prices for the last trading day of March, June, September, and December. Securities added during the quarter are assigned to the appropriate portfolio when two consecutive month-end prices are available. If the final NYSE price of a security that becomes delisted is a month-end price, then that month's return is included in the quarterly return of the security's portfolio. When a month-end NYSE price is missing, the month-end value of the security is derived from merger terms, quotations on regional exchanges, and other sources. If a month-end value still is not determined, the last available daily price is used.

Base security returns are monthly holding period returns. All distributions are added to the month-end prices, and appropriate price adjustments are made to account for stock splits and dividends. The return on a portfolio for one month is calculated as the weighted average of the returns for its individual stocks. Annual portfolio returns are calculated by compounding the monthly portfolio returns.

Size of the Deciles

Table 7-1 reveals that the top three deciles of the NYSE/AMEX/NASDAQ account for most of the total market value of its stocks. Approximately two-thirds of the market value is represented by the first decile, which currently consists of 168 stocks, while the smallest decile accounts for less than one percent of the market value. The data in the second column of Table 7-1 are averages across all

---

[1] Rolf W. Banz was the first to document this phenomenon. See Banz, Rolf W. "The Relationship Between Returns and Market Value of Common Stocks," *Journal of Financial Economics*, Vol. 9, 1981, pp. 3–18.

77 years. Of course, the proportion of market value represented by the various deciles varies from year to year.

Columns three and four give recent figures on the number of companies and their market capitalization, presenting a snapshot of the structure of the deciles near the end of 2002.

Table 7-1

Size-Decile Portfolios of the NYSE/AMEX/NASDAQ Size and Composition
1926-2002

Decile	Historical Average Percentage of Total Capitalization	Recent Number of Companies	Recent Decile Market Capitalization (in thousands)	Recent Percentage of Total Capitalization
1-Largest	63.27%	168	$6,099,523,614	66.27%
2	14.01%	182	1,174,194,524	12.76%
3	7.60%	197	584,693,698	6.35%
4	4.75%	200	344,651,829	3.74%
5	3.25%	244	282,490,634	3.07%
6	2.37%	268	206,453,954	2.24%
7	1.72%	347	175,969,268	1.91%
8	1.27%	427	136,629,517	1.48%
9	0.97%	703	117,578,857	1.28%
10-Smallest	0.79%	1,994	81,984,379	0.89%
Mid-Cap 3–5	15.59%	641	1,211,836,161	13.17%
Low-Cap 6–8	5.36%	1,042	519,052,738	5.64%
Micro-Cap 9–10	1.76%	2,697	199,563,236	2.17%

Source: Center for Research in Security Prices, University of Chicago.

Historical average percentage of total capitalization shows the average, over the last 77 years, of the decile market values as a percentage of the total NYSE/AMEX/NASDAQ calculated each month. Number of companies in deciles, recent market capitalization of deciles, and recent percentage of total capitalization are as of September 30, 2002.

Table 7-2 gives the current breakpoints that define the composition of the NYSE/AMEX/NASDAQ size deciles. The largest company and its market capitalization are presented for each decile. Table 7-3 shows the historical breakpoints for each of the three size groupings presented throughout this chapter. Mid-cap stocks are defined here as the aggregate of deciles 3–5. Based on the most recent data (Table 7-2), companies within this mid-cap range have market capitalizations at or below $5,012,705,000 but greater than $1,143,845,000. Low-cap stocks include deciles 6–8 and currently include all companies in the NYSE/AMEX/NASDAQ with market capitalizations at or below $1,143,845,000 but greater than $314,042,000. Micro-cap stocks include deciles 9–10 and include companies with market capitalizations at or below $314,042,000. The market capitalization of the smallest company included in the micro-capitalization group is currently $501 thousand.

Table 7-2

Size-Decile Portfolios of the NYSE/AMEX/NASDAQ, Largest Company
and Its Market Capitalization by Decile
September 30, 2002

Decile	Market Capitalization of Largest Company (in thousands)	Company Name
1-Largest	$293,137,304	Microsoft Corp.
2	11,628,735	KeyCorp New
3	5,012,705	Rockwell Collins Inc.
4	2,680,573	Diebold Inc.
5	1,691,210	Smucker JM Co.
6	1,143,845	CEC Entertainment Inc.
7	791,336	Playtex Products Inc.
8	521,298	Buckle Inc.
9	314,042	Guess? Inc.
10-Smallest	141,459	NYMAGIC Inc.

Source: Center for Research in Security Prices, University of Chicago.

Presentation of the Decile Data

Summary statistics of annual returns of the 10 deciles over 1926–2002 are presented in Table 7-4. Note from this exhibit that both the average return and the total risk, or standard deviation of annual returns, tend to increase as one moves from the largest decile to the smallest. Furthermore, the serial correlations of returns are near zero for all but the smallest two deciles. Serial correlations and their significance will be discussed in detail later in this chapter.

Graph 7-1 depicts the growth of one dollar invested in each of three NYSE/AMEX/NASDAQ groups broken down into mid-cap, low-cap, and micro-cap stocks. The index value of the entire NYSE/AMEX/NASDAQ is also included. All returns presented are value-weighted based on the market capitalizations of the deciles contained in each subgroup. The sheer magnitude of the size effect in some years is noteworthy. While the largest stocks actually declined in 1977, the smallest stocks rose more than 20 percent. A more extreme case occurred in the depression-recovery year of 1933, when the difference between the first and tenth decile returns was far more substantial. This divergence in the performance of small and large company stocks is a common occurrence.

Table 7-3

Size-Decile Portfolios of the NYSE/AMEX/NASDAQ
Largest and Smallest Company by Size Group

from 1926 to1965

Date (Sept 30)	Capitalization of Largest Company (in thousands)			Capitalization of Smallest Company (in thousands)		
	Mid-Cap 3-5	Low-Cap 6-8	Micro-Cap 9-10	Mid-Cap 3-5	Low-Cap 6-8	Micro-Cap 9-10
1926	$61,490	$14,040	$4,305	$14,100	$4,325	$43
1927	$65,281	$14,746	$4,450	$15,311	$4,496	$72
1928	$81,998	$18,975	$5,074	$19,050	$5,119	$135
1929	$107,085	$24,328	$5,875	$24,480	$5,915	$126
1930	$67,808	$13,050	$3,219	$13,068	$3,264	$30
1931	$42,607	$8,142	$1,905	$8,222	$1,927	$15
1932	$12,431	$2,170	$473	$2,196	$477	$19
1933	$40,298	$7,210	$1,830	$7,280	$1,875	$100
1934	$38,129	$6,669	$1,669	$6,734	$1,673	$68
1935	$37,631	$6,519	$1,350	$6,549	$1,383	$38
1936	$46,920	$11,505	$2,660	$11,526	$2,668	$98
1937	$51,750	$13,601	$3,500	$13,635	$3,539	$68
1938	$36,102	$8,325	$2,125	$8,372	$2,145	$60
1939	$35,784	$7,367	$1,697	$7,389	$1,800	$75
1940	$31,050	$7,990	$1,861	$8,007	$1,872	$51
1941	$31,744	$8,316	$2,086	$8,336	$2,087	$72
1942	$26,135	$6,870	$1,779	$6,875	$1,788	$82
1943	$43,218	$11,475	$3,847	$11,480	$3,903	$395
1944	$46,621	$13,066	$4,800	$13,068	$4,812	$309
1945	$55,268	$17,325	$6,413	$17,575	$6,428	$225
1946	$79,158	$24,192	$10,013	$24,199	$10,051	$829
1947	$57,830	$17,735	$6,373	$17,872	$6,380	$747
1948	$67,238	$19,575	$7,313	$19,651	$7,329	$784
1949	$55,506	$14,549	$5,037	$14,577	$5,108	$379
1950	$65,881	$18,675	$6,176	$18,750	$6,201	$303
1951	$82,517	$22,750	$7,567	$22,860	$7,598	$668
1952	$97,936	$25,452	$8,428	$25,532	$8,480	$480
1953	$98,595	$25,374	$8,156	$25,395	$8,168	$459
1954	$125,834	$29,645	$8,484	$29,707	$8,488	$463
1955	$170,829	$41,445	$12,353	$41,681	$12,366	$553
1956	$183,434	$46,805	$13,481	$46,886	$13,524	$1,122
1957	$192,861	$47,658	$13,844	$48,509	$13,848	$925
1958	$195,083	$46,774	$13,789	$46,871	$13,816	$550
1959	$253,644	$64,221	$19,500	$64,372	$19,548	$1,804
1960	$246,202	$61,485	$19,344	$61,529	$19,385	$831
1961	$296,261	$79,058	$23,562	$79,422	$23,613	$2,455
1962	$250,433	$58,866	$18,952	$59,143	$18,968	$1,018
1963	$308,438	$71,846	$23,819	$71,971	$23,822	$296
1964	$344,033	$79,343	$25,594	$79,508	$25,595	$223
1965	$363,759	$84,479	$28,365	$84,600	$28,375	$250

Source: Center for Research in Security Prices, University of Chicago.

Table 7-3 (continued)

Size-Decile Portfolios of the NYSE/AMEX/NASDAQ
Largest and Smallest Company by Size Group

from 1966 to 2002

Date (Sept 30)	Capitalization of Largest Company (in thousands)			Capitalization of Smallest Company (in thousands)		
	Mid-Cap 3-5	Low-Cap 6-8	Micro-Cap 9-10	Mid-Cap 3-5	Low-Cap 6-8	Micro-Cap 9-10
1966	$399,455	$99,578	$34,884	$99,935	$34,966	$381
1967	$459,170	$117,985	$42,267	$118,329	$42,313	$381
1968	$528,326	$149,261	$60,351	$150,128	$60,397	$592
1969	$517,452	$144,770	$54,273	$145,684	$54,280	$2,119
1970	$380,246	$94,025	$29,910	$94,047	$29,916	$822
1971	$542,517	$145,340	$45,571	$145,673	$45,589	$865
1972	$545,211	$139,647	$46,728	$139,710	$46,757	$1,031
1973	$424,584	$94,809	$29,601	$95,378	$29,606	$561
1974	$344,013	$75,272	$22,475	$75,853	$22,481	$444
1975	$465,763	$96,954	$28,140	$97,266	$28,144	$540
1976	$551,071	$116,184	$31,987	$116,212	$32,002	$564
1977	$573,084	$135,804	$39,192	$137,323	$39,254	$513
1978	$572,967	$159,778	$46,621	$160,524	$46,629	$830
1979	$661,336	$174,480	$49,088	$174,517	$49,172	$948
1980	$754,562	$194,012	$48,671	$194,241	$48,953	$549
1981	$954,665	$259,028	$71,276	$261,059	$71,289	$1,446
1982	$762,028	$205,590	$54,675	$206,536	$54,883	$1,060
1983	$1,200,680	$352,698	$103,443	$352,944	$103,530	$2,025
1984	$1,068,972	$314,650	$90,419	$315,214	$90,659	$2,093
1985	$1,432,342	$367,413	$93,810	$368,249	$94,000	$760
1986	$1,857,621	$444,827	$109,956	$445,648	$109,975	$706
1987	$2,059,143	$467,430	$112,035	$468,948	$112,125	$1,277
1988	$1,957,926	$420,257	$94,268	$421,340	$94,302	$696
1989	$2,147,608	$480,975	$100,285	$483,623	$100,384	$96
1990	$2,164,185	$472,003	$93,627	$474,065	$93,750	$132
1991	$2,129,863	$457,958	$87,586	$458,853	$87,733	$278
1992	$2,428,671	$500,346	$103,352	$501,050	$103,500	$510
1993	$2,711,068	$608,520	$137,945	$608,825	$137,987	$602
1994	$2,497,073	$601,552	$149,435	$602,552	$149,532	$598
1995	$2,793,761	$653,178	$158,011	$654,019	$158,063	$89
1996	$3,150,685	$763,377	$195,188	$763,812	$195,326	$1,043
1997	$3,511,132	$818,299	$230,472	$821,028	$230,554	$480
1998	$4,216,707	$934,264	$253,329	$936,727	$253,336	$1,671
1999	$4,251,741	$875,309	$218,336	$875,582	$218,368	$1,502
2000	$4,143,902	$840,000	$192,598	$840,730	$192,721	$1,462
2001	$5,252,063	$1,114,792	$269,275	$1,115,200	$270,391	$443
2002	$5,012,705	$1,143,845	$314,042	$1,144,452	$314,174	$501

Source: Center for Research in Security Prices, University of Chicago.

Table 7-4

Size-Decile Portfolios of the NYSE/AMEX/NASDAQ, Summary Statistics of Annual Returns
1926–2002

Decile	Geometric Mean	Arithmetic Mean	Standard Deviation	Serial Correlation
1-Largest	9.4%	11.2%	19.44%	0.11
2	10.5	12.9	22.13	0.05
3	10.9	13.5	24.02	−0.01
4	11.0	14.0	26.26	0.00
5	11.1	14.5	27.06	0.00
6	11.3	14.9	28.11	0.06
7	11.1	15.2	30.33	0.02
8	11.3	16.2	34.03	0.06
9	11.5	17.1	36.90	0.07
10-Smallest	13.1	20.8	45.37	0.17
Mid-Cap, 3–5	11.0	13.8	25.08	−0.01
Low-Cap, 6–8	11.2	15.2	29.86	0.05
Micro-Cap, 9–10	12.1	18.2	39.32	0.10
NYSE/AMEX/NASDAQ Total Value-Weighted Index	9.8	11.8	20.48	0.05

Aspects of the Firm Size Effect

The firm size phenomenon is remarkable in several ways. First, the greater risk of small stocks does not, in the context of the capital asset pricing model (CAPM), fully account for their higher returns over the long term. In the CAPM, only systematic or beta risk is rewarded; small company stocks have had returns in excess of those implied by their betas.

Second, the calendar annual return differences between small and large companies are serially correlated. This suggests that past annual returns may be of some value in predicting future annual returns. Such serial correlation, or autocorrelation, is practically unknown in the market for large stocks and in most other equity markets but is evident in the size premia.

Third, the firm size effect is seasonal. For example, small company stocks outperformed large company stocks in the month of January in a large majority of the years. Such predictability is surprising and suspicious in light of modern capital market theory. These three aspects of the firm size effect—long-term returns in excess of systematic risk, serial correlation, and seasonality—will be analyzed thoroughly in the following sections.

Graph 7-1

Size-Decile Portfolios of the NYSE/AMEX/NASDAQ: Wealth Indices of Investments in Mid-, Low-, Micro- and Total Capitalization Stocks

1925–2002*

*Year-end 1925 = $1.00

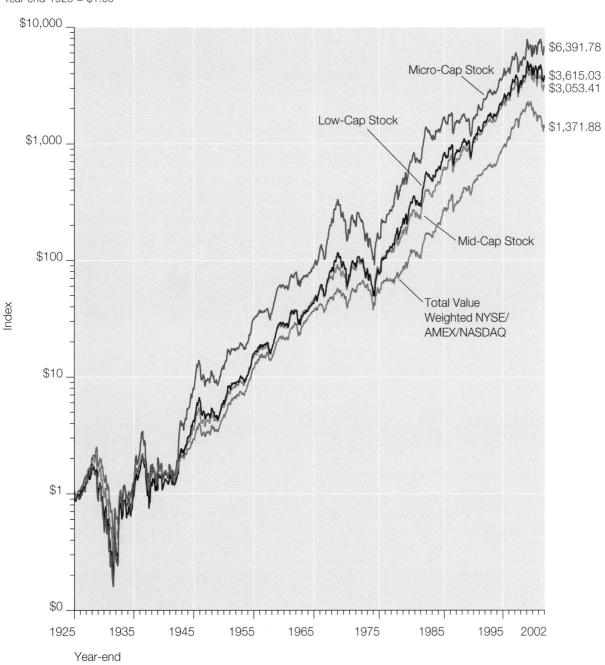

Long-Term Returns in Excess of Systematic Risk

The capital asset pricing model (CAPM) does not fully account for the higher returns of small company stocks. Table 7-5 shows the returns in excess of systematic risk over the past 77 years for each decile of the NYSE/AMEX/NASDAQ. Recall that the CAPM is expressed as follows:

$$k_s = r_f + (\beta_s \times ERP)$$

Table 7-5 uses the CAPM to estimate the return in excess of the riskless rate and compares this estimate to historical performance. According to the CAPM, the expected return on a security should consist of the riskless rate plus an additional return to compensate for the systematic risk of the security. The return in excess of the riskless rate is estimated in the context of the CAPM by multiplying the equity risk premium by β (beta). The equity risk premium is the return that compensates investors for taking on risk equal to the risk of the market as a whole (systematic risk).[2] Beta measures the extent to which a security or portfolio is exposed to systematic risk.[3] The beta of each decile indicates the degree to which the decile's return moves with that of the overall market.

A beta greater than one indicates that the security or portfolio has greater systematic risk than the market; according to the CAPM equation, investors are compensated for taking on this additional risk. Yet, Table 7-5 illustrates that the smaller deciles have had returns that are not fully explainable by their higher betas. This return in excess of that predicted by CAPM increases as one moves from the largest companies in decile 1 to the smallest in decile 10. The excess return is especially pronounced for micro-cap stocks (deciles 9–10). This size-related phenomenon has prompted a revision to the CAPM, which includes a size premium. Chapter 4 presents this modified CAPM theory and its application in more detail.

This phenomenon can also be viewed graphically, as depicted in the Graph 7-2. The security market line is based on the pure CAPM without adjustment for the size premium. Based on the risk (or beta) of a security, the expected return lies on the security market line. However, the actual historic returns for the smaller deciles of the NYSE/AMEX/NASDAQ lie above the line, indicating that these deciles have had returns in excess of that which is appropriate for their systematic risk.

2 The equity risk premium is estimated by the 77-year arithmetic mean return on large company stocks, 12.20 percent, less the 77-year arithmetic mean income-return component of 20-year government bonds as the historical riskless rate, in this case 5.23 percent. (It is appropriate, however, to match the maturity, or duration, of the riskless asset with the investment horizon.) See Chapter 5 for more detail on equity risk premium estimation.
3 Historical betas were calculated using a simple regression of the monthly portfolio (decile) total returns in excess of the 30-day U.S. Treasury bill total returns versus the S&P 500 total returns in excess of the 30-day U.S. Treasury bill, January 1926–December 2002. See Chapter 6 for more detail on beta estimation.

Table 7-5

Long-Term Returns in Excess of CAPM Estimation for Decile Portfolios of the NYSE/AMEX/NASDAQ
1926–2002

Decile	Beta*	Arithmetic Mean Return	Realized Return in Excess of Riskless Rate**	Estimated Return in Excess of Riskless Rate†	Size Premium (Return in Excess of CAPM)
1-Largest	0.91	11.25%	6.01%	6.34%	−0.32%
2	1.03	12.86%	7.63%	7.21%	0.42%
3	1.09	13.51%	8.28%	7.62%	0.66%
4	1.13	14.03%	8.80%	7.85%	0.95%
5	1.16	14.48%	9.25%	8.08%	1.16%
6	1.18	14.93%	9.70%	8.22%	1.48%
7	1.23	15.16%	9.92%	8.58%	1.35%
8	1.27	16.17%	10.94%	8.88%	2.06%
9	1.34	17.12%	11.89%	9.33%	2.56%
10-Smallest	1.41	20.75%	15.52%	9.85%	5.67%
Mid-Cap, 3-5	1.11	13.82%	8.59%	7.77%	0.82%
Low-Cap, 6-8	1.22	15.23%	9.99%	8.47%	1.52%
Micro-Cap, 9-10	1.35	18.20%	12.96%	9.44%	3.53%

*Betas are estimated from monthly portfolio total returns in excess of the 30-day U.S. Treasury bill total return versus the S&P 500 total returns in excess of the 30-day U.S. Treasury bill, January 1926–December 2002.

**Historical riskless rate is measured by the 77-year arithmetic mean income return component of 20-year government bonds (5.23 percent).

†Calculated in the context of the CAPM by multiplying the equity risk premium by beta. The equity risk premium is estimated by the arithmetic mean total return of the S&P 500 (12.20 percent) minus the arithmetic mean income return component of 20-year government bonds (5.23 percent) from 1926–2002.

Graph 7-2

Security Market Line versus Size-Decile Portfolios of the NYSE/AMEX/NASDAQ
1926–2002

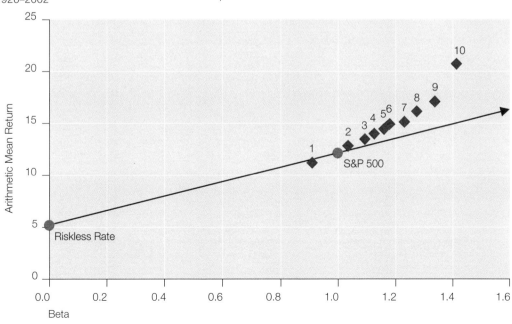

Further Analysis of the 10th Decile

The size premia presented thus far do a great deal to explain the return due solely to size in publicly traded companies. However, by splitting the 10th decile into two size groupings we can get a closer look at the smallest companies. This magnification of the smallest companies will demonstrate whether the company size to size premia relationship continues to hold true.

As previously discussed, the method for determining the size groupings for size premia analysis was to take the stocks traded on the NYSE and break them up into 10 deciles, after which stocks traded on the AMEX and NASDAQ were allocated into the same size groupings. This same methodology was used to split the 10th decile into two parts: 10a and 10b, with 10b being the smaller of the two. This is equivalent to breaking the stocks down into 20 size groupings, with portfolios 19 and 20 representing 10a and 10b.

Table 7-7 shows that the pattern continues; as companies get smaller their size premium increases. There is a noticeable increase in size premium from 10a to 10b, which can also be demonstrated visually in Graph 7-3. This can be useful in valuing companies that are extremely small. Table 7-6 presents the size, composition, and breakpoints of deciles 10a and 10b. First, the recent number of companies and total decile market capitalization are presented. Then the largest company and its market capitalization are presented.

Breaking the smallest decile down lowers the significance of the results compared to results for the 10th decile taken as a whole, however. The same holds true for comparing the 10th decile with the Micro-Cap aggregation of the 9th and 10th deciles. The more stocks included in a sample the more significance can be placed on the results. While this is not as much of a factor with the recent years of data, these size premia are constructed with data back to 1926. By breaking the 10th decile down into smaller components we have cut the number of stocks included in each grouping. The change over time of the number of stocks included in the 10th decile for the NYSE/AMEX/NASDAQ is presented in Table 7-8. With fewer stocks included in the analysis early on, there is a strong possibility that just a few stocks can dominate the returns for those early years.

While the number of companies included in the 10th decile for the early years of our analysis is low, it is not too low to still draw meaningful results even when broken down into subdivisions 10a and 10b. All things considered, size premia developed for deciles 10a and 10b are significant and can be used in cost of capital analysis. These size premia should greatly enhance the development of cost of capital analysis for very small companies.

Table 7-6

Size-Decile Portfolios 10a and 10b of the NYSE/AMEX/NASDAQ,
Largest Company and Its Market Capitalization
September 30, 2002

Decile	Recent Number of Companies	Recent Decile Market Capitalization (in thousands)	Market Capitalization of Largest Company (in thousands)	Company Name
10a	584	$49,010,627	$141,459	NYMAGIC, Inc.
10b	1,314	$38,115,236	$64,767	Hartmarx Corp.

Note: These numbers may not aggregate to equal decile 10 figures.

Table 7-7

Long-Term Returns in Excess of CAPM Estimation for Decile Portfolios of the NYSE/AMEX/NASDAQ, with 10th Decile Split

1926–2002

	Beta*	Arithmetic Mean Return	Realized Return in Excess of Riskless Rate**	Estimated Return in Excess of Riskless Rate†	Size Premium (Return in Excess of CAPM)
1-Largest	0.91	11.25%	6.01%	6.34%	–0.32%
2	1.03	12.86%	7.63%	7.21%	0.42%
3	1.09	13.51%	8.28%	7.62%	0.66%
4	1.13	14.03%	8.80%	7.85%	0.95%
5	1.16	14.48%	9.25%	8.08%	1.16%
6	1.18	14.93%	9.70%	8.22%	1.48%
7	1.23	15.16%	9.92%	8.58%	1.35%
8	1.27	16.17%	10.94%	8.88%	2.06%
9	1.34	17.12%	11.89%	9.33%	2.56%
10a	1.42	19.11%	13.88%	9.90%	3.98%
10b-Smallest	1.40	24.13%	18.89%	9.73%	9.16%
Mid-Cap, 3–5	1.11	13.82%	8.59%	7.77%	0.82%
Low-Cap, 6–8	1.22	15.23%	9.99%	8.47%	1.52%
Micro-Cap, 9-10	1.35	18.20%	12.96%	9.44%	3.53%

*Betas are estimated from monthly portfolio total returns in excess of the 30-day U.S. Treasury bill total return versus the S&P 500 total returns in excess of the 30-day U.S. Treasury bill, January 1926–December 2002.

**Historical riskless rate is measured by the 77-year arithmetic mean income return component of 20-year government bonds (5.23 percent).

†Calculated in the context of the CAPM by multiplying the equity risk premium by beta. The equity risk premium is estimated by the arithmetic mean total return of the S&P 500 (12.20 percent) minus the arithmetic mean income return component of 20-year government bonds (5.23 percent) from 1926–2002.

Graph 7-3

Security Market Line versus Size-Decile Portfolios of the NYSE/AMEX/NASDAQ, with 10th Decile Split

1926-2002

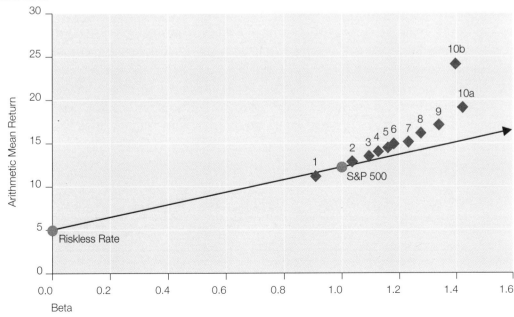

Table 7-8

Historical Number of Companies for NYSE/AMEX/NASDAQ Decile 10

Sept.	Number of Companies
1926	52*
1930	72
1940	78
1950	100
1960	109
1970	865
1980	685
1990	1,814
2000	1,927
2002	1,994

*The fewest number of companies was 49 in March, 1926

Alternative Methods of Calculating the Size Premia

The size premia estimation method presented above makes several assumptions with respect to the market benchmark and the measurement of beta. The impact of these assumptions can best be examined by looking at some alternatives. In this section we will examine the impact on the size premia of using a different market benchmark for estimating the equity risk premia and beta. We will also examine the effect on the size premia study of using sum beta or an annual beta.[4]

Changing the Market Benchmark

In the original size premia study, the S&P 500 is used as the market benchmark in the calculation of the realized historical equity risk premium and of each size group's beta. The NYSE total value-weighted index is a common alternative market benchmark used to calculate beta. Table 7-9 uses this market benchmark in the calculation of beta. In order to isolate the size effect, we require an equity risk premium based on a large company stock benchmark. The NYSE deciles 1–2 large company index offers a mutually exclusive set of portfolios for the analysis of the smaller company groups: mid-cap deciles 3–5, low-cap deciles 6–8, and micro-cap deciles 9–10. The size premia analyses using these benchmarks are summarized in Table 7-9 and depicted graphically in Graph 7-4.

For the entire period analyzed, 1926–2002, the betas obtained using the NYSE total value-weighted index are higher than those obtained using the S&P 500. Since smaller companies had higher betas using the NYSE benchmark, one would expect the size premia to shrink. However, as was illustrated in Chapter 5, the equity risk premium calculated using the NYSE deciles 1–2 benchmark results in a value of 6.24, as opposed to 6.97 when using the S&P 500. The effect of the higher betas and lower equity risk premium cancel each other out, and the resulting size premia in Table 7-9 are slightly higher than those resulting from the original study.

---

4 Sum beta is the method of beta estimation described in Chapter 6 that was developed to better account for the lagged reaction of small stocks to market movements. The sum beta methodology was developed for the same reason that the size premia were developed; small company betas were too small to account for all of their excess returns.

Table 7-9

Long-Term Returns in Excess of CAPM Estimation for Decile Portfolios of the NYSE/AMEX/NASDAQ, with NYSE Market Benchmarks
1926–2002

Decile	Beta*	Arithmetic Mean Return	Realized Return in Excess of Riskless Rate**	Estimated Return in Excess of Riskless Rate†	Size Premium (Return in Excess of CAPM)
1-Largest	0.93	11.25%	6.01%	5.82%	0.19%
2	1.08	12.86%	7.63%	6.73%	0.90%
3	1.14	13.51%	8.28%	7.14%	1.13%
4	1.19	14.03%	8.80%	7.42%	1.38%
5	1.23	14.48%	9.25%	7.66%	1.59%
6	1.26	14.93%	9.70%	7.85%	1.85%
7	1.32	15.16%	9.92%	8.22%	1.71%
8	1.37	16.17%	10.94%	8.55%	2.39%
9	1.44	17.12%	11.89%	8.97%	2.91%
10-Smallest	1.52	20.75%	15.52%	9.46%	6.06%
Mid-Cap, 3-5	1.17	13.82%	8.59%	7.32%	1.27%
Low-Cap, 6-8	1.30	15.23%	9.99%	8.11%	1.89%
Micro-Cap, 9-10	1.45	18.20%	12.96%	9.08%	3.89%

*Betas are estimated from monthly portfolio total returns in excess of the 30-day U.S. Treasury bill total return versus the NYSE total capitalization-weighted index total returns in excess of the 30-day U.S. Treasury bill, January 1926–December 2002.

**Historical riskless rate is measured by the 77-year arithmetic mean income return component of 20-year government bonds (5.23 percent).

†Calculated in the context of the CAPM by multiplying the equity risk premium by beta. The equity risk premium is estimated by the arithmetic mean total return of the NYSE deciles 1–2 (11.47 percent) minus the arithmetic mean income return component of 20-year government bonds (5.23 percent) from 1926–2002.

Graph 7-4

Security Market Line versus Size-Decile Portfolios of the NYSE/AMEX/NASDAQ with NYSE Market Benchmarks
1926-2002

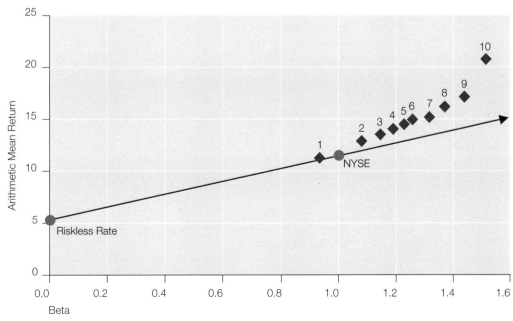

Measuring Beta with Sum Beta

The sum beta method attempts to provide a better measure of beta for small stocks by taking into account their lagged price reaction to movements in the market. [See Chapter 6.] Table 7-10 shows that using this method of beta estimation results in larger betas for the smaller size deciles of the NYSE/AMEX/NASDAQ while those of the larger size deciles remain relatively stable. From these results, it appears that the sum beta method corrects for possible errors that are made when estimating small company betas without adjusting for the lagged price reaction of small stocks. However, the sum beta, when applied to the CAPM, still does not account for all of the returns in excess of the riskless rate historically found for small stocks. Table 7-10 demonstrates that a size premium is still necessary to estimate the expected returns using sum beta in conjunction with the CAPM, though the premium is smaller than that needed when using the typical calculation of beta.

Graph 7-5 compares the 10 deciles of the NYSE/AMEX/NASDAQ to the security market line. There are two sets of decile portfolios—one set is plotted using the single variable regression method of calculating beta, as in Graph 7-2, and the second set uses the sum beta method. The portfolios plotted using sum beta more closely resemble the security market line. Again, this demonstrates that the sum beta method results in the desired effect: a higher estimate of returns for small companies. Yet the smaller portfolios still lie above the security market line, indicating that an additional premium may be required.

Table 7-10

Long-Term Returns in Excess of CAPM for Decile Portfolios of the NYSE/AMEX/NASDAQ, with Sum Beta
1926–2002

Decile	Sum Beta*	Arithmetic Mean Return	Realized Return in Excess of Riskless Rate**	Estimated Return in Excess of Riskless Rate†	Size Premium (Return in Excess of CAPM)
1-Largest	0.91	11.25%	6.01%	6.34%	–0.33%
2	1.06	12.86%	7.63%	7.37%	0.26%
3	1.13	13.51%	8.28%	7.85%	0.43%
4	1.19	14.03%	8.80%	8.32%	0.47%
5	1.24	14.48%	9.25%	8.64%	0.61%
6	1.30	14.93%	9.70%	9.05%	0.65%
7	1.37	15.16%	9.92%	9.58%	0.34%
8	1.48	16.17%	10.94%	10.31%	0.63%
9	1.55	17.12%	11.89%	10.80%	1.09%
10-Smallest	1.71	20.75%	15.52%	11.90%	3.61%
Mid-Cap, 3-5	1.17	13.82%	8.59%	8.13%	0.46%
Low-Cap, 6-8	1.36	15.23%	9.99%	9.47%	0.52%
Micro-Cap, 9-10	1.59	18.20%	12.96%	11.11%	1.86%

*Betas are estimated from monthly portfolio total returns in excess of the 30-day U.S. Treasury bill total return versus the S&P 500 index total returns in excess of the 30-day U.S. Treasury bill, January 1926–December 2002.

**Historical riskless rate is measured by the 77-year arithmetic mean income return component of 20-year government bonds (5.23 percent).

†Calculated in the context of the CAPM by multiplying the equity risk premium by beta. The equity risk premium is estimated by the arithmetic mean total return of the S&P 500 (12.20 percent) minus the arithmetic mean income return component of 20-year government bonds (5.23 percent) from 1926–2002.

Graph 7-5

Security Market Line versus Size-Decile Portfolios of the NYSE/AMEX/NASDAQ, Sum Beta (with Lag) versus Unadjusted Beta (without Lag)
1926–2002

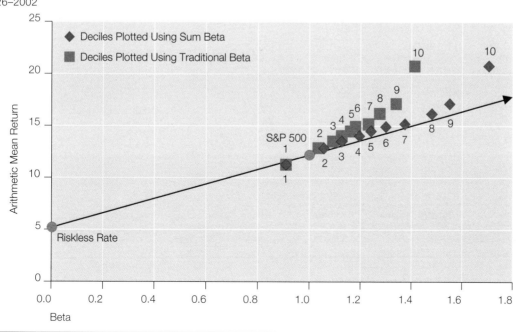

Annual Data versus Monthly Data

Another potential way to correct for the low beta estimates of small company stocks is to calculate the long-term beta with annual data instead of monthly data. Using annual data may eliminate the infrequent trading argument because of the long period of time covered. However, Table 7-11 and Graph 7-6 illustrate that the size premium is still present when estimating beta with annual data.

Table 7-11

Long-Term Returns in Excess of CAPM Estimation for Decile Portfolios of the NYSE/AMEX/NASDAQ, with Annual Beta
1926–2002

Decile	Annual Beta*	Arithmetic Mean Return	Realized Return in Excess of Riskless Rate**	Estimated Return in Excess of Riskless Rate†	Size Premium (Return in Excess of CAPM)
1-Largest	0.94	11.25%	6.01%	6.54%	–0.53%
2	1.04	12.86%	7.63%	7.26%	0.37%
3	1.08	13.51%	8.28%	7.56%	0.72%
4	1.16	14.03%	8.80%	8.09%	0.70%
5	1.20	14.48%	9.25%	8.36%	0.89%
6	1.19	14.93%	9.70%	8.32%	1.37%
7	1.30	15.16%	9.92%	9.03%	0.90%
8	1.37	16.17%	10.94%	9.53%	1.41%
9	1.45	17.12%	11.89%	10.07%	1.81%
10-Smallest	1.62	20.75%	15.52%	11.29%	4.23%
Mid-Cap, 3-5	1.13	13.82%	8.59%	7.87%	0.72%
Low-Cap, 6-8	1.26	15.23%	9.99%	8.80%	1.19%
Micro-Cap, 9-10	1.49	18.20%	12.96%	10.41%	2.55%

*Betas are estimated from annual portfolio total returns in excess of the 30-day U.S. Treasury bill total return versus the S&P 500 index total returns in excess of the 30-day U.S. Treasury bill, January 1926–December 2002.

**Historical riskless rate is measured by the 77-year arithmetic mean income return component of 20-year government bonds (5.23 percent).

†Calculated in the context of the CAPM by multiplying the equity risk premium by beta. The equity risk premium is estimated by the arithmetic mean total return of the S&P 500 (12.20 percent) minus the arithmetic mean income return component of 20-year government bonds (5.23 percent) from 1926–2002.

Graph 7-6

Security Market Line versus Size-Decile Portfolios of the NYSE/AMEX/NASDAQ Annual Beta versus Monthly Beta
1926–2002

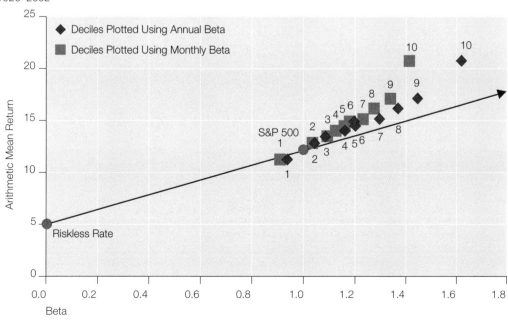

Serial Correlation in Small Company Stock Returns

In six of the last ten years, large-capitalization stocks have outperformed small-capitalization stocks. This recent role reversal has led some to speculate that there is no size premium, but statistical evidence suggests that periods of underperformance should be expected.

History tells us that small companies are riskier than large companies. Table 7-4 shows the standard deviation (a measure of risk) for each decile of the NYSE/AMEX/NASDAQ. As one moves from larger to smaller deciles, the standard deviation of return grows. Investors are compensated for taking on this additional risk by the higher returns provided by small companies. It is important to note, however, that the risk/return profile is over the long term. If small companies did not provide higher long-term returns, investors would be more inclined to invest in the less risky stocks of large companies.

The increased risk faced by investors in small stocks is quite real. The long-term expected return for any asset class is quite different than short-term expected returns, and investors in small-capitalization stocks should expect losses and periods of underperformance. Graph 7-7 shows five-year rolling period returns of four size groups: large-cap (deciles 1–2), mid-cap (deciles 3–5), low-cap (deciles 6–8), and micro-cap (deciles 9–10). There have been a number of five-year periods in which the large-cap group outperformed some or all of the small-cap groups.

Graph 7-7

Five-Year Rolling Period Returns for the Size-Decile Portfolios of the NYSE/AMEX/NASDAQ
1926–2002

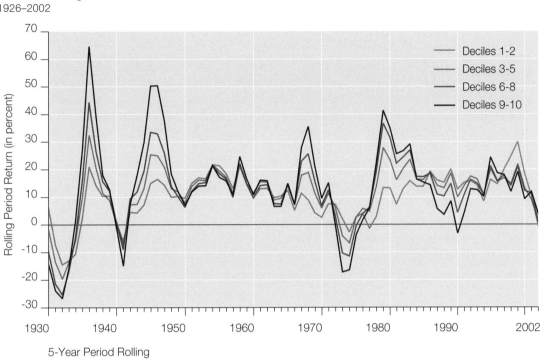

5-Year Period Rolling

Serial correlation, or first-order autocorrelation, measures the degree to which the return of a given series is related from period to period. Serial correlation, like cross-correlation, ranges from positive one to negative one. A positive serial correlation can be an indicator of a trend in a return series. A serial correlation of positive one indicates that returns from one period have a perfectly positive relationship to the returns of the next period; returns are therefore perfectly predictable from one period to the next. A negative serial correlation can be an indicator of a cycle in a return series. A serial correlation of negative one indicates that returns from one period have a perfectly negative relationship to the next period. A serial correlation near zero indicates that returns are random or unpredictable.

If stock returns have a positive or a negative serial correlation, one can gain some information about future performance based on prior period returns. The serial correlation of returns on large-capitalization stocks is near zero. [See Table 7-4.] For the smallest deciles of stocks, the serial correlation is near or above 0.1. This observation bears further examination.

To remove the randomizing effect of the market as a whole, the returns for decile 1 are geometrically subtracted from the returns for each decile 2 through 10. The result illustrates that these series in excess of decile 1 exhibit greater serial correlation than the individual decile series themselves. Table 7-12 presents the serial correlations of the excess returns for deciles 2 through 10. These serial correlations suggest some predictability of smaller company excess returns; however, caution is necessary. The serial correlation of small company excess returns for non-calendar years (February through January, etc.) do not always confirm the results shown here for calendar years (January through December). Therefore, predicting small company excess returns may not be easy.

Table 7-12

Size-Decile Portfolios of the NYSE/AMEX/NASDAQ,
Serial Correlation of Annual Returns
in Excess of Decile 1 Returns
1926–2002

Decile	Serial Correlation of Annual Returns in Excess of Decile 1 Returns
2	0.23
3	0.29
4	0.23
5	0.26
6	0.35
7	0.28
8	0.34
9	0.32
10	0.40

The size premia developed in this chapter also remove the randomizing effect of the market as a whole and appear to be serially correlated. Graph 7-8 shows the size premia for rolling five-year periods for each of the three size groups: mid-cap, low-cap, and micro-cap. (A five-year period is necessary to calculate the beta for each portfolio, which is then used to calculate the size premia.) There are periods in which the size premia are positive and periods in which they are negative. However, none of these periods appears to continue for an extended time. Basing a long-term estimate of the size premia on the most recent periods would therefore be inappropriate.

Graph 7-8

Five-Year Rolling Period Size Premia for Decile Portfolios of the NYSE/AMEX/NASDAQ
1926–2002

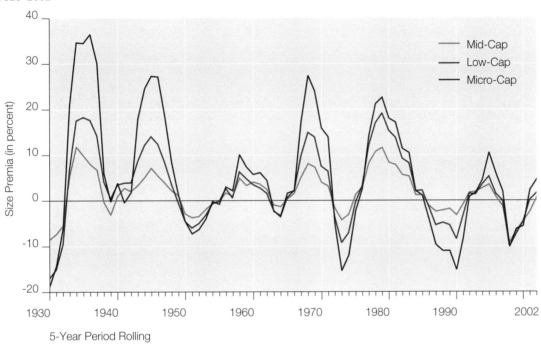

5-Year Period Rolling

The logic behind using a long history to estimate the size premia is similar to the argument for using a long history in estimating the equity risk premium (see Chapter 5). Longer historical periods provide more stable estimates of the size premia because unique events are not weighted heavily, and the probability of such events occurring is better represented by an average that covers a long period of time. Graph 7-9 demonstrates the calculation of the size premia using different starting dates. It shows the realized size premia for a series of time periods through 2002. In other words, the first value on the graph represents the average realized size premium over the period 1926–2002. The next value on the graph represents the average realized size premium over the period 1927–2002, and so on, with the last value representing the average over the most recent five years, 1998–2002. Concentrating on the left side of Graph 7-9, one notices that the realized size premia, when measured over long periods of time, are relatively stable. The increased volatility of the size premia in more recent periods is due to their cyclical nature.

Graph 7-9

Size Premia for Decile Portfolios of the NYSE/AMEX/NASDAQ Calculated with Different Starting Dates
1926–2002

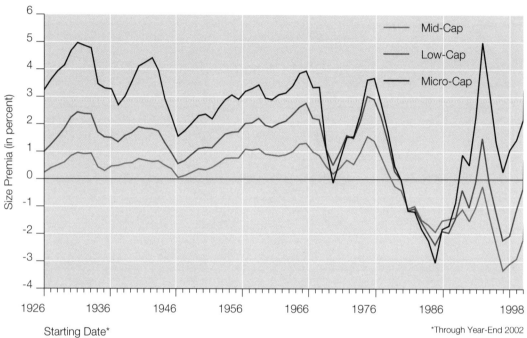

Starting Date*

*Through Year-End 2002

Seasonality

Unlike the returns on large company stocks, the returns on small company stocks appear to be seasonal. The January effect denotes the empirical regularity with which rates of return for small stocks have historically been higher in January than in the other months of the year. Small company stocks furthermore often outperform larger stocks by amounts in January far greater than in any other month.

Table 7-13 shows the returns of capitalization deciles 2 through 10 in excess of the return on decile 1; the excess returns are segregated into months. For each decile and for each month, the exhibit shows both the average excess return and the number of times the excess return was positive. These two statistics measure the seasonality of the excess return in different ways—the average excess return illustrates the size of the seasonality effect, while the number of positive excess returns shows its reliability.

Table 7-13

Returns in Excess of First Decile, Size-Decile Portfolios of the NYSE/AMEX/NASDAQ

1926–2002

Decile	Jan	Feb	Mar	Apr	May	Jun	Jul	Aug	Sep	Oct	Nov	Dec	Total (Jan–Dec)
2	0.84%	0.48%	–0.07%	–0.32%	0.02%	–0.11%	–0.06%	0.23%	0.04%	–0.29%	0.08%	0.38%	1.27%
	56	49	34	28	36	38	35	44	41	35	40	41	
3	1.18%	0.33%	0.01%	–0.08%	–0.27%	–0.18%	–0.02%	0.37%	–0.07%	–0.40%	0.50%	0.32%	1.75%
	58	50	37	30	32	33	38	46	41	32	42	46	
4	1.36%	0.59%	–0.12%	–0.20%	–0.02%	–0.09%	–0.06%	0.31%	0.10%	–0.82%	0.31%	0.52%	1.98%
	55	50	37	34	37	35	35	47	39	26	44	45	
5	2.23%	0.58%	–0.13%	–0.30%	–0.27%	–0.06%	–0.08%	0.30%	0.11%	–0.86%	0.31%	0.35%	2.29%
	57	47	35	30	31	34	37	44	40	29	43	41	
6	2.64%	0.56%	–0.26%	–0.13%	0.12%	–0.20%	–0.11%	0.54%	0.17%	–1.28%	0.18%	0.26%	2.69%
	58	49	39	32	35	34	40	44	41	29	40	41	
7	3.26%	0.68%	–0.24%	–0.12%	–0.01%	–0.39%	–0.12%	0.19%	0.26%	–1.08%	0.11%	0.04%	2.62%
	60	51	39	36	32	31	34	35	42	29	39	37	
8	4.50%	0.79%	–0.46%	–0.42%	0.33%	–0.51%	0.03%	0.03%	0.08%	–1.15%	0.17%	–0.30%	3.39%
	59	47	34	32	29	33	34	35	40	30	34	34	
9	5.99%	1.03%	–0.21%	–0.25%	0.13%	–0.49%	–0.02%	0.12%	–0.09%	–1.34%	0.06%	–1.07%	4.10%
	62	44	38	31	30	30	33	39	35	27	32	32	
10	9.35%	1.08%	–0.86%	0.08%	0.40%	–0.81%	0.47%	–0.13%	0.56%	–1.48%	–0.49%	–1.80%	7.10%
	70	41	33	35	33	29	35	28	39	26	29	27	

First row: average excess return in percent.
Second row: number of times excess return was positive (in 77 years).

Virtually all of the small stock effect occurs in January, as the excess outcomes for small company stocks are mostly negative in the other months of the year. Excess returns in January relate to size in a precisely rank-ordered fashion, and the January effect seems to pervade all size groups. Yet, simply demonstrating that the size premium is largely produced by the January effect does nothing to refute the existence of such a premium.

Possible Explanations for the January Effect

There is no generally accepted explanation of the January effect. One potential explanation is that it results from year-end window dressing by portfolio managers. Window dressing is the process of dumping money-losing stocks just before year-end so that such stocks are not included in the portfolio managers' annual reports.

Another explanation of the January effect is that it results from tax-loss selling at year-end, whereby money-losing stocks are sold at the end of the year for tax purposes. They are then repurchased in the market in January. Investors who have earned a capital loss on a security may be motivated to sell their shares shortly before the end of December in order to realize the capital loss for income tax purposes. This creates a preponderance of sellers in need of willing buyers at year-end. Amid such selling pressure, transactions will generally occur at the bid price, or the price a buyer is willing to pay for a particular stock, which is generally lower than the ask price. Therefore, a preponderance of sell orders will register more transactions at lower bid prices, which may create some temporary downward pressure on the prices of these stocks. They will only appear to recover in January, when trading returns to a more balanced mix of buy and sell orders, though there may be some actual recovery of prices as money generated by tax-loss selling returns to the market, driving up demand.

How does this cause "small" stocks to have higher apparent returns? Stocks that are "losers" will tend to have depressed stock prices. Also, stocks whose prices are quoted at the "bid" price will tend to have lower apparent market values than stocks quoted at the "ask" price. These two effects may lead to a bias when we use the market value of equity as our measure of "size." If losing stocks have both depressed prices and a tendency to sell at the "bid" at year-end, then they will likely be pushed down in the rankings according to market value. At the same time, winners will be pushed up. Thus, portfolios composed of "small" market value companies will tend to have more "losers" whose returns in January are distorted by tax-loss selling.

This argument vanishes if one uses a non-value criterion (such as net sales, total assets, or number of employees) to measure "size." As long as the "size" measure is not based on market value, there will be no tendency for firms with depressed stock prices to be ranked lower than other firms or for "small" stock portfolios to include a preponderance of "bid" prices at year-end. One study that corroborates the effect of different size measures is the PricewaterhouseCoopers study.[5] The PricewaterhouseCoopers study focuses on different measures of size and finds size premia for these different measures. The measures of size considered by the study are market value of equity, book value of equity, five-year average net income, market value of invested capital, total assets, five-year average EBITDA, sales, and number of employees. This study is updated annually and now sold as the Standard and Poor's Corporate Value Consulting Risk Premium Report.[6]

---

5 Grabowski, Roger, and David W. King. "New Evidence on Size Effects and Rates of Return," *Business Valuation Review*, September 1996, p. 103.
6 For more information on the "S&P CVC Risk Premium Report" see Ibbotson's Cost of Capital Center at http://www.ibbotson.com.

The Size Phenomena Across Industries

One question regularly raised concerning the size premium is whether it is relevant for specific industries. In the past there has been no concrete evidence to counter the contention that a size effect exists for the economy as a whole but may not be relevant to a specific industry. The problem of supporting a size premia for a specific industry has been made difficult by a lack of data for companies in individual industries.

We have attempted to answer this question by performing an industry-specific size effect study. The study uses the Center for Research in Security Prices (CRSP) database and the following methodology:

1. Industries are defined at the two-digit SIC (Standard Industrial Classification) code level. Companies are sorted into industries using the CRSP SIC code classification system. In order to be included in the study, an industry must have a minimum of ten companies for all periods. Any industry containing less than 30 years of data was not included in the study.

2. On a calendar year-end basis, companies are ranked by market capitalization within each industry from largest to smallest. Each industry is split into a "large" and a "small" portfolio with an equal number of companies.

3. A capitalization-weighted return series is calculated for each "large" and "small" portfolio. The excess return for each industry is represented by the "small" portfolio arithmetic return less the "large" portfolio arithmetic return.

The results of the study can be found in Table 7-14. Note that a large majority of industries exhibit returns where small company stocks outperform large company stocks over extended periods.

The excess returns presented in this table should not be construed as size premia. Due to limited data, we have defined size in rather general terms. In addition, the population of companies in most industries is very small. These data only provide evidence that smaller companies have generally out-performed larger companies across industries. The size premium study presented earlier in this chapter provides more reliable statistics as they relate to the size premium. In addition, measures of industry risk for use in the buildup model are presented in Table 3-5.

Table 7-14

Size Effect within Industries
Summary Statistics and Excess Returns

(Through Year-end 2002)

SIC Code	Description	Years	Large Company Group		
			Geometric Mean	Arithmetic Mean	Standard Deviation
10	Metal Mining	77	7.21%	10.77%	29.04%
13	Oil and Gas Extraction	40	9.48%	12.34%	25.76%
15	Building Construction-General Contractors & Op. Builders	31	10.23%	16.54%	38.09%
16	Hvy. Construction Other than Bldg. Construction-Contractors	32	5.05%	8.60%	30.33%
20	Food and Kindred Spirits	77	11.14%	12.83%	19.30%
22	Textile Mill Products	77	6.87%	11.92%	33.55%
23	Apparel & other Finished Products Made from Fabrics & Similar	43	7.77%	12.71%	33.92%
24	Lumber and Wood Products, Except Furniture	40	8.45%	10.99%	24.67%
25	Furniture and Fixtures	33	10.03%	12.50%	22.90%
26	Paper & Allied Products	74	10.53%	13.67%	27.25%
27	Printing, Publishing and Allied Products	44	11.32%	13.48%	21.33%
28	Chemicals and Allied Products	77	11.90%	14.11%	22.82%
29	Petroleum Refining & Related Industries	77	10.93%	13.10%	21.71%
30	Rubber & Miscellaneous Plastics Products	56	10.34%	13.11%	25.66%
31	Leather & Leather Products	40	11.56%	16.10%	33.90%
32	Stone, Clay, Glass & Concrete Products	74	8.18%	12.17%	32.20%
33	Primary Metal Industries	77	7.13%	11.15%	30.74%
34	Fabricated Metal Products, Except Machinery & Trans. Equip.	75	8.68%	11.28%	23.49%
35	Industrial & Commercial Machinery & Computer Equipment	77	10.43%	13.94%	28.05%
36	Electrical Equipment & Components, Except Computer	77	9.54%	13.24%	28.34%
37	Transportation Equipment	77	10.63%	15.01%	32.63%
38	Measuring, Analyzing & Controlling Instruments	66	11.82%	13.97%	22.29%
39	Miscellaneous Manufacturing Industries	43	9.01%	13.17%	30.02%
40	Railroad Transportation	77	8.72%	11.75%	24.93%
42	Motor Freight Transportation & Warehousing	39	9.35%	12.97%	28.99%
45	Transport by Air	57	6.84%	11.46%	33.22%
48	Communications	40	8.92%	11.38%	22.85%
49	Electric, Gas & Sanitary Services	77	8.35%	10.53%	21.94%
50	Wholesale Trade-Durable Goods	57	9.54%	11.76%	22.65%
51	Wholesale Trade-Nondurable Goods	35	9.81%	13.00%	25.92%
53	General Merchandise Stores	77	10.03%	13.38%	27.09%
54	Food Stores	46	11.35%	14.00%	24.07%
56	Apparel & Accessory Stores	56	13.57%	17.83%	32.87%
57	Home Furniture, Furnishings, and Equipment Stores	30	11.72%	23.91%	62.89%
58	Eating and Drinking Places	34	9.73%	14.49%	34.17%
59	Miscellaneous Retail	40	12.08%	15.52%	27.67%
60	Depository Institutions	34	11.04%	13.27%	21.82%
61	Nondepository Credit Institutions	53	12.82%	15.73%	26.91%
62	Security and Commod. Brokers, Dealers, Exchanges	30	17.11%	24.47%	45.05%
63	Insurance Carriers	34	9.81%	11.81%	21.07%
64	Insurance Agents, Brokers, and Service	30	14.67%	16.28%	19.15%
65	Real Estate	40	6.31%	10.83%	30.79%
67	Holding & Other Investment Offices	73	9.72%	12.99%	25.65%
70	Hotels, Rooming Houses, Camps, & Other Lodging	33	8.45%	14.32%	35.82%
72	Personal Services	33	7.55%	12.42%	31.29%
73	Business Services	40	9.88%	15.00%	33.64%
78	Motion Pictures	53	11.67%	16.35%	33.60%
79	Amusement and Recreation Services	30	11.82%	15.66%	27.97%
80	Health Services	31	11.83%	18.05%	37.43%

Table 7-14 (continued)

Size Effect within Industries
Summary Statistics and Excess Returns

(Through Year-end 2002)

SIC Code	Description	Small Company Group			Excess Return
		Geometric Mean	Arithmetic Mean	Standard Deviation	
10	Metal Mining	7.26%	14.63%	43.59%	3.86%
13	Oil and Gas Extraction	9.38%	17.64%	47.01%	5.30%
15	Building Construction-General Contractors & Op. Builders	3.57%	13.12%	44.17%	−3.42%
16	Hvy. Construction Other than Bldg. Construction-Contractors	15.95%	20.58%	35.16%	11.98%
20	Food and Kindred Spirits	11.50%	15.02%	29.58%	2.19%
22	Textile Mill Products	9.40%	15.06%	34.99%	3.14%
23	Apparel & other Finished Products Made from Fabrics & Similar	5.13%	11.27%	39.13%	−1.44%
24	Lumber and Wood Products, Except Furniture	10.65%	21.32%	54.76%	10.33%
25	Furniture and Fixtures	6.92%	11.10%	30.09%	−1.40%
26	Paper & Allied Products	11.27%	17.43%	41.36%	3.76%
27	Printing, Publishing and Allied Products	16.06%	18.80%	24.32%	5.32%
28	Chemicals and Allied Products	12.77%	18.14%	39.09%	4.03%
29	Petroleum Refining & Related Industries	11.61%	16.01%	31.65%	2.91%
30	Rubber & Miscellaneous Plastics Products	13.11%	17.48%	32.72%	4.37%
31	Leather & Leather Products	9.98%	14.96%	33.92%	−1.14%
32	Stone, Clay, Glass & Concrete Products	9.16%	14.04%	33.37%	1.87%
33	Primary Metal Industries	11.20%	16.55%	36.52%	5.40%
34	Fabricated Metal Products, Except Machinery & Trans. Equip.	10.30%	15.81%	36.86%	4.53%
35	Industrial & Commercial Machinery & Computer Equipment	11.04%	16.13%	33.84%	2.19%
36	Electrical Equipment & Components, Except Computer	11.33%	19.05%	44.63%	5.81%
37	Transportation Equipment	11.72%	18.04%	38.46%	3.03%
38	Measuring, Analyzing & Controlling Instruments	12.05%	16.60%	32.76%	2.63%
39	Miscellaneous Manufacturing Industries	8.56%	13.33%	33.03%	0.16%
40	Railroad Transportation	7.89%	14.21%	36.39%	2.46%
42	Motor Freight Transportation & Warehousing	5.27%	11.25%	39.03%	−1.72%
45	Transport by Air	7.30%	15.65%	48.22%	4.19%
48	Communications	16.68%	24.44%	44.34%	13.06%
49	Electric, Gas & Sanitary Services	9.74%	13.47%	30.17%	2.94%
50	Wholesale Trade-Durable Goods	9.92%	15.18%	36.50%	3.42%
51	Wholesale Trade-Nondurable Goods	8.04%	11.72%	28.40%	−1.28%
53	General Merchandise Stores	8.23%	15.80%	43.61%	2.42%
54	Food Stores	7.98%	11.61%	28.58%	−2.39%
56	Apparel & Accessory Stores	10.95%	17.32%	39.73%	−0.51%
57	Home Furniture, Furnishings, and Equipment Stores	14.86%	26.25%	53.47%	2.34%
58	Eating and Drinking Places	−0.17%	6.02%	37.93%	−8.47%
59	Miscellaneous Retail	11.71%	17.35%	36.89%	1.83%
60	Depository Institutions	14.77%	17.55%	25.65%	4.28%
61	Nondepository Credit Institutions	11.22%	15.32%	30.35%	−0.41%
62	Security and Commod. Brokers, Dealers, Exchanges	13.20%	20.07%	40.90%	−4.40%
63	Insurance Carriers	12.23%	15.12%	24.16%	3.31%
64	Insurance Agents, Brokers, and Service	11.24%	18.19%	39.67%	1.91%
65	Real Estate	4.97%	9.89%	34.93%	−0.94%
67	Holding & Other Investment Offices	11.21%	15.69%	32.17%	2.70%
70	Hotels, Rooming Houses, Camps, & Other Lodging	4.53%	10.96%	38.33%	−3.36%
72	Personal Services	14.98%	18.56%	27.53%	6.14%
73	Business Services	12.35%	22.04%	60.11%	7.04%
78	Motion Pictures	3.18%	10.03%	41.37%	−6.32%
79	Amusement and Recreation Services	12.01%	17.01%	37.77%	1.35%
80	Health Services	13.56%	20.04%	41.03%	1.99%

Other Criticisms of the Size Premium

Bid/Ask Spread

All stocks have a bid/ask spread that represents the differential between the highest price a prospective buyer is prepared to pay (bid) and the lowest price a seller is willing to take (ask). Market makers in a particular security make their money off of this spread. The spread is a form of transaction cost and is a function of the liquidity of a particular security; the greater the liquidity, the lower the bid/ask spread. In general, larger companies have more trading activity and therefore have greater liquidity and a lower bid/ask spread.

Some argue that the existence of such a spread adds a bias to all stock returns but particularly so to portfolios of less liquid (generally smaller) companies that have higher bid/ask spreads. The bias arises because the movement from a bid price to an ask price creates a measured rate of return that is higher in absolute value than a movement from one ask price to another ask price. Since trades occur randomly at either the bid or the ask price, some bias may slip into the measured returns. This bias can be especially pronounced if one is measuring rates of return on a daily basis. Most studies (e.g., Ibbotson Associates and PricewaterhouseCoopers) calculate returns at the portfolio level on a monthly basis and then compound the portfolio returns for each of the 12 months of the year to obtain an annual rate of return.

The "bid/ask bias" is a valid concern that deserves some consideration. Most studies of the small stock effect use the Center for Research in Security Prices (CRSP) database to measure rates of return. CRSP generally uses the closing price, which will be either a "bid" or an "ask," to measure the rates of return. If there are no trades on a given day, CRSP will use the average of the "bid" and "ask" prices. Note that the most illiquid stocks (those with the highest bid/ask spreads) will be the least likely to trade on a given day. For these stocks, CRSP uses the bid/ask average, which automatically rectifies the "bias" to some extent.

The "bid/ask bias" has only a trivial impact on the observed size/return relationship. Average bid/ask spreads are less than four percent of the underlying stock price for all but the very smallest portfolios of stocks.[7] Spreads of under 4 percent could give rise to biases in measured returns that are at most 50 basis points (assuming that annual returns are being compounded from monthly portfolio results, as in the Ibbotson and PricewaterhouseCoopers studies), yet the size/return relationship is manifest even for mid-sized public companies.

Geometric versus Arithmetic Averages

It has been suggested that using geometric averages to formulate discount rates will correct for the alleged "bid/ask bias." This argument is completely spurious. The difference between the geometric and arithmetic averages has nothing whatsoever to do with the bid/ask bounce. Both measures are built up from the same underlying monthly return measurements. Geometric averages are always less than arithmetic averages as a matter of mathematical law, not as a result of the bid/ask spread. Though using geometric averages produces a lower discount rate, the lower rate cannot be attributed to a correction of the bid/ask spread.

Infrequent Trading and Small Stock Betas

It has been argued that betas for smaller, less frequently traded stocks are mismeasured; in particular, they tend to be too low. If small stock betas were sufficiently high to measure their true systematic risk, then the small stock premium might disappear. This possibility has been offered as an argument against the use of a small stock premium in calculating discount rates.

With a little bit of thought, one should come to a very different conclusion. If small stocks have high returns because they have high betas, and if methods of measuring betas for smaller companies produce betas that are too low, then in the context of the CAPM some sort of adjustment is necessary in order to produce a discount rate of the right magnitude. A small stock premium is one such adjustment.

The Ibbotson Associates size premia study presented earlier in this chapter demonstrates this concept. Beta is calculated for each decile for the entire history back to 1926. These betas are then plugged into the capital asset pricing model to produce decile costs of equity under CAPM, which are then compared to the actual returns that the deciles achieved over this period of history. For all but the largest decile, CAPM underestimates the cost of equity. The amount of this underestimation is termed the size premium.

As was noted earlier in this chapter, it is possible to estimate beta with a different regression equation to take into account the infrequent trading of small-capitalization stocks. One can accomplish this either by using the sum beta technique or by measuring beta with annual data. As seen in Tables 7-10 and 7-11, these techniques increase the cost of equity as predicted by CAPM but fail to completely eradicate the size premium.

Transaction Costs

It has been argued that, because of high bid/ask spreads and other transaction costs, an investor in publicly traded small stocks is not able to realize returns as high as those we observe in the historical record. According to one theory, small stocks earn high returns in order to compensate investors for high transaction costs. However, in valuing a business, one typically applies to cash flows a discount rate that does not reflect the buyer's or the seller's transaction costs. It would be inconsistent to also use a discount rate that reflects a rate of return on a "net of transaction cost" basis.

Delisted Return Bias

Tyler Shumway published some evidence that the CRSP database omits delisting returns for a large number of companies.[8] This creates a potential bias because stocks generally experience negative returns upon delisting. Since delisting is concentrated in firms with small market values, this has been offered as a partial explanation of the observed size effect.

Shumway's data revealed that the possible bias is trivial for all but the very smallest companies, yet the historical size effect is still evident in mid-cap companies. Therefore, this bias would explain little of the observed historical relationship.

PricewaterhouseCoopers revised its methodology to take into account the Shumway evidence. Shumway reported that the average delisting rate of return for companies for which he could find data was approximately minus 30 percent. The PricewaterhouseCoopers calculations thus assumed a rate of return upon delisting of minus 30 percent for any company for which CRSP lacks delisting return data. This adjustment did not greatly affect the results of the 25 size portfolios in the *PricewaterhouseCoopers Risk Premia Study*. Even for the very smallest (25th) portfolio, the adjustment lowered the observed average return by only 22 basis points (less than one percent). For the rest of the portfolios, the adjustment was even smaller or non-existent. Starting in 2001, the PricewaterhouseCoopers Risk Premia Study became the S&P Corporate Value Consulting Risk Premium Report.

CRSP questions, in its *CRSP Delisting Returns study*, "whether or not using one replacement value for all missing delisting returns associated with poor performance delists is the most appropriate solution." CRSP further implies that using one single replacement value may create more bias in the data than would otherwise have existed because of the "significant variation in the average delisting returns for individual delist codes..." The "codes" represent groupings of firms that were delisted from an exchange for the same reason.

In the table below borrowed from the study, geometric annual returns of the 10 deciles are calculated over the 1926–2000 period in three ways: (1) Without Replacements – calculated without any substitution of the missing returns, as outlined on page 117 of this chapter, (2) Treating partial-month returns as delisting returns; partial-month returns are calculated by using the last daily trade price or bid-ask spread for the month in which the security delisted, if no post-delist value can be found, and (3) Using one of the three single-replacement values, based on the assumption "that all issues with missing delisting returns lost an additional 30, 55, or 100 percent of their pre-delist value after leaving the exchange."

Table 7-15

Size-Decile Portfolios of the NYSE/AMEX/NASDAQ, Geometric Annual Returns With or Without Single-replacement Values
1926–2000

	Without Replacements	Partial	–30%	–55%	–100%
1 – Largest	10.31%	10.31%	10.31%	10.31%	10.31%
2	11.28	11.27	11.27	11.27	11.27
3	11.58	11.58	11.58	11.58	11.57
4	11.53	11.53	11.53	11.53	11.53
5	11.81	11.81	11.81	11.81	11.81
6	11.82	11.84	11.83	11.83	11.82
7	11.57	11.57	11.57	11.56	11.55
8	11.65	11.66	11.65	11.64	11.63
9	11.75	11.75	11.74	11.74	11.72
10 – Smallest	13.11	13.11	13.05	13.00	12.92

The highest difference between the returns calculated using a single-replacement value and no replacement value is 19 basis points in the case of the smallest decile portfolio (Decile 10: 13.11%–12.92%); hence, single-replacement values have little impact on the overall decile portfolios. Consequently, the potential upward bias in the size premia–constructed by applying Ibbotson Associates' methodology to CRSP's NYSE/AMEX/NASDAQ Size-Decile Portfolios–is not evident, since the bias of the missing delisting returns (discussed by

Shumway) does not manifest when decile portfolio returns are calculated with and without single-replacement value. For more information on delisting returns, visit CRSP's web site at http://www.crsp.uchicago.edu/ or directly download the CRSP Delisting Returns study at http://gsbwww.uchicago.edu/research/crsp/news/announcements.html.

Small Stock Returns Are Unpredictable

Since investors cannot predict when small stock returns will be higher than large stock returns, it has been argued that they do not expect higher rates of return for small stocks. As was illustrated earlier in this chapter, even over periods of many years, investors in small stocks do not always earn returns that are higher than those of investors in large stocks. By simple definition, one cannot expect risky companies to always outperform less risky companies; otherwise they would not be risky. Over the long-term, however, investors do expect small stocks to outperform large stocks.

The unpredictability of small stock returns has given rise to another argument against the existence of a size premium: the argument that markets have changed so that there is no longer such a thing as a size premium. As evidence, one might observe the last 20 years of market data to see that small-capitalization stocks have not outperformed large-capitalization stocks. In fact, large-capitalization stocks have outperformed small-capitalization stocks in five of the last eight years.

While the 20-year returns of small-capitalization stocks currently seem low in comparison to large-capitalization stocks, the same relationship has been true in the past. Graph 7-10 shows the excess returns of small stocks versus large stocks over historical rolling 20-year time periods. (Small stocks are represented by the CRSP NYSE/AMEX/NASDAQ deciles 9 and 10. The S&P 500 represents large stocks. The excess return is calculated by subtracting the large stock returns from the small ones.) The graph clearly shows that, over the most recent 20-year period, small-capitalization stocks have not outperformed large-capitalization stocks. What is also clear from the graph is that this has happened before.

As was noted earlier in this chapter, one thing that we do know about the size premium is that it is cyclical in nature. Most market returns (including those of large- and small-capitalization stocks) have no historical pattern; however, this is not true of the size premium. It is not unusual for the size premium to follow several years of consistently positive values with several years of consistently negative values. Given the cyclical nature of the size premium, it is therefore not surprising that, in recent years, large-capitalization stocks have dominated small-capitalization stocks. We should actually expect periods of small stock underperformance as well as overperformance in the future.

Graph 7-10

Small Stock Excess Returns over 20-year Rolling Periods

1926–2002

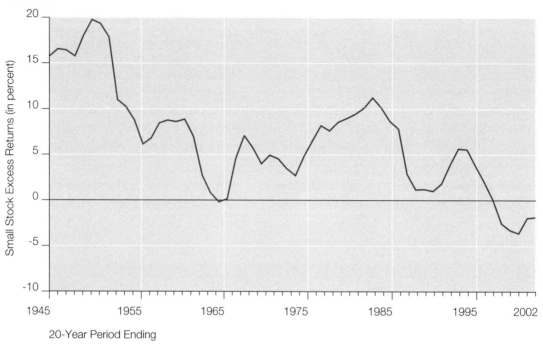

20-Year Period Ending

Conclusion

Most criticisms of the use of size premia do not address the underlying reason for the existence of size premia. Small-capitalization stocks are still considered riskier investments than large company stocks. Investors require an additional reward, in the form of additional return, to take on the added risk of an investment in small-capitalization stock. It is unlikely that in the future investors will require no compensation for taking on this additional risk.

The size premium will undoubtedly continue to be questioned in some quarters. The goal of this section was to review the most common arguments against its existence. Most criticisms presented to date, however, have not provided sufficient evidence to disprove the existence of a size premium.

Chapter 8

Fama-French Three Factor Model

In 1992 Eugene Fama and Kenneth French published a landmark paper in the *Journal of Finance* titled "The Cross-Section of Expected Returns." In this paper, Fama and French criticized the traditional capital asset pricing model (CAPM) for not adequately measuring asset returns. They found that the relationship between beta and average return disappears over the 1963–1990 period and is weak for the 1941–1990 period. Their findings did not support the key assumption of the CAPM: that returns on stocks are not positively related to market betas.[1]

After critiquing CAPM, Fama and French went on to identify two other characteristics that they claim better describe security returns—market value and the book-value-to-market-value ratio. While Fama and French at the time offered no explicit replacement for CAPM, their 1992 paper was the start of a series of critiques and arguments among academics that persists today.

The 1992 paper was followed that same year by an academic study conducted by Kothari, Shanken, and Sloan that seemed to contradict the findings of Fama and French. Kothari, Shanken, and Sloan concluded in their paper that returns do reflect significant compensation for beta risk, both statistically and economically, when beta is measured on an annual basis. (Fama and French used monthly data in their study.) However, they went on to say that the variation in expected returns may not be accounted for by beta alone.[2]

There were two more papers of importance published in 1993 in *The Journal of Portfolio Management*. "Are Reports of Beta's Death Premature?" was written by Chan and Lakonishok who detailed the influence of sample period selection on the conclusion of prior studies. They found a strong relationship between beta and return for the years of their study up to 1982. Though Chan and Lakonishok are not ardent supporters of beta, they "do not feel that the evidence for discarding beta is clear-cut and overwhelming."[3]

The second noteworthy article, written by Fischer Black, was titled "Beta and Return." In this article, Black refuted the conclusions of Fama and French and stated that "beta is alive and well."[4] Black's main point was that Fama and French did not prove what they claimed to have proven—that beta has no explanatory power. Like Chan and Lakonishok, Black pointed to the selection of time period. He also showed that Fama and French's own results still showed a relationship, albeit weak, between beta and return for the selected period.

Finally, Fama and French revisited the issue in 1994.[5] Building on their prior work, they proposed a three factor model for security expected returns:

1. Covariance with the market
2. Size
3. Financial risk as determined by the book-to-market ratio

---

1 Fama, Eugene F., and Kenneth R. French. "The Cross-Section of Expected Stock Returns," *Journal of Finance*, Vol. 47, 1992a, pp. 427–465.
2 Kothari, S.P., Jay Shanken, and Richard G. Sloan. "Another Look at the Cross-Section of Expected Stock Returns," Working Paper, December 1992.
3 Chan, Louis K.C., and Josef Lakonishok. "Are Reports of Beta's Death Premature?" *Journal of Portfolio Management*, Summer 1993, pp. 51–61.
4 Black, Fischer. "Beta and Return," *Journal of Portfolio Management*, Fall 1993, pp. 8–18.
5 Fama, Eugene F., and Kenneth French. "Industry Costs of Equity," Working Paper 396, University of Chicago, July 1994.

In addition to the market factor present in the CAPM, both size and financial risk were introduced as factors that determine a security's expected returns. Fama and French found that the returns on stocks are better explained as a function of a company's size (capturing the size effect) and its book-to-market ratio (capturing the financial distress of a firm) in addition to the single market factor of the CAPM.

Within the context of the Fama-French model, size is measured by market capitalization. Many studies, including one by Ibbotson Associates, have looked at firm size as a determinant of expected returns. The underlying notion is that small companies are viewed as riskier than large companies and therefore should reward investors for taking on the additional risk. Firms with a higher book-to-market ratio (the more "financially distressed" companies) also demonstrate more risk than firms with a low book-to-market ratio. Again, investors should be rewarded with a higher cost of equity for taking on additional risk.

The Fama-French three factor model is represented by the following formula:

$$E(R_i) - R_f = \beta_m RP_m + \beta_s RP_s + \beta_v RP_v$$

where:

$E(R_i)$ = expected return on security i;

R_f = rate on risk-free asset;

β_m = market coefficient in the Fama-French regression;

RP_m = expected market risk premium;

β_s = small-minus-big (SMB) coefficient in the Fama-French regression;

RP_s = the expected SMB risk premium, estimated as the difference between the historical average annual returns on the small-capitalization and large-capitalization portfolios;

β_v = high-minus-low (HML) coefficient in the Fama-French regression; and

RP_v = the expected HML risk premium, estimated as the difference between the historical average annual returns on the high book-to-market stocks and the low book-to-market stocks.

The HML (RP_v) portfolios require the use of financial statement data making it possible to construct the portfolios back to 1962 (using Compustat data). Therefore, the Fama-French model can only be tested from 1962 to present.

The HML (RP_v) and SMB (RP_s) portfolios are formed using stocks from the New York Stock Exchange (NYSE), the American Stock Exchange (AMEX), and the National Association of Securities Dealers Automated Quotation System (NASDAQ). To form the SMB portfolios, all stocks are sorted into two portfolios based on whether their market value of equity is below or above the median market value for the NYSE. Therefore, there are more companies in the "small" SMB portfolio than the "big" SMB portfolio. To form the HML portfolios, all stocks are sorted by book-to-market value of equity and split into three portfolios using the breakpoints of the NYSE at the top 30 percent of values, the middle 40 percent of values, and the bottom 30 percent of values.

Fama and French form their portfolios annually from data through June of each year. From the two size portfolios and three book-to-market portfolios, Fama and French create six capitalization-weighted return series from the intersection of companies in the two groups (size and book-to-market). The six return series are:

1. Small size and low book-to-market
2. Small size and medium book-to-market
3. Small size and high book-to-market
4. Big size and low book-to-market
5. Big size and medium book-to-market
6. Big size and high book-to-market

SMB represents the average monthly return of the three "small" size-oriented portfolios less the average returns on the three "big" size-oriented portfolios. HML is the difference between the average of the returns on the two "high" book-to-market portfolios and the average of the returns on the two "low" book-to-market portfolios.

As a result of this academic debate, Fama and French created a model that can be viewed as an extension of the CAPM. Where the traditional CAPM focuses only on the covariance of security returns with the market as a whole, Fama and French add two additional elements: size and book-to-market value.

Fama-French versus CAPM

Now that we have a functioning Fama-French model, we can compare results from the model to results from the CAPM. Graph 8-1 shows a distribution of cost of equity statistics for the *Cost of Capital Yearbook* company population. The chart shows cost of equity distributions for the traditional CAPM, the CAPM with a size premium, and the Fama-French model.

As we would expect, the narrowest distribution is represented by the traditional CAPM. As the different models consider more factors, the distributions broaden. Adding a size premium to the traditional CAPM shifts its distribution to the right and adds positive skewness to the distribution. The Fama-French model, which considers three factors in calculating the cost of equity, has the broadest distribution. The fact that a large number of companies have high costs of equity under the Fama-French model is intuitively appealing. Small companies dominate the *Cost of Capital Yearbook* population of companies. Because of the documented size effect, higher costs of equity would be expected with a properly functioning model.

Graph 8-1

Cost of Equity Distribution Using CAPM, CAPM with Size Premium, and Fama-French
September 30, 2002

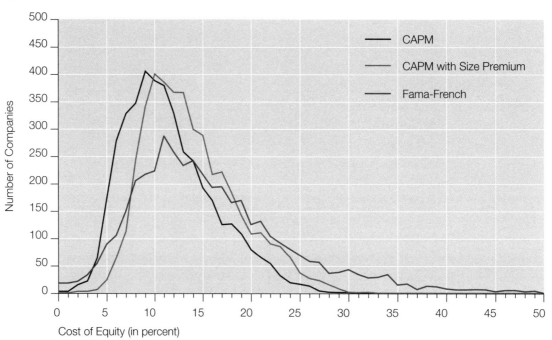

What is questionable about the Fama-French cost of equity distribution in Graph 8-1 is the number of companies with very high costs of equity. There are a number of companies with cost of equity numbers that exceed 30 percent. It may be that the Fama-French model over-corrects for size and/or financial distress in the time period covered.

Graph 8-2

Cost of Equity by Company Size Using CAPM, CAPM with Size Premium, and Fama-French
September 30, 2002

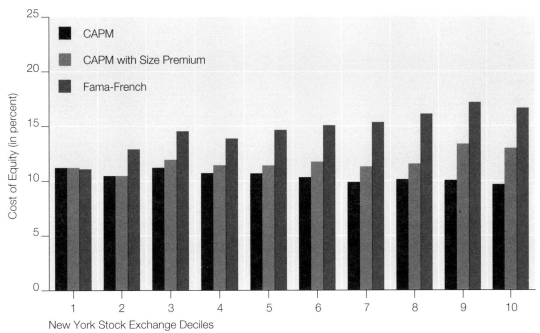

Graph 8-2 shows comparable CAPM and Fama-French cost of equity statistics for the NYSE deciles as of September 2002. In the aggregate, CAPM is not reflecting higher systematic risk for small companies for this time period. The Fama-French model does show a size effect.

Stability

In Chapter 6 we looked at the stability of beta across selected NYSE deciles. In that chapter, we showed that small company betas are less stable than large company betas and therefore produce less stable cost of equity estimates. Graphs 8-3 and 8-4 show rolling cost of equity estimates for Decile 10 and Decile 1, respectively, using CAPM, CAPM with size premium, and Fama-French. Decile 1 of the NYSE contains the largest 10 percent of companies, ranked by market capitalization, traded on the NYSE. Decile 10 contains the smallest 10 percent. (For more detail on the construction of the NYSE decile portfolios, see Chapter 7. Note that Graph 8-4 does not include the CAPM plus size premium, since these large companies do not require a size premium adjustment.) Since the Fama-French model requires financial statement data, the period studied is limited to the longest common period of available data for the three models shown.

Graph 8-3

60-Month Rolling Cost of Equity for Decile 10 of the NYSE Using CAPM, CAPM with Size Premium, and Fama-French
September 30, 1968 through September 30, 2002

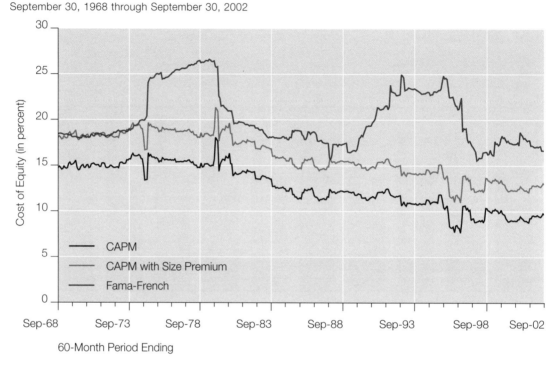

We can make a couple of observations about Graphs 8-3 and 8-4. First, for most of the historical time period, Fama-French provides a higher cost of equity for smaller companies. Second, Fama-French appears to be less stable than CAPM. This is not an unanticipated result. As more factors are added to the analysis, less stability is also added because changes in any of the three factors can have an impact on the cost of equity produced by the model.

Graph 8-4

60-Month Rolling Cost of Equity for Decile 1 of the NYSE Using CAPM and Fama-French
September 30, 1968 through September 30, 2002

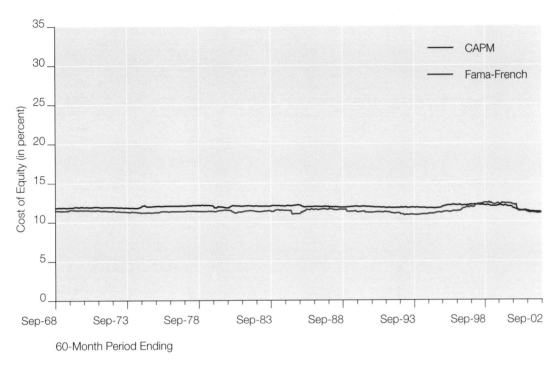

60-Month Period Ending

Both the CAPM and Fama-French produce similar estimates for large-cap companies. Moreover, these estimates are relatively stable over time.

Graph 8-5

60-Month Rolling Cost of Equity Comparisons for General Motors
September 30, 1997 through September 30, 2002

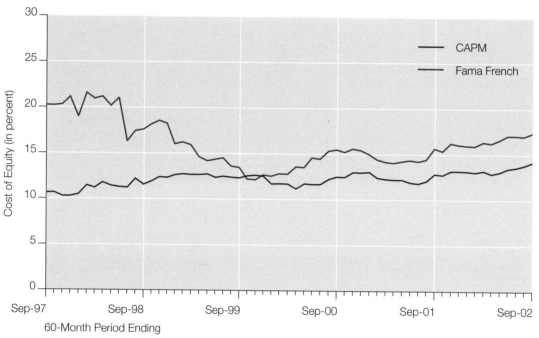

On a company-specific basis, the CAPM model again produces results that are more stable than Fama-French. Graph 8-5 shows rolling Fama-French and CAPM statistics for General Motors. For this company, the CAPM model produces a very stable cost of equity estimate. The cost of equity estimate for the Fama-French model is initially much higher than that of the CAPM, but then decreases significantly.

Graph 8-6

60-Month Rolling Cost of Equity Comparisons for Boise Cascade
September 30, 1997 through September 30, 2002

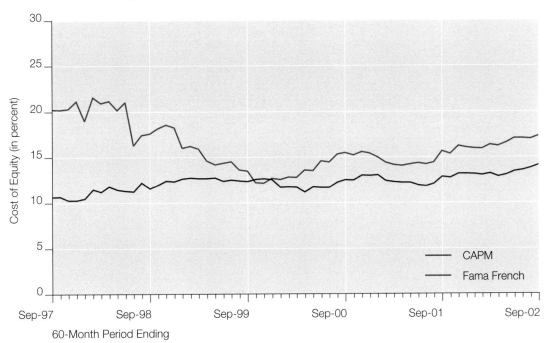

Boise Cascade provides another example, in Graph 8-6, where the CAPM model provides slightly more stable cost of equity estimates. However, both CAPM and Fama-French estimates experience fluctuation over time, with the Fama-French model exhibiting relatively more fluctuation.

Graph 8-7

60-Month Rolling Cost of Equity Comparisons for Abbott Laboratories
September 30, 1997 through September 30, 2002

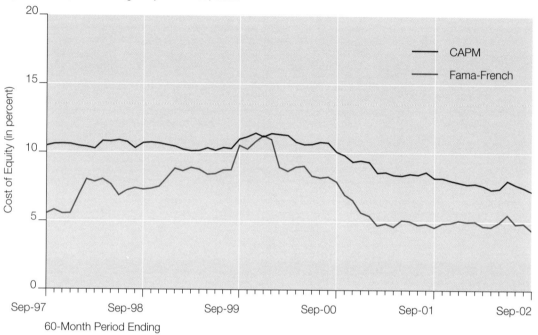

60-Month Period Ending

Graphs 8-7 and 8-8 show similar calculations for Abbott Laboratories and Georgia Pacific, which serve as large company examples. In the case of Abbott, CAPM provides a higher cost of equity over much of the time horizon shown. In the case of Georgia Pacific, the CAPM is more stable but both models produce estimates which move together over time. This indicates that Georgia Pacific has risk characteristics which have shifted significantly over the period shown, and that these shifts have been captured by both models.

Graph 8-8

60-Month Rolling Cost of Equity Comparisons for Georgia Pacific
September 30, 1997 through September 30, 2002

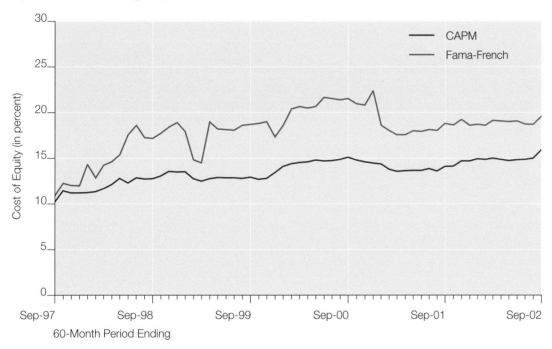

What conclusions can we draw from this analysis? The Fama-French model provides a different approach to calculating the cost of equity. It is not possible to say whether the numbers provided by the Fama-French model are better or more reliable than the cost of equity estimates provided by the CAPM. Both models fail to produce logical results for a large number of entities. The Fama-French model should be viewed as an additional tool available to analysts in determining the cost of equity.

Chapter 9

International Cost of Capital

Calculating the cost of capital for a domestic enterprise can be a difficult proposition because of limited data or the poor statistical quality of the models being used. Applying cost of capital principles to international markets is even more challenging due to additional data limitations and the lack of integrated markets.

We begin this chapter by addressing a fundamental cost of capital issue: Should companies be concerned with international cost of capital issues? Consider a U.S. manufacturing company that raises its debt and equity through U.S. markets. Should it be concerned with applying a discount rate to operations in international markets that differs from its domestic cost of capital? The answer to this question is yes.

Assume this U.S. manufacturing company is considering opening a factory in Mexico. Also assume the economics driving the purchase or construction of a Mexican facility are access to cheaper labor and a less regulated infrastructure. These are cash flow issues that would be addressed in the numerator of the discounted cash flow analysis. However, the risks associated with this venture would differ significantly from the risks associated with a similar facility located in the United States.

Mexico is a distinct economy with its own equity markets, political system, and market regulations. While the investment in the Mexican factory might be made with equity raised in the U.S., that equity would be in Mexico and subject to the market fluctuations of the Mexican economy. In order for a U.S. investor to receive similar cash flows, the investor would have to buy a factory in Mexico. Therefore, a market-specific cost of capital should be determined for use in evaluating the Mexican investment. In other words, a Mexico-specific cost of capital should be used.

Calculating the International Cost of Capital

Because international data on companies and industries is so difficult to obtain, international cost of capital calculations are typically done on a country-specific basis. Therefore, instead of attempting to determine the risk of the auto-parts industry in Brazil or the chemical industry in Germany, we typically focus on the risk of the general Brazilian and German markets.

In analyzing markets, it is important to consider the size of the market being analyzed. For example, with the U.S. market it is possible to examine returns on thousands of publicly traded entities diversified across multiple industries. From an international perspective, the U.S. market has been large for a number of years. The tapes of the Center for Research in Security Prices (CRSP) contain the 1926 return on approximately 500 separate U.S. companies.

In comparison, many international markets are much smaller and much less diversified. For example, one commonly cited provider of international market data, Morgan Stanley Capital International (MSCI), based its 1998 Austrian equity market index on the returns of only 35 individual companies. The banking industry, which consisted of only three companies, represents over 20 percent of the total capitalization of the 1998 Austrian index. One energy company represented over 10 percent of the index. This demonstrates that the Austrian market is not only less diversified than the U.S. market, but also more concentrated. In addition, MSCI only has data from 1970 to the present, making long-term historical analysis impossible.

Emerging markets data tend to be even more concentrated. The International Finance Corporation (IFC) is another commonly cited international data provider. The IFC Argentine index had over 47 percent of its capitalization weighted in mining companies in 1998. The IFC Indian index was over

85 percent weighted toward manufacturing companies. As with MSCI, the IFC database also has a limited history of return data.

International Equity Risk Premia

It is possible to calculate historical equity risk premium statistics similar to the calculations provided for the U.S. in Chapter 5 for any international market. The limiting factor in these calculations is finding historical data. Listed below are the historical risk premia for some selected international markets.[1]

Table 9-1

Equity Risk Premia by Country
1970–2001

	Local Currency	U.S. Dollars
Canada	3.17	2.13
U.K.	7.14	5.47
U.S.	5.28	5.28

Source: International Risk Premia Report 2002, Ibbotson Associates (http://vwww.ibbotson.com).

The risk premia shown above are presented both in local currency and in U.S. dollar terms. In calculating historical international risk premia, it is essential to keep in perspective the investor's location, because this is a crucial element in cost of capital analysis. For instance, a Canadian investor valuing a Canadian business would be interested in the Canadian equity risk premium in Canadian dollar terms.

An international investor's local currency risk premia and the U.S. dollar risk premia are different because of exchange rate gains and losses. These currency gains and losses impact the returns of the equity market and the risk-free asset in different magnitudes. For example: Suppose that in one year Canada had an equity return of 10 percent and a risk-free return of 5 percent. Also suppose Canada's currency depreciated against the U.S. dollar by 2 percent. The equity risk premium in Canadian dollars would be 5.0 percent (10 percent – 5 percent). However, the equity risk premium in U.S. dollar terms would be 5.1 percent (10.2 percent – 5.1 percent).

Also note that it is possible for historical risk premia to be very low or negative. Low or negative risk premia are most commonly seen in high-inflation economies. A negative risk premium would indicate that the country's equities are less risky than its risk-free asset (represented here by each country's government bond). Though it is possible for equities to have lower returns than government bonds for periods of time, a negative historical equity risk premium is nonsensical for a long-term, forward-looking estimate of the equity risk premium.

It is also interesting to compare the historical U.S. equity risk premium in the table above to the results obtained using the full history of available U.S. market data. The figure of 5.28 percent is substantially lower than the U.S. equity risk premium calculated over a longer time horizon in Chapter 5.

1 Note that data is only through year-end 2001 as complete international data was unavailable at time of publication.

This illustrates another danger in using international data. Using a limited data window (1970 to present) can significantly understate or overstate the expected equity risk premium. Again, as was addressed in Chapter 5, longer periods of time are preferable in estimating the future equity risk premium from historical data. For many international markets, long-term data is not available.

International Cost of Equity Models

The measurement of cost of equity estimates for international markets is a developing area of academia. The remainder of this chapter will provide an overview of some of the more commonly discussed international cost of equity models. Parties interested in obtaining additional international data should look for the Ibbotson "International Cost of Capital Report" on the Cost of Capital Center at http://www.ibbotson.com.

International CAPM

The principles of the capital asset pricing model (CAPM) can also be applied to the international market. The definition of the market portfolio can be expanded to include the equity markets of all countries of the world. The CAPM states that the expected return on a security, asset, or country is equal to the risk-free rate plus the beta multiplied by the equity risk premium. The CAPM can be stated mathematically as follows:

$$k_s = r_f + (\beta_s \times ERP)$$

where:

k_s = the cost of equity for company s;

r_f = the expected return on the riskless asset;

β_s = the beta of the stock of company s; and

ERP = the expected equity risk premium, or the amount by which investors expect the future return on equities to exceed that on the riskless asset.

To convert CAPM to a country-specific international format, the model can be modified so that the risk-free rate and beta are specific to the country being analyzed and the equity risk premium is calculated on a worldwide basis. Beta would be estimated using the world equity market as the market benchmark.

As was stated in the previous section, one limiting factor with international data is the historical time period over which data is available. Key to the calculation of the CAPM is the estimation of the world equity risk premium. For reasons outlined in Chapter 5, equity risk premium estimations using historical data should cover a long time period. However, data for many international markets is only available over much shorter time periods.

Since extensive historical data is available in the U.S., it is desirable to estimate the world equity risk premium by relating it to the U.S. data. To do this we can divide the U.S. equity risk premium by the beta of the U.S. market in relation to the world market:

$$ERP_W = \frac{ERP_{U.S.}}{\beta_{U.S.}}$$

where:

ERP_W = the world equity risk premium;

$ERP_{U.S.}$ = the U.S. equity risk premium measured over the full history of available data; and

$\beta_{U.S.}$ = the U.S. market beta measured over the common history of available data.

We know from our analysis of the equity risk premium in Chapter 5 that the expected U.S. value is 6.97 percent, using data from 1926 through 2002. If we assume that the Morgan Stanley Capital International (MSCI) world index represents a good proxy for world markets, we can regress the U.S. returns against the returns of the world index. The MSCI data is available from 1970 to the present. The U.S. beta for 1970 through 2002 using monthly returns is 0.92. If the U.S. equity risk premium is 6.97 percent and the U.S. market has a beta with the world of 0.92, then it follows that the equity risk premium of the world is 7.58 percent (6.97 percent divided by 0.92).

The next step in the application of an international CAPM is the calculation of a country-specific beta. The beta calculation methodology for international markets is similar to the calculation methodology for domestic companies. Probably the most important assumption in this calculation is the selection of the appropriate historical time period. While a five-year window may be relevant for an established economy, such as the United Kingdom, it might be desirable to focus on shorter data windows for developing markets or markets in transition, such as Indonesia.

Table 9-2 shows the impact of using different time periods to measure beta for a developed market, the U.K., versus less developed markets, Indonesia and Mexico. Less developed markets tend to have less stable betas over time than developed markets.

Table 9-2

Betas for Selected Countries over Various Periods
Through September 2002

Period	Beta U.K.	Indonesia	Mexico
60 months	0.74	1.54	1.39
48 months	0.75	1.71	1.22
36 months	0.78	0.92	1.32
24 months	0.79	0.37	1.24

Statistics calculated from the monthly total return indices of Morgan Stanley Capital International.

The same problems that plague domestic beta calculations also plague international betas, only they are more pronounced.[2] The statistical quality of international betas is especially low, which calls into question the usefulness of the standard CAPM in the international arena.

Tables 9-3 and 9-4 show the beta, t-statistic, R-squared, and standard error for a selection of developing markets and developed markets, respectively. Unfortunately, foreign markets that intuitively have more risk often have lower betas than foreign markets that are seen as less risky. The regression statistics for the developing markets indicate less confidence in their beta measures than in those of the developed countries. The higher standard error and lower t-statistic of the developing market betas also indicates less statistical confidence in the beta estimates than those for the developed markets. The lower R-squared of these betas demonstrates that less of the developing market returns can be explained by changes in the world market.

Table 9-3

Beta, t-Statistic, R-Squared, and Standard Error for Developing Markets
October 1997–September 2002

	Colombia	India	Indonesia	Poland	Venezuela
Beta	0.30	0.55	1.54	1.39	0.81
t-Statistic	1.00	12.82	3.01	5.39	2.28
R-Squared	0.02	0.09	0.14	0.33	0.08
Standard Error	0.30	0.23	0.51	0.26	0.36

Statistics calculated from the monthly total return indices of Morgan Stanley Capital International.

Table 9-4

Beta, t-Statistic, R-Squared, and Standard Error for Developed Markets
October 1997–September 2002

	Canada	Germany	Japan	U.K.	U.S.
Beta	1.24	1.24	0.89	0.74	1.04
t-Statistic	13.03	10.74	6.96	13.16	25.54
R-Squared	0.75	0.67	0.45	0.75	0.92
Standard Error	0.10	0.12	0.13	0.06	0.04

Statistics calculated from the monthly total return indices of Morgan Stanley Capital International.

Globally Nested CAPM

One potential solution to the CAPM in international markets is to expand the model. While we might obtain data on country risk by the interaction of a specific country with the world, we may gather more information by examining the interaction of the country with the geographic region in which it is located.

Clare and Kaplan recently explored this topic using a "globally nested CAPM."[3] The idea behind this model is that if markets are not fully integrated, then regional risk will matter. For

---

2 See Chapter 6 for more details on the tools used to evaluate beta.
3 Clare, Andrew D., and Paul Kaplan. "A Globally Nested Capital Asset Pricing Model," Ibbotson Associates' Working Paper, July 1998.

instance, if we were trying to calculate a cost of equity for Mexico, we would look not only at how Mexico reacts to the rest of the world, but also in how Mexico reacts to the Latin American region.

This model is expressed as:

$$k_C = r_f + (\beta_{CW} \times ERP_W) + (\beta_{CR} \times \delta_R)$$

where:

k_C = the cost of equity for country C;

r_f = the expected return on the riskless asset;

β_{CW} = the country's covariance with world market risk;

ERP_W = the expected world equity risk premium;

β_{CR} = the country's covariance with regional risk; and

δ_R = the risk premium associated with region R that is not part of the world equity risk premium.

The full model, which is beyond the scope of this book, focuses on measuring the country's sensitivity to both a world and a regional proxy. It is important to note that the regional risk measured here is residual regional risk that is not included in the world market risk.

For Mexico, the model works as follows:

$$k_C = r_f + (\beta_{CW} \times ERP_W) + (\beta_{CR} \times \delta_R) = 4.84 + (1.07 \times 7.58) + (0.61 \times 12.94) = 20.84\%$$

The advantage of this model is that it allows for other elements of risk to improve the statistical quality of the regression equation. The Clare-Kaplan study found that this model worked particularly well for the Latin American region. Unfortunately, other regional results using the MSCI regional data were not as encouraging. One line of reasoning for the poor regional performance of the model is the country makeup of the MSCI benchmarks currently used. The MSCI regions are constructed for the most part along geographic lines. However, regions that combine countries along economic lines would intuitively be better suited for this model. Additional study of this model is being pursued using modified regional benchmarks.

Country Risk Rating Model

One problem with market-based models is that they can only be applied to market-based economies. In a worldwide context, there are few countries that have the data necessary to provide a CAPM cost of equity. As a solution to this and other modeling problems, Erb, Harvey, and Viskanta have proposed a model based on country credit ratings.[4]

Twice each year, *Institutional Investor* produces a country risk rating based on a survey of lenders around the world for well over 100 countries. The survey provides a forward-looking measure of risk for a broad sample of markets.

4 Erb, Claude, Campbell R. Harvey, and Tadas Viskanta. "Country Credit Risk and Global Portfolio Selection," *Journal of Portfolio Management*, Winter 1995, pp. 74–83.

The idea behind this approach is that, given the risk ratings and financial returns of developed market economies, we should be able to make inferences about expected returns in developing markets or non-market-based economies. From the entire sample of market-based economies that have available returns and country credit ratings, a regression is performed with the return as the dependent variable and the natural logarithm of the country credit rating for the prior period as the independent variable. Country credit ratings are available for many countries on a semiannual basis back to 1979. The entire history of available data is used for added statistical confidence. The resulting regression equation allows one to estimate the expected return of any country, given its country credit rating, regardless of whether the country has available return data. Table 9-5 shows the risk rating and expected return for a sample of developed countries using this model. Table 9-6 shows a sample of emerging market and non-market country expected returns.

Table 9-5

Country Credit Ratings and Expected Returns for Developed Markets
Through September 2002

	Canada	Germany	Japan	U.K.	U.S.
Country Credit Rating	89.4	94	82.7	94.1	93.1
Expected Return	8.54%	7.72%	9.81%	7.70%	7.88%

Regression uses Country Credit Ratings from *Institutional Investor* and market returns from Morgan Stanley Capital International.

Table 9-6

Country Credit Ratings and Expected Returns for Emerging Markets
Through September 2002

	Colombia	India	Indonesia	Poland	Venezuela
Country Credit Rating	38.7	47.3	23.8	60.1	30.6
Expected Return	22.19%	18.92%	30.12%	15.01%	26.02%

Regression uses Country Credit Ratings from *Institutional Investor* and market returns from Morgan Stanley Capital International.

Country-Spread Model

Another international model in current use is the country-spread model. While it takes many forms, this model adds a country-specific spread to a cost of equity determined from more conventional means. Typically, a cost of equity is determined using U.S. data, then a spread is added to the cost of equity to "internationalize" it. Ideally, the spread is between the yield on dollar-denominated foreign bonds (Brady bonds) and the yield on the U.S. Treasury bond.

The spread between the bonds is intended to measure the additional return required to compensate for the additional risk inherent in the foreign investment. However, though the spread may capture incremental returns due to currency risk and other country-specific risks, it is important to note that there may be additional risks inherent in the equity market of a particular country that are not captured in the yield spread. The model nonetheless provides a good reference point to check against other models.

For example, suppose a dollar denominated foreign bond of an emerging-market country has a current yield that is 12.0 percent higher than the yield on a U.S. Treasury bond. The estimated U.S. cost of equity using the CAPM is determined to be 11.81 percent (the current U.S. Treasury yield, 4.84 percent, plus the U.S. equity risk premium, 6.97 percent). The estimated cost of equity for this emerging-market country would be 23.81 percent (the U.S. cost of equity, 11.81 percent, plus the spread of 12.0 percent) using the country-spread model. Table 9-7 illustrates the use of the country-spread model for a sample of emerging markets.

Table 9-7

Country-Spread Model Expected Returns for Emerging Markets

	Argentina	Brazil	Colombia	Panama	Russia
Expected Return	63.00	23.68	17.55	15.73	16.15

Based on Brady bond yield spreads as of December 2002.

Relative Standard Deviation Model

A more simplistic approach to calculating the international cost of equity is through the standard deviation model. In this model, the standard deviations of international markets are indexed to the standard deviation of the U.S. market. Countries with higher standard deviations than the U.S. are given a higher equity risk premium in proportion to their relative standard deviation. In other words, a country that has twice the standard deviation of returns is assumed to be twice as risky as the U.S. market.

$$\sigma_{j,R} = \frac{\sigma_j}{\sigma_{U.S.}}$$

where:

$\sigma_{j,R}$ = the relative standard deviation of country j;

σ_j = the standard deviation of excess returns for country j; and

$\sigma_{U.S.}$ = the standard deviation of excess returns for the U.S.

For example, the relative standard deviation of excess returns for Canada is 1.24 (5.63 percent / 4.55 percent). Therefore, the equity risk premium for Canada would be 8.64 percent (6.97 percent × 1.24). The difficulty with this model is that it produces unreasonably high measures of the equity risk premium for many international markets. Developed markets such as the U.K. and Japan have relative standard deviation statistics in excess of 1.45. Less developed markets have relative standard deviation statistics even higher (e.g., Poland at 3.95). Table 9-8 shows the relative standard deviations for a sample of developed and emerging markets.

Table 9-8

Relative Standard Deviations
Through September 2002

Developed Country	Relative Standard Deviation	Emerging Country	Relative Standard Deviation
Canada	1.24	Colombia	1.95
Germany	1.35	India	1.80
Japan	1.45	Indonesia	3.30
U.K.	1.49	Poland	3.95
U.S.	1.00	Venezuela	3.06

Statistics for the developed countries were derived from the monthly total return indices of Morgan Stanley Capital International. Statistics for the emerging countries were derived from the monthly total return indices of S&P/IFCG.

Conclusion

Determining appropriate cost of capital estimates for international markets is a problem for which the solution continues to be developed. While cost of capital models in general are plagued by statistical inaccuracy and limited data, these problems are compounded in the international arena.

Which International Model Is Best?

While no cost of equity model produces reliable numbers in every situation, the Country Risk Rating Model offers a number of advantages that the other international models are unable to overcome. These advantages include:

1. Breadth of coverage
2. Reasonable results
3. Stability of results

Trying to evaluate an investment in the Middle East, Central America, or Africa? Most of the models we have discussed require data that does not exist for many countries of the world. Most countries lack organized equity markets. Others have equity markets, but do not have either significant history or a broad enough market to produce reliable market benchmarks.

The Country Risk Rating Model requires only a credit rating to produce a cost of equity estimate. Therefore, the model can be applied to almost every country in the world.

Another advantage of the Country Risk Rating Model is that it consistently produces results that are reasonable. The model works by using data from the developed world and extrapolating that data to developing markets. This methodology avoids using data from developing markets that may be inconsistent or incomplete, thereby producing results that do not make sense.

One example of an international cost of equity model producing nonsensical results is the international CAPM. This model recently produced single-digit cost of equity values for countries such as China and Colombia that were dramatically smaller than comparable figures for the U.S., U.K., Germany or Japan.

Finally, the Country Risk Rating Model produces results that are relatively stable. Cost of equity estimates should vary across time as conditions change, but they should not vary radically from one time period to the next unless country-specific conditions change dramatically from one period to the next. Market-based models or macro-economic based models can become unstable if the data underlying the models is erratic in any way. For many developing markets, it is not unusual to have higher volatility and lower correlation with world market benchmarks. These data issues impact the results of market based and macro-economic based models.

This chapter has explored the challenges and potential solutions for determining international market cost of capital. Though all the models explored have some flaws, for most countries there is at least one model that produces a reasonable cost of equity estimate.

Stocks, Bonds, Bills, and Inflation
Valuation Edition

−7.2	7.2	−6.7	6.1	−6.4	−7.1
7.2	7.2	6.7	6.1	6.4	7.1
7.3	−7.3	6.8	6.2	−6.5	−7.2
7.1	7.1	6.6	6.0	6.3	7.0
7.3	7.3	−6.9	−6.3	6.6	7.2
7.4	−7.3	6.9	6.3	−6.6	−7.3
−7.2	7.2	−6.7	6.2	−6.5	7.1
7.2	−7.2	6.8	−6.2	−6.5	7.1

Appendix A

7.3	−7.3	−6.9	6.3	6.6	−7.2
−7.2	7.2	6.8	−6.3	−6.6	7.1
7.0	−7.0	−6.6	−6.1	6.4	−6.9
−7.4	7.4	−7.0	−6.5	6.7	−7.3
7.5	−7.5	−7.1	6.6	−6.9	7.4
−7.8	7.8	−7.4	−6.9	−7.2	−7.7
−8.0	8.0	−7.6	7.1	−7.4	7.9
8.1	−8.1	7.7	−7.3	7.5	−8.0
9.2	−9.2	8.7	−8.5	−8.9	9.1

IbbotsonAssociates

Appendix A

Risk Premia Over Time (S&P 500 Market Benchmark): 1926–2002

Risk Premia Over Time (S&P 500 Market Benchmark)

Each table in this section consists of six pages.

Table A-1 (Page 1 of 6)

Long-Horizon Equity Risk Premia*

Percent per annum arithmetic mean risk premia
for all historical time periods.

from 1926 to 2002

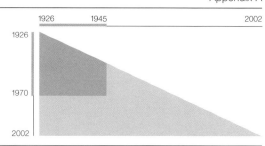

To the end of	From the beginning of 1926	1927	1928	1929	1930	1931	1932	1933	1934	1935	1936	1937	1938	1939	1940	1941	1942	1943	1944	1945
1926	7.9																			
1927	21.0	34.1																		
1928	27.5	37.2	40.4																	
1929	17.6	20.9	14.3	−11.9																
1930	8.5	8.6	0.1	−20.1	−28.2															
1931	−0.7	−2.5	−11.6	−28.9	−37.4	−46.7														
1932	−2.3	−4.0	−11.7	−24.7	−28.9	−29.3	−11.9													
1933	4.3	3.8	−1.2	−9.6	−9.0	−2.6	19.5	50.9												
1934	3.3	2.8	−1.7	−8.7	−8.1	−3.1	11.5	23.1	−4.6											
1935	7.5	7.4	4.1	−1.1	0.7	6.5	19.8	30.4	20.1	44.9										
1936	9.6	9.8	7.1	3.0	5.1	10.6	22.1	30.6	23.8	38.0	31.1									
1937	5.7	5.5	2.6	−1.6	−0.3	3.7	12.1	16.9	8.4	12.8	−3.3	−37.7								
1938	7.4	7.4	5.0	1.4	2.9	6.8	14.5	18.8	12.4	16.7	7.3	−4.6	28.5							
1939	6.7	6.6	4.3	1.1	2.3	5.7	12.3	15.7	9.9	12.8	4.8	−4.0	12.8	−2.8						
1940	5.5	5.3	3.1	0.0	1.0	4.0	9.6	12.3	6.8	8.7	1.4	−6.0	4.6	−7.4	−12.0					
1941	4.3	4.0	1.9	−1.1	−0.2	2.4	7.3	9.4	4.2	5.5	−1.1	−7.5	0.0	−9.5	−12.8	−13.5				
1942	5.1	4.9	3.0	0.3	1.2	3.7	8.2	10.3	5.7	7.0	1.6	−3.3	3.6	−2.6	−2.6	2.2	17.9			
1943	6.1	6.0	4.2	1.8	2.8	5.2	9.5	11.5	7.5	8.9	4.4	0.5	6.9	2.6	3.9	9.3	20.7	23.5		
1944	6.7	6.6	5.0	2.8	3.8	6.1	10.1	11.9	8.4	9.7	5.8	2.6	8.4	5.0	6.6	11.3	19.5	20.4	17.3	
1945	8.1	8.1	6.6	4.6	5.7	7.9	11.8	13.6	10.5	11.9	8.6	6.1	11.6	9.2	11.2	15.8	23.2	24.9	25.7	34.1
1946	7.2	7.2	5.7	3.8	4.7	6.8	10.4	12.0	9.0	10.1	6.9	4.5	9.2	6.8	8.2	11.5	16.5	16.2	13.8	12.0
1947	7.0	7.0	5.6	3.8	4.7	6.6	9.9	11.4	8.6	9.6	6.6	4.4	8.6	6.4	7.6	10.4	14.4	13.7	11.2	9.2
1948	6.9	6.8	5.5	3.8	4.6	6.4	9.5	10.9	8.2	9.1	6.4	4.3	8.1	6.1	7.1	9.5	12.8	11.9	9.6	7.7
1949	7.3	7.2	6.0	4.4	5.2	6.9	9.9	11.2	8.7	9.6	7.1	5.3	8.8	7.0	8.0	10.3	13.2	12.6	10.7	9.4
1950	8.2	8.2	7.0	5.5	6.4	8.1	11.0	12.2	10.0	10.9	8.6	7.0	10.4	8.9	10.0	12.2	15.0	14.7	13.4	12.8
1951	8.7	8.7	7.6	6.2	7.0	8.7	11.5	12.7	10.6	11.5	9.4	8.0	11.2	9.9	11.0	13.0	15.7	15.5	14.5	14.1
1952	8.9	9.0	8.0	6.6	7.4	9.0	11.7	12.9	10.9	11.7	9.8	8.5	11.5	10.3	11.3	13.3	15.7	15.5	14.6	14.3
1953	8.5	8.5	7.5	6.2	7.0	8.5	11.0	12.1	10.1	10.9	9.0	7.7	10.6	9.4	10.2	12.0	14.1	13.7	12.8	12.3
1954	9.9	10.0	9.1	7.9	8.7	10.2	12.7	13.8	12.0	12.9	11.2	10.1	12.9	11.9	12.9	14.7	16.8	16.7	16.1	16.0
1955	10.5	10.6	9.8	8.7	9.4	10.9	13.4	14.4	12.8	13.6	12.1	11.1	13.8	12.9	13.9	15.6	17.7	17.7	17.2	17.2
1956	10.3	10.4	9.6	8.5	9.2	10.7	13.0	14.0	12.4	13.2	11.7	10.7	13.2	12.4	13.3	14.9	16.7	16.7	16.1	16.0
1957	9.5	9.6	8.8	7.7	8.4	9.7	11.9	12.9	11.3	12.0	10.5	9.5	11.9	11.0	11.7	13.1	14.8	14.6	14.0	13.7
1958	10.5	10.5	9.8	8.8	9.5	10.8	13.0	13.9	12.4	13.1	11.8	10.9	13.2	12.4	13.2	14.6	16.3	16.2	15.7	15.6
1959	10.4	10.5	9.7	8.7	9.4	10.7	12.8	13.7	12.3	12.9	11.6	10.8	13.0	12.2	13.0	14.3	15.8	15.7	15.2	15.1
1960	10.0	10.0	9.3	8.4	9.0	10.2	12.2	13.1	11.7	12.3	11.0	10.2	12.2	11.5	12.2	13.4	14.8	14.6	14.1	13.9
1961	10.4	10.4	9.7	8.8	9.4	10.7	12.6	13.4	12.1	12.7	11.5	10.7	12.7	12.0	12.7	13.8	15.2	15.1	14.6	14.4
1962	9.7	9.8	9.1	8.2	8.8	9.9	11.8	12.5	11.2	11.8	10.6	9.8	11.7	11.0	11.6	12.6	13.9	13.7	13.2	12.9
1963	10.0	10.0	9.4	8.5	9.1	10.2	12.0	12.7	11.5	12.0	10.9	10.1	11.9	11.3	11.9	12.9	14.1	13.9	13.5	13.3
1964	10.0	10.1	9.4	8.6	9.2	10.3	12.0	12.7	11.5	12.0	10.9	10.2	12.0	11.3	11.9	12.9	14.0	13.9	13.4	13.2
1965	10.0	10.0	9.4	8.6	9.1	10.2	11.9	12.6	11.4	11.9	10.8	10.1	11.8	11.2	11.7	12.7	13.8	13.6	13.2	13.0
1966	9.4	9.4	8.8	8.0	8.5	9.5	11.1	11.8	10.6	11.1	10.0	9.3	10.9	10.3	10.8	11.7	12.7	12.4	12.0	11.7
1967	9.6	9.7	9.1	8.3	8.8	9.8	11.4	12.0	10.9	11.3	10.3	9.6	11.2	10.6	11.1	11.9	12.9	12.7	12.3	12.1
1968	9.5	9.6	9.0	8.2	8.7	9.7	11.2	11.8	10.7	11.2	10.2	9.5	11.0	10.4	10.9	11.7	12.6	12.4	12.0	11.8
1969	9.0	9.0	8.4	7.6	8.1	9.1	10.5	11.1	10.0	10.4	9.4	8.8	10.2	9.6	10.0	10.8	11.7	11.4	11.0	10.7
1970	8.7	8.7	8.2	7.4	7.9	8.8	10.2	10.8	9.7	10.1	9.1	8.4	9.8	9.2	9.6	10.4	11.2	10.9	10.5	10.2

*S&P 500 total returns minus long-term government bond income returns.

Table A-1 (Page 2 of 6)

Long-Horizon Equity Risk Premia*

Percent per annum arithmetic mean risk premia
for all historical time periods.

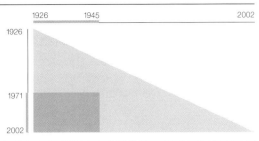

from 1926 to 2002

To the end of	From the beginning of 1926	1927	1928	1929	1930	1931	1932	1933	1934	1935	1936	1937	1938	1939	1940	1941	1942	1943	1944	1945
1971	8.7	8.7	8.2	7.4	7.9	8.7	10.1	10.7	9.6	10.0	9.1	8.4	9.8	9.2	9.6	10.3	11.1	10.8	10.4	10.1
1972	8.8	8.8	8.3	7.5	8.0	8.8	10.2	10.8	9.7	10.1	9.2	8.5	9.9	9.3	9.7	10.4	11.1	10.9	10.5	10.2
1973	8.2	8.2	7.6	6.9	7.3	8.1	9.5	10.0	8.9	9.3	8.4	7.7	9.0	8.5	8.8	9.4	10.1	9.9	9.4	9.2
1974	7.3	7.3	6.7	6.0	6.4	7.2	8.4	8.9	7.9	8.2	7.3	6.7	7.9	7.3	7.6	8.1	8.8	8.5	8.0	7.7
1975	7.8	7.8	7.2	6.5	6.9	7.7	8.9	9.4	8.4	8.7	7.8	7.2	8.4	7.9	8.2	8.7	9.4	9.1	8.7	8.4
1976	7.9	7.9	7.4	6.7	7.1	7.9	9.1	9.6	8.6	8.9	8.0	7.5	8.6	8.1	8.4	8.9	9.6	9.3	8.9	8.7
1977	7.5	7.5	7.0	6.3	6.6	7.4	8.6	9.0	8.1	8.4	7.5	6.9	8.0	7.5	7.8	8.3	8.9	8.7	8.2	8.0
1978	7.3	7.3	6.8	6.1	6.5	7.2	8.4	8.8	7.9	8.1	7.3	6.7	7.8	7.3	7.5	8.1	8.6	8.4	8.0	7.7
1979	7.4	7.4	6.8	6.2	6.5	7.3	8.4	8.8	7.9	8.2	7.3	6.8	7.8	7.3	7.6	8.1	8.7	8.4	8.0	7.7
1980	7.6	7.6	7.1	6.5	6.9	7.6	8.7	9.1	8.2	8.5	7.7	7.1	8.2	7.7	8.0	8.5	9.0	8.8	8.4	8.1
1981	7.2	7.2	6.7	6.1	6.4	7.1	8.2	8.6	7.7	8.0	7.2	6.6	7.6	7.1	7.4	7.9	8.4	8.1	7.7	7.5
1982	7.2	7.2	6.7	6.1	6.4	7.1	8.2	8.6	7.7	8.0	7.2	6.6	7.6	7.2	7.4	7.9	8.4	8.1	7.7	7.5
1983	7.3	7.3	6.8	6.2	6.5	7.2	8.2	8.6	7.8	8.0	7.3	6.8	7.7	7.3	7.5	8.0	8.5	8.2	7.9	7.6
1984	7.1	7.1	6.6	6.0	6.3	7.0	8.0	8.4	7.5	7.8	7.0	6.5	7.5	7.0	7.2	7.6	8.1	7.9	7.5	7.3
1985	7.3	7.3	6.9	6.3	6.6	7.2	8.2	8.6	7.8	8.0	7.3	6.8	7.7	7.3	7.5	7.9	8.4	8.2	7.8	7.6
1986	7.4	7.3	6.9	6.3	6.6	7.3	8.2	8.6	7.8	8.1	7.3	6.9	7.8	7.3	7.6	8.0	8.5	8.2	7.9	7.7
1987	7.2	7.2	6.7	6.2	6.5	7.1	8.0	8.4	7.6	7.9	7.1	6.7	7.6	7.1	7.3	7.7	8.2	8.0	7.6	7.4
1988	7.2	7.2	6.8	6.2	6.5	7.1	8.0	8.4	7.6	7.9	7.2	6.7	7.6	7.1	7.3	7.8	8.2	8.0	7.7	7.4
1989	7.4	7.4	7.0	6.5	6.8	7.4	8.3	8.6	7.9	8.1	7.4	7.0	7.9	7.4	7.7	8.1	8.5	8.3	8.0	7.8
1990	7.2	7.1	6.7	6.2	6.5	7.1	8.0	8.3	7.6	7.8	7.1	6.7	7.5	7.1	7.3	7.7	8.1	7.9	7.6	7.4
1991	7.4	7.4	7.0	6.4	6.7	7.3	8.2	8.5	7.8	8.0	7.4	6.9	7.8	7.4	7.6	8.0	8.4	8.2	7.9	7.7
1992	7.3	7.3	6.9	6.3	6.6	7.2	8.1	8.4	7.7	7.9	7.3	6.8	7.6	7.2	7.4	7.8	8.2	8.0	7.7	7.5
1993	7.2	7.2	6.8	6.3	6.6	7.1	8.0	8.3	7.6	7.8	7.2	6.8	7.5	7.2	7.4	7.7	8.1	7.9	7.6	7.4
1994	7.0	7.0	6.6	6.1	6.4	6.9	7.8	8.1	7.4	7.6	7.0	6.5	7.3	6.9	7.1	7.5	7.9	7.7	7.4	7.2
1995	7.4	7.4	7.0	6.5	6.7	7.3	8.1	8.4	7.8	8.0	7.3	6.9	7.7	7.3	7.5	7.9	8.3	8.1	7.8	7.6
1996	7.5	7.5	7.1	6.6	6.9	7.4	8.3	8.6	7.9	8.1	7.5	7.1	7.9	7.5	7.7	8.0	8.4	8.3	8.0	7.8
1997	7.8	7.8	7.4	6.9	7.2	7.7	8.5	8.9	8.2	8.4	7.8	7.4	8.2	7.8	8.0	8.4	8.8	8.6	8.3	8.2
1998	8.0	8.0	7.6	7.1	7.4	7.9	8.7	9.1	8.4	8.6	8.0	7.7	8.4	8.1	8.3	8.6	9.0	8.8	8.6	8.4
1999	8.1	8.1	7.7	7.3	7.5	8.0	8.8	9.2	8.5	8.7	8.2	7.8	8.5	8.2	8.4	8.7	9.1	9.0	8.7	8.6
2000	7.8	7.8	7.4	6.9	7.2	7.7	8.5	8.8	8.2	8.4	7.8	7.4	8.1	7.8	8.0	8.3	8.7	8.5	8.3	8.1
2001	7.4	7.4	7.1	6.6	6.9	7.4	8.1	8.4	7.8	8.0	7.4	7.1	7.7	7.4	7.6	7.9	8.3	8.1	7.8	7.7
2002	7.0	7.0	6.6	6.1	6.4	6.9	7.6	7.9	7.3	7.5	6.9	6.5	7.2	6.9	7.0	7.3	7.7	7.5	7.2	7.1

*S&P 500 total returns minus long-term government bond income returns.

Table A-1 (Page 3 of 6)

Long-Horizon Equity Risk Premia*

Percent per annum arithmetic mean risk premia
for all historical time periods.

from 1926 to 2002

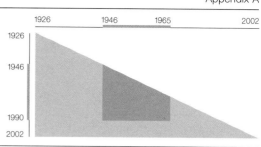

To the end of	From the beginning of 1946	1947	1948	1949	1950	1951	1952	1953	1954	1955	1956	1957	1958	1959	1960	1961	1962	1963	1964	1965
1946	-10.1																			
1947	-3.3	3.6																		
1948	-1.1	3.3	3.1																	
1949	3.3	7.7	9.8	16.5																
1950	8.5	13.2	16.4	23.1	29.6															
1951	10.7	14.9	17.7	22.6	25.6	21.6														
1952	11.4	15.0	17.3	20.9	22.3	18.7	15.7													
1953	9.5	12.3	13.8	15.9	15.8	11.2	5.9	-3.8												
1954	14.0	17.0	18.9	21.6	22.6	20.8	20.6	23.0	49.8											
1955	15.5	18.3	20.2	22.6	23.6	22.4	22.6	24.9	39.3	28.8										
1956	14.4	16.9	18.3	20.2	20.8	19.3	18.8	19.6	27.4	16.2	3.6									
1957	12.0	14.0	15.1	16.4	16.4	14.5	13.3	12.8	17.0	6.1	-5.3	-14.2								
1958	14.2	16.2	17.3	18.8	19.0	17.7	17.1	17.4	21.6	14.6	9.8	12.9	40.1							
1959	13.7	15.6	16.6	17.8	17.9	16.6	16.0	16.0	19.3	13.2	9.3	11.3	24.0	7.9						
1960	12.6	14.2	15.0	16.0	15.9	14.6	13.8	13.6	16.0	10.4	6.7	7.5	14.7	2.1	-3.8					
1961	13.2	14.8	15.6	16.5	16.5	15.3	14.7	14.6	16.9	12.2	9.4	10.6	16.8	9.1	9.6	23.1				
1962	11.7	13.1	13.7	14.4	14.3	13.0	12.2	11.9	13.6	9.1	6.3	6.7	10.9	3.6	2.2	5.2	-12.7			
1963	12.1	13.4	14.0	14.7	14.6	13.5	12.8	12.5	14.1	10.2	7.9	8.5	12.2	6.7	6.4	9.7	3.1	18.9		
1964	12.1	13.3	13.9	14.6	14.5	13.4	12.7	12.5	14.0	10.4	8.4	9.0	12.3	7.6	7.6	10.4	6.2	15.6	12.3	
1965	11.9	13.1	13.6	14.2	14.1	13.0	12.4	12.2	13.5	10.2	8.3	8.9	11.8	7.7	7.7	10.0	6.7	13.2	10.3	8.3
1966	10.7	11.7	12.1	12.6	12.4	11.3	10.6	10.3	11.3	8.1	6.3	6.5	8.8	4.9	4.5	5.9	2.4	6.2	2.0	-3.1
1967	11.1	12.1	12.5	13.0	12.8	11.8	11.2	10.9	11.9	9.0	7.4	7.7	9.9	6.5	6.4	7.8	5.3	8.9	6.4	4.4
1968	10.8	11.8	12.2	12.6	12.4	11.4	10.8	10.5	11.5	8.8	7.2	7.5	9.5	6.4	6.3	7.5	5.3	8.3	6.2	4.7
1969	9.8	10.6	10.9	11.3	11.1	10.1	9.4	9.1	9.9	7.2	5.7	5.8	7.5	4.5	4.2	5.1	2.8	5.1	2.8	0.8
1970	9.3	10.1	10.3	10.7	10.4	9.4	8.8	8.4	9.1	6.6	5.1	5.2	6.7	3.9	3.6	4.3	2.2	4.1	2.0	0.2
1971	9.2	10.0	10.3	10.6	10.3	9.4	8.8	8.4	9.1	6.7	5.3	5.4	6.8	4.2	3.9	4.6	2.8	4.5	2.7	1.4
1972	9.4	10.1	10.4	10.7	10.4	9.5	9.0	8.6	9.3	7.0	5.7	5.9	7.2	4.9	4.6	5.3	3.7	5.4	3.9	2.8
1973	8.3	8.9	9.2	9.4	9.1	8.2	7.6	7.2	7.8	5.5	4.3	4.3	5.5	3.1	2.8	3.3	1.7	3.0	1.4	0.2
1974	6.8	7.4	7.6	7.7	7.4	6.5	5.8	5.3	5.8	3.6	2.3	2.2	3.1	0.8	0.4	0.7	-1.1	-0.1	-1.8	-3.2
1975	7.6	8.2	8.3	8.5	8.2	7.4	6.8	6.4	6.8	4.8	3.6	3.6	4.6	2.5	2.2	2.6	1.1	2.2	0.8	-0.3
1976	7.8	8.4	8.6	8.8	8.5	7.7	7.1	6.8	7.2	5.3	4.2	4.2	5.2	3.3	3.0	3.4	2.1	3.1	1.9	1.1
1977	7.1	7.7	7.8	8.0	7.7	6.9	6.3	5.9	6.3	4.5	3.3	3.3	4.2	2.3	2.0	2.4	1.1	2.0	0.8	-0.1
1978	6.9	7.4	7.5	7.7	7.4	6.6	6.0	5.7	6.0	4.2	3.1	3.1	4.0	2.1	1.8	2.2	0.9	1.8	0.6	-0.2
1979	7.0	7.5	7.6	7.7	7.5	6.7	6.2	5.8	6.2	4.4	3.4	3.4	4.2	2.5	2.2	2.5	1.4	2.2	1.2	0.4
1980	7.4	7.9	8.1	8.2	7.9	7.2	6.7	6.4	6.8	5.1	4.2	4.2	5.0	3.4	3.2	3.5	2.5	3.4	2.4	1.8
1981	6.7	7.2	7.3	7.5	7.2	6.5	5.9	5.6	5.9	4.3	3.4	3.4	4.1	2.5	2.3	2.6	1.6	2.3	1.4	0.7
1982	6.8	7.2	7.3	7.5	7.2	6.5	6.0	5.7	6.0	4.5	3.5	3.5	4.3	2.8	2.5	2.8	1.9	2.6	1.7	1.1
1983	6.9	7.4	7.5	7.6	7.3	6.7	6.2	5.9	6.2	4.7	3.9	3.9	4.6	3.1	2.9	3.2	2.3	3.0	2.3	1.7
1984	6.6	7.0	7.1	7.2	7.0	6.3	5.8	5.5	5.8	4.4	3.5	3.5	4.2	2.8	2.6	2.9	2.0	2.7	1.9	1.4
1985	7.0	7.4	7.5	7.6	7.4	6.7	6.3	6.0	6.3	4.9	4.1	4.1	4.8	3.5	3.3	3.6	2.8	3.5	2.8	2.3
1986	7.0	7.4	7.5	7.7	7.4	6.8	6.4	6.1	6.4	5.1	4.3	4.3	4.9	3.7	3.5	3.8	3.0	3.7	3.0	2.6
1987	6.8	7.2	7.3	7.4	7.2	6.6	6.1	5.9	6.1	4.8	4.1	4.1	4.7	3.5	3.3	3.6	2.8	3.5	2.8	2.4
1988	6.8	7.2	7.3	7.4	7.2	6.6	6.2	5.9	6.2	4.9	4.2	4.2	4.8	3.6	3.5	3.7	3.0	3.6	3.0	2.6
1989	7.2	7.6	7.7	7.8	7.6	7.0	6.6	6.4	6.6	5.4	4.7	4.8	5.4	4.2	4.1	4.4	3.7	4.3	3.8	3.4
1990	6.8	7.1	7.2	7.3	7.1	6.5	6.2	5.9	6.2	4.9	4.3	4.3	4.8	3.7	3.6	3.9	3.2	3.8	3.2	2.9

*S&P 500 total returns minus long-term government bond income returns.

Table A-1 (Page 4 of 6)

Long-Horizon Equity Risk Premia*

Percent per annum arithmetic mean risk premia
for all historical time periods.

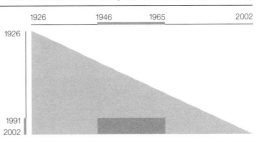

from 1926 to 2002

To the end of	From the beginning of																			
	1946	1947	1948	1949	1950	1951	1952	1953	1954	1955	1956	1957	1958	1959	1960	1961	1962	1963	1964	1965
1991	7.1	7.5	7.6	7.7	7.5	6.9	6.6	6.3	6.6	5.4	4.8	4.8	5.4	4.3	4.2	4.5	3.8	4.4	3.9	3.6
1992	7.0	7.3	7.4	7.5	7.3	6.8	6.4	6.2	6.4	5.3	4.7	4.7	5.2	4.2	4.1	4.3	3.7	4.3	3.8	3.5
1993	6.9	7.2	7.3	7.4	7.2	6.7	6.3	6.1	6.3	5.2	4.6	4.6	5.2	4.2	4.0	4.3	3.7	4.2	3.7	3.4
1994	6.6	7.0	7.0	7.1	6.9	6.4	6.0	5.8	6.1	5.0	4.3	4.4	4.9	3.9	3.8	4.0	3.4	3.9	3.4	3.1
1995	7.1	7.4	7.5	7.6	7.4	6.9	6.6	6.4	6.6	5.6	5.0	5.0	5.5	4.6	4.5	4.7	4.2	4.7	4.3	4.0
1996	7.3	7.6	7.7	7.8	7.6	7.1	6.8	6.6	6.9	5.8	5.3	5.3	5.8	4.9	4.8	5.1	4.6	5.1	4.7	4.4
1997	7.7	8.0	8.1	8.2	8.0	7.6	7.3	7.1	7.3	6.3	5.8	5.8	6.3	5.5	5.4	5.7	5.2	5.7	5.3	5.1
1998	7.9	8.3	8.4	8.5	8.3	7.9	7.6	7.4	7.7	6.7	6.2	6.2	6.7	5.9	5.9	6.1	5.7	6.2	5.8	5.6
1999	8.1	8.4	8.5	8.6	8.5	8.0	7.7	7.6	7.8	6.9	6.4	6.5	7.0	6.1	6.1	6.4	5.9	6.4	6.1	5.9
2000	7.6	8.0	8.1	8.2	8.0	7.6	7.3	7.1	7.3	6.4	5.9	6.0	6.4	5.6	5.6	5.8	5.4	5.8	5.5	5.3
2001	7.2	7.5	7.6	7.7	7.5	7.1	6.8	6.6	6.8	5.9	5.4	5.4	5.9	5.1	5.0	5.2	4.8	5.2	4.9	4.7
2002	6.6	6.9	6.9	7.0	6.8	6.4	6.1	5.9	6.1	5.2	4.7	4.7	5.1	4.3	4.3	4.5	4.0	4.4	4.0	3.8

*S&P 500 total returns minus long-term government bond income returns.

Table A-1 (Page 5 of 6)

Long-Horizon Equity Risk Premia*

Percent per annum arithmetic mean risk premia
for all historical time periods.

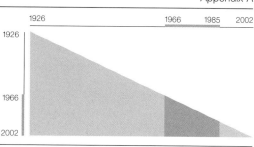

from 1926 to 2002

To the end of	From the beginning of 1966	1967	1968	1969	1970	1971	1972	1973	1974	1975	1976	1977	1978	1979	1980	1981	1982	1983	1984	1985
1966	-14.6																			
1967	2.4	19.4																		
1968	3.5	12.5	5.6																	
1969	-1.0	3.5	-4.4	-14.5																
1970	-1.4	1.9	-3.9	-8.6	-2.7															
1971	0.2	3.2	-0.9	-3.1	2.6	8.0														
1972	2.0	4.8	1.9	1.0	6.1	10.6	13.1													
1973	-0.9	1.1	-1.9	-3.5	-0.7	0.0	-4.0	-21.2												
1974	-4.5	-3.3	-6.5	-8.5	-7.3	-8.5	-13.9	-27.5	-33.7											
1975	-1.1	0.4	-2.0	-3.1	-1.2	-0.9	-3.1	-8.6	-2.3	29.2										
1976	0.4	1.9	0.0	-0.7	1.2	1.9	0.7	-2.4	3.8	22.6	16.0									
1977	-0.8	0.4	-1.5	-2.2	-0.7	-0.4	-1.8	-4.8	-0.7	10.3	0.8	-14.3								
1978	-0.9	0.3	-1.4	-2.1	-0.8	-0.5	-1.8	-4.2	-0.8	7.4	0.1	-7.8	-1.3							
1979	-0.1	1.0	-0.5	-1.1	0.3	0.6	-0.3	-2.3	0.9	7.8	2.5	-2.0	4.1	9.6						
1980	1.4	2.5	1.2	0.9	2.3	2.8	2.2	0.8	4.0	10.3	6.5	4.1	10.2	16.0	22.4					
1981	0.3	1.3	0.0	-0.5	0.7	1.0	0.3	-1.1	1.4	6.4	2.6	0.0	3.6	5.2	3.0	-16.5				
1982	0.7	1.7	0.5	0.1	1.3	1.6	1.0	-0.2	2.1	6.6	3.4	1.3	4.4	5.9	4.6	-4.3	7.9			
1983	1.4	2.3	1.2	0.9	2.0	2.4	1.9	0.9	3.1	7.2	4.5	2.9	5.7	7.1	6.5	1.2	10.0	12.1		
1984	1.0	1.9	0.8	0.5	1.5	1.8	1.4	0.4	2.4	6.0	3.4	1.8	4.1	5.0	4.1	-0.5	4.9	3.3	-5.5	
1985	2.0	2.9	2.0	1.7	2.8	3.1	2.8	2.0	3.9	7.3	5.1	3.9	6.2	7.3	6.9	3.8	8.9	9.2	7.7	20.9
1986	2.4	3.2	2.3	2.2	3.1	3.5	3.2	2.5	4.3	7.5	5.5	4.5	6.6	7.6	7.3	4.8	9.0	9.3	8.3	15.2
1987	2.1	2.9	2.1	1.9	2.8	3.2	2.8	2.2	3.8	6.7	4.8	3.8	5.7	6.4	6.0	3.7	7.0	6.9	5.6	9.2
1988	2.4	3.1	2.4	2.2	3.1	3.4	3.1	2.5	4.1	6.8	5.1	4.2	5.9	6.6	6.2	4.2	7.2	7.0	6.0	8.9
1989	3.2	4.0	3.3	3.2	4.1	4.4	4.2	3.7	5.3	7.9	6.3	5.6	7.3	8.0	7.9	6.3	9.1	9.3	8.8	11.6
1990	2.6	3.4	2.7	2.5	3.3	3.6	3.4	2.9	4.3	6.7	5.2	4.4	5.8	6.4	6.1	4.5	6.8	6.7	5.9	7.8
1991	3.4	4.1	3.5	3.4	4.2	4.5	4.4	3.9	5.3	7.6	6.2	5.6	7.0	7.6	7.5	6.1	8.4	8.4	8.0	9.9
1992	3.3	4.0	3.4	3.3	4.0	4.3	4.2	3.7	5.0	7.2	5.9	5.3	6.6	7.1	6.9	5.6	7.7	7.6	7.1	8.7
1993	3.3	3.9	3.3	3.2	4.0	4.3	4.1	3.7	4.9	7.0	5.7	5.1	6.3	6.8	6.6	5.4	7.3	7.2	6.7	8.0
1994	3.0	3.6	3.0	2.9	3.6	3.9	3.7	3.3	4.4	6.3	5.1	4.5	5.6	6.1	5.8	4.7	6.3	6.2	5.6	6.7
1995	3.9	4.5	4.0	3.9	4.6	4.9	4.8	4.4	5.6	7.5	6.4	5.9	7.0	7.5	7.3	6.3	8.0	8.0	7.6	8.8
1996	4.3	4.9	4.4	4.4	5.1	5.4	5.3	4.9	6.1	7.9	6.9	6.4	7.5	8.0	7.9	7.0	8.6	8.6	8.3	9.5
1997	5.0	5.6	5.2	5.1	5.8	6.2	6.1	5.8	6.9	8.7	7.8	7.4	8.5	9.0	9.0	8.2	9.7	9.8	9.7	10.8
1998	5.5	6.2	5.7	5.7	6.4	6.8	6.7	6.5	7.6	9.3	8.4	8.1	9.1	9.7	9.7	9.0	10.5	10.6	10.5	11.7
1999	5.8	6.4	6.0	6.0	6.7	7.1	7.0	6.8	7.9	9.5	8.7	8.4	9.4	10.0	10.0	9.3	10.7	10.9	10.8	11.9
2000	5.2	5.8	5.4	5.4	6.0	6.3	6.2	6.0	7.0	8.6	7.7	7.4	8.3	8.8	8.8	8.8	8.1	9.4	9.3	10.2
2001	4.6	5.1	4.7	4.7	5.3	5.5	5.5	5.2	6.1	7.6	6.8	6.4	7.3	7.6	7.6	6.9	8.0	8.0	7.8	8.6
2002	3.7	4.2	3.8	3.7	4.3	4.5	4.4	4.1	5.0	6.3	5.5	5.1	5.9	6.2	6.0	5.3	6.3	6.2	5.9	6.6

*S&P 500 total returns minus long-term government bond income returns.

Table A-1 (Page 6 of 6)

Long-Horizon Equity Risk Premia*

Percent per annum arithmetic mean risk premia
for all historical time periods.

from 1926 to 2002

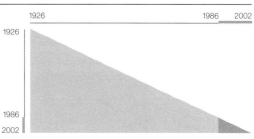

To the end of	From the beginning of																
	1986	1987	1988	1989	1990	1991	1992	1993	1994	1995	1996	1997	1998	1999	2000	2001	2002
1986	9.5																
1987	3.4	−2.7															
1988	4.9	2.6	7.8														
1989	9.3	9.3	15.3	22.7													
1990	5.2	4.1	6.4	5.7	−11.4												
1991	8.0	7.8	10.4	11.2	5.5	22.3											
1992	7.0	6.5	8.4	8.5	3.8	11.4	0.4										
1993	6.4	6.0	7.5	7.4	3.5	8.5	1.6	2.8									
1994	5.1	4.6	5.6	5.3	1.8	5.1	−0.7	−1.2	−5.3								
1995	7.6	7.4	8.7	8.8	6.5	10.0	6.9	9.1	12.3	29.8							
1996	8.5	8.3	9.6	9.8	7.9	11.2	8.9	11.1	13.8	23.4	16.9						
1997	10.0	10.0	11.3	11.7	10.3	13.4	11.9	14.2	17.0	24.5	21.8	26.7					
1998	11.0	11.1	12.3	12.8	11.7	14.6	13.4	15.6	18.2	24.1	22.1	24.7	22.7				
1999	11.3	11.4	12.6	13.0	12.1	14.7	13.7	15.6	17.7	22.3	20.5	21.6	19.1	15.5			
2000	9.5	9.5	10.4	10.6	9.5	11.6	10.4	11.7	13.0	16.0	13.2	12.3	7.5	−0.1	−15.6		
2001	7.8	7.7	8.4	8.5	7.3	9.0	7.7	8.5	9.2	11.2	8.1	6.4	1.3	−5.8	−16.5	−17.4	
2002	5.7	5.5	6.0	5.9	4.6	5.9	4.4	4.8	5.1	6.4	3.0	0.7	−4.5	−11.3	−20.2	−22.6	−27.7

*S&P 500 total returns minus long-term government bond income returns.

Table A-2 (Page 1 of 6)

Intermediate-Horizon Equity Risk Premia*

Percent per annum arithmetic mean risk premia
for all historical time periods.

from 1926 to 2002

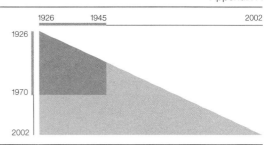

To the end of	1926	1927	1928	1929	1930	1931	1932	1933	1934	1935	1936	1937	1938	1939	1940	1941	1942	1943	1944	1945
1926	7.8																			
1927	20.9	34.0																		
1928	27.3	37.0	40.0																	
1929	17.3	20.5	13.7	−12.5																
1930	8.2	8.3	−0.2	−20.3	−28.2															
1931	−0.9	−2.6	−11.8	−29.1	−37.3	−46.5														
1932	−2.5	−4.2	−11.8	−24.7	−28.8	−29.2	−11.8													
1933	4.2	3.7	−1.3	−9.6	−8.8	−2.4	19.7	51.2												
1934	3.3	2.7	−1.7	−8.7	−7.9	−2.9	11.7	23.4	−4.4											
1935	7.5	7.5	4.2	−0.9	1.0	6.8	20.2	30.8	20.6	45.6										
1936	9.8	10.0	7.3	3.2	5.5	11.1	22.6	31.2	24.6	39.1	32.5									
1937	5.9	5.8	2.9	−1.2	0.2	4.3	12.8	17.7	9.3	13.9	−2.0	−36.5								
1938	7.7	7.7	5.3	1.9	3.5	7.4	15.1	19.6	13.3	17.7	8.4	−3.6	29.3							
1939	7.1	7.0	4.7	1.5	2.9	6.4	13.0	16.6	10.8	13.8	5.9	−3.0	13.8	−1.7						
1940	5.9	5.7	3.6	0.5	1.7	4.7	10.4	13.2	7.7	9.8	2.6	−4.9	5.6	−6.2	−10.7					
1941	4.7	4.5	2.4	−0.5	0.5	3.2	8.1	10.3	5.2	6.6	0.1	−6.4	1.2	−8.2	−11.5	−12.3				
1942	5.6	5.5	3.6	1.0	2.0	4.5	9.2	11.3	6.8	8.2	2.9	−2.0	4.8	−1.3	−1.1	3.7	19.6			
1943	6.7	6.6	4.9	2.5	3.6	6.0	10.4	12.5	8.6	10.0	5.6	1.7	8.1	3.8	5.2	10.6	22.0	24.3		
1944	7.3	7.2	5.7	3.5	4.6	6.9	11.0	12.9	9.5	10.8	7.0	3.8	9.6	6.3	7.9	12.5	20.7	21.3	18.3	
1945	8.7	8.7	7.3	5.4	6.5	8.8	12.8	14.7	11.6	13.1	9.8	7.3	12.8	10.4	12.4	17.0	24.4	26.0	26.8	35.2
1946	7.8	7.8	6.4	4.6	5.6	7.7	11.3	13.0	10.0	11.2	8.1	5.6	10.3	8.0	9.3	12.7	17.7	17.2	14.8	13.0
1947	7.7	7.7	6.3	4.6	5.5	7.5	10.9	12.4	9.6	10.7	7.8	5.5	9.7	7.6	8.7	11.5	15.5	14.6	12.2	10.2
1948	7.5	7.5	6.2	4.5	5.4	7.3	10.5	11.9	9.2	10.2	7.5	5.4	9.2	7.2	8.2	10.6	13.8	12.9	10.6	8.6
1949	7.9	7.9	6.7	5.2	6.0	7.8	10.9	12.2	9.8	10.7	8.2	6.3	9.9	8.1	9.1	11.3	14.3	13.5	11.7	10.4
1950	8.8	8.9	7.8	6.3	7.2	9.0	11.9	13.2	11.0	11.9	9.7	8.0	11.5	10.0	11.1	13.2	16.1	15.6	14.4	13.7
1951	9.3	9.4	8.4	7.0	7.9	9.6	12.4	13.7	11.6	12.5	10.4	9.0	12.2	10.9	12.0	14.0	16.7	16.3	15.3	14.9
1952	9.6	9.6	8.7	7.4	8.2	9.9	12.6	13.8	11.8	12.7	10.8	9.4	12.5	11.3	12.3	14.2	16.6	16.3	15.4	15.1
1953	9.1	9.2	8.2	6.9	7.7	9.3	11.8	13.0	11.1	11.9	10.0	8.7	11.5	10.3	11.2	12.8	14.9	14.5	13.5	13.0
1954	10.6	10.7	9.8	8.6	9.5	11.0	13.5	14.7	13.0	13.8	12.1	11.0	13.8	12.8	13.8	15.6	17.7	17.6	16.9	16.8
1955	11.2	11.3	10.5	9.4	10.2	11.8	14.2	15.3	13.7	14.6	13.0	12.0	14.7	13.8	14.8	16.5	18.5	18.4	18.0	17.9
1956	10.9	11.0	10.2	9.2	10.0	11.4	13.8	14.8	13.2	14.0	12.5	11.5	14.1	13.2	14.1	15.7	17.5	17.4	16.8	16.7
1957	10.1	10.2	9.4	8.4	9.1	10.5	12.7	13.7	12.1	12.8	11.3	10.3	12.7	11.8	12.5	13.9	15.5	15.3	14.6	14.3
1958	11.1	11.2	10.4	9.4	10.2	11.6	13.7	14.7	13.2	14.0	12.6	11.7	14.0	13.2	14.0	15.4	17.0	16.8	16.3	16.2
1959	11.0	11.1	10.3	9.4	10.1	11.4	13.5	14.4	13.0	13.7	12.4	11.5	13.7	13.0	13.7	15.0	16.5	16.3	15.8	15.6
1960	10.5	10.6	9.9	9.0	9.7	10.9	12.9	13.8	12.4	13.0	11.7	10.9	12.9	12.2	12.9	14.0	15.4	15.2	14.7	14.4
1961	10.9	11.0	10.3	9.4	10.1	11.3	13.3	14.1	12.8	13.4	12.2	11.4	13.4	12.7	13.3	14.5	15.8	15.6	15.1	14.9
1962	10.3	10.3	9.7	8.8	9.4	10.6	12.4	13.2	11.9	12.5	11.3	10.5	12.3	11.6	12.2	13.3	14.5	14.2	13.7	13.4
1963	10.5	10.6	9.9	9.1	9.7	10.8	12.6	13.4	12.2	12.7	11.6	10.8	12.6	11.9	12.5	13.5	14.7	14.4	14.0	13.7
1964	10.5	10.6	10.0	9.2	9.8	10.9	12.6	13.4	12.2	12.7	11.6	10.8	12.6	12.0	12.5	13.5	14.6	14.4	13.9	13.7
1965	10.5	10.6	9.9	9.1	9.7	10.8	12.5	13.2	12.1	12.6	11.5	10.8	12.4	11.8	12.3	13.3	14.3	14.1	13.6	13.4
1966	9.9	9.9	9.3	8.5	9.1	10.1	11.7	12.4	11.2	11.7	10.6	9.9	11.5	10.9	11.3	12.2	13.1	12.9	12.4	12.1
1967	10.1	10.1	9.5	8.8	9.3	10.3	11.9	12.6	11.5	11.9	10.9	10.2	11.7	11.1	11.6	12.4	13.4	13.1	12.7	12.4
1968	10.0	10.0	9.4	8.7	9.2	10.2	11.7	12.4	11.3	11.8	10.7	10.0	11.6	11.0	11.4	12.2	13.1	12.8	12.4	12.1
1969	9.4	9.4	8.9	8.1	8.6	9.6	11.0	11.7	10.6	11.0	10.0	9.3	10.7	10.1	10.5	11.2	12.1	11.8	11.3	11.0
1970	9.1	9.2	8.6	7.8	8.3	9.2	10.7	11.3	10.2	10.6	9.6	8.9	10.3	9.7	10.1	10.8	11.5	11.3	10.8	10.5

*S&P 500 total returns minus intermediate-term government bond income returns.

Table A-2 (Page 2 of 6)

Intermediate-Horizon Equity Risk Premia*

Percent per annum arithmetic mean risk premia
for all historical time periods.

from 1926 to 2002

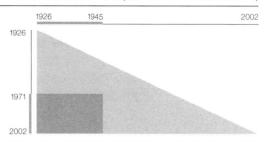

To the end of	From the beginning of 1926	1927	1928	1929	1930	1931	1932	1933	1934	1935	1936	1937	1938	1939	1940	1941	1942	1943	1944	1945
1971	9.1	9.1	8.6	7.8	8.3	9.2	10.6	11.2	10.1	10.5	9.6	8.9	10.2	9.7	10.0	10.7	11.4	11.2	10.7	10.4
1972	9.2	9.2	8.7	8.0	8.4	9.3	10.7	11.2	10.2	10.6	9.7	9.0	10.3	9.8	10.1	10.8	11.5	11.2	10.8	10.5
1973	8.6	8.6	8.0	7.3	7.8	8.6	9.9	10.4	9.4	9.8	8.8	8.2	9.4	8.9	9.2	9.8	10.5	10.2	9.7	9.4
1974	7.7	7.7	7.1	6.4	6.8	7.6	8.9	9.4	8.4	8.7	7.7	7.1	8.3	7.7	8.0	8.5	9.1	8.8	8.3	8.0
1975	8.1	8.2	7.6	6.9	7.3	8.1	9.4	9.9	8.9	9.2	8.3	7.7	8.8	8.3	8.6	9.1	9.7	9.5	9.0	8.7
1976	8.3	8.3	7.8	7.1	7.5	8.3	9.5	10.0	9.1	9.4	8.5	7.9	9.0	8.5	8.8	9.3	9.9	9.7	9.2	8.9
1977	7.9	7.9	7.4	6.7	7.1	7.9	9.0	9.5	8.6	8.9	8.0	7.4	8.5	7.9	8.2	8.7	9.3	9.0	8.5	8.3
1978	7.7	7.7	7.2	6.5	6.9	7.7	8.8	9.3	8.3	8.6	7.8	7.2	8.2	7.7	8.0	8.4	9.0	8.7	8.3	8.0
1979	7.8	7.7	7.2	6.6	7.0	7.7	8.8	9.3	8.4	8.6	7.8	7.2	8.3	7.8	8.0	8.5	9.0	8.7	8.3	8.0
1980	8.0	8.0	7.5	6.9	7.3	8.0	9.1	9.5	8.6	8.9	8.1	7.6	8.6	8.1	8.3	8.8	9.3	9.1	8.7	8.4
1981	7.5	7.5	7.0	6.4	6.8	7.5	8.6	9.0	8.1	8.4	7.5	7.0	8.0	7.5	7.7	8.2	8.7	8.4	8.0	7.7
1982	7.6	7.6	7.1	6.5	6.8	7.5	8.6	9.0	8.1	8.4	7.6	7.0	8.0	7.5	7.7	8.2	8.7	8.4	8.0	7.7
1983	7.6	7.6	7.2	6.6	6.9	7.6	8.6	9.0	8.2	8.4	7.7	7.1	8.1	7.6	7.8	8.3	8.7	8.5	8.1	7.8
1984	7.4	7.4	6.9	6.4	6.7	7.3	8.4	8.8	7.9	8.2	7.4	6.9	7.8	7.3	7.5	7.9	8.4	8.2	7.8	7.5
1985	7.7	7.7	7.2	6.6	7.0	7.6	8.6	9.0	8.2	8.4	7.7	7.2	8.1	7.6	7.8	8.3	8.7	8.5	8.1	7.8
1986	7.7	7.7	7.3	6.7	7.0	7.7	8.7	9.0	8.2	8.5	7.7	7.3	8.1	7.7	7.9	8.3	8.8	8.5	8.2	7.9
1987	7.6	7.5	7.1	6.5	6.9	7.5	8.5	8.8	8.0	8.3	7.6	7.1	7.9	7.5	7.7	8.1	8.5	8.3	7.9	7.7
1988	7.6	7.6	7.1	6.6	6.9	7.5	8.5	8.8	8.1	8.3	7.6	7.1	8.0	7.5	7.7	8.1	8.5	8.3	7.9	7.7
1989	7.8	7.8	7.4	6.9	7.2	7.8	8.7	9.1	8.3	8.5	7.9	7.4	8.2	7.8	8.0	8.4	8.8	8.6	8.3	8.0
1990	7.5	7.5	7.1	6.6	6.9	7.5	8.4	8.7	8.0	8.2	7.5	7.1	7.9	7.5	7.6	8.0	8.4	8.2	7.8	7.6
1991	7.8	7.8	7.3	6.8	7.1	7.7	8.6	9.0	8.2	8.5	7.8	7.3	8.2	7.8	7.9	8.3	8.7	8.5	8.2	7.9
1992	7.7	7.7	7.2	6.7	7.0	7.6	8.5	8.8	8.1	8.3	7.7	7.2	8.0	7.6	7.8	8.2	8.6	8.4	8.0	7.8
1993	7.6	7.6	7.2	6.7	7.0	7.6	8.4	8.8	8.1	8.3	7.6	7.2	8.0	7.6	7.8	8.1	8.5	8.3	8.0	7.7
1994	7.4	7.4	7.0	6.5	6.8	7.4	8.2	8.5	7.8	8.1	7.4	7.0	7.7	7.4	7.5	7.9	8.2	8.0	7.7	7.5
1995	7.8	7.8	7.4	6.9	7.2	7.7	8.6	8.9	8.2	8.4	7.8	7.4	8.1	7.8	7.9	8.3	8.7	8.5	8.1	7.9
1996	7.9	7.9	7.5	7.0	7.3	7.9	8.7	9.0	8.4	8.6	8.0	7.5	8.3	7.9	8.1	8.4	8.8	8.6	8.3	8.1
1997	8.2	8.2	7.8	7.3	7.6	8.2	9.0	9.3	8.7	8.9	8.3	7.9	8.6	8.3	8.4	8.8	9.1	9.0	8.7	8.5
1998	8.4	8.4	8.0	7.6	7.9	8.4	9.2	9.5	8.9	9.1	8.5	8.1	8.9	8.5	8.7	9.0	9.4	9.2	8.9	8.8
1999	8.5	8.5	8.1	7.7	8.0	8.5	9.3	9.6	9.0	9.2	8.6	8.2	9.0	8.6	8.8	9.1	9.5	9.3	9.1	8.9
2000	8.2	8.2	7.8	7.4	7.6	8.2	8.9	9.2	8.6	8.8	8.3	7.9	8.6	8.2	8.4	8.7	9.1	8.9	8.6	8.5
2001	7.8	7.8	7.5	7.0	7.3	7.8	8.6	8.9	8.3	8.4	7.9	7.5	8.2	7.9	8.0	8.3	8.7	8.5	8.2	8.0
2002	7.4	7.4	7.0	6.6	6.9	7.3	8.1	8.4	7.8	7.9	7.4	7.0	7.7	7.3	7.5	7.8	8.1	7.9	7.6	7.4

*S&P 500 total returns minus intermediate-term government bond income returns.

Table A-2 (Page 3 of 6)

Intermediate-Horizon Equity Risk Premia*

Percent per annum arithmetic mean risk premia
for all historical time periods.

from 1926 to 2002

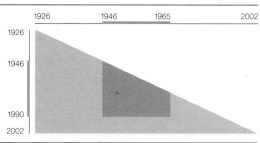

To the end of	From the beginning of																			
	1946	1947	1948	1949	1950	1951	1952	1953	1954	1955	1956	1957	1958	1959	1960	1961	1962	1963	1964	1965
1946	-9.2																			
1947	-2.3	4.5																		
1948	-0.2	4.2	3.9																	
1949	4.2	8.6	10.7	17.4																
1950	9.4	14.0	17.2	23.9	30.3															
1951	11.5	15.6	18.4	23.3	26.2	22.0														
1952	12.2	15.7	18.0	21.5	22.8	19.1	16.2													
1953	10.2	13.0	14.4	16.5	16.2	11.6	6.3	-3.5												
1954	14.7	17.7	19.6	22.2	23.2	21.4	21.2	23.7	51.0											
1955	16.2	19.0	20.8	23.2	24.2	23.0	23.2	25.5	40.1	29.1										
1956	15.0	17.4	18.9	20.8	21.2	19.7	19.3	20.0	27.9	16.3	3.5									
1957	12.6	14.6	15.6	16.9	16.8	14.8	13.7	13.1	17.3	6.1	-5.4	-14.4								
1958	14.7	16.7	17.8	19.2	19.4	18.0	17.5	17.7	21.9	14.7	9.9	13.0	40.4							
1959	14.2	16.0	17.0	18.2	18.2	16.9	16.3	16.3	19.6	13.3	9.3	11.3	24.1	7.8						
1960	13.0	14.6	15.4	16.4	16.3	14.8	14.0	13.8	16.3	10.5	6.7	7.5	14.8	2.1	-3.7					
1961	13.7	15.2	16.0	16.9	16.8	15.6	15.0	14.8	17.1	12.3	9.5	10.7	17.0	9.2	9.8	23.3				
1962	12.1	13.5	14.1	14.8	14.6	13.3	12.5	12.1	13.9	9.2	6.4	6.8	11.1	3.7	2.4	5.4	-12.5			
1963	12.5	13.8	14.4	15.1	14.9	13.7	13.0	12.7	14.4	10.3	8.0	8.6	12.4	6.8	6.6	10.0	3.3	19.1		
1964	12.5	13.7	14.3	14.9	14.7	13.6	13.0	12.7	14.2	10.5	8.5	9.1	12.4	7.8	7.8	10.6	6.4	15.8	12.5	
1965	12.3	13.4	13.9	14.5	14.3	13.3	12.7	12.4	13.7	10.3	8.4	9.0	11.9	7.8	7.8	10.2	6.9	13.3	10.4	8.3
1966	11.0	12.0	12.4	12.9	12.6	11.5	10.8	10.4	11.5	8.2	6.3	6.6	8.9	5.0	4.6	6.0	2.5	6.2	1.9	-3.3
1967	11.4	12.4	12.8	13.2	13.0	12.0	11.3	11.0	12.0	9.0	7.4	7.7	9.9	6.6	6.4	7.8	5.3	8.8	6.2	4.1
1968	11.1	12.0	12.4	12.8	12.6	11.6	11.0	10.7	11.6	8.8	7.2	7.5	9.5	6.5	6.3	7.6	5.3	8.3	6.1	4.5
1969	10.0	10.9	11.2	11.5	11.2	10.2	9.5	9.1	9.9	7.2	5.6	5.8	7.5	4.5	4.2	5.0	2.7	4.9	2.6	0.6
1970	9.5	10.3	10.5	10.8	10.5	9.5	8.9	8.4	9.2	6.5	5.0	5.1	6.6	3.8	3.5	4.2	2.0	3.9	1.7	-0.1
1971	9.5	10.2	10.4	10.7	10.4	9.5	8.8	8.5	9.1	6.7	5.3	5.4	6.8	4.2	3.9	4.6	2.7	4.4	2.5	1.1
1972	9.6	10.3	10.6	10.8	10.5	9.6	9.0	8.7	9.3	7.0	5.7	5.9	7.2	4.8	4.6	5.3	3.7	5.3	3.7	2.6
1973	8.5	9.1	9.3	9.5	9.2	8.3	7.7	7.3	7.8	5.5	4.2	4.3	5.4	3.1	2.8	3.3	1.6	2.9	1.2	0.0
1974	7.0	7.6	7.7	7.9	7.5	6.5	5.9	5.4	5.8	3.6	2.2	2.2	3.1	0.8	0.3	0.6	-1.1	-0.2	-1.9	-3.4
1975	7.8	8.4	8.5	8.7	8.4	7.5	6.9	6.5	6.9	4.8	3.6	3.6	4.6	2.5	2.2	2.6	1.1	2.1	0.7	-0.4
1976	8.1	8.7	8.8	9.0	8.7	7.8	7.3	6.9	7.3	5.4	4.2	4.3	5.3	3.3	3.0	3.5	2.1	3.2	1.9	1.1
1977	7.4	7.9	8.1	8.2	7.9	7.0	6.5	6.1	6.5	4.5	3.4	3.4	4.3	2.4	2.1	2.4	1.1	2.0	0.8	-0.1
1978	7.1	7.7	7.8	7.9	7.6	6.7	6.2	5.8	6.2	4.3	3.2	3.2	4.0	2.2	1.9	2.2	1.0	1.8	0.7	-0.2
1979	7.2	7.7	7.8	7.9	7.6	6.8	6.3	5.9	6.3	4.5	3.5	3.5	4.3	2.6	2.3	2.6	1.5	2.3	1.2	0.5
1980	7.6	8.1	8.2	8.4	8.1	7.3	6.8	6.5	6.9	5.2	4.2	4.2	5.0	3.4	3.2	3.6	2.5	3.4	2.4	1.8
1981	6.9	7.4	7.5	7.6	7.3	6.5	6.0	5.7	6.0	4.3	3.4	3.4	4.1	2.5	2.3	2.6	1.5	2.3	1.3	0.7
1982	7.0	7.4	7.5	7.6	7.3	6.6	6.1	5.8	6.1	4.5	3.6	3.6	4.3	2.8	2.5	2.8	1.9	2.6	1.7	1.1
1983	7.1	7.5	7.6	7.7	7.4	6.8	6.3	6.0	6.3	4.7	3.9	3.9	4.6	3.1	2.9	3.2	2.3	3.0	2.2	1.7
1984	6.8	7.2	7.3	7.4	7.1	6.4	5.9	5.6	5.9	4.4	3.5	3.5	4.2	2.8	2.6	2.9	2.0	2.6	1.9	1.3
1985	7.2	7.6	7.7	7.8	7.5	6.8	6.4	6.1	6.4	5.0	4.2	4.2	4.8	3.5	3.4	3.6	2.8	3.5	2.8	2.3
1986	7.2	7.7	7.7	7.8	7.6	6.9	6.5	6.2	6.5	5.1	4.4	4.4	5.0	3.8	3.6	3.9	3.1	3.8	3.1	2.7
1987	7.0	7.4	7.5	7.6	7.3	6.7	6.3	6.0	6.3	4.9	4.2	4.2	4.8	3.6	3.4	3.7	2.9	3.5	2.9	2.5
1988	7.1	7.4	7.5	7.6	7.4	6.7	6.3	6.1	6.3	5.0	4.3	4.3	4.9	3.7	3.6	3.9	3.1	3.7	3.1	2.7
1989	7.4	7.8	7.9	8.0	7.7	7.2	6.8	6.5	6.8	5.5	4.8	4.9	5.5	4.4	4.2	4.5	3.8	4.4	3.9	3.5
1990	7.0	7.4	7.4	7.5	7.3	6.7	6.3	6.1	6.3	5.1	4.4	4.4	5.0	3.9	3.7	4.0	3.3	3.9	3.3	3.0

*S&P 500 total returns minus intermediate-term government bond income returns.

Table A-2 (Page 4 of 6)

Intermediate-Horizon Equity Risk Premia*

Percent per annum arithmetic mean risk premia
for all historical time periods.

from 1926 to 2002

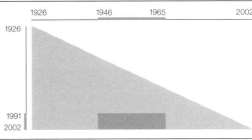

To the end of	From the beginning of																			
	1946	1947	1948	1949	1950	1951	1952	1953	1954	1955	1956	1957	1958	1959	1960	1961	1962	1963	1964	1965
1991	7.4	7.7	7.8	7.9	7.7	7.1	6.7	6.5	6.8	5.6	4.9	4.9	5.5	4.5	4.3	4.6	4.0	4.5	4.0	3.7
1992	7.2	7.6	7.7	7.7	7.5	7.0	6.6	6.4	6.6	5.4	4.8	4.8	5.4	4.4	4.3	4.5	3.9	4.4	3.9	3.6
1993	7.2	7.5	7.6	7.7	7.4	6.9	6.5	6.3	6.6	5.4	4.8	4.8	5.4	4.4	4.3	4.5	3.9	4.4	4.0	3.7
1994	6.9	7.3	7.3	7.4	7.2	6.6	6.3	6.1	6.3	5.2	4.6	4.6	5.1	4.1	4.0	4.2	3.7	4.2	3.7	3.4
1995	7.4	7.7	7.8	7.9	7.7	7.2	6.8	6.6	6.9	5.8	5.2	5.3	5.8	4.8	4.7	5.0	4.4	5.0	4.5	4.3
1996	7.6	7.9	8.0	8.1	7.9	7.4	7.1	6.9	7.1	6.1	5.5	5.6	6.1	5.2	5.1	5.3	4.8	5.3	4.9	4.7
1997	8.0	8.3	8.4	8.5	8.3	7.8	7.5	7.3	7.6	6.6	6.0	6.1	6.6	5.7	5.7	5.9	5.4	5.9	5.6	5.4
1998	8.3	8.6	8.7	8.8	8.6	8.1	7.8	7.7	7.9	6.9	6.4	6.5	7.0	6.2	6.1	6.4	5.9	6.4	6.1	5.9
1999	8.4	8.7	8.8	8.9	8.7	8.3	8.0	7.8	8.1	7.1	6.6	6.7	7.2	6.4	6.4	6.6	6.2	6.7	6.3	6.2
2000	8.0	8.3	8.4	8.4	8.3	7.8	7.5	7.4	7.6	6.6	6.1	6.2	6.7	5.9	5.8	6.1	5.6	6.1	5.8	5.6
2001	7.5	7.8	7.9	8.0	7.8	7.4	7.1	6.9	7.1	6.2	5.7	5.7	6.2	5.4	5.3	5.5	5.1	5.5	5.2	5.0
2002	6.9	7.2	7.3	7.3	7.2	6.7	6.4	6.2	6.4	5.5	5.0	5.0	5.4	4.7	4.6	4.8	4.3	4.7	4.4	4.2

*S&P 500 total returns minus intermediate-term government bond income returns.

Table A-2 (Page 5 of 6)

Intermediate-Horizon Equity Risk Premia*

Percent per annum arithmetic mean risk premia
for all historical time periods.

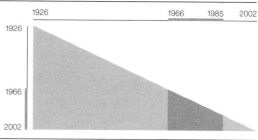

from 1926 to 2002

To the end of	From the beginning of																			
	1966	1967	1968	1969	1970	1971	1972	1973	1974	1975	1976	1977	1978	1979	1980	1981	1982	1983	1984	1985
1966	-15.0																			
1967	2.1	19.1																		
1968	3.2	12.3	5.6																	
1969	-1.4	3.2	-4.8	-15.2																
1970	-1.8	1.5	-4.4	-9.3	-3.5															
1971	-0.1	2.9	-1.1	-3.4	2.5	8.6														
1972	1.8	4.6	1.7	0.8	6.1	10.9	13.2													
1973	-1.0	0.9	-2.1	-3.6	-0.7	0.2	-4.0	-21.2												
1974	-4.7	-3.4	-6.6	-8.6	-7.3	-8.3	-13.9	-27.5	-33.7											
1975	-1.2	0.3	-2.0	-3.1	-1.1	-0.7	-3.0	-8.4	-1.9	29.9										
1976	0.4	1.9	0.0	-0.7	1.4	2.2	1.0	-2.1	4.3	23.3	16.7									
1977	-0.8	0.5	-1.3	-2.1	-0.5	0.0	-1.5	-4.4	-0.2	11.0	1.5	-13.7								
1978	-0.8	0.4	-1.3	-2.0	-0.6	-0.2	-1.4	-3.9	-0.4	7.9	0.6	-7.5	-1.3							
1979	-0.1	1.1	-0.4	-1.0	0.4	0.9	-0.1	-2.0	1.2	8.2	2.8	-1.8	4.1	9.4						
1980	1.4	2.6	1.3	0.9	2.4	3.0	2.4	1.0	4.2	10.5	6.6	4.1	10.0	15.6	21.9					
1981	0.2	1.2	-0.1	-0.5	0.7	1.1	0.3	-1.1	1.4	6.4	2.5	-0.3	3.0	4.5	2.0	-17.9				
1982	0.7	1.7	0.5	0.1	1.3	1.7	1.1	-0.1	2.2	6.7	3.4	1.2	4.1	5.5	4.2	-4.6	8.6			
1983	1.3	2.3	1.2	0.9	2.1	2.5	2.0	1.0	3.2	7.3	4.5	2.7	5.5	6.8	6.2	1.0	10.4	12.2		
1984	1.0	1.8	0.8	0.5	1.6	1.9	1.4	0.5	2.4	6.0	3.4	1.7	3.9	4.8	3.9	-0.6	5.1	3.4	-5.4	
1985	2.0	2.9	2.0	1.8	2.9	3.3	2.9	2.1	4.0	7.5	5.2	4.0	6.2	7.2	6.9	3.9	9.3	9.5	8.2	21.9
1986	2.4	3.3	2.5	2.3	3.3	3.7	3.4	2.7	4.6	7.8	5.7	4.6	6.7	7.7	7.4	5.0	9.6	9.8	9.1	16.3
1987	2.2	3.0	2.2	2.1	3.0	3.4	3.1	2.4	4.1	7.0	5.1	4.0	5.8	6.6	6.2	4.0	7.6	7.4	6.2	10.1
1988	2.5	3.3	2.5	2.4	3.3	3.7	3.4	2.8	4.4	7.1	5.3	4.4	6.0	6.8	6.5	4.6	7.8	7.6	6.7	9.7
1989	3.3	4.1	3.5	3.4	4.3	4.7	4.5	4.0	5.5	8.2	6.6	5.8	7.5	8.2	8.1	6.6	9.7	9.8	9.4	12.4
1990	2.8	3.5	2.8	2.7	3.5	3.9	3.6	3.1	4.5	6.9	5.4	4.6	6.0	6.6	6.4	4.8	7.3	7.2	6.5	8.4
1991	3.5	4.3	3.7	3.6	4.4	4.8	4.6	4.2	5.6	7.9	6.5	5.8	7.2	7.9	7.8	6.5	8.9	8.9	8.5	10.5
1992	3.5	4.2	3.6	3.5	4.3	4.7	4.5	4.0	5.4	7.5	6.2	5.6	6.8	7.4	7.3	6.1	8.2	8.2	7.8	9.4
1993	3.5	4.2	3.6	3.5	4.3	4.6	4.5	4.1	5.3	7.4	6.1	5.5	6.7	7.2	7.1	5.9	7.9	7.9	7.4	8.8
1994	3.2	3.9	3.3	3.2	3.9	4.3	4.1	3.7	4.8	6.8	5.5	4.9	6.0	6.5	6.3	5.2	6.9	6.8	6.3	7.5
1995	4.1	4.8	4.3	4.2	5.0	5.3	5.2	4.8	6.0	7.9	6.8	6.3	7.4	7.9	7.8	6.9	8.6	8.6	8.3	9.6
1996	4.6	5.2	4.7	4.7	5.4	5.8	5.7	5.3	6.5	8.3	7.3	6.8	7.9	8.4	8.4	7.5	9.2	9.3	9.0	10.2
1997	5.3	5.9	5.5	5.5	6.2	6.6	6.5	6.2	7.4	9.2	8.2	7.8	8.9	9.4	9.4	8.7	10.3	10.5	10.3	11.5
1998	5.8	6.5	6.0	6.1	6.8	7.2	7.1	6.9	8.0	9.7	8.9	8.5	9.6	10.1	10.1	9.5	11.1	11.3	11.2	12.4
1999	6.1	6.7	6.4	6.4	7.1	7.5	7.4	7.2	8.3	10.0	9.2	8.8	9.8	10.4	10.4	9.8	11.4	11.5	11.5	12.6
2000	5.5	6.1	5.7	5.7	6.4	6.7	6.6	6.4	7.4	9.0	8.2	7.8	8.8	9.2	9.2	8.6	10.0	10.0	9.9	10.9
2001	4.9	5.5	5.1	5.0	5.7	6.0	5.9	5.6	6.6	8.1	7.2	6.9	7.7	8.1	8.0	7.4	8.7	8.7	8.5	9.3
2002	4.1	4.6	4.2	4.1	4.7	5.0	4.8	4.6	5.5	6.9	6.0	5.6	6.4	6.7	6.6	5.9	7.0	6.9	6.6	7.3

*S&P 500 total returns minus intermediate-term government bond income returns.

Table A-2 (Page 6 of 6)

Intermediate-Horizon Equity Risk Premia*

Percent per annum arithmetic mean risk premia
for all historical time periods.

from 1926 to 2002

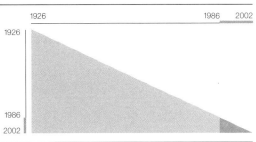

To the end of	From the beginning of																
	1986	1987	1988	1989	1990	1991	1992	1993	1994	1995	1996	1997	1998	1999	2000	2001	2002
1986	10.8																
1987	4.3	−2.2															
1988	5.7	3.2	8.6														
1989	10.0	9.8	15.8	23.0													
1990	5.8	4.5	6.8	5.8	−11.3												
1991	8.7	8.2	10.8	11.6	5.9	23.1											
1992	7.6	7.1	9.0	9.1	4.4	12.3	1.4										
1993	7.2	6.7	8.2	8.1	4.4	9.7	2.9	4.5									
1994	5.9	5.3	6.4	6.0	2.6	6.1	0.4	−0.1	−4.8								
1995	8.4	8.1	9.4	9.5	7.3	11.0	8.0	10.1	13.0	30.7							
1996	9.2	9.0	10.3	10.5	8.7	12.0	9.8	11.9	14.4	24.0	17.3						
1997	10.7	10.7	12.0	12.3	11.0	14.2	12.7	15.0	17.6	25.1	22.2	27.2					
1998	11.7	11.7	13.0	13.4	12.4	15.3	14.2	16.4	18.7	24.6	22.6	25.3	23.3				
1999	11.9	12.0	13.2	13.7	12.7	15.4	14.4	16.3	18.2	22.8	20.9	22.1	19.5	15.7			
2000	10.1	10.1	11.0	11.2	10.2	12.3	11.1	12.3	13.5	16.5	13.6	12.7	7.9	0.2	−15.3		
2001	8.5	8.3	9.1	9.1	8.0	9.7	8.4	9.2	9.8	11.8	8.7	7.0	1.9	−5.2	−15.7	−16.2	
2002	6.5	6.2	6.7	6.6	5.4	6.7	5.3	5.6	5.8	7.1	3.7	1.5	−3.7	−10.4	−19.2	−21.1	−26.1

*S&P 500 total returns minus intermediate-term government bond income returns.

Table A-3 (Page 1 of 6)

Short-Horizon Equity Risk Premia*

Percent per annum arithmetic mean risk premia
for all historical time periods.

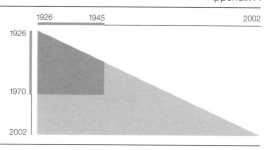

from 1926 to 2002

To the end of	From the beginning of 1926	1927	1928	1929	1930	1931	1932	1933	1934	1935	1936	1937	1938	1939	1940	1941	1942	1943	1944	1945
1926	8.4																			
1927	21.4	34.4																		
1928	27.6	37.2	40.1																	
1929	17.4	20.4	13.4	−13.2																
1930	8.5	8.5	−0.1	−20.2	−27.3															
1931	−0.4	−2.1	−11.2	−28.3	−35.9	−44.4														
1932	−1.6	−3.3	−10.8	−23.5	−27.0	−26.8	−9.2													
1933	5.3	4.9	0.0	−8.1	−6.8	0.0	22.3	53.7												
1934	4.5	4.1	−0.3	−7.0	−5.8	−0.4	14.3	26.0	−1.6											
1935	8.8	8.9	5.7	0.8	3.1	9.2	22.6	33.2	22.9	47.5										
1936	11.1	11.4	8.8	4.9	7.5	13.3	24.8	33.3	26.5	40.6	33.7									
1937	7.2	7.1	4.4	0.4	2.1	6.3	14.8	19.6	11.1	15.3	−0.8	−35.3								
1938	9.1	9.1	6.8	3.5	5.4	9.4	17.1	21.5	15.1	19.3	9.8	−2.1	31.1							
1939	8.4	8.4	6.2	3.2	4.8	8.3	14.9	18.4	12.5	15.3	7.3	−1.5	15.4	−0.4						
1940	7.2	7.1	5.0	2.1	3.5	6.5	12.2	14.9	9.3	11.1	3.9	−3.6	7.0	−5.1	−9.8					
1941	6.0	5.8	3.8	1.0	2.2	4.9	9.8	11.9	6.7	7.9	1.3	−5.2	2.3	−7.3	−10.7	−11.7				
1942	6.8	6.7	4.9	2.4	3.6	6.1	10.7	12.7	8.2	9.4	4.0	−1.0	5.9	−0.4	−0.5	4.2	20.1			
1943	7.9	7.8	6.2	3.9	5.1	7.6	12.0	13.9	9.9	11.2	6.7	2.8	9.1	4.8	6.0	11.3	22.8	25.6		
1944	8.5	8.5	7.0	4.9	6.1	8.5	12.6	14.4	10.8	12.0	8.1	4.9	10.6	7.2	8.7	13.3	21.7	22.5	19.4	
1945	9.9	9.9	8.6	6.7	8.0	10.3	14.2	16.0	12.9	14.2	10.9	8.3	13.8	11.3	13.3	17.9	25.3	27.0	27.8	36.1
1946	9.0	9.0	7.7	5.9	7.0	9.2	12.7	14.3	11.3	12.3	9.1	6.7	11.3	8.9	10.2	13.5	18.5	18.2	15.7	13.8
1947	8.8	8.8	7.6	5.9	6.9	8.9	12.3	13.7	10.8	11.8	8.8	6.5	10.7	8.5	9.6	12.3	16.3	15.6	13.1	11.0
1948	8.6	8.6	7.4	5.8	6.8	8.7	11.8	13.1	10.4	11.3	8.5	6.4	10.2	8.1	9.0	11.4	14.7	13.8	11.4	9.4
1949	9.0	9.0	7.9	6.4	7.3	9.2	12.1	13.4	10.9	11.7	9.1	7.2	10.8	8.9	9.9	12.1	15.0	14.3	12.4	11.1
1950	9.9	9.9	8.9	7.5	8.4	10.2	13.1	14.3	12.0	12.9	10.6	8.9	12.3	10.7	11.8	13.9	16.8	16.3	15.0	14.3
1951	10.4	10.4	9.4	8.1	9.1	10.8	13.6	14.8	12.6	13.4	11.3	9.8	13.0	11.7	12.7	14.7	17.3	17.0	16.0	15.5
1952	10.6	10.7	9.7	8.5	9.4	11.1	13.7	14.9	12.8	13.6	11.6	10.2	13.3	12.0	13.0	14.9	17.3	17.0	16.0	15.6
1953	10.1	10.2	9.3	8.0	8.9	10.5	13.0	14.0	12.0	12.8	10.8	9.5	12.3	11.0	11.8	13.5	15.6	15.2	14.2	13.6
1954	11.6	11.7	10.8	9.7	10.6	12.2	14.7	15.7	13.9	14.7	13.0	11.8	14.6	13.6	14.5	16.2	18.4	18.2	17.6	17.4
1955	12.2	12.3	11.5	10.5	11.4	12.9	15.3	16.4	14.7	15.4	13.8	12.8	15.5	14.5	15.5	17.2	19.2	19.1	18.6	18.5
1956	11.9	12.0	11.3	10.2	11.1	12.6	14.8	15.8	14.2	14.9	13.4	12.4	14.9	14.0	14.8	16.3	18.2	18.1	17.5	17.3
1957	11.1	11.2	10.4	9.4	10.2	11.6	13.7	14.7	13.0	13.7	12.1	11.1	13.4	12.5	13.2	14.6	16.2	15.9	15.3	14.9
1958	12.0	12.1	11.4	10.5	11.3	12.7	14.8	15.7	14.2	14.8	13.4	12.5	14.8	14.0	14.7	16.1	17.7	17.6	17.0	16.9
1959	11.9	12.0	11.4	10.4	11.2	12.5	14.6	15.5	14.0	14.6	13.2	12.3	14.5	13.7	14.4	15.7	17.2	17.1	16.5	16.3
1960	11.5	11.6	10.9	10.0	10.8	12.1	14.0	14.8	13.4	14.0	12.6	11.7	13.8	13.0	13.6	14.8	16.2	16.0	15.4	15.2
1961	11.9	12.0	11.3	10.5	11.2	12.5	14.4	15.2	13.8	14.4	13.1	12.3	14.2	13.5	14.1	15.3	16.6	16.4	15.9	15.7
1962	11.3	11.4	10.7	9.8	10.5	11.7	13.5	14.3	12.9	13.4	12.2	11.3	13.2	12.5	13.0	14.1	15.3	15.1	14.5	14.2
1963	11.5	11.6	10.9	10.1	10.8	12.0	13.7	14.5	13.1	13.7	12.4	11.7	13.5	12.8	13.3	14.3	15.5	15.3	14.8	14.5
1964	11.5	11.6	11.0	10.2	10.9	12.0	13.7	14.4	13.1	13.6	12.5	11.7	13.4	12.8	13.3	14.3	15.4	15.2	14.7	14.4
1965	11.5	11.5	10.9	10.1	10.8	11.9	13.5	14.2	13.0	13.5	12.3	11.6	13.3	12.6	13.1	14.0	15.1	14.9	14.4	14.2
1966	10.8	10.9	10.3	9.5	10.1	11.1	12.7	13.4	12.2	12.6	11.5	10.7	12.3	11.6	12.1	12.9	13.9	13.6	13.1	12.8
1967	11.0	11.1	10.5	9.8	10.4	11.4	12.9	13.6	12.4	12.8	11.7	11.0	12.5	11.9	12.3	13.2	14.1	13.9	13.4	13.1
1968	10.9	11.0	10.4	9.7	10.2	11.2	12.7	13.3	12.2	12.6	11.5	10.8	12.3	11.7	12.1	12.9	13.8	13.6	13.1	12.8
1969	10.3	10.4	9.8	9.1	9.6	10.6	12.0	12.6	11.4	11.8	10.8	10.1	11.5	10.8	11.2	11.9	12.8	12.5	12.0	11.7
1970	10.0	10.1	9.5	8.8	9.3	10.2	11.6	12.2	11.1	11.4	10.4	9.7	11.1	10.4	10.8	11.5	12.3	12.0	11.5	11.2

*S&P 500 total returns minus 30-day Treasury bill total returns. For 30-day Treasury bills, the income return and total return are the same.

Table A-3 (Page 2 of 6)

Short-Horizon Equity Risk Premia*

Percent per annum arithmetic mean risk premia
for all historical time periods.

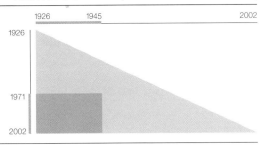

from 1926 to 2002

To the end of	From the beginning of 1926	1927	1928	1929	1930	1931	1932	1933	1934	1935	1936	1937	1938	1939	1940	1941	1942	1943	1944	1945
1971	10.0	10.1	9.5	8.8	9.3	10.2	11.6	12.1	11.0	11.4	10.4	9.7	11.0	10.4	10.7	11.4	12.2	11.9	11.4	11.1
1972	10.1	10.2	9.6	8.9	9.5	10.3	11.7	12.2	11.1	11.5	10.5	9.8	11.1	10.5	10.9	11.5	12.3	12.0	11.5	11.3
1973	9.5	9.5	9.0	8.3	8.8	9.6	10.9	11.4	10.3	10.6	9.6	9.0	10.2	9.6	9.9	10.5	11.2	10.9	10.4	10.1
1974	8.6	8.6	8.0	7.3	7.8	8.6	9.8	10.3	9.2	9.5	8.5	7.9	9.0	8.4	8.7	9.2	9.8	9.5	9.0	8.6
1975	9.0	9.1	8.5	7.9	8.3	9.1	10.3	10.8	9.7	10.0	9.1	8.5	9.6	9.0	9.3	9.8	10.5	10.2	9.7	9.4
1976	9.2	9.2	8.7	8.1	8.5	9.3	10.5	11.0	10.0	10.2	9.3	8.7	9.8	9.3	9.5	10.1	10.7	10.4	10.0	9.7
1977	8.8	8.8	8.3	7.7	8.1	8.9	10.0	10.4	9.5	9.7	8.8	8.2	9.3	8.7	9.0	9.5	10.1	9.8	9.3	9.0
1978	8.6	8.6	8.1	7.5	7.9	8.7	9.8	10.2	9.2	9.5	8.6	8.0	9.0	8.5	8.7	9.2	9.8	9.5	9.0	8.7
1979	8.6	8.6	8.1	7.5	7.9	8.6	9.7	10.1	9.2	9.4	8.6	8.0	9.0	8.5	8.7	9.2	9.7	9.5	9.0	8.7
1980	8.9	8.9	8.4	7.8	8.2	8.9	10.0	10.4	9.5	9.7	8.9	8.3	9.3	8.8	9.0	9.5	10.0	9.8	9.3	9.1
1981	8.3	8.3	7.9	7.3	7.6	8.3	9.4	9.8	8.9	9.1	8.2	7.7	8.6	8.1	8.3	8.8	9.3	9.0	8.6	8.3
1982	8.4	8.4	7.9	7.3	7.7	8.4	9.4	9.8	8.9	9.1	8.3	7.7	8.7	8.2	8.4	8.8	9.3	9.1	8.6	8.3
1983	8.5	8.5	8.0	7.4	7.8	8.5	9.5	9.9	9.0	9.2	8.4	7.9	8.8	8.3	8.5	8.9	9.4	9.2	8.8	8.5
1984	8.3	8.3	7.8	7.2	7.6	8.3	9.3	9.6	8.7	8.9	8.2	7.6	8.5	8.1	8.2	8.7	9.1	8.9	8.5	8.2
1985	8.5	8.5	8.1	7.5	7.9	8.6	9.5	9.9	9.0	9.3	8.5	8.0	8.9	8.4	8.6	9.0	9.5	9.2	8.8	8.6
1986	8.6	8.6	8.2	7.6	8.0	8.6	9.6	9.9	9.1	9.3	8.6	8.1	8.9	8.5	8.7	9.1	9.5	9.3	8.9	8.7
1987	8.5	8.5	8.0	7.5	7.8	8.5	9.4	9.7	8.9	9.1	8.4	7.9	8.8	8.3	8.5	8.9	9.3	9.1	8.7	8.5
1988	8.5	8.5	8.1	7.5	7.9	8.5	9.4	9.8	9.0	9.2	8.4	7.9	8.8	8.3	8.5	8.9	9.3	9.1	8.7	8.5
1989	8.7	8.7	8.3	7.8	8.1	8.7	9.7	10.0	9.2	9.4	8.7	8.2	9.1	8.6	8.8	9.2	9.6	9.4	9.1	8.8
1990	8.4	8.4	8.0	7.5	7.8	8.4	9.3	9.6	8.9	9.0	8.3	7.9	8.7	8.3	8.4	8.8	9.2	9.0	8.6	8.4
1991	8.7	8.7	8.3	7.8	8.1	8.7	9.6	9.9	9.1	9.3	8.6	8.2	9.0	8.6	8.7	9.1	9.5	9.3	9.0	8.8
1992	8.6	8.6	8.2	7.7	8.0	8.6	9.5	9.8	9.1	9.2	8.6	8.1	8.9	8.5	8.7	9.0	9.4	9.2	8.9	8.7
1993	8.6	8.6	8.2	7.7	8.0	8.6	9.4	9.8	9.0	9.2	8.5	8.1	8.9	8.5	8.6	9.0	9.4	9.2	8.8	8.6
1994	8.4	8.4	8.0	7.5	7.9	8.4	9.3	9.6	8.8	9.0	8.4	7.9	8.7	8.3	8.4	8.8	9.2	8.9	8.6	8.4
1995	8.8	8.8	8.4	7.9	8.2	8.8	9.6	9.9	9.2	9.4	8.7	8.3	9.1	8.7	8.8	9.2	9.6	9.4	9.1	8.9
1996	8.9	8.9	8.5	8.1	8.4	8.9	9.7	10.0	9.3	9.5	8.9	8.5	9.2	8.8	9.0	9.3	9.7	9.5	9.2	9.0
1997	9.2	9.2	8.8	8.3	8.7	9.2	10.0	10.3	9.6	9.8	9.2	8.8	9.5	9.2	9.3	9.7	10.1	9.9	9.6	9.4
1998	9.4	9.4	9.0	8.6	8.9	9.4	10.2	10.5	9.8	10.0	9.4	9.0	9.8	9.4	9.6	9.9	10.3	10.1	9.8	9.7
1999	9.4	9.5	9.1	8.7	9.0	9.5	10.3	10.6	9.9	10.1	9.5	9.2	9.9	9.5	9.7	10.0	10.4	10.2	10.0	9.8
2000	9.1	9.1	8.8	8.3	8.7	9.2	9.9	10.2	9.6	9.7	9.2	8.8	9.5	9.1	9.3	9.6	10.0	9.8	9.5	9.3
2001	8.8	8.8	8.5	8.0	8.3	8.8	9.6	9.8	9.2	9.4	8.8	8.4	9.1	8.7	8.9	9.2	9.5	9.4	9.1	8.9
2002	8.4	8.4	8.0	7.6	7.9	8.4	9.1	9.4	8.7	8.9	8.3	7.9	8.6	8.2	8.4	8.7	9.0	8.8	8.5	8.3

*S&P 500 total returns minus 30-day Treasury bill total returns. For 30-day Treasury bills, the income return and total return are the same.

Table A-3 (Page 3 of 6)

Short-Horizon Equity Risk Premia*

Percent per annum arithmetic mean risk premia
for all historical time periods.

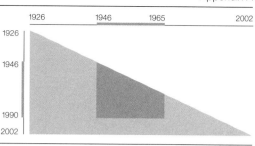

from 1926 to 2002

To the end of	From the beginning of 1946	1947	1948	1949	1950	1951	1952	1953	1954	1955	1956	1957	1958	1959	1960	1961	1962	1963	1964	1965
1946	-8.4																			
1947	-1.6	5.2																		
1948	0.5	4.9	4.7																	
1949	4.8	9.2	11.2	17.7																
1950	9.9	14.5	17.6	24.1	30.5															
1951	12.0	16.1	18.9	23.6	26.5	22.5														
1952	12.7	16.2	18.4	21.9	23.3	19.6	16.7													
1953	10.8	13.5	14.9	16.9	16.7	12.1	6.9	-2.8												
1954	15.3	18.3	20.2	22.7	23.7	22.0	21.9	24.5	51.8											
1955	16.8	19.6	21.4	23.8	24.8	23.6	23.9	26.3	40.9	30.0										
1956	15.6	18.0	19.5	21.3	21.8	20.4	19.9	20.8	28.6	17.0	4.1									
1957	13.2	15.1	16.1	17.4	17.4	15.5	14.3	13.8	18.0	6.7	-4.9	-13.9								
1958	15.4	17.4	18.5	19.8	20.1	18.8	18.2	18.5	22.7	15.5	10.7	14.0	41.8							
1959	14.9	16.7	17.7	18.9	19.0	17.7	17.1	17.1	20.5	14.2	10.3	12.3	25.4	9.0						
1960	13.8	15.4	16.1	17.1	17.0	15.7	14.9	14.7	17.2	11.5	7.8	8.7	16.2	3.4	-2.2					
1961	14.5	16.0	16.8	17.7	17.7	16.5	15.9	15.8	18.2	13.4	10.6	11.9	18.3	10.5	11.3	24.8				
1962	12.9	14.3	14.9	15.6	15.4	14.2	13.4	13.1	14.9	10.3	7.4	8.0	12.4	5.0	3.7	6.6	-11.5			
1963	13.3	14.6	15.2	15.9	15.7	14.6	14.0	13.7	15.4	11.3	9.0	9.7	13.6	8.0	7.7	11.0	4.1	19.7		
1964	13.3	14.5	15.0	15.7	15.6	14.5	13.9	13.6	15.1	11.5	9.4	10.1	13.5	8.8	8.7	11.5	7.1	16.3	12.9	
1965	13.1	14.2	14.7	15.3	15.1	14.1	13.5	13.2	14.6	11.2	9.3	9.9	12.9	8.8	8.7	10.9	7.4	13.7	10.7	8.5
1966	11.7	12.7	13.1	13.6	13.4	12.3	11.6	11.2	12.3	9.0	7.1	7.4	9.8	5.8	5.3	6.6	3.0	6.6	2.2	-3.1
1967	12.1	13.1	13.5	13.9	13.7	12.7	12.1	11.8	12.9	9.9	8.2	8.6	10.8	7.4	7.2	8.5	5.8	9.2	6.6	4.5
1968	11.8	12.7	13.1	13.5	13.3	12.3	11.7	11.4	12.4	9.6	8.0	8.3	10.4	7.2	7.0	8.2	5.8	8.7	6.5	4.8
1969	10.7	11.5	11.8	12.2	11.9	10.9	10.3	9.9	10.7	7.9	6.4	6.5	8.2	5.2	4.8	5.6	3.2	5.3	2.9	0.8
1970	10.2	10.9	11.2	11.5	11.2	10.2	9.6	9.2	9.9	7.3	5.8	5.9	7.4	4.5	4.1	4.8	2.5	4.3	2.1	0.3
1971	10.2	10.9	11.1	11.4	11.1	10.2	9.6	9.2	9.9	7.4	6.0	6.2	7.6	5.0	4.6	5.2	3.3	4.9	3.1	1.7
1972	10.3	11.1	11.3	11.6	11.3	10.4	9.9	9.5	10.2	7.9	6.6	6.7	8.1	5.7	5.4	6.1	4.4	5.9	4.4	3.3
1973	9.2	9.9	10.0	10.3	9.9	9.0	8.4	8.0	8.6	6.3	5.0	5.0	6.2	3.9	3.5	3.9	2.2	3.4	1.8	0.6
1974	7.7	8.3	8.4	8.5	8.2	7.2	6.6	6.1	6.5	4.3	2.9	2.9	3.8	1.5	1.0	1.2	-0.6	0.3	-1.5	-2.9
1975	8.5	9.1	9.2	9.4	9.1	8.2	7.6	7.2	7.7	5.6	4.3	4.4	5.4	3.2	2.9	3.2	1.7	2.7	1.3	0.2
1976	8.8	9.4	9.5	9.7	9.4	8.6	8.1	7.7	8.1	6.2	5.0	5.1	6.1	4.1	3.8	4.2	2.8	3.8	2.6	1.7
1977	8.2	8.7	8.8	9.0	8.6	7.8	7.3	6.9	7.3	5.4	4.2	4.2	5.2	3.2	2.9	3.2	1.9	2.7	1.5	0.7
1978	7.9	8.4	8.5	8.6	8.3	7.5	7.0	6.6	7.0	5.1	4.0	4.0	4.9	3.0	2.7	3.0	1.7	2.5	1.4	0.6
1979	7.9	8.4	8.5	8.6	8.3	7.5	7.0	6.7	7.0	5.2	4.2	4.2	5.0	3.3	3.0	3.3	2.1	2.9	1.8	1.1
1980	8.3	8.8	8.9	9.0	8.7	8.0	7.5	7.2	7.5	5.8	4.9	4.9	5.7	4.1	3.9	4.2	3.1	3.9	2.9	2.3
1981	7.5	8.0	8.0	8.1	7.8	7.1	6.6	6.3	6.6	4.9	3.9	3.9	4.7	3.1	2.8	3.0	1.9	2.6	1.7	1.0
1982	7.6	8.0	8.1	8.2	7.9	7.2	6.7	6.4	6.7	5.1	4.2	4.2	4.9	3.4	3.1	3.4	2.4	3.1	2.2	1.6
1983	7.8	8.2	8.3	8.4	8.1	7.4	7.0	6.6	7.0	5.4	4.5	4.5	5.3	3.8	3.6	3.8	2.9	3.6	2.8	2.2
1984	7.5	7.9	8.0	8.0	7.8	7.1	6.6	6.3	6.6	5.1	4.3	4.3	4.9	3.5	3.3	3.5	2.6	3.2	2.5	1.9
1985	7.9	8.3	8.4	8.5	8.2	7.6	7.2	6.9	7.2	5.7	4.9	5.0	5.6	4.3	4.1	4.4	3.5	4.2	3.5	3.0
1986	8.0	8.4	8.5	8.6	8.3	7.7	7.3	7.0	7.3	5.9	5.2	5.2	5.9	4.6	4.4	4.7	3.9	4.5	3.8	3.4
1987	7.8	8.2	8.3	8.4	8.1	7.5	7.1	6.8	7.1	5.8	5.0	5.0	5.7	4.4	4.2	4.5	3.7	4.3	3.7	3.3
1988	7.9	8.3	8.3	8.4	8.2	7.6	7.2	6.9	7.2	5.9	5.2	5.2	5.8	4.6	4.5	4.7	4.0	4.5	3.9	3.6
1989	8.2	8.6	8.7	8.8	8.6	8.0	7.6	7.4	7.6	6.4	5.7	5.7	6.4	5.2	5.1	5.3	4.6	5.2	4.7	4.3
1990	7.8	8.2	8.2	8.3	8.1	7.5	7.1	6.9	7.1	5.9	5.2	5.2	5.8	4.7	4.6	4.8	4.1	4.7	4.1	3.8

*S&P 500 total returns minus 30-day Treasury bill total returns. For 30-day Treasury bills, the income return and total return are the same.

Table A-3 (Page 4 of 6)

Short-Horizon Equity Risk Premia*

Percent per annum arithmetic mean risk premia
for all historical time periods.

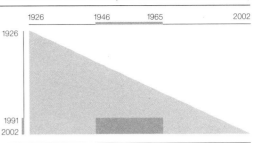

from 1926 to 2002

To the end of	From the beginning of																			
	1946	1947	1948	1949	1950	1951	1952	1953	1954	1955	1956	1957	1958	1959	1960	1961	1962	1963	1964	1965
1991	8.2	8.5	8.6	8.7	8.5	7.9	7.6	7.3	7.6	6.4	5.8	5.8	6.4	5.3	5.2	5.4	4.8	5.4	4.8	4.5
1992	8.1	8.4	8.5	8.6	8.4	7.9	7.5	7.3	7.5	6.4	5.7	5.8	6.3	5.3	5.2	5.4	4.8	5.3	4.8	4.5
1993	8.1	8.4	8.5	8.6	8.3	7.8	7.5	7.3	7.5	6.4	5.8	5.8	6.3	5.3	5.2	5.4	4.8	5.4	4.9	4.6
1994	7.8	8.2	8.2	8.3	8.1	7.6	7.2	7.0	7.3	6.2	5.5	5.6	6.1	5.1	5.0	5.2	4.6	5.1	4.7	4.4
1995	8.3	8.7	8.7	8.8	8.6	8.1	7.8	7.6	7.8	6.8	6.2	6.3	6.8	5.8	5.7	6.0	5.4	5.9	5.5	5.3
1996	8.5	8.8	8.9	9.0	8.8	8.3	8.0	7.8	8.1	7.0	6.5	6.5	7.1	6.2	6.1	6.3	5.8	6.3	5.9	5.7
1997	8.9	9.2	9.3	9.4	9.2	8.8	8.5	8.3	8.5	7.5	7.0	7.1	7.6	6.7	6.7	6.9	6.4	6.9	6.5	6.3
1998	9.2	9.5	9.6	9.7	9.5	9.1	8.8	8.6	8.9	7.9	7.4	7.5	8.0	7.1	7.1	7.3	6.9	7.4	7.0	6.8
1999	9.3	9.6	9.7	9.8	9.7	9.2	8.9	8.8	9.0	8.1	7.6	7.7	8.2	7.4	7.3	7.6	7.1	7.6	7.3	7.1
2000	8.9	9.2	9.2	9.3	9.2	8.7	8.5	8.3	8.5	7.6	7.1	7.2	7.6	6.8	6.8	7.0	6.5	7.0	6.7	6.5
2001	8.4	8.7	8.8	8.9	8.7	8.3	8.0	7.8	8.0	7.1	6.6	6.6	7.1	6.3	6.2	6.4	6.0	6.4	6.1	5.9
2002	7.8	8.1	8.2	8.3	8.1	7.6	7.4	7.2	7.4	6.4	5.9	6.0	6.4	5.6	5.5	5.7	5.3	5.7	5.3	5.1

*S&P 500 total returns minus 30-day Treasury bill total returns. For 30-day Treasury bills, the income return and total return are the same.

Table A-3 (Page 5 of 6)

Short-Horizon Equity Risk Premia*

Percent per annum arithmetic mean risk premia
for all historical time periods.

from 1926 to 2002

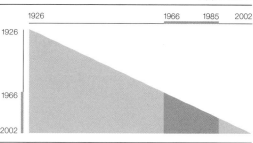

To the end of	From the beginning of																			
	1966	1967	1968	1969	1970	1971	1972	1973	1974	1975	1976	1977	1978	1979	1980	1981	1982	1983	1984	1985
1966	-14.8																			
1967	2.5	19.8																		
1968	3.6	12.8	5.9																	
1969	-1.1	3.5	-4.6	-15.1																
1970	-1.4	2.0	-3.9	-8.8	-2.5															
1971	0.5	3.6	-0.5	-2.6	3.7	9.9														
1972	2.6	5.5	2.7	1.9	7.5	12.5	15.1													
1973	-0.4	1.6	-1.4	-2.8	0.2	1.2	-3.2	-21.6												
1974	-4.2	-2.9	-6.1	-8.1	-6.7	-7.7	-13.6	-28.0	-34.5											
1975	-0.6	0.9	-1.4	-2.5	-0.4	0.1	-2.4	-8.2	-1.5	31.4										
1976	1.1	2.7	0.8	0.2	2.4	3.2	1.8	-1.5	5.2	25.1	18.8									
1977	0.0	1.4	-0.5	-1.2	0.5	1.0	-0.5	-3.6	0.8	12.6	3.2	-12.3								
1978	0.0	1.2	-0.5	-1.1	0.4	0.8	-0.5	-3.1	0.6	9.3	1.9	-6.5	-0.6							
1979	0.5	1.7	0.2	-0.3	1.2	1.6	0.5	-1.5	1.8	9.1	3.5	-1.6	3.7	8.1						
1980	1.9	3.1	1.8	1.5	3.0	3.5	2.8	1.3	4.6	11.1	7.0	4.1	9.5	14.6	21.2					
1981	0.6	1.6	0.3	-0.1	1.1	1.4	0.6	-1.0	1.5	6.7	2.6	-0.7	2.3	3.2	0.8	-19.6				
1982	1.2	2.2	1.0	0.7	1.9	2.2	1.5	0.2	2.6	7.2	3.8	1.3	4.0	5.1	4.1	-4.4	10.9			
1983	1.9	2.9	1.8	1.5	2.7	3.1	2.5	1.4	3.7	7.9	5.0	3.0	5.6	6.8	6.5	1.7	12.3	13.7		
1984	1.6	2.5	1.5	1.2	2.3	2.6	2.1	1.0	3.0	6.8	4.1	2.2	4.3	5.1	4.5	0.3	7.0	5.1	-3.6	
1985	2.7	3.6	2.8	2.6	3.7	4.1	3.7	2.8	4.8	8.4	6.1	4.7	6.8	7.9	7.8	5.2	11.4	11.5	10.4	24.4
1986	3.2	4.1	3.3	3.1	4.2	4.6	4.2	3.5	5.4	8.7	6.7	5.4	7.4	8.4	8.5	6.4	11.5	11.7	11.1	18.4
1987	3.0	3.9	3.1	2.9	3.9	4.3	4.0	3.2	5.0	8.0	6.1	4.9	6.7	7.5	7.4	5.4	9.6	9.3	8.2	12.2
1988	3.3	4.2	3.4	3.3	4.3	4.7	4.3	3.7	5.4	8.2	6.4	5.4	7.0	7.8	7.7	6.0	9.7	9.5	8.7	11.7
1989	4.2	5.0	4.3	4.3	5.2	5.6	5.4	4.8	6.5	9.2	7.6	6.8	8.3	9.2	9.3	7.9	11.4	11.5	11.1	14.0
1990	3.6	4.3	3.7	3.6	4.4	4.8	4.5	3.9	5.4	7.9	6.4	5.5	6.9	7.5	7.4	6.0	8.9	8.7	7.9	9.9
1991	4.4	5.2	4.5	4.5	5.4	5.8	5.5	5.0	6.5	8.9	7.5	6.8	8.1	8.8	8.9	7.8	10.5	10.5	10.1	12.0
1992	4.4	5.1	4.5	4.5	5.3	5.7	5.5	5.0	6.4	8.7	7.3	6.6	7.9	8.5	8.5	7.5	9.9	9.8	9.4	11.0
1993	4.5	5.2	4.6	4.6	5.4	5.7	5.6	5.1	6.4	8.6	7.3	6.6	7.8	8.4	8.4	7.4	9.7	9.6	9.2	10.6
1994	4.2	4.9	4.4	4.3	5.1	5.4	5.2	4.8	6.0	8.0	6.8	6.1	7.2	7.7	7.7	6.7	8.7	8.6	8.1	9.3
1995	5.2	5.8	5.3	5.3	6.1	6.5	6.3	5.9	7.2	9.2	8.1	7.5	8.6	9.1	9.2	8.4	10.4	10.4	10.1	11.3
1996	5.6	6.2	5.8	5.8	6.5	6.9	6.8	6.4	7.6	9.6	8.5	8.0	9.1	9.6	9.7	9.0	10.9	10.9	10.7	11.9
1997	6.3	6.9	6.5	6.5	7.3	7.7	7.6	7.3	8.5	10.4	9.4	9.0	10.0	10.6	10.7	10.1	12.0	12.0	11.9	13.1
1998	6.8	7.5	7.1	7.1	7.9	8.3	8.2	7.9	9.1	10.9	10.0	9.6	10.7	11.2	11.4	10.9	12.7	12.8	12.7	13.9
1999	7.1	7.7	7.4	7.4	8.2	8.5	8.5	8.2	9.4	11.1	10.3	9.9	10.9	11.5	11.7	11.2	12.9	13.0	12.9	14.0
2000	6.4	7.1	6.7	6.7	7.4	7.7	7.7	7.4	8.5	10.1	9.3	8.9	9.8	10.3	10.4	9.8	11.4	11.4	11.3	12.2
2001	5.8	6.4	6.0	6.0	6.7	7.0	6.9	6.6	7.6	9.2	8.3	7.9	8.7	9.2	9.2	8.6	10.0	10.0	9.8	10.6
2002	5.0	5.6	5.2	5.2	5.8	6.0	5.9	5.6	6.5	8.0	7.1	6.7	7.4	7.8	7.8	7.2	8.4	8.3	8.0	8.7

*S&P 500 total returns minus 30-day Treasury bill total returns. For 30-day Treasury bills, the income return and total return are the same.

Table A-3 (Page 6 of 6)

Short-Horizon Equity Risk Premia*

Percent per annum arithmetic mean risk premia
for all historical time periods.

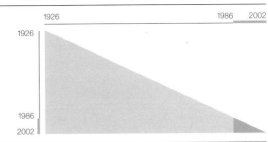

from 1926 to 2002

To the end of	From the beginning of 1986	1987	1988	1989	1990	1991	1992	1993	1994	1995	1996	1997	1998	1999	2000	2001	2002
1986	12.3																
1987	6.0	-0.2															
1988	7.5	5.1	10.5														
1989	11.4	11.1	16.8	23.1													
1990	6.9	5.6	7.5	6.1	-11.0												
1991	9.9	9.5	11.9	12.4	7.0	25.0											
1992	9.1	8.6	10.3	10.3	6.0	14.6	4.2										
1993	8.9	8.4	9.8	9.7	6.3	12.1	5.6	7.1									
1994	7.6	7.0	8.0	7.6	4.5	8.4	2.9	2.2	-2.6								
1995	10.0	9.8	11.0	11.1	9.1	13.1	10.1	12.1	14.6	31.8							
1996	10.7	10.6	11.8	11.9	10.3	13.9	11.7	13.5	15.7	24.9	17.9						
1997	12.2	12.2	13.4	13.7	12.6	15.9	14.4	16.5	18.8	25.9	23.0	28.1					
1998	13.1	13.1	14.3	14.7	13.8	16.9	15.7	17.7	19.8	25.4	23.2	25.9	23.7				
1999	13.3	13.4	14.5	14.9	14.1	16.8	15.8	17.5	19.2	23.6	21.5	22.7	20.0	16.4			
2000	11.4	11.3	12.2	12.4	11.4	13.7	12.4	13.4	14.3	17.1	14.2	13.3	8.4	0.7	-15.0		
2001	9.7	9.5	10.2	10.2	9.2	11.0	9.6	10.2	10.6	12.5	9.2	7.5	2.3	-4.8	-15.4	-15.7	
2002	7.7	7.5	8.0	7.8	6.6	8.1	6.6	6.8	6.8	7.9	4.5	2.3	-2.9	-9.5	-18.2	-19.7	-23.8

*S&P 500 total returns minus 30-day Treasury bill total returns. For 30-day Treasury bills, the income return and total return are the same.

Table A-4 (Page 1 of 6)

Mid-Cap Size Premia*

Percent per annum risk premia for all historical time periods.

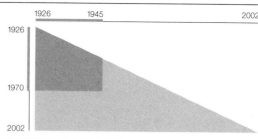

from 1926 to 2002

To the end of	From the beginning of																			
	1926	1927	1928	1929	1930	1931	1932	1933	1934	1935	1936	1937	1938	1939	1940	1941	1942	1943	1944	1945
1926																				
1927																				
1928																				
1929																				
1930	-8.5																			
1931	-7.7	-7.4																		
1932	-6.2	-5.6	-5.5																	
1933	0.0	1.6	3.1	5.4																
1934	1.5	3.0	4.6	6.9	11.8															
1935	0.1	1.3	2.4	4.0	7.4	9.9														
1936	-0.1	1.0	1.9	3.2	6.0	7.8	8.0													
1937	-0.2	0.8	1.6	2.7	5.2	6.6	6.7	6.7												
1938	0.0	0.9	1.6	2.7	4.8	6.0	5.9	5.9	-0.3											
1939	-0.1	0.7	1.5	2.4	4.3	5.3	5.1	4.8	-0.6	-3.1										
1940	0.3	1.1	1.8	2.7	4.5	5.4	5.3	5.2	0.5	-1.5	0.9									
1941	0.6	1.4	2.1	2.9	4.5	5.4	5.3	5.3	1.2	-0.5	1.7	2.7								
1942	0.5	1.2	1.7	2.5	4.0	4.7	4.6	4.5	0.7	-0.7	1.0	1.6	2.0							
1943	0.9	1.6	2.2	2.9	4.3	5.0	4.9	4.8	1.5	0.3	2.0	2.6	3.1	3.4						
1944	1.3	1.9	2.5	3.2	4.5	5.1	5.0	4.9	2.0	1.0	2.5	3.1	3.5	3.9	5.1					
1945	2.0	2.6	3.2	3.9	5.1	5.7	5.6	5.5	3.0	2.2	3.7	4.4	4.9	5.3	6.9	7.1				
1946	1.8	2.5	3.0	3.6	4.8	5.4	5.3	5.2	2.7	2.0	3.3	3.9	4.3	4.6	5.7	5.5	5.4			
1947	1.5	2.1	2.6	3.2	4.2	4.8	4.6	4.5	2.2	1.4	2.6	3.1	3.3	3.5	4.3	3.9	3.4	3.9		
1948	1.2	1.8	2.2	2.7	3.7	4.2	4.0	3.9	1.7	1.0	2.0	2.4	2.6	2.7	3.3	3.0	2.6	3.0	2.1	
1949	1.2	1.8	2.2	2.7	3.6	4.0	3.8	3.7	1.7	1.0	2.0	2.3	2.5	2.5	3.2	2.8	2.4	2.7	2.0	1.1
1950	1.0	1.4	1.8	2.3	3.1	3.5	3.3	3.1	1.2	0.6	1.4	1.7	1.8	1.8	2.4	2.0	1.6	1.6	0.9	0.0
1951	0.6	1.0	1.4	1.8	2.6	2.9	2.7	2.5	0.7	0.1	0.8	1.0	1.1	1.0	1.6	1.2	0.8	0.7	-0.1	-1.0
1952	0.3	0.7	1.0	1.4	2.1	2.4	2.1	1.9	0.2	-0.4	0.3	0.4	0.4	0.4	1.0	0.6	0.1	0.0	-0.8	-1.7
1953	0.3	0.7	1.0	1.3	2.0	2.3	2.1	1.9	0.3	-0.3	0.3	0.4	0.5	0.5	1.0	0.7	0.3	0.2	-0.4	-1.2
1954	0.2	0.6	0.8	1.2	1.8	2.1	1.8	1.6	0.2	-0.3	0.2	0.3	0.4	0.4	1.0	0.8	0.6	0.4	-0.1	-0.8
1955	-0.3	0.0	0.3	0.5	1.1	1.4	1.1	0.9	-0.4	-0.9	-0.4	-0.4	-0.3	-0.3	0.5	0.4	0.2	0.0	-0.5	-1.2
1956	-0.2	0.1	0.3	0.6	1.2	1.4	1.2	1.1	-0.2	-0.6	-0.2	-0.2	-0.1	0.0	0.7	0.7	0.6	0.5	0.1	-0.6
1957	-0.2	0.1	0.3	0.6	1.1	1.4	1.2	1.1	-0.2	-0.6	-0.2	-0.2	0.0	0.1	0.7	0.7	0.6	0.5	0.0	-0.6
1958	0.0	0.3	0.6	0.8	1.3	1.6	1.4	1.3	0.1	-0.2	0.2	0.2	0.4	0.5	1.2	1.3	1.2	1.1	0.8	0.3
1959	0.1	0.4	0.6	0.9	1.4	1.6	1.4	1.3	0.2	-0.1	0.3	0.3	0.5	0.6	1.3	1.4	1.3	1.3	1.0	0.5
1960	0.2	0.5	0.7	0.9	1.4	1.6	1.5	1.4	0.3	0.0	0.4	0.4	0.6	0.8	1.4	1.5	1.4	1.4	1.1	0.7
1961	0.1	0.4	0.6	0.9	1.3	1.5	1.4	1.3	0.3	0.0	0.4	0.4	0.6	0.7	1.4	1.4	1.4	1.3	1.1	0.7
1962	0.1	0.4	0.5	0.8	1.2	1.4	1.3	1.2	0.2	-0.1	0.3	0.3	0.4	0.5	1.1	1.1	1.0	1.0	0.6	0.2
1963	-0.2	0.1	0.3	0.5	0.9	1.1	0.9	0.9	-0.1	-0.3	0.0	0.0	0.1	0.2	0.7	0.7	0.6	0.6	0.3	-0.1
1964	-0.2	0.1	0.3	0.5	0.9	1.1	0.9	0.9	0.0	-0.3	0.0	0.0	0.1	0.2	0.8	0.8	0.7	0.6	0.4	0.0
1965	0.2	0.4	0.6	0.8	1.2	1.4	1.2	1.2	0.3	0.1	0.4	0.4	0.6	0.7	1.2	1.2	1.2	1.2	0.9	0.6
1966	0.3	0.6	0.8	0.9	1.4	1.5	1.4	1.4	0.5	0.3	0.6	0.6	0.8	0.9	1.4	1.4	1.3	1.3	1.0	0.7
1967	0.6	0.9	1.1	1.3	1.7	1.9	1.7	1.7	0.9	0.7	1.0	1.0	1.2	1.3	1.8	1.9	1.8	1.8	1.6	1.3
1968	0.8	1.1	1.3	1.5	1.8	2.0	1.9	1.9	1.1	0.9	1.2	1.3	1.4	1.6	2.0	2.1	2.0	2.0	1.8	1.6
1969	0.7	0.9	1.1	1.3	1.7	1.9	1.8	1.7	0.9	0.7	1.0	1.0	1.2	1.3	1.7	1.7	1.6	1.6	1.4	1.1
1970	0.5	0.8	0.9	1.1	1.5	1.7	1.5	1.5	0.7	0.5	0.7	0.8	0.9	0.9	1.3	1.2	1.1	1.1	0.9	0.6

*Beta and equity risk premium estimated from the S&P 500. Estimates based on a minimum of five years of data.

Table A-4 (Page 2 of 6)

Mid-Cap Size Premia*

Percent per annum risk premia for all historical time periods.

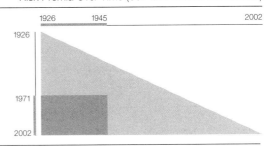

from 1926 to 2002

To the end of	From the beginning of 1926	1927	1928	1929	1930	1931	1932	1933	1934	1935	1936	1937	1938	1939	1940	1941	1942	1943	1944	1945
1971	0.6	0.9	1.0	1.2	1.6	1.7	1.6	1.6	0.8	0.6	0.9	0.9	1.0	1.1	1.4	1.3	1.2	1.2	1.0	0.8
1972	0.4	0.6	0.7	0.9	1.3	1.4	1.3	1.2	0.5	0.3	0.5	0.6	0.6	0.7	1.0	0.9	0.8	0.8	0.6	0.3
1973	0.1	0.3	0.5	0.7	1.0	1.1	1.0	0.9	0.1	-0.1	0.2	0.2	0.2	0.2	0.5	0.3	0.2	0.2	-0.1	-0.3
1974	0.3	0.5	0.7	0.8	1.2	1.3	1.2	1.2	0.4	0.2	0.4	0.5	0.5	0.6	0.8	0.7	0.6	0.6	0.3	0.1
1975	0.6	0.8	1.0	1.1	1.5	1.6	1.5	1.4	0.7	0.5	0.8	0.8	0.9	0.9	1.1	1.0	0.9	1.0	0.7	0.5
1976	0.8	1.1	1.2	1.4	1.7	1.9	1.8	1.7	1.0	0.8	1.1	1.1	1.2	1.2	1.5	1.4	1.3	1.3	1.1	0.9
1977	1.1	1.3	1.5	1.6	2.0	2.1	2.0	2.0	1.3	1.1	1.4	1.4	1.5	1.6	1.8	1.7	1.6	1.7	1.5	1.3
1978	1.2	1.4	1.5	1.7	2.0	2.2	2.1	2.1	1.4	1.2	1.5	1.5	1.6	1.6	1.8	1.8	1.7	1.7	1.5	1.4
1979	1.4	1.6	1.8	1.9	2.3	2.4	2.3	2.3	1.6	1.5	1.7	1.8	1.9	1.9	2.1	2.1	2.0	2.0	1.9	1.7
1980	1.3	1.5	1.7	1.8	2.1	2.3	2.2	2.2	1.5	1.4	1.6	1.7	1.8	1.8	2.0	1.9	1.9	1.9	1.7	1.6
1981	1.5	1.7	1.8	2.0	2.3	2.5	2.4	2.4	1.7	1.6	1.8	1.9	2.0	2.0	2.2	2.1	2.1	2.1	2.0	1.8
1982	1.5	1.7	1.9	2.0	2.3	2.5	2.4	2.4	1.8	1.6	1.8	1.9	2.0	2.0	2.2	2.2	2.1	2.1	2.0	1.8
1983	1.5	1.7	1.9	2.0	2.3	2.5	2.4	2.4	1.8	1.6	1.9	1.9	2.0	2.0	2.2	2.2	2.1	2.2	2.0	1.9
1984	1.4	1.6	1.7	1.9	2.2	2.3	2.2	2.2	1.6	1.4	1.7	1.7	1.8	1.8	2.0	2.0	1.9	1.9	1.8	1.6
1985	1.3	1.5	1.6	1.8	2.1	2.2	2.1	2.1	1.5	1.3	1.6	1.6	1.7	1.7	1.9	1.9	1.8	1.8	1.7	1.5
1986	1.2	1.4	1.6	1.7	2.0	2.1	2.0	2.0	1.4	1.3	1.5	1.6	1.6	1.7	1.9	1.8	1.7	1.8	1.6	1.5
1987	1.2	1.4	1.5	1.6	1.9	2.0	2.0	2.0	1.4	1.2	1.4	1.5	1.6	1.6	1.8	1.7	1.6	1.7	1.5	1.4
1988	1.2	1.4	1.5	1.7	1.9	2.3	2.0	2.0	1.4	1.3	1.5	1.5	1.6	1.7	1.8	1.8	1.7	1.7	1.6	1.5
1989	1.1	1.2	1.4	1.5	1.8	1.9	1.8	1.8	1.3	1.1	1.3	1.4	1.4	1.5	1.6	1.6	1.5	1.6	1.4	1.3
1990	0.9	1.1	1.2	1.4	1.6	1.7	1.7	1.7	1.1	1.0	1.2	1.2	1.3	1.3	1.5	1.4	1.3	1.4	1.2	1.1
1991	1.1	1.2	1.4	1.5	1.7	1.9	1.8	1.8	1.3	1.1	1.3	1.3	1.4	1.5	1.6	1.6	1.5	1.5	1.4	1.2
1992	1.2	1.4	1.5	1.6	1.8	2.0	1.9	1.9	1.4	1.3	1.4	1.5	1.6	1.6	1.7	1.7	1.6	1.7	1.5	1.4
1993	1.3	1.4	1.5	1.7	1.9	2.0	2.0	2.0	1.5	1.3	1.5	1.6	1.6	1.7	1.8	1.8	1.7	1.8	1.6	1.5
1994	1.2	1.4	1.5	1.6	1.8	1.9	1.9	1.9	1.4	1.3	1.4	1.5	1.6	1.6	1.7	1.7	1.6	1.7	1.5	1.4
1995	1.1	1.2	1.3	1.5	1.7	1.8	1.7	1.7	1.3	1.1	1.3	1.3	1.4	1.4	1.6	1.5	1.5	1.5	1.4	1.3
1996	0.9	1.1	1.2	1.3	1.6	1.7	1.6	1.6	1.1	1.0	1.2	1.2	1.3	1.3	1.5	1.4	1.4	1.4	1.2	1.1
1997	0.8	0.9	1.0	1.1	1.4	1.5	1.4	1.4	1.0	0.8	1.0	1.0	1.1	1.1	1.3	1.2	1.2	1.2	1.1	0.9
1998	0.4	0.6	0.7	0.8	1.0	1.1	1.0	1.0	0.6	0.4	0.6	0.6	0.7	0.7	0.8	0.8	0.7	0.7	0.6	0.5
1999	0.5	0.7	0.8	0.9	1.1	1.2	1.1	1.1	0.7	0.6	0.7	0.7	0.8	0.8	1.0	0.9	0.9	0.9	0.7	0.6
2000	0.6	0.7	0.8	0.9	1.1	1.2	1.2	1.2	0.8	0.7	0.8	0.8	0.9	0.9	1.1	1.0	1.0	1.0	0.8	0.7
2001	0.7	0.9	1.0	1.1	1.3	1.4	1.3	1.3	0.9	0.8	0.9	0.9	1.0	1.0	1.2	1.1	1.1	1.1	0.9	0.8
2002	0.8	1.0	1.1	1.2	1.4	1.5	1.4	1.4	1.0	0.9	1.0	1.0	1.1	1.1	1.3	1.2	1.2	1.2	1.1	0.9

*Beta and equity risk premium estimated from the S&P 500. Estimates based on a minimum of five years of data.

Table A-4 (Page 3 of 6)

Mid-Cap Size Premia*

Percent per annum risk premia for all historical time periods.

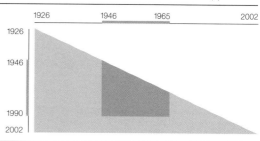

from 1926 to 2002

To the end of	1946	1947	1948	1949	1950	1951	1952	1953	1954	1955	1956	1957	1958	1959	1960	1961	1962	1963	1964	1965
1946																				
1947																				
1948																				
1949																				
1950	-2.9																			
1951	-3.6	-3.7																		
1952	-4.1	-4.0	-3.5																	
1953	-3.3	-3.2	-2.6	-1.9																
1954	-2.6	-2.1	-1.3	-0.3	-0.7															
1955	-3.0	-2.2	-1.5	0.0	-0.3	-0.1														
1956	-2.2	-1.4	-0.7	0.7	0.4	0.6	1.6													
1957	-2.1	-1.5	-0.9	0.1	-0.3	-0.4	0.1	0.9												
1958	-1.0	-0.2	0.5	1.6	1.5	1.7	2.6	3.8	5.0											
1959	-0.6	0.1	0.8	1.8	1.7	2.0	2.8	3.9	4.8	3.4										
1960	-0.5	0.2	0.8	1.7	1.6	1.8	2.4	3.3	3.9	2.6	4.1									
1961	-0.4	0.3	0.9	1.7	1.6	1.8	2.4	3.2	3.7	2.8	3.8	3.6								
1962	-0.8	-0.4	0.1	0.6	0.4	0.6	1.0	1.6	1.8	1.0	2.2	2.0	2.4							
1963	-1.1	-0.7	-0.3	0.2	0.0	0.1	0.5	1.0	1.1	0.3	1.2	0.7	0.8	-1.0						
1964	-0.9	-0.5	-0.1	0.4	0.2	0.3	0.7	1.1	1.3	0.6	1.3	0.9	0.9	-0.6	-1.4					
1965	-0.3	0.2	0.6	1.1	1.0	1.1	1.5	2.0	2.2	1.6	2.4	2.1	2.3	1.2	0.9	0.3				
1966	0.0	0.3	0.7	1.2	1.0	1.2	1.6	2.0	2.2	1.7	2.5	2.4	2.6	1.7	1.5	1.3	1.5			
1967	0.6	1.0	1.4	1.9	1.8	2.0	2.4	2.9	3.1	2.8	3.6	3.5	3.8	3.1	3.1	3.1	3.6	5.2		
1968	0.9	1.3	1.7	2.1	2.1	2.2	2.7	3.1	3.3	3.1	3.9	3.8	4.1	3.6	3.7	3.7	4.3	5.5	8.1	
1969	0.5	0.8	1.1	1.4	1.3	1.5	1.9	2.3	2.4	2.2	3.0	3.0	3.1	2.7	2.7	2.6	3.1	3.8	5.9	7.3
1970	0.0	0.2	0.5	0.7	0.6	0.8	1.1	1.5	1.6	1.5	2.3	2.2	2.2	1.8	1.8	1.7	2.1	2.5	4.3	5.2
1971	0.2	0.4	0.6	0.9	0.8	1.0	1.3	1.7	1.7	1.7	2.4	2.4	2.4	2.1	2.1	2.0	2.4	2.7	4.3	5.1
1972	-0.2	-0.1	0.2	0.4	0.3	0.4	0.7	1.1	1.1	1.0	1.6	1.5	1.5	1.1	1.0	0.8	1.0	1.2	2.4	2.8
1973	-0.9	-0.8	-0.6	-0.4	-0.5	-0.4	-0.1	0.2	0.1	0.1	0.8	0.7	0.6	0.3	0.2	-0.1	0.2	0.2	1.4	1.8
1974	-0.5	-0.4	-0.2	0.0	-0.1	0.0	0.3	0.6	0.6	0.5	1.2	1.2	1.2	0.9	0.8	0.7	0.8	1.1	2.1	2.3
1975	0.0	0.1	0.3	0.5	0.4	0.6	0.9	1.2	1.2	1.2	1.9	1.9	2.0	1.7	1.7	1.6	1.8	2.1	3.1	3.5
1976	0.4	0.5	0.8	1.0	0.9	1.1	1.4	1.7	1.7	1.8	2.5	2.5	2.6	2.3	2.4	2.3	2.6	2.9	3.9	4.3
1977	0.8	1.0	1.2	1.4	1.3	1.5	1.8	2.2	2.2	2.3	3.0	3.0	3.1	3.0	3.0	3.0	3.3	3.7	4.6	5.0
1978	0.9	1.0	1.2	1.4	1.4	1.6	1.9	2.2	2.3	2.4	3.1	3.1	3.2	3.0	3.1	3.1	3.4	3.7	4.6	5.0
1979	1.3	1.4	1.6	1.8	1.8	2.0	2.3	2.6	2.7	2.8	3.5	3.6	3.7	3.5	3.6	3.7	4.0	4.3	5.2	5.6
1980	1.2	1.3	1.5	1.7	1.7	1.8	2.1	2.4	2.5	2.6	3.2	3.2	3.3	3.2	3.3	3.3	3.5	3.8	4.6	4.9
1981	1.4	1.5	1.7	1.9	1.9	2.1	2.4	2.7	2.8	2.9	3.5	3.6	3.7	3.6	3.6	3.7	3.9	4.2	5.0	5.3
1982	1.5	1.6	1.8	2.0	1.9	2.1	2.4	2.7	2.8	2.9	3.5	3.5	3.6	3.5	3.6	3.6	3.8	4.1	4.9	5.1
1983	1.5	1.6	1.8	2.0	2.0	2.1	2.4	2.7	2.8	2.9	3.5	3.5	3.6	3.5	3.5	3.5	3.8	4.0	4.7	5.0
1984	1.3	1.4	1.6	1.7	1.7	1.9	2.1	2.4	2.5	2.5	3.1	3.1	3.2	3.1	3.1	3.1	3.3	3.6	4.2	4.4
1985	1.2	1.3	1.4	1.6	1.6	1.7	2.0	2.3	2.3	2.4	2.9	2.9	3.0	2.8	2.8	2.8	3.0	3.2	3.8	4.0
1986	1.1	1.2	1.4	1.5	1.5	1.7	1.9	2.2	2.2	2.2	2.7	2.7	2.8	2.6	2.7	2.6	2.8	3.0	3.5	3.7
1987	1.0	1.1	1.3	1.4	1.4	1.5	1.8	2.0	2.0	2.1	2.6	2.6	2.6	2.5	2.5	2.5	2.6	2.8	3.3	3.4
1988	1.1	1.2	1.3	1.5	1.5	1.6	1.8	2.1	2.1	2.2	2.6	2.6	2.7	2.5	2.5	2.5	2.6	2.8	3.3	3.4
1989	0.9	1.0	1.2	1.3	1.3	1.4	1.6	1.8	1.9	1.9	2.3	2.3	2.3	2.2	2.2	2.1	2.2	2.4	2.8	2.9
1990	0.7	0.8	0.9	1.1	1.0	1.2	1.4	1.6	1.6	1.6	2.0	2.0	2.1	1.9	1.9	1.9	1.9	2.1	2.5	2.6

*Beta and equity risk premium estimated from the S&P 500. Estimates based on a minimum of five years of data.

Table A-4 (Page 4 of 6)

Mid-Cap Size Premia*

Percent per annum risk premia for all historical time periods.

1926   1946   1965   2002

from 1926 to 2002

To the end of	From the beginning of																			
	1946	1947	1948	1949	1950	1951	1952	1953	1954	1955	1956	1957	1958	1959	1960	1961	1962	1963	1964	1965
1991	0.9	1.0	1.1	1.3	1.2	1.4	1.6	1.8	1.8	1.8	2.2	2.2	2.3	2.1	2.1	2.1	2.2	2.3	2.7	2.8
1992	1.1	1.2	1.3	1.4	1.4	1.5	1.7	2.0	2.0	2.0	2.4	2.4	2.5	2.3	2.3	2.3	2.4	2.5	2.9	3.0
1993	1.2	1.3	1.4	1.6	1.5	1.6	1.8	2.1	2.1	2.1	2.5	2.5	2.6	2.4	2.4	2.4	2.5	2.7	3.0	3.1
1994	1.1	1.2	1.3	1.4	1.4	1.5	1.7	1.9	2.0	2.0	2.4	2.4	2.4	2.2	2.2	2.2	2.3	2.5	2.8	2.9
1995	1.0	1.0	1.2	1.3	1.3	1.4	1.6	1.8	1.8	1.8	2.1	2.1	2.2	2.0	2.0	2.0	2.0	2.2	2.5	2.6
1996	0.8	0.9	1.0	1.1	1.1	1.2	1.4	1.6	1.6	1.6	1.9	1.9	1.9	1.8	1.8	1.7	1.8	1.9	2.2	2.3
1997	0.6	0.7	0.8	1.0	0.9	1.0	1.2	1.3	1.4	1.3	1.7	1.6	1.6	1.5	1.4	1.4	1.4	1.6	1.9	1.9
1998	0.1	0.2	0.3	0.4	0.4	0.5	0.6	0.8	0.8	0.7	1.0	1.0	1.0	0.8	0.8	0.7	0.7	0.8	1.1	1.1
1999	0.3	0.4	0.5	0.6	0.6	0.6	0.8	0.9	0.9	0.9	1.2	1.2	1.2	1.0	1.0	0.9	0.9	1.0	1.3	1.3
2000	0.4	0.5	0.6	0.7	0.7	0.7	0.9	1.0	1.0	1.0	1.3	1.3	1.3	1.1	1.1	1.0	1.1	1.2	1.4	1.4
2001	0.5	0.6	0.7	0.8	0.8	0.9	1.0	1.2	1.2	1.2	1.5	1.4	1.5	1.3	1.3	1.2	1.3	1.4	1.6	1.6
2002	0.7	0.7	0.8	0.9	0.9	1.0	1.1	1.3	1.3	1.3	1.6	1.6	1.6	1.4	1.4	1.4	1.4	1.5	1.8	1.8

*Beta and equity risk premium estimated from the S&P 500. Estimates based on a minimum of five years of data.

Table A-4 (Page 5 of 6)

Mid-Cap Size Premia*

Percent per annum risk premia for all historical time periods.

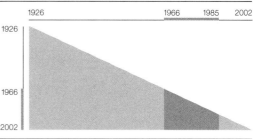

from 1926 to 2002

To the end of	From the beginning of 1966	1967	1968	1969	1970	1971	1972	1973	1974	1975	1976	1977	1978	1979	1980	1981	1982	1983	1984	1985
1966																				
1967																				
1968																				
1969																				
1970	4.0																			
1971	4.1	3.3																		
1972	1.6	0.5	−1.6																	
1973	0.6	−0.5	−2.2	−4.2																
1974	1.3	0.6	−1.1	−3.0	2.9															
1975	2.7	2.1	0.9	−0.2	0.2	1.4														
1976	3.6	3.2	2.3	1.5	2.1	3.4	3.1													
1977	4.5	4.2	3.5	2.9	3.6	4.9	4.8	8.2												
1978	4.5	4.3	3.6	3.0	3.7	4.9	4.8	7.6	10.7											
1979	5.2	5.0	4.4	4.0	4.7	5.9	6.0	8.6	11.4	11.6										
1980	4.5	4.3	3.7	3.2	3.9	4.8	4.8	6.9	9.3	9.0	8.3									
1981	4.9	4.8	4.3	3.9	4.5	5.4	5.5	7.4	9.4	9.5	8.8	7.8								
1982	4.8	4.6	4.1	3.7	4.3	5.2	5.1	6.8	8.7	8.7	7.9	6.9	5.6							
1983	4.6	4.5	4.0	3.6	4.1	4.9	4.9	6.4	8.1	8.0	7.2	6.3	5.1	5.3						
1984	4.0	3.9	3.4	3.0	3.4	4.1	4.0	5.3	6.7	6.5	5.7	4.7	3.4	3.3	1.2					
1985	3.6	3.4	2.9	2.6	3.0	3.6	3.5	4.6	5.9	5.6	4.8	3.8	2.6	2.3	0.5	1.2				
1986	3.3	3.1	2.6	2.3	2.6	3.2	3.1	4.1	5.3	5.0	4.2	3.2	2.1	1.9	0.2	0.7	−1.1			
1987	3.0	2.9	2.3	2.0	2.3	2.9	2.7	3.6	4.7	4.5	3.6	2.6	1.6	1.3	−0.2	0.0	−1.6	−2.4		
1988	3.1	2.9	2.4	2.1	2.4	2.9	2.8	3.7	4.7	4.5	3.7	2.8	1.9	1.7	0.3	0.6	−0.7	−1.2	−2.1	
1989	2.6	2.4	1.9	1.5	1.9	2.3	2.2	2.9	3.9	3.7	2.9	2.0	1.1	0.9	−0.4	−0.2	−1.4	−2.0	−2.9	−1.9
1990	2.2	2.0	1.5	1.2	1.5	1.9	1.7	2.4	3.2	3.0	2.2	1.3	0.4	0.1	−1.1	−1.0	-2.2	−2.8	−3.6	-3.0
1991	2.5	2.3	1.8	1.5	1.8	2.2	2.1	2.8	3.6	3.4	2.7	1.9	1.1	0.9	−0.2	0.0	−1.0	−1.4	−1.9	−1.1
1992	2.7	2.5	2.1	1.8	2.1	2.5	2.4	3.1	3.9	3.7	3.0	2.3	1.6	1.4	0.5	0.7	−0.1	−0.3	−0.7	0.1
1993	2.8	2.7	2.3	2.0	2.3	2.7	2.5	3.2	4.0	3.8	3.2	2.5	1.9	1.7	0.9	1.1	0.4	0.3	−0.1	0.8
1994	2.6	2.5	2.1	1.8	2.1	2.4	2.3	2.9	3.6	3.4	2.8	2.2	1.6	1.4	0.6	0.8	0.1	−0.1	−0.4	0.3
1995	2.3	2.1	1.7	1.5	1.7	2.1	1.9	2.5	3.2	3.0	2.4	1.8	1.2	1.0	0.2	0.4	−0.2	−0.4	−0.7	−0.1
1996	2.0	1.8	1.4	1.1	1.4	1.7	1.6	2.1	2.8	2.6	2.0	1.4	0.8	0.6	−0.1	0.0	−0.6	−0.8	−1.1	−0.6
1997	1.6	1.4	1.0	0.7	1.0	1.3	1.1	1.6	2.3	2.1	1.5	0.9	0.3	0.2	−0.5	−0.4	−1.0	−1.2	−1.6	−1.0
1998	0.8	0.6	0.2	−0.1	0.1	0.4	0.2	0.6	1.2	0.9	0.4	−0.3	−0.9	−1.1	−1.9	−1.8	−2.5	−2.8	−3.2	−2.8
1999	1.0	0.8	0.4	0.2	0.4	0.7	0.5	0.9	1.5	1.3	0.7	0.1	−0.4	−0.6	−1.3	−1.2	−1.8	−2.1	−2.4	−2.0
2000	1.1	1.0	0.6	0.3	0.5	0.8	0.7	1.1	1.7	1.4	0.9	0.3	−0.2	−0.3	−1.0	−0.9	−1.5	−1.6	−2.0	−1.5
2001	1.3	1.2	0.8	0.6	0.8	1.1	0.9	1.3	1.9	1.7	1.2	0.6	0.1	0.0	−0.6	−0.6	−1.1	−1.2	−1.5	−1.1
2002	1.5	1.4	1.0	0.8	1.0	1.2	1.1	1.5	2.0	1.9	1.4	0.8	0.4	0.2	−0.4	−0.3	−0.7	−0.9	−1.1	−0.8

*Beta and equity risk premium estimated from the S&P 500. Estimates based on a minimum of five years of data.

Table A-4 (Page 6 of 6)

Mid-Cap Size Premia*

Percent per annum risk premia for all historical time periods.

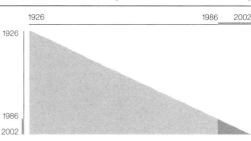

from 1926 to 2002

To the end of	From the beginning of 1986	1987	1988	1989	1990	1991	1992	1993	1994	1995	1996	1997	1998
1986													
1987													
1988													
1989													
1990	−3.2												
1991	−1.0	−0.8											
1992	0.4	0.8	1.7										
1993	1.2	1.5	2.4	1.9									
1994	0.6	0.9	1.6	1.0	2.8								
1995	0.1	0.3	0.8	0.2	1.3	3.6							
1996	−0.4	−0.4	0.1	−0.5	0.2	2.3	0.9						
1997	−1.0	−1.0	−0.3	−0.9	−0.4	1.7	0.5	−1.2					
1998	−2.9	−3.1	−2.9	−3.7	−3.5	−2.4	−4.2	−6.5	−9.2				
1999	−2.0	−2.1	−1.8	−2.5	−2.2	−1.1	−2.5	−4.3	−6.1	−6.7			
2000	−1.5	−1.6	−1.2	−1.8	−1.4	−0.4	−1.6	−2.9	−4.3	−4.2	−4.6		
2001	−1.1	−1.1	−0.8	−1.2	−0.8	0.0	−1.1	−2.2	−3.2	−3.1	−3.0	−2.5	
2002	−0.7	−0.6	−0.4	−0.8	−0.3	0.4	−0.6	−1.5	−2.4	−2.2	−2.0	−1.4	0.7

*Beta and equity risk premium estimated from the S&P 500. Estimates based on a minimum of five years of data.

Table A-5 (Page 1 of 6)

Low-Cap Size Premia*

Percent per annum risk premia for all historical time periods.

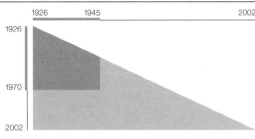

from 1926 to 2002

To the end of	From the beginning of 1926	1927	1928	1929	1930	1931	1932	1933	1934	1935	1936	1937	1938	1939	1940	1941	1942	1943	1944	1945
1926																				
1927																				
1928																				
1929																				
1930	-17.0																			
1931	-14.8	-15.1																		
1932	-11.5	-11.0	-9.5																	
1933	-3.0	-1.3	1.8	6.8																
1934	-0.2	1.7	4.9	9.8	17.5															
1935	-0.1	1.5	4.3	8.3	14.3	18.3														
1936	0.7	2.2	4.7	8.2	13.2	16.5	17.6													
1937	0.3	1.6	3.9	6.9	11.3	13.8	14.3	14.2												
1938	0.3	1.6	3.6	6.4	10.1	12.1	12.3	11.8	4.2											
1939	0.5	1.7	3.6	6.2	9.5	11.2	11.1	10.3	3.8	0.4										
1940	1.0	2.2	4.0	6.3	9.4	10.9	10.9	10.4	5.0	2.2	3.5									
1941	1.3	2.4	4.1	6.3	9.2	10.5	10.5	10.1	5.3	2.9	4.1	4.0								
1942	1.4	2.4	3.9	6.0	8.5	9.7	9.6	9.2	4.8	2.8	3.6	3.2	4.0							
1943	2.7	3.7	5.2	7.2	9.6	10.8	10.8	10.4	6.5	5.0	6.1	6.1	7.2	8.7						
1944	3.5	4.5	6.0	7.9	10.2	11.3	11.3	10.9	7.4	6.2	7.3	7.5	8.6	10.0	12.2					
1945	4.2	5.2	6.6	8.4	10.6	11.6	11.6	11.2	8.0	7.1	8.1	8.3	9.4	10.7	13.5	14.1				
1946	3.9	4.9	6.3	7.9	9.9	10.9	10.8	10.5	7.5	6.5	7.4	7.5	8.4	9.5	11.2	11.4	12.4			
1947	3.3	4.2	5.5	7.0	8.8	9.7	9.5	9.1	6.2	5.2	5.9	5.9	6.6	7.3	8.6	8.3	8.5	8.4		
1948	2.8	3.6	4.7	6.1	7.8	8.6	8.4	8.0	5.2	4.3	4.8	4.6	5.2	5.7	6.7	6.5	6.6	6.5	3.6	
1949	2.5	3.3	4.4	5.7	7.3	8.0	7.7	7.3	4.7	3.8	4.2	4.0	4.5	4.9	5.9	5.5	5.5	5.1	2.6	-0.5
1950	2.3	3.0	4.0	5.3	6.7	7.4	7.1	6.6	4.1	3.3	3.6	3.4	3.8	4.2	5.3	4.8	4.7	4.1	2.0	-0.6
1951	1.7	2.3	3.3	4.4	5.7	6.3	6.0	5.5	3.0	2.2	2.5	2.2	2.5	2.8	3.9	3.3	3.1	2.4	0.4	-2.2
1952	1.2	1.8	2.6	3.7	4.9	5.4	5.1	4.6	2.2	1.5	1.7	1.3	1.6	1.8	2.9	2.3	2.1	1.3	-0.5	-2.9
1953	1.1	1.7	2.5	3.5	4.7	5.2	4.9	4.4	2.1	1.4	1.6	1.2	1.5	1.8	2.7	2.2	2.1	1.4	-0.3	-2.4
1954	0.8	1.4	2.1	3.1	4.2	4.6	4.3	3.8	1.7	1.0	1.1	0.8	1.1	1.4	2.6	2.2	2.1	1.4	0.0	-1.9
1955	0.2	0.8	1.5	2.3	3.3	3.8	3.4	2.9	0.9	0.4	0.4	0.0	0.3	0.7	2.0	1.8	1.8	1.1	-0.2	-1.9
1956	0.3	0.8	1.5	2.3	3.2	3.7	3.3	2.9	1.1	0.6	0.6	0.1	0.5	1.0	2.2	2.2	2.3	1.7	0.5	-1.1
1957	0.2	0.7	1.3	2.1	3.0	3.4	3.1	2.8	1.0	0.5	0.5	0.0	0.4	0.8	1.9	1.8	1.9	1.4	0.1	-1.4
1958	0.4	0.9	1.5	2.3	3.2	3.6	3.3	2.9	1.3	0.8	0.8	0.4	0.8	1.3	2.5	2.5	2.7	2.2	1.2	-0.2
1959	0.5	1.0	1.6	2.3	3.2	3.6	3.3	3.0	1.4	1.0	1.0	0.6	1.0	1.5	2.7	2.7	2.9	2.4	1.5	0.3
1960	0.5	0.9	1.5	2.2	3.0	3.4	3.1	2.9	1.3	0.9	0.9	0.5	1.0	1.4	2.5	2.5	2.6	2.2	1.3	0.1
1961	0.4	0.8	1.3	2.0	2.8	3.2	2.9	2.6	1.1	0.7	0.8	0.4	0.8	1.2	2.3	2.3	2.4	2.0	1.2	0.1
1962	0.2	0.7	1.2	1.8	2.6	2.9	2.7	2.4	1.0	0.6	0.6	0.2	0.6	0.9	1.8	1.8	1.8	1.4	0.5	-0.6
1963	0.0	0.4	0.9	1.5	2.3	2.6	2.3	2.1	0.7	0.3	0.3	-0.1	0.3	0.6	1.5	1.5	1.5	1.1	0.2	-0.8
1964	-0.1	0.3	0.8	1.4	2.1	2.4	2.1	1.9	0.5	0.2	0.2	-0.2	0.2	0.5	1.4	1.4	1.4	1.0	0.2	-0.8
1965	0.4	0.8	1.3	1.9	2.6	2.9	2.7	2.4	1.2	0.8	0.8	0.5	0.9	1.3	2.2	2.1	2.2	1.8	1.1	0.2
1966	0.6	1.0	1.5	2.0	2.7	3.0	2.8	2.6	1.3	1.0	1.0	0.7	1.1	1.4	2.2	2.2	2.2	1.9	1.2	0.3
1967	1.4	1.8	2.3	2.9	3.5	3.9	3.7	3.5	2.3	2.0	2.1	1.8	2.2	2.5	3.4	3.4	3.4	3.2	2.5	1.8
1968	1.8	2.2	2.7	3.3	3.9	4.3	4.1	3.9	2.8	2.5	2.6	2.3	2.7	3.1	3.9	3.9	4.0	3.8	3.1	2.5
1969	1.5	1.9	2.4	2.9	3.6	3.9	3.7	3.5	2.3	2.1	2.1	1.9	2.2	2.5	3.2	3.1	3.1	2.9	2.3	1.6
1970	1.2	1.5	2.0	2.5	3.2	3.4	3.2	3.0	1.9	1.6	1.6	1.4	1.7	1.9	2.5	2.4	2.3	2.1	1.4	0.7

*Beta and equity risk premium estimated from the S&P 500. Estimates based on a minimum of five years of data.

Table A-5 (Page 2 of 6)

Low-Cap Size Premia*

Percent per annum risk premia for all historical time periods.

from 1926 to 2002

To the end of	1926	1927	1928	1929	1930	1931	1932	1933	1934	1935	1936	1937	1938	1939	1940	1941	1942	1943	1944	1945
1971	1.2	1.6	2.0	2.6	3.2	3.4	3.2	3.0	1.9	1.6	1.7	1.5	1.7	2.0	2.5	2.4	2.3	2.1	1.5	0.8
1972	0.8	1.2	1.6	2.1	2.7	3.0	2.7	2.5	1.4	1.2	1.2	1.0	1.2	1.4	2.0	1.8	1.8	1.5	0.9	0.2
1973	0.5	0.8	1.2	1.7	2.3	2.5	2.3	2.0	0.9	0.6	0.6	0.4	0.6	0.7	1.1	0.9	0.8	0.6	−0.1	−0.7
1974	0.7	1.0	1.5	1.9	2.5	2.8	2.6	2.4	1.4	1.0	1.0	0.8	1.0	1.2	1.5	1.4	1.3	1.2	0.5	−0.2
1975	1.0	1.3	1.8	2.2	2.8	3.0	2.9	2.7	1.7	1.4	1.4	1.2	1.4	1.6	1.9	1.8	1.7	1.6	0.9	0.3
1976	1.4	1.7	2.2	2.6	3.2	3.4	3.3	3.1	2.1	1.8	1.9	1.7	1.9	2.1	2.5	2.3	2.3	2.1	1.5	1.0
1977	2.0	2.3	2.7	3.2	3.7	4.0	3.9	3.7	2.8	2.5	2.5	2.4	2.6	2.8	3.2	3.1	3.0	2.9	2.4	1.8
1978	2.1	2.4	2.8	3.3	3.9	4.1	4.0	3.8	2.9	2.7	2.7	2.5	2.8	2.9	3.3	3.2	3.2	3.1	2.5	2.0
1979	2.5	2.8	3.2	3.7	4.2	4.5	4.4	4.2	3.3	3.1	3.1	3.0	3.2	3.4	3.7	3.7	3.6	3.6	3.0	2.6
1980	2.4	2.7	3.1	3.5	4.1	4.3	4.2	4.0	3.2	2.9	3.0	2.8	3.1	3.2	3.6	3.5	3.5	3.4	2.8	2.4
1981	2.5	2.9	3.3	3.7	4.2	4.5	4.4	4.2	3.4	3.1	3.2	3.1	3.3	3.4	3.8	3.7	3.7	3.6	3.1	2.6
1982	2.6	2.9	3.3	3.8	4.3	4.5	4.4	4.3	3.5	3.2	3.3	3.1	3.4	3.5	3.8	3.8	3.8	3.7	3.2	2.8
1983	2.6	2.9	3.3	3.7	4.3	4.5	4.4	4.3	3.5	3.2	3.3	3.2	3.4	3.5	3.8	3.8	3.8	3.7	3.2	2.8
1984	2.5	2.8	3.1	3.6	4.1	4.3	4.2	4.1	3.3	3.0	3.1	2.9	3.2	3.3	3.6	3.5	3.5	3.4	2.9	2.5
1985	2.4	2.6	3.0	3.4	3.9	4.1	4.0	3.9	3.1	2.9	2.9	2.8	3.0	3.2	3.4	3.4	3.4	3.3	2.8	2.4
1986	2.2	2.4	2.8	3.2	3.7	3.9	3.8	3.7	2.9	2.7	2.7	2.6	2.8	2.9	3.2	3.1	3.1	3.0	2.6	2.2
1987	2.0	2.2	2.6	3.0	3.4	3.6	3.5	3.5	2.7	2.5	2.5	2.3	2.5	2.7	2.9	2.8	2.8	2.7	2.3	1.9
1988	2.0	2.3	2.6	3.0	3.5	3.7	3.6	3.5	2.8	2.5	2.6	2.4	2.6	2.8	3.0	2.9	2.9	2.8	2.4	2.0
1989	1.7	2.0	2.3	2.7	3.1	3.3	3.2	3.2	2.4	2.2	2.2	2.1	2.3	2.4	2.7	2.6	2.6	2.5	2.1	1.7
1990	1.5	1.8	2.1	2.5	2.9	3.1	3.0	2.9	2.2	2.0	2.0	1.8	2.0	2.1	2.4	2.3	2.2	2.2	1.7	1.3
1991	1.7	2.0	2.3	2.6	3.1	3.3	3.2	3.1	2.4	2.2	2.2	2.0	2.2	2.4	2.6	2.5	2.5	2.4	2.0	1.6
1992	1.8	2.1	2.4	2.7	3.2	3.4	3.3	3.2	2.5	2.3	2.3	2.2	2.4	2.5	2.8	2.7	2.7	2.6	2.2	1.8
1993	1.9	2.2	2.5	2.8	3.2	3.4	3.3	3.3	2.6	2.4	2.4	2.3	2.5	2.6	2.8	2.8	2.8	2.7	2.3	1.9
1994	1.9	2.1	2.4	2.8	3.2	3.4	3.3	3.2	2.6	2.4	2.4	2.2	2.4	2.6	2.8	2.7	2.7	2.6	2.2	1.9
1995	1.7	1.9	2.2	2.5	2.9	3.1	3.0	2.9	2.3	2.1	2.1	2.0	2.2	2.3	2.5	2.5	2.4	2.4	1.9	1.6
1996	1.5	1.7	2.0	2.3	2.7	2.9	2.8	2.8	2.1	2.0	2.0	1.8	2.0	2.1	2.4	2.3	2.3	2.2	1.8	1.5
1997	1.4	1.6	1.9	2.2	2.6	2.7	2.7	2.6	2.0	1.8	1.8	1.7	1.9	2.0	2.2	2.2	2.2	2.1	1.7	1.3
1998	0.9	1.1	1.4	1.7	2.0	2.2	2.1	2.1	1.5	1.3	1.3	1.1	1.3	1.4	1.7	1.6	1.6	1.5	1.1	0.7
1999	1.0	1.2	1.5	1.8	2.1	2.3	2.2	2.2	1.6	1.4	1.4	1.3	1.4	1.6	1.8	1.7	1.7	1.6	1.2	0.9
2000	1.1	1.3	1.5	1.8	2.2	2.3	2.3	2.3	1.7	1.5	1.5	1.3	1.5	1.7	1.9	1.8	1.8	1.7	1.3	1.0
2001	1.4	1.6	1.9	2.2	2.5	2.7	2.7	2.6	2.1	1.9	1.9	1.7	1.9	2.0	2.3	2.2	2.2	2.1	1.7	1.4
2002	1.5	1.7	2.0	2.3	2.6	2.8	2.8	2.7	2.2	2.0	2.0	1.8	2.0	2.1	2.3	2.3	2.3	2.2	1.8	1.5

*Beta and equity risk premium estimated from the S&P 500. Estimates based on a minimum of five years of data.

Table A-5 (Page 3 of 6)

Low-Cap Size Premia*

Percent per annum risk premia for all historical time periods.

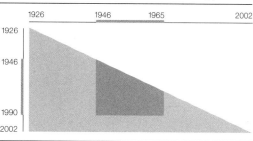

from 1926 to 2002

To the end of	From the beginning of 1946	1947	1948	1949	1950	1951	1952	1953	1954	1955	1956	1957	1958	1959	1960	1961	1962	1963	1964	1965
1946																				
1947																				
1948																				
1949																				
1950	−4.5																			
1951	−5.7	−5.9																		
1952	−6.1	−6.1	−5.0																	
1953	−5.3	−5.1	−4.1	−3.2																
1954	−4.4	−3.7	−2.5	−1.3	−0.7															
1955	−4.3	−3.2	−2.0	−0.2	0.5	−0.1														
1956	−3.2	−2.1	−0.9	0.9	1.5	0.8	2.6													
1957	−3.5	−2.6	−1.7	−0.4	−0.3	−1.2	−0.3	0.6												
1958	−1.9	−0.9	0.2	1.7	2.1	1.7	3.2	4.6	6.3											
1959	−1.3	−0.3	0.8	2.2	2.7	2.4	3.7	5.0	6.5	4.8										
1960	−1.4	−0.5	0.4	1.6	1.9	1.5	2.5	3.5	4.4	2.8	3.5									
1961	−1.3	−0.5	0.4	1.4	1.7	1.5	2.4	3.3	4.1	2.9	3.3	2.8								
1962	−2.0	−1.4	−0.8	0.0	0.1	−0.3	0.4	1.0	1.3	0.3	1.1	0.7	1.6							
1963	−2.1	−1.6	−1.0	−0.3	−0.2	−0.5	0.1	0.7	0.9	−0.1	0.4	−0.1	0.4	−2.2						
1964	−2.0	−1.5	−0.9	−0.2	−0.2	−0.5	0.2	0.7	0.9	0.0	0.3	−0.3	0.2	−2.0	−3.5					
1965	−0.9	−0.3	0.3	1.0	1.1	1.0	1.6	2.2	2.5	1.9	2.4	2.0	2.6	1.2	0.5	0.6				
1966	−0.7	−0.3	0.3	0.9	1.0	0.9	1.5	2.0	2.3	1.8	2.4	2.2	2.8	1.6	1.1	1.5	2.2			
1967	0.9	1.4	2.0	2.7	2.9	2.9	3.6	4.2	4.6	4.4	5.1	5.1	5.9	5.2	5.2	6.1	7.6	9.9		
1968	1.6	2.1	2.8	3.4	3.6	3.6	4.4	5.0	5.4	5.3	6.1	6.2	7.0	6.6	6.7	7.6	9.2	11.3	14.9	
1969	0.7	1.1	1.7	2.1	2.3	2.3	2.9	3.5	3.8	3.7	4.5	4.6	5.1	4.7	4.8	5.4	6.6	7.8	10.8	14.0
1970	−0.1	0.2	0.7	1.1	1.2	1.1	1.7	2.2	2.4	2.4	3.2	3.2	3.5	3.1	3.1	3.5	4.4	5.2	7.5	9.6
1971	0.0	0.3	0.7	1.1	1.2	1.2	1.7	2.3	2.4	2.4	3.2	3.2	3.5	3.2	3.1	3.5	4.3	5.0	7.0	8.7
1972	−0.5	−0.3	0.1	0.4	0.5	0.5	1.0	1.4	1.5	1.5	2.1	2.0	2.2	1.8	1.6	1.8	2.3	2.8	4.2	5.3
1973	−1.5	−1.3	−1.0	−0.8	−0.7	−0.8	−0.3	0.1	0.1	0.2	0.8	0.7	0.8	0.5	0.3	0.4	0.9	1.1	2.5	3.4
1974	−0.9	−0.8	−0.5	−0.1	−0.1	−0.2	0.2	0.6	0.7	0.7	1.4	1.4	1.7	1.2	1.0	1.3	1.6	2.2	3.2	3.9
1975	−0.4	−0.2	0.1	0.4	0.5	0.5	0.9	1.3	1.4	1.5	2.2	2.2	2.5	2.1	2.0	2.3	2.7	3.3	4.3	5.1
1976	0.3	0.5	0.9	1.2	1.3	1.3	1.8	2.2	2.3	2.4	3.1	3.2	3.5	3.2	3.2	3.5	4.0	4.5	5.6	6.4
1977	1.2	1.4	1.8	2.1	2.2	2.3	2.8	3.2	3.4	3.6	4.3	4.4	4.8	4.6	4.6	5.0	5.5	6.2	7.3	8.2
1978	1.4	1.6	2.0	2.3	2.4	2.5	3.0	3.4	3.6	3.8	4.5	4.7	5.0	4.8	4.9	5.3	5.8	6.4	7.5	8.3
1979	2.0	2.2	2.6	2.9	3.1	3.1	3.6	4.1	4.3	4.5	5.3	5.4	5.8	5.7	5.8	6.2	6.8	7.4	8.5	9.3
1980	1.9	2.0	2.4	2.7	2.8	2.9	3.4	3.9	4.0	4.2	4.9	5.0	5.3	5.2	5.3	5.6	6.1	6.7	7.6	8.3
1981	2.1	2.3	2.7	3.0	3.1	3.2	3.7	4.1	4.3	4.5	5.2	5.3	5.7	5.6	5.6	6.0	6.5	7.0	8.0	8.7
1982	2.3	2.4	2.8	3.1	3.2	3.3	3.8	4.2	4.4	4.6	5.2	5.4	5.7	5.6	5.7	6.0	6.5	7.0	7.9	8.5
1983	2.3	2.5	2.8	3.2	3.3	3.4	3.8	4.2	4.4	4.6	5.2	5.3	5.6	5.5	5.6	5.9	6.3	6.8	7.6	8.2
1984	2.1	2.2	2.5	2.8	2.9	3.0	3.4	3.8	4.0	4.2	4.8	4.9	5.2	5.0	5.1	5.4	5.7	6.2	6.9	7.4
1985	1.9	2.1	2.4	2.7	2.8	2.9	3.3	3.6	3.8	3.9	4.5	4.6	4.8	4.7	4.7	5.0	5.3	5.7	6.4	6.9
1986	1.7	1.9	2.2	2.4	2.5	2.6	2.9	3.3	3.4	3.5	4.0	4.1	4.4	4.2	4.2	4.4	4.7	5.1	5.7	6.1
1987	1.4	1.5	1.8	2.1	2.1	2.2	2.5	2.9	3.0	3.1	3.6	3.7	3.9	3.7	3.7	3.9	4.1	4.5	5.0	5.3
1988	1.5	1.7	2.0	2.2	2.3	2.3	2.7	3.0	3.1	3.2	3.7	3.8	4.0	3.8	3.8	4.0	4.2	4.6	5.1	5.4
1989	1.2	1.3	1.6	1.9	1.9	1.9	2.3	2.6	2.7	2.7	3.2	3.2	3.4	3.2	3.1	3.3	3.5	3.8	4.3	4.5
1990	0.9	1.0	1.2	1.5	1.5	1.5	1.8	2.1	2.2	2.3	2.7	2.7	2.9	2.7	2.6	2.8	2.9	3.2	3.6	3.9

*Beta and equity risk premium estimated from the S&P 500. Estimates based on a minimum of five years of data.

Table A-5 (Page 4 of 6)

Low-Cap Size Premia*

Percent per annum risk premia for all historical time periods.

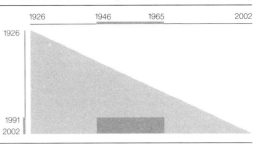

from 1926 to 2002

To the end of	From the beginning of																			
	1946	1947	1948	1949	1950	1951	1952	1953	1954	1955	1956	1957	1958	1959	1960	1961	1962	1963	1964	1965
1991	1.2	1.3	1.5	1.8	1.8	1.9	2.2	2.5	2.5	2.6	3.0	3.1	3.2	3.0	3.0	3.1	3.3	3.6	4.0	4.3
1992	1.4	1.5	1.7	2.0	2.0	2.1	2.4	2.7	2.7	2.8	3.2	3.3	3.4	3.2	3.2	3.4	3.5	3.8	4.2	4.5
1993	1.5	1.6	1.9	2.1	2.2	2.2	2.5	2.8	2.9	2.9	3.3	3.4	3.6	3.3	3.3	3.5	3.7	3.9	4.3	4.6
1994	1.5	1.6	1.8	2.0	2.1	2.1	2.4	2.7	2.8	2.8	3.2	3.3	3.4	3.2	3.2	3.4	3.5	3.8	4.2	4.4
1995	1.2	1.3	1.5	1.8	1.8	1.8	2.1	2.4	2.4	2.5	2.8	2.8	3.0	2.8	2.7	2.9	3.0	3.3	3.6	3.8
1996	1.1	1.2	1.4	1.6	1.7	1.7	1.9	2.2	2.2	2.3	2.6	2.6	2.8	2.5	2.5	2.6	2.7	3.0	3.3	3.5
1997	1.0	1.1	1.3	1.5	1.5	1.5	1.8	2.0	2.1	2.1	2.4	2.4	2.5	2.3	2.2	2.4	2.5	2.7	3.0	3.1
1998	0.3	0.4	0.6	0.8	0.8	0.8	1.1	1.3	1.3	1.3	1.6	1.6	1.7	1.4	1.4	1.4	1.5	1.7	2.0	2.1
1999	0.5	0.6	0.8	1.0	1.0	1.0	1.3	1.5	1.5	1.5	1.8	1.8	1.9	1.7	1.6	1.7	1.7	2.0	2.2	2.3
2000	0.6	0.7	0.9	1.1	1.1	1.1	1.3	1.6	1.6	1.6	1.9	1.8	2.0	1.7	1.7	1.7	1.8	2.0	2.3	2.4
2001	1.0	1.1	1.4	1.5	1.6	1.6	1.8	2.0	2.1	2.1	2.4	2.4	2.5	2.3	2.2	2.3	2.4	2.7	2.9	3.0
2002	1.1	1.2	1.4	1.6	1.6	1.6	1.9	2.1	2.1	2.2	2.4	2.5	2.6	2.4	2.3	2.4	2.5	2.7	3.0	3.1

*Beta and equity risk premium estimated from the S&P 500. Estimates based on a minimum of five years of data.

Table A-5 (Page 5 of 6)

Low-Cap Size Premia*

Percent per annum risk premia for all historical time periods.

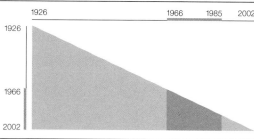

from 1926 to 2002

To the end of	From the beginning of 1966	1967	1968	1969	1970	1971	1972	1973	1974	1975	1976	1977	1978	1979	1980	1981	1982	1983	1984	1985
1966																				
1967																				
1968																				
1969																				
1970	7.6																			
1971	6.9	6.5																		
1972	3.3	2.3	−3.5																	
1973	1.5	0.3	−4.7	−9.3																
1974	2.0	1.5	−3.4	−7.5	−7.1															
1975	3.5	3.2	−0.7	−3.6	−2.6	−0.5														
1976	5.2	5.0	1.8	−0.4	1.0	3.4	3.2													
1977	7.1	7.2	4.5	2.8	4.4	6.9	7.2	12.0												
1978	7.4	7.4	5.0	3.6	5.1	7.3	7.7	11.8	17.0											
1979	8.5	8.6	6.6	5.4	6.9	9.1	9.7	13.6	18.3	19.3										
1980	7.6	7.6	5.6	4.5	5.8	7.7	8.1	11.2	15.2	15.2	15.5									
1981	7.9	8.0	6.2	5.1	6.4	8.2	8.6	11.4	14.7	15.2	15.2	14.0								
1982	7.8	7.9	6.1	5.2	6.3	8.0	8.3	10.8	13.8	14.2	14.0	12.6	9.5							
1983	7.5	7.6	5.9	5.0	6.1	7.6	7.9	10.1	12.8	13.0	12.7	11.3	8.5	8.4						
1984	6.7	6.8	5.2	4.2	5.2	6.6	6.7	8.7	11.0	11.0	10.4	9.0	6.2	5.7	2.2					
1985	6.2	6.2	4.6	3.7	4.7	5.9	6.0	7.7	9.8	9.6	9.0	7.6	5.0	4.4	1.5	2.4				
1986	5.4	5.3	3.8	2.9	3.8	4.9	4.9	6.4	8.3	8.2	7.4	5.9	3.5	2.9	0.1	0.5	−1.3			
1987	4.6	4.6	3.1	2.2	3.0	4.0	3.9	5.2	6.9	6.8	5.9	4.4	2.0	1.3	−1.5	−1.4	−3.3	−5.3		
1988	4.7	4.7	3.2	2.4	3.2	4.1	4.1	5.3	6.9	6.8	6.0	4.6	2.5	1.9	−0.5	−0.3	−1.7	−3.2	−4.8	
1989	3.9	3.8	2.4	1.5	2.2	3.1	3.0	4.1	5.6	5.4	4.6	3.2	1.2	0.5	−1.7	−1.6	−3.0	−4.4	−6.1	−5.4
1990	3.2	3.1	1.7	0.9	1.5	2.3	2.2	3.2	4.5	4.2	3.3	1.9	0.0	−0.7	−2.9	−3.0	−4.4	−5.9	−7.4	−7.2
1991	3.6	3.5	2.2	1.5	2.1	2.9	2.8	3.8	5.1	4.9	4.1	2.8	1.1	0.5	−1.3	−1.2	−2.4	−3.4	−4.5	−3.8
1992	3.9	3.8	2.5	1.8	2.4	3.2	3.2	4.1	5.4	5.2	4.4	3.3	1.7	1.2	−0.4	−0.3	−1.2	−2.0	−2.8	−2.0
1993	4.0	3.9	2.7	2.1	2.7	3.4	3.4	4.3	5.5	5.3	4.6	3.6	2.1	1.7	0.1	0.3	−0.5	−1.1	−1.8	−0.9
1994	3.8	3.7	2.6	1.9	2.5	3.2	3.2	4.0	5.1	5.0	4.3	3.3	1.9	1.5	0.0	0.2	−0.6	−1.2	−1.8	−1.0
1995	3.2	3.2	2.0	1.4	1.9	2.6	2.5	3.3	4.4	4.2	3.5	2.5	1.1	0.8	−0.6	−0.5	−1.2	−1.8	−2.4	−1.8
1996	2.9	2.8	1.7	1.1	1.6	2.3	2.2	2.9	4.0	3.7	3.1	2.1	0.8	0.4	−0.9	−0.8	−1.5	−2.1	−2.6	−2.0
1997	2.6	2.5	1.4	0.8	1.3	1.9	1.9	2.5	3.6	3.4	2.7	1.8	0.5	0.2	−1.0	−0.9	−1.6	−2.1	−2.6	−2.0
1998	1.5	1.4	0.3	−0.3	0.2	0.7	0.6	1.2	2.2	1.9	1.2	0.3	−1.0	−1.4	−2.7	−2.7	−3.4	−4.0	−4.6	−4.3
1999	1.8	1.7	0.6	0.0	0.5	1.1	1.0	1.6	2.5	2.2	1.6	0.7	−0.5	−0.8	−2.0	−1.9	−2.6	−3.1	−3.6	−3.2
2000	1.9	1.8	0.8	0.2	0.6	1.2	1.1	1.6	2.6	2.4	1.8	0.9	−0.3	−0.6	−1.7	−1.6	−2.2	−2.7	−3.2	−2.7
2001	2.5	2.5	1.5	1.0	1.4	2.0	1.9	2.5	3.3	3.2	2.6	1.8	0.8	0.5	−0.6	−0.5	−1.0	−1.4	−1.7	−1.3
2002	2.6	2.6	1.6	1.1	1.5	2.0	2.0	2.5	3.3	3.2	2.7	1.9	0.9	0.6	−0.4	−0.4	−0.8	−1.2	−1.5	−1.1

*Beta and equity risk premium estimated from the S&P 500. Estimates based on a minimum of five years of data.

Table A-5 (Page 6 of 6)

Low-Cap Size Premia*

Percent per annum risk premia for all historical time periods.

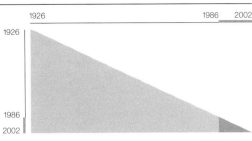

from 1926 to 2002

To the end of	From the beginning of												
	1986	1987	1988	1989	1990	1991	1992	1993	1994	1995	1996	1997	1998
1986													
1987													
1988													
1989													
1990	−8.4												
1991	−4.3	−3.4											
1992	−2.2	−1.1	1.5										
1993	−0.9	0.2	2.5	1.4									
1994	−1.0	−0.1	1.9	0.8	3.5								
1995	−1.8	−1.2	0.6	−0.5	1.1	5.3							
1996	−2.1	−1.6	0.1	−1.0	0.3	4.0	1.6						
1997	−2.1	−1.7	0.2	−0.8	0.1	3.8	1.8	0.0					
1998	−4.5	−4.3	−3.1	−4.3	−3.7	−1.6	−4.2	−6.9	−10.0				
1999	−3.3	−3.1	−1.8	−2.8	−2.2	0.0	−2.1	−4.1	−6.2	−7.3			
2000	−2.9	−2.5	−1.3	−2.1	−1.5	0.5	−1.4	−2.9	−4.5	−4.7	−4.6		
2001	−1.3	−0.9	0.2	−0.4	0.4	2.1	0.6	−0.5	−1.6	−1.4	−0.5	0.3	
2002	−1.1	−0.7	0.3	−0.3	0.5	2.0	0.5	−0.5	−1.4	−1.2	−0.4	0.3	1.6

*Beta and equity risk premium estimated from the S&P 500. Estimates based on a minimum of five years of data.

Table A-6 (Page 1 of 6)

Micro-Cap Size Premia*

Percent per annum risk premia for all historical time periods.

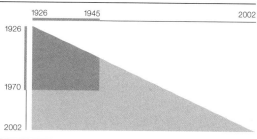

from 1926 to 2002

To the end of	From the beginning of 1926	1927	1928	1929	1930	1931	1932	1933	1934	1935	1936	1937	1938	1939	1940	1941	1942	1943	1944	1945
1926																				
1927																				
1928																				
1929																				
1930	−18.8																			
1931	−15.6	−14.3																		
1932	−10.2	−8.0	−5.9																	
1933	5.1	9.2	14.3	20.8																
1934	7.6	11.5	16.4	22.5	34.7															
1935	6.6	10.0	14.1	18.8	27.9	34.5														
1936	9.2	12.5	16.4	20.7	28.6	34.3	36.5													
1937	8.4	11.4	14.8	18.6	25.5	29.8	30.9	30.2												
1938	6.2	8.7	11.6	14.6	20.1	23.3	23.3	21.6	6.0											
1939	5.6	7.9	10.6	13.4	18.2	20.6	20.0	17.6	4.1	−0.2										
1940	5.5	7.7	10.1	12.7	17.0	19.1	18.5	16.7	5.1	1.5	3.9									
1941	5.5	7.5	9.8	12.2	16.1	18.0	17.4	15.7	5.5	2.4	4.5	−0.5								
1942	6.5	8.4	10.6	12.8	16.4	18.2	17.6	16.2	7.0	4.6	6.5	2.6	1.8							
1943	9.5	11.5	13.7	15.9	19.5	21.3	21.0	19.7	11.8	10.3	12.8	10.6	10.9	18.0						
1944	10.6	12.5	14.7	16.9	20.2	22.0	21.6	20.4	13.2	12.1	14.6	12.8	13.4	19.3	24.6					
1945	11.4	13.3	15.4	17.4	20.5	22.2	21.9	20.6	13.9	13.2	15.4	13.9	14.7	19.4	25.4	27.3				
1946	10.9	12.7	14.6	16.5	19.4	20.9	20.5	19.3	13.2	12.3	14.3	12.8	13.4	17.6	21.8	23.4	27.2			
1947	9.9	11.6	13.3	15.1	17.7	19.0	18.5	17.3	11.4	10.5	12.2	10.6	10.9	14.4	17.6	18.3	20.4	18.5		
1948	9.0	10.5	12.1	13.7	16.1	17.3	16.8	15.6	10.0	9.1	10.4	8.8	9.0	12.0	14.7	15.4	17.2	15.3	8.3	
1949	8.4	9.8	11.3	12.7	15.0	16.0	15.4	14.2	8.9	8.0	9.1	7.5	7.6	10.2	12.7	13.1	14.3	12.2	6.2	1.2
1950	8.0	9.3	10.7	12.1	14.1	15.1	14.4	13.1	8.0	7.3	8.2	6.7	6.8	9.0	11.7	11.8	12.9	10.6	5.7	1.6
1951	6.7	7.9	9.2	10.4	12.3	13.1	12.4	11.0	6.1	5.4	6.1	4.5	4.5	6.3	9.0	8.9	9.7	7.2	2.7	−1.3
1952	5.8	6.9	8.1	9.2	10.9	11.6	10.9	9.5	4.8	4.1	4.7	3.1	3.0	4.7	7.2	7.1	7.8	5.3	1.2	−2.5
1953	5.5	6.6	7.7	8.7	10.3	11.0	10.3	9.0	4.6	3.8	4.4	2.8	2.8	4.3	6.6	6.6	7.2	5.0	1.1	−2.3
1954	4.9	5.9	7.0	7.9	9.4	10.0	9.3	8.0	3.7	3.1	3.6	2.0	2.1	3.5	6.2	6.3	7.0	4.8	1.5	−1.4
1955	4.1	5.0	6.0	6.8	8.1	8.7	8.0	6.7	2.7	2.2	2.5	0.9	1.0	2.5	5.3	5.5	6.3	4.2	1.3	−1.5
1956	3.9	4.8	5.7	6.5	7.8	8.3	7.6	6.5	2.7	2.2	2.4	1.0	1.2	2.6	5.3	5.7	6.5	4.6	1.8	−0.7
1957	3.9	4.8	5.7	6.4	7.7	8.2	7.6	6.6	2.9	2.4	2.7	1.2	1.5	2.9	5.2	5.6	6.4	4.7	1.9	−0.6
1958	4.0	4.9	5.7	6.4	7.6	8.2	7.5	6.5	3.1	2.7	2.9	1.6	1.8	3.2	5.9	6.3	7.1	5.5	3.1	1.0
1959	4.0	4.8	5.6	6.3	7.4	8.0	7.3	6.4	3.1	2.7	2.9	1.7	2.0	3.3	5.9	6.3	7.1	5.6	3.4	1.4
1960	3.8	4.7	5.4	6.1	7.2	7.7	7.1	6.2	3.1	2.7	2.9	1.6	2.0	3.3	5.7	6.1	6.9	5.5	3.3	1.4
1961	3.5	4.3	5.0	5.6	6.7	7.2	6.6	5.7	2.7	2.4	2.5	1.3	1.6	2.9	5.3	5.8	6.5	5.1	3.1	1.3
1962	3.5	4.2	4.9	5.5	6.5	7.0	6.5	5.7	2.8	2.4	2.6	1.4	1.7	2.9	5.0	5.4	6.0	4.7	2.5	0.8
1963	2.9	3.6	4.3	4.8	5.8	6.2	5.7	4.9	2.1	1.8	1.9	0.7	1.0	2.2	4.3	4.7	5.2	4.0	1.9	0.3
1964	2.7	3.4	4.1	4.6	5.5	5.9	5.4	4.6	1.9	1.6	1.7	0.6	0.9	2.1	4.1	4.5	5.0	3.8	1.9	0.3
1965	3.2	3.9	4.5	5.0	6.0	6.4	5.8	5.1	2.5	2.3	2.4	1.3	1.7	2.8	4.9	5.2	5.8	4.6	2.9	1.4
1966	3.4	4.0	4.7	5.2	6.1	6.5	6.0	5.3	2.8	2.5	2.6	1.6	1.9	3.0	4.9	5.2	5.7	4.6	2.9	1.5
1967	5.0	5.7	6.3	6.8	7.7	8.2	7.7	7.1	4.7	4.6	4.7	3.8	4.2	5.4	7.3	7.7	8.2	7.3	5.7	4.5
1968	5.7	6.4	7.1	7.6	8.5	8.9	8.6	8.0	5.7	5.6	5.8	4.9	5.3	6.5	8.3	8.8	9.4	8.5	7.1	6.0
1969	5.2	5.8	6.4	6.9	7.8	8.2	7.8	7.2	5.0	4.8	4.9	4.1	4.5	5.5	7.1	7.4	7.8	7.0	5.5	4.3
1970	4.6	5.3	5.9	6.3	7.2	7.6	7.2	6.6	4.4	4.2	4.3	3.4	3.8	4.7	6.2	6.4	6.8	5.9	4.3	3.2

*Beta and equity risk premium estimated from the S&P 500. Estimates based on a minimum of five years of data.

Table A-6 (Page 2 of 6)

Micro-Cap Size Premia*

Percent per annum risk premia for all historical time periods.

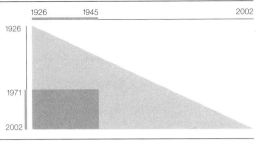

from 1926 to 2002

To the end of	From the beginning of 1926	1927	1928	1929	1930	1931	1932	1933	1934	1935	1936	1937	1938	1939	1940	1941	1942	1943	1944	1945
1971	4.5	5.1	5.7	6.2	7.0	7.4	7.0	6.4	4.2	4.0	4.2	3.3	3.6	4.5	5.9	6.1	6.5	5.6	4.1	3.0
1972	3.9	4.5	5.0	5.5	6.2	6.6	6.2	5.6	3.5	3.3	3.4	2.5	2.8	3.7	5.0	5.2	5.5	4.7	3.2	2.1
1973	3.4	4.0	4.5	4.9	5.7	6.0	5.6	5.0	2.9	2.6	2.7	1.9	2.1	2.9	4.0	4.1	4.3	3.5	1.9	0.8
1974	3.7	4.3	4.8	5.2	6.0	6.4	6.0	5.6	3.5	3.2	3.3	2.4	2.7	3.5	4.4	4.6	4.8	4.0	2.4	1.4
1975	4.0	4.6	5.1	5.5	6.3	6.6	6.3	5.8	3.8	3.5	3.6	2.8	3.1	3.9	4.9	5.0	5.2	4.5	3.0	2.0
1976	4.4	5.0	5.5	5.9	6.6	6.9	6.6	6.2	4.2	4.0	4.1	3.3	3.6	4.4	5.3	5.5	5.7	5.0	3.6	2.6
1977	5.0	5.6	6.1	6.5	7.2	7.6	7.3	6.9	5.0	4.8	4.9	4.2	4.4	5.2	6.1	6.3	6.5	5.9	4.5	3.6
1978	5.2	5.8	6.3	6.7	7.4	7.8	7.5	7.1	5.2	5.0	5.1	4.4	4.7	5.4	6.3	6.5	6.7	6.1	4.7	3.8
1979	5.5	6.1	6.6	7.0	7.7	8.0	7.8	7.4	5.6	5.4	5.5	4.8	5.1	5.8	6.7	6.9	7.1	6.5	5.2	4.3
1980	5.3	5.8	6.3	6.7	7.4	7.7	7.5	7.1	5.3	5.1	5.2	4.6	4.8	5.6	6.4	6.6	6.8	6.2	4.9	4.1
1981	5.6	6.1	6.6	7.0	7.7	8.0	7.8	7.4	5.7	5.5	5.6	4.9	5.2	5.9	6.7	6.9	7.1	6.5	5.3	4.5
1982	5.6	6.1	6.6	6.9	7.6	8.0	7.7	7.4	5.7	5.5	5.6	5.0	5.3	6.0	6.7	6.9	7.1	6.6	5.3	4.6
1983	5.6	6.1	6.6	6.9	7.6	7.9	7.7	7.4	5.7	5.6	5.7	5.0	5.3	6.0	6.8	7.0	7.2	6.7	5.4	4.7
1984	5.2	5.7	6.2	6.5	7.2	7.5	7.2	6.9	5.3	5.1	5.2	4.6	4.9	5.5	6.2	6.4	6.6	6.1	4.8	4.1
1985	4.9	5.4	5.8	6.2	6.8	7.1	6.9	6.6	5.0	4.8	4.9	4.3	4.5	5.2	5.9	6.1	6.2	5.7	4.5	3.8
1986	4.6	5.1	5.5	5.8	6.4	6.7	6.5	6.2	4.6	4.5	4.5	3.9	4.2	4.8	5.5	5.7	5.9	5.3	4.2	3.5
1987	4.3	4.8	5.2	5.5	6.1	6.4	6.2	5.9	4.4	4.2	4.2	3.6	3.9	4.5	5.1	5.3	5.4	4.9	3.7	3.0
1988	4.3	4.7	5.1	5.4	6.0	6.3	6.1	5.9	4.3	4.2	4.2	3.6	3.9	4.5	5.1	5.2	5.4	4.9	3.7	3.0
1989	3.8	4.2	4.5	4.8	5.4	5.7	5.5	5.3	3.8	3.6	3.6	3.0	3.3	3.9	4.5	4.7	4.8	4.3	3.2	2.5
1990	3.4	3.8	4.2	4.5	5.0	5.3	5.1	4.9	3.4	3.2	3.2	2.6	2.9	3.4	4.0	4.1	4.3	3.8	2.6	1.9
1991	3.6	4.0	4.3	4.6	5.1	5.4	5.2	5.0	3.6	3.4	3.4	2.8	3.1	3.7	4.3	4.4	4.6	4.1	3.0	2.3
1992	3.8	4.2	4.6	4.8	5.4	5.7	5.5	5.3	3.9	3.7	3.8	3.2	3.4	4.0	4.6	4.8	4.9	4.4	3.4	2.7
1993	3.9	4.3	4.6	4.9	5.4	5.7	5.6	5.4	4.0	3.8	3.9	3.3	3.6	4.1	4.7	4.9	5.0	4.5	3.5	2.8
1994	3.8	4.2	4.6	4.8	5.3	5.6	5.4	5.3	3.9	3.8	3.8	3.2	3.5	4.0	4.6	4.7	4.9	4.4	3.4	2.7
1995	3.6	3.9	4.3	4.5	5.0	5.3	5.1	5.0	3.6	3.5	3.5	2.9	3.2	3.7	4.4	4.5	4.6	4.2	3.2	2.5
1996	3.4	3.8	4.1	4.3	4.8	5.1	4.9	4.7	3.5	3.3	3.3	2.8	3.0	3.6	4.2	4.3	4.5	4.0	3.0	2.4
1997	3.1	3.5	3.8	4.0	4.5	4.7	4.6	4.5	3.2	3.1	3.1	2.5	2.8	3.3	4.0	4.1	4.3	3.8	2.8	2.2
1998	2.5	2.8	3.1	3.3	3.8	4.0	3.9	3.8	2.5	2.4	2.4	1.8	2.1	2.6	3.3	3.4	3.5	3.0	2.1	1.5
1999	2.6	2.9	3.2	3.4	3.8	4.1	3.9	3.8	2.6	2.5	2.5	2.0	2.2	2.8	3.4	3.5	3.6	3.2	2.3	1.7
2000	2.6	3.0	3.2	3.4	3.9	4.1	4.0	3.9	2.7	2.6	2.6	2.0	2.3	2.8	3.4	3.6	3.7	3.3	2.3	1.7
2001	3.3	3.6	3.9	4.1	4.6	4.8	4.7	4.7	3.5	3.4	3.3	2.8	3.1	3.6	4.2	4.3	4.4	4.0	3.1	2.5
2002	3.5	3.9	4.1	4.3	4.8	5.1	5.0	4.9	3.7	3.6	3.6	3.0	3.3	3.8	4.3	4.4	4.6	4.2	3.2	2.7

*Beta and equity risk premium estimated from the S&P 500. Estimates based on a minimum of five years of data.

Table A-6 (Page 3 of 6)

Micro-Cap Size Premia*

Percent per annum risk premia for all historical time periods.

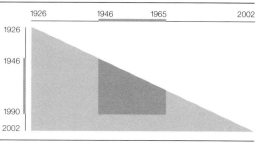

from 1926 to 2002

To the end of	From the beginning of 1946	1947	1948	1949	1950	1951	1952	1953	1954	1955	1956	1957	1958	1959	1960	1961	1962	1963	1964	1965
1946																				
1947																				
1948																				
1949																				
1950	−4.6																			
1951	−7.0	−7.3																		
1952	−7.7	−7.6	−6.3																	
1953	−6.9	−6.6	−5.5	−4.0																
1954	−5.5	−4.6	−3.1	−1.1	−0.2															
1955	−5.3	−3.9	−2.4	0.1	1.1	−0.8														
1956	−4.2	−2.7	−1.3	1.2	1.9	0.1	3.0													
1957	−3.8	−2.7	−1.5	0.5	0.7	−1.2	0.7	2.1												
1958	−1.8	−0.4	1.0	3.1	3.8	2.7	5.1	7.1	10.1											
1959	−1.1	0.3	1.6	3.6	4.3	3.4	5.5	7.3	9.8	7.4										
1960	−1.1	0.2	1.4	3.2	3.7	2.7	4.4	5.8	7.7	5.2	5.7									
1961	−0.9	0.3	1.4	3.1	3.6	2.8	4.4	5.6	7.2	5.2	5.7	6.2								
1962	−1.4	−0.5	0.4	1.6	1.9	0.9	2.2	3.2	4.1	2.3	3.0	3.3	4.4							
1963	−1.8	−1.0	−0.1	1.0	1.2	0.3	1.4	2.3	3.0	1.3	1.6	1.6	2.2	−2.4						
1964	−1.7	−0.8	0.0	1.1	1.3	0.5	1.6	2.4	3.1	1.5	1.8	1.6	2.1	−1.6	−3.3					
1965	−0.4	0.5	1.4	2.5	2.7	2.1	3.2	4.0	4.8	3.6	4.0	4.1	4.7	2.1	1.2	1.6				
1966	−0.3	0.5	1.3	2.2	2.4	1.8	2.8	3.6	4.2	3.1	3.6	3.8	4.4	2.0	1.3	1.9	2.1			
1967	3.0	3.9	4.8	5.9	6.3	6.0	7.2	8.2	9.1	8.6	9.5	10.1	11.1	9.9	10.4	11.9	14.1	17.3		
1968	4.6	5.5	6.4	7.5	7.9	7.7	9.0	10.0	11.0	10.7	11.7	12.4	13.6	12.8	13.5	15.2	17.5	20.9	27.3	
1969	3.0	3.6	4.4	5.2	5.6	5.3	6.4	7.3	8.0	7.7	8.7	9.2	9.8	9.1	9.4	10.6	12.3	14.1	19.2	23.9
1970	1.9	2.4	3.0	3.7	4.0	3.7	4.6	5.5	6.0	5.7	6.6	7.0	7.4	6.6	6.7	7.6	8.8	10.1	13.9	16.8
1971	1.7	2.2	2.8	3.4	3.6	3.4	4.3	5.1	5.5	5.3	6.2	6.5	6.8	6.1	6.2	6.9	8.0	8.9	12.1	14.4
1972	0.8	1.3	1.8	2.4	2.6	2.2	3.1	3.7	4.1	3.8	4.5	4.7	4.8	4.0	3.9	4.3	5.1	5.5	7.9	9.4
1973	−0.4	−0.1	0.3	0.8	0.9	0.6	1.3	1.9	2.2	2.0	2.7	2.8	2.8	2.1	2.0	2.2	2.9	3.1	5.4	6.5
1974	0.1	0.4	0.8	1.3	1.4	1.0	1.7	2.3	2.6	2.3	3.0	3.3	3.5	2.6	2.5	3.0	3.4	4.0	5.9	6.6
1975	0.8	1.1	1.5	2.0	2.1	1.8	2.6	3.2	3.5	3.4	4.1	4.4	4.6	3.9	3.9	4.3	4.9	5.4	7.3	8.2
1976	1.5	1.8	2.3	2.7	2.9	2.7	3.5	4.1	4.4	4.3	5.1	5.4	5.6	5.1	5.1	5.6	6.2	6.8	8.6	9.5
1977	2.5	2.9	3.3	3.8	4.0	3.8	4.6	5.3	5.6	5.6	6.4	6.8	7.1	6.6	6.7	7.3	8.0	8.7	10.5	11.5
1978	2.8	3.1	3.6	4.1	4.3	4.1	4.9	5.6	5.9	5.9	6.8	7.1	7.4	7.0	7.2	7.7	8.4	9.1	10.8	11.8
1979	3.4	3.7	4.2	4.6	4.8	4.7	5.5	6.2	6.5	6.6	7.4	7.8	8.1	7.7	7.9	8.5	9.2	9.8	11.5	12.5
1980	3.2	3.5	3.9	4.4	4.6	4.4	5.2	5.8	6.1	6.2	7.0	7.3	7.5	7.2	7.3	7.8	8.4	9.0	10.5	11.3
1981	3.6	3.9	4.3	4.8	5.0	4.8	5.6	6.2	6.5	6.6	7.4	7.7	8.0	7.7	7.8	8.3	8.9	9.5	11.0	11.8
1982	3.7	4.0	4.4	4.9	5.0	4.9	5.6	6.2	6.6	6.6	7.3	7.7	7.9	7.6	7.7	8.2	8.7	9.3	10.7	11.4
1983	3.8	4.1	4.6	5.0	5.2	5.1	5.8	6.4	6.7	6.7	7.4	7.7	8.0	7.6	7.8	8.2	8.7	9.3	10.5	11.2
1984	3.3	3.5	3.9	4.3	4.5	4.4	5.0	5.6	5.8	5.9	6.5	6.8	7.0	6.6	6.7	7.1	7.6	8.0	9.2	9.7
1985	3.0	3.2	3.6	4.0	4.2	4.0	4.7	5.2	5.4	5.4	6.0	6.2	6.4	6.1	6.1	6.5	6.8	7.3	8.3	8.8
1986	2.6	2.9	3.2	3.6	3.7	3.6	4.2	4.6	4.9	4.8	5.4	5.6	5.7	5.3	5.3	5.6	5.9	6.3	7.2	7.6
1987	2.2	2.4	2.7	3.1	3.2	3.0	3.6	4.0	4.2	4.2	4.7	4.9	5.0	4.5	4.5	4.8	5.1	5.4	6.3	6.6
1988	2.2	2.4	2.8	3.1	3.2	3.1	3.6	4.0	4.2	4.2	4.6	4.8	5.0	4.5	4.5	4.8	5.0	5.4	6.1	6.4
1989	1.6	1.8	2.2	2.5	2.6	2.4	2.9	3.3	3.5	3.4	3.8	3.9	4.0	3.6	3.5	3.7	3.9	4.2	4.9	5.1
1990	1.1	1.3	1.6	1.9	2.0	1.8	2.2	2.6	2.8	2.7	3.1	3.2	3.3	2.8	2.7	2.9	3.0	3.3	3.9	4.1

*Beta and equity risk premium estimated from the S&P 500. Estimates based on a minimum of five years of data.

Table A-6 (Page 4 of 6)

Micro-Cap Size Premia*

Percent per annum risk premia for all historical time periods.

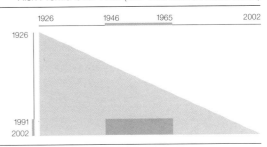

from 1926 to 2002

To the end of	From the beginning of																			
	1946	1947	1948	1949	1950	1951	1952	1953	1954	1955	1956	1957	1958	1959	1960	1961	1962	1963	1964	1965
1991	1.5	1.7	2.0	2.3	2.4	2.2	2.7	3.0	3.2	3.1	3.5	3.6	3.7	3.2	3.1	3.3	3.5	3.8	4.4	4.5
1992	1.9	2.1	2.4	2.7	2.8	2.6	3.1	3.5	3.7	3.6	3.9	4.1	4.2	3.7	3.7	3.9	4.0	4.3	4.9	5.1
1993	2.1	2.3	2.6	2.9	3.0	2.8	3.3	3.6	3.8	3.7	4.1	4.2	4.3	3.9	3.9	4.1	4.2	4.5	5.1	5.3
1994	2.0	2.2	2.5	2.8	2.9	2.7	3.1	3.5	3.7	3.6	3.9	4.0	4.2	3.7	3.7	3.9	4.0	4.3	4.8	5.0
1995	1.8	2.0	2.3	2.6	2.6	2.5	2.9	3.2	3.4	3.3	3.6	3.7	3.8	3.4	3.3	3.5	3.6	3.9	4.4	4.5
1996	1.7	1.9	2.1	2.4	2.5	2.3	2.7	3.1	3.2	3.1	3.4	3.5	3.6	3.2	3.1	3.2	3.4	3.6	4.1	4.2
1997	1.5	1.7	2.0	2.3	2.3	2.2	2.5	2.8	3.0	2.8	3.1	3.2	3.3	2.8	2.8	2.9	3.0	3.2	3.7	3.8
1998	0.8	0.9	1.2	1.4	1.5	1.3	1.7	1.9	2.1	1.9	2.1	2.2	2.3	1.8	1.7	1.8	1.8	2.0	2.4	2.5
1999	1.0	1.1	1.4	1.6	1.7	1.5	1.9	2.2	2.3	2.1	2.4	2.4	2.5	2.0	1.9	2.0	2.1	2.3	2.7	2.7
2000	1.0	1.2	1.5	1.7	1.8	1.6	1.9	2.2	2.3	2.1	2.4	2.4	2.5	2.0	1.9	2.1	2.1	2.3	2.7	2.8
2001	1.8	2.0	2.3	2.5	2.6	2.4	2.8	3.1	3.2	3.1	3.3	3.4	3.5	3.1	3.0	3.2	3.2	3.5	3.9	3.9
2002	2.0	2.2	2.4	2.7	2.7	2.6	2.9	3.2	3.4	3.2	3.5	3.6	3.7	3.3	3.2	3.4	3.4	3.7	4.1	4.2

*Beta and equity risk premium estimated from the S&P 500. Estimates based on a minimum of five years of data.

Table A-6 (Page 5 of 6)

Micro-Cap Size Premia*

Percent per annum risk premia for all historical time periods.

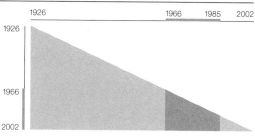

from 1926 to 2002

To the end of	From the beginning of																			
	1966	1967	1968	1969	1970	1971	1972	1973	1974	1975	1976	1977	1978	1979	1980	1981	1982	1983	1984	1985
1966																				
1967																				
1968																				
1969																				
1970	15.8																			
1971	13.1	13.9																		
1972	7.6	7.2	−5.2																	
1973	4.7	3.9	−6.9	−15.4																
1974	4.8	4.6	−5.6	−13.0	−12.0															
1975	6.7	6.7	−1.6	−7.1	−5.2	−2.2														
1976	8.4	8.4	1.4	−3.0	−0.8	2.4	2.7													
1977	10.6	10.9	4.7	1.1	3.6	6.9	7.8	14.2												
1978	11.0	11.3	5.8	2.6	5.0	8.1	9.0	14.7	21.2											
1979	11.8	12.1	7.1	4.4	6.7	9.7	10.8	15.8	21.6	22.6										
1980	10.6	10.8	6.1	3.5	5.6	8.1	9.0	13.1	18.0	17.8	17.9									
1981	11.1	11.4	7.0	4.7	6.7	9.1	9.9	13.7	17.9	18.5	18.4	17.1								
1982	10.7	10.9	6.8	4.6	6.5	8.7	9.4	12.7	16.5	17.1	16.5	15.0	11.4							
1983	10.5	10.7	6.9	4.9	6.6	8.7	9.3	12.3	15.8	16.2	15.6	14.2	11.0	10.5						
1984	9.0	9.1	5.4	3.4	5.0	6.7	7.2	9.7	12.6	12.8	11.8	10.1	6.8	5.5	2.1					
1985	8.1	8.1	4.5	2.6	4.1	5.7	6.0	8.3	10.9	10.7	9.8	8.1	4.9	3.7	0.6	1.2				
1986	6.9	6.9	3.4	1.5	2.9	4.4	4.6	6.5	8.9	8.8	7.7	5.9	2.9	1.7	−1.3	−1.3	−4.1			
1987	5.8	5.8	2.4	0.6	1.8	3.1	3.2	4.9	7.0	7.0	5.6	3.7	0.8	−0.6	−3.6	−4.0	−7.0	−9.7		
1988	5.7	5.7	2.5	0.7	1.9	3.1	3.2	4.8	6.8	6.8	5.5	3.7	1.2	−0.1	−2.6	−2.9	−5.2	−7.2	−10.9	
1989	4.3	4.3	1.1	−0.6	0.5	1.6	1.6	3.0	4.9	4.7	3.4	1.6	−0.9	−2.1	−4.6	−5.0	−7.3	−9.3	−12.7	−11.0
1990	3.3	3.2	0.2	−1.6	−0.6	0.4	0.4	1.6	3.3	3.1	1.6	−0.1	−2.6	−3.9	−6.4	−7.0	−9.2	−11.2	−14.4	−13.3
1991	3.8	3.8	0.8	−0.8	0.2	1.2	1.3	2.5	4.1	4.0	2.7	1.1	−1.0	−2.1	−4.2	−4.5	−6.2	−7.7	−10.1	−8.5
1992	4.4	4.4	1.6	0.1	1.1	2.1	2.2	3.4	5.0	4.9	3.8	2.4	0.4	−0.4	−2.2	−2.4	−3.7	−4.8	−6.6	−4.8
1993	4.6	4.6	1.9	0.5	1.5	2.5	2.5	3.7	5.2	5.2	4.1	2.8	1.0	0.3	−1.4	−1.4	−2.6	−3.4	−4.9	−3.1
1994	4.4	4.3	1.7	0.3	1.3	2.2	2.3	3.4	4.8	4.8	3.7	2.5	0.8	0.0	−1.5	−1.6	−2.7	−3.5	−4.8	−3.2
1995	3.9	3.9	1.4	0.0	0.9	1.8	1.9	2.9	4.3	4.2	3.3	2.1	0.4	−0.2	−1.7	−1.7	−2.7	−3.4	−4.7	−3.1
1996	3.6	3.6	1.1	−0.2	0.7	1.6	1.6	2.6	4.0	3.8	2.9	1.8	0.2	−0.4	−1.7	−1.8	−2.7	−3.4	−4.5	−3.0
1997	3.2	3.1	0.7	−0.5	0.4	1.2	1.2	2.1	3.5	3.4	2.5	1.4	−0.1	−0.7	−1.9	−1.9	−2.8	−3.4	−4.5	−3.0
1998	1.9	1.8	−0.5	−1.8	−1.0	−0.3	−0.3	0.5	1.8	1.6	0.7	−0.4	−2.0	−2.6	−3.9	−4.0	−4.9	−5.7	−6.8	−5.7
1999	2.1	2.1	−0.2	−1.4	−0.6	0.2	0.2	0.9	2.2	2.0	1.2	0.2	−1.3	−1.8	−3.0	−3.0	−3.9	−4.5	−5.5	−4.4
2000	2.1	2.1	−0.1	−1.3	−0.5	0.2	0.2	1.0	2.2	2.1	1.3	0.2	−1.1	−1.6	−2.8	−2.8	−3.6	−4.1	−5.1	−4.0
2001	3.4	3.4	1.3	0.1	1.0	1.7	1.7	2.5	3.7	3.7	2.9	1.9	0.7	0.3	−0.7	−0.8	−1.4	−1.8	−2.6	−1.4
2002	3.6	3.6	1.6	0.5	1.3	2.0	2.0	2.8	3.9	3.9	3.1	2.2	1.0	0.6	−0.4	−0.5	−1.0	−1.4	−2.1	−1.0

*Beta and equity risk premium estimated from the S&P 500. Estimates based on a minimum of five years of data.

Table A-6 (Page 6 of 6)

Micro-Cap Size Premia*

Percent per annum risk premia for all historical time periods.

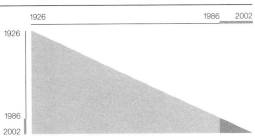

from 1926 to 2002

To the end of	From the beginning of 1986	1987	1988	1989	1990	1991	1992	1993	1994	1995	1996	1997	1998
1986													
1987													
1988													
1989													
1990	−15.2												
1991	−9.2	−8.3											
1992	−4.9	−3.5	0.7										
1993	−3.0	−1.5	2.3	1.5									
1994	−3.1	−1.8	1.3	0.5	4.4								
1995	−3.0	−2.0	1.2	0.4	3.4	10.5							
1996	−2.9	−2.0	1.0	0.3	2.8	8.8	6.0						
1997	−3.0	−2.1	0.9	0.3	2.3	8.0	5.5	2.0					
1998	−5.8	−5.3	−3.1	−4.1	−2.6	1.0	−2.2	−6.6	−10.2				
1999	−4.4	−3.8	−1.6	−2.3	−0.8	2.6	0.1	−3.3	−5.7	−6.2			
2000	−4.0	−3.4	−1.4	−2.0	−0.7	2.5	0.1	−2.6	−4.5	−4.3	−5.6		
2001	−1.3	−0.5	1.3	1.0	2.6	5.4	3.6	1.7	0.6	1.4	1.6	2.2	
2002	−0.9	−0.2	1.4	1.1	2.6	5.1	3.5	1.8	0.9	1.6	1.9	2.6	4.7

*Beta and equity risk premium estimated from the S&P 500. Estimates based on a minimum of five years of data.

Stocks, Bonds, Bills, and Inflation
Valuation Edition

0.0478	0.0013	−0.0103	0.0096	0.0424
−0.0071	−0.0176	0.0020	0.0571	0.0382
−0.0501	0.0034	0.0540	0.0204	0.0052
0.0589	−0.0275	0.0851	−0.0167	0.0909
0.0197	0.0098	−0.0030	0.0396	0.0055
−0.0328	−0.0440	0.0066	−0.0050	0.0370
0.0449	0.0176	0.0501	0.0270	0.0284

Appendix B

0.0209	−0.0046	−0.0607	−0.0811	−0.0803
−0.0022	0.0535	−0.0097	0.0339	−0.0046
0.0162	0.0178	0.0195	−0.0118	0.0301
−0.0133	0.0356	−0.0030	−0.0473	0.0147
0.0334	0.0289	−0.0031	0.0106	0.1245
−0.0120	−0.0725	−0.0053	0.0494	0.0095
0.0190	0.0468	−0.0070	0.0342	−0.0276
0.0105	−0.0172	0.0164	0.0400	0.0876

IbbotsonAssociates

Appendix B

Monthly and Annual Returns on Basic Series

Basic Series

Table B-1

Large Company Stocks: Total Returns

from January 1926 to December 1970

Year	Jan	Feb	Mar	Apr	May	Jun	Jul	Aug	Sep	Oct	Nov	Dec	Year	Jan-Dec*
1926	0.0000	−0.0385	−0.0575	0.0253	0.0179	0.0457	0.0479	0.0248	0.0252	−0.0284	0.0347	0.0196	1926	0.1162
1927	−0.0193	0.0537	0.0087	0.0201	0.0607	−0.0067	0.0670	0.0515	0.0450	−0.0502	0.0721	0.0279	1927	0.3749
1928	−0.0040	−0.0125	0.1101	0.0345	0.0197	−0.0385	0.0141	0.0803	0.0259	0.0168	0.1292	0.0049	1928	0.4361
1929	0.0583	−0.0019	−0.0012	0.0176	−0.0362	0.1140	0.0471	0.1028	−0.0476	−0.1973	−0.1246	0.0282	1929	−0.0842
1930	0.0639	0.0259	0.0812	−0.0080	−0.0096	−0.1625	0.0386	0.0141	−0.1282	−0.0855	−0.0089	−0.0706	1930	−0.2490
1931	0.0502	0.1193	−0.0675	−0.0935	−0.1279	0.1421	−0.0722	0.0182	−0.2973	0.0896	−0.0798	−0.1400	1931	−0.4334
1932	−0.0271	0.0570	−0.1158	−0.1997	−0.2196	−0.0022	0.3815	0.3869	−0.0346	−0.1349	−0.0417	0.0565	1932	−0.0819
1933	0.0087	−0.1772	0.0353	0.4256	0.1683	0.1338	−0.0862	0.1206	−0.1118	−0.0855	0.1127	0.0253	1933	0.5399
1934	0.1069	−0.0322	0.0000	−0.0251	−0.0736	0.0229	−0.1132	0.0611	−0.0033	−0.0286	0.0942	−0.0010	1934	−0.0144
1935	−0.0411	−0.0341	−0.0286	0.0980	0.0409	0.0699	0.0850	0.0280	0.0256	0.0777	0.0474	0.0394	1935	0.4767
1936	0.0670	0.0224	0.0268	−0.0751	0.0545	0.0333	0.0701	0.0151	0.0031	0.0775	0.0134	−0.0029	1936	0.3392
1937	0.0390	0.0191	−0.0077	−0.0809	−0.0024	−0.0504	0.1045	−0.0483	−0.1403	−0.0981	−0.0866	−0.0459	1937	−0.3503
1938	0.0152	0.0674	−0.2487	0.1447	−0.0330	0.2503	0.0744	−0.0226	0.0166	0.0776	−0.0273	0.0401	1938	0.3112
1939	−0.0674	0.0390	−0.1339	−0.0027	0.0733	−0.0612	0.1105	−0.0648	0.1673	−0.0123	−0.0398	0.0270	1939	−0.0041
1940	−0.0336	0.0133	0.0124	−0.0024	−0.2289	0.0809	0.0341	0.0350	0.0123	0.0422	−0.0316	0.0009	1940	−0.0978
1941	−0.0463	−0.0060	0.0071	−0.0612	0.0183	0.0578	0.0579	0.0010	−0.0068	−0.0657	−0.0284	−0.0407	1941	−0.1159
1942	0.0161	−0.0159	−0.0652	−0.0399	0.0796	0.0221	0.0337	0.0164	0.0290	0.0678	−0.0021	0.0549	1942	0.2034
1943	0.0737	0.0583	0.0545	0.0035	0.0552	0.0223	−0.0526	0.0171	0.0263	−0.0108	−0.0654	0.0617	1943	0.2590
1944	0.0171	0.0042	0.0195	−0.0100	0.0505	0.0543	−0.0193	0.0157	−0.0008	0.0023	0.0133	0.0374	1944	0.1975
1945	0.0158	0.0683	−0.0441	0.0902	0.0195	−0.0007	−0.0180	0.0641	0.0438	0.0322	0.0396	0.0116	1945	0.3644
1946	0.0714	−0.0641	0.0480	0.0393	0.0288	−0.0370	−0.0239	−0.0674	−0.0997	−0.0060	−0.0027	0.0457	1946	−0.0807
1947	0.0255	−0.0077	−0.0149	−0.0363	0.0014	0.0554	0.0381	−0.0203	−0.0111	0.0238	−0.0175	0.0233	1947	0.0571
1948	−0.0379	−0.0388	0.0793	0.0292	0.0879	0.0054	−0.0508	0.0158	−0.0276	0.0710	−0.0961	0.0346	1948	0.0550
1949	0.0039	−0.0296	0.0328	−0.0179	−0.0258	0.0014	0.0650	0.0219	0.0263	0.0340	0.0175	0.0486	1949	0.1879
1950	0.0197	0.0199	0.0070	0.0486	0.0509	−0.0548	0.0119	0.0443	0.0592	0.0093	0.0169	0.0513	1950	0.3171
1951	0.0637	0.0157	−0.0156	0.0509	−0.0299	−0.0228	0.0711	0.0478	0.0013	−0.0103	0.0096	0.0424	1951	0.2402
1952	0.0181	−0.0282	0.0503	−0.0402	0.0343	0.0490	0.0196	−0.0071	−0.0176	0.0020	0.0571	0.0382	1952	0.1837
1953	−0.0049	−0.0106	−0.0212	−0.0237	0.0077	−0.0134	0.0273	−0.0501	0.0034	0.0540	0.0204	0.0052	1953	−0.0099
1954	0.0536	0.0111	0.0325	0.0516	0.0418	0.0031	0.0589	−0.0275	0.0851	−0.0167	0.0909	0.0534	1954	0.5262
1955	0.0197	0.0098	−0.0030	0.0396	0.0055	0.0841	0.0622	−0.0025	0.0130	−0.0284	0.0827	0.0015	1955	0.3156
1956	−0.0347	0.0413	0.0710	−0.0004	−0.0593	0.0409	0.0530	−0.0328	−0.0440	0.0066	−0.0050	0.0370	1956	0.0656
1957	−0.0401	−0.0264	0.0215	0.0388	0.0437	0.0004	0.0131	−0.0505	−0.0602	−0.0302	0.0231	−0.0395	1957	−0.1078
1958	0.0445	−0.0141	0.0328	0.0337	0.0212	0.0279	0.0449	0.0176	0.0501	0.0270	0.0284	0.0535	1958	0.4336
1959	0.0053	0.0049	0.0020	0.0402	0.0240	−0.0022	0.0363	−0.0102	−0.0443	0.0128	0.0186	0.0292	1959	0.1196
1960	−0.0700	0.0147	−0.0123	−0.0161	0.0326	0.0211	−0.0234	0.0317	−0.0590	−0.0007	0.0465	0.0479	1960	0.0047
1961	0.0645	0.0319	0.0270	0.0051	0.0239	−0.0275	0.0342	0.0243	−0.0184	0.0298	0.0447	0.0046	1961	0.2689
1962	−0.0366	0.0209	−0.0046	−0.0607	−0.0811	−0.0803	0.0652	0.0208	−0.0465	0.0064	0.1086	0.0153	1962	−0.0873
1963	0.0506	−0.0239	0.0370	0.0500	0.0193	−0.0188	−0.0022	0.0535	−0.0097	0.0339	−0.0046	0.0262	1963	0.2280
1964	0.0283	0.0147	0.0165	0.0075	0.0162	0.0178	0.0195	−0.0118	0.0301	0.0096	0.0005	0.0056	1964	0.1648
1965	0.0345	0.0031	−0.0133	0.0356	−0.0030	−0.0473	0.0147	0.0272	0.0334	0.0289	−0.0031	0.0106	1965	0.1245
1966	0.0062	−0.0131	−0.0205	0.0220	−0.0492	−0.0146	−0.0120	−0.0725	−0.0053	0.0494	0.0095	0.0002	1966	−0.1006
1967	0.0798	0.0072	0.0409	0.0437	−0.0477	0.0190	0.0468	−0.0070	0.0342	−0.0276	0.0065	0.0278	1967	0.2398
1968	−0.0425	−0.0261	0.0110	0.0834	0.0161	0.0105	−0.0172	0.0164	0.0400	0.0087	0.0531	−0.0402	1968	0.1106
1969	−0.0068	−0.0426	0.0359	0.0229	0.0026	−0.0542	−0.0587	0.0454	−0.0236	0.0459	−0.0297	−0.0177	1969	−0.0850
1970	−0.0743	0.0586	0.0030	−0.0889	−0.0547	−0.0482	0.0752	0.0509	0.0347	−0.0097	0.0536	0.0584	1970	0.0401

*Compound annual return

Table B–1 (continued)

Large Company Stocks: Total Returns

from January 1971 to December 2002

Year	Jan	Feb	Mar	Apr	May	Jun	Jul	Aug	Sep	Oct	Nov	Dec	Year	Jan–Dec*
1971	0.0419	0.0141	0.0382	0.0377	−0.0367	0.0021	−0.0399	0.0412	−0.0056	−0.0404	0.0027	0.0877	1971	0.1431
1972	0.0194	0.0299	0.0072	0.0057	0.0219	−0.0205	0.0036	0.0391	−0.0036	0.0107	0.0505	0.0131	1972	0.1898
1973	−0.0159	−0.0333	−0.0002	−0.0395	−0.0139	−0.0051	0.0394	−0.0318	0.0415	0.0003	−0.1082	0.0183	1973	−0.1466
1974	−0.0085	0.0019	−0.0217	−0.0373	−0.0272	−0.0128	−0.0759	−0.0828	−0.1170	0.1657	−0.0448	−0.0177	1974	−0.2647
1975	0.1251	0.0674	0.0237	0.0493	0.0509	0.0462	−0.0659	−0.0144	−0.0328	0.0637	0.0313	−0.0096	1975	0.3720
1976	0.1199	−0.0058	0.0326	−0.0099	−0.0073	0.0427	−0.0068	0.0014	0.0247	−0.0206	−0.0009	0.0540	1976	0.2384
1977	−0.0489	−0.0151	−0.0119	0.0014	−0.0150	0.0475	−0.0151	−0.0133	0.0000	−0.0415	0.0370	0.0048	1977	−0.0718
1978	−0.0596	−0.0161	0.0276	0.0870	0.0136	−0.0152	0.0560	0.0340	−0.0048	−0.0891	0.0260	0.0172	1978	0.0656
1979	0.0421	−0.0284	0.0575	0.0036	−0.0168	0.0410	0.0110	0.0611	0.0025	−0.0656	0.0514	0.0192	1979	0.1844
1980	0.0610	0.0031	−0.0987	0.0429	0.0562	0.0296	0.0676	0.0131	0.0281	0.0187	0.1095	−0.0315	1980	0.3242
1981	−0.0438	0.0208	0.0380	−0.0213	0.0062	−0.0080	0.0007	−0.0554	−0.0502	0.0528	0.0441	−0.0265	1981	−0.0491
1982	−0.0163	−0.0512	−0.0060	0.0414	−0.0288	−0.0174	−0.0215	0.1267	0.0110	0.1126	0.0438	0.0173	1982	0.2141
1983	0.0348	0.0260	0.0365	0.0758	−0.0052	0.0382	−0.0313	0.0170	0.0136	−0.0134	0.0233	−0.0061	1983	0.2251
1984	−0.0065	−0.0328	0.0171	0.0069	−0.0534	0.0221	−0.0143	0.1125	0.0002	0.0026	−0.0101	0.0253	1984	0.0627
1985	0.0768	0.0137	0.0018	−0.0032	0.0615	0.0159	−0.0026	−0.0061	−0.0321	0.0447	0.0716	0.0467	1985	0.3216
1986	0.0044	0.0761	0.0554	−0.0124	0.0549	0.0166	−0.0569	0.0748	−0.0822	0.0556	0.0256	−0.0264	1986	0.1847
1987	0.1343	0.0413	0.0272	−0.0088	0.0103	0.0499	0.0498	0.0385	−0.0220	−0.2152	−0.0819	0.0738	1987	0.0523
1988	0.0427	0.0470	−0.0302	0.0108	0.0078	0.0464	−0.0040	−0.0331	0.0424	0.0273	−0.0142	0.0181	1988	0.1681
1989	0.0723	−0.0249	0.0236	0.0516	0.0402	−0.0054	0.0898	0.0193	−0.0039	−0.0233	0.0208	0.0236	1989	0.3149
1990	−0.0671	0.0129	0.0263	−0.0247	0.0975	−0.0070	−0.0032	−0.0903	−0.0492	−0.0037	0.0644	0.0274	1990	−0.0317
1991	0.0442	0.0716	0.0238	0.0028	0.0428	−0.0457	0.0468	0.0235	−0.0164	0.0134	−0.0404	0.1143	1991	0.3055
1992	−0.0186	0.0128	−0.0196	0.0291	0.0054	−0.0145	0.0403	−0.0202	0.0115	0.0036	0.0337	0.0131	1992	0.0767
1993	0.0073	0.0135	0.0215	−0.0245	0.0270	0.0033	−0.0047	0.0381	−0.0074	0.0203	−0.0094	0.0123	1993	0.0999
1994	0.0335	−0.0270	−0.0435	0.0130	0.0163	−0.0247	0.0331	0.0407	−0.0241	0.0229	−0.0367	0.0146	1994	0.0131
1995	0.0260	0.0388	0.0296	0.0291	0.0395	0.0235	0.0333	0.0027	0.0419	−0.0035	0.0440	0.0185	1995	0.3743
1996	0.0344	0.0096	0.0096	0.0147	0.0258	0.0041	−0.0445	0.0212	0.0562	0.0274	0.0759	−0.0196	1996	0.2307
1997	0.0621	0.0081	−0.0416	0.0597	0.0614	0.0446	0.0794	−0.0556	0.0548	−0.0334	0.0463	0.0172	1997	0.3336
1998	0.0111	0.0721	0.0512	0.0101	−0.0172	0.0406	−0.0107	−0.1446	0.0641	0.0813	0.0606	0.0576	1998	0.2858
1999	0.0418	−0.0311	0.0400	0.0387	−0.0236	0.0555	−0.0312	−0.0050	−0.0274	0.0633	0.0203	0.0589	1999	0.2104
2000	−0.0502	−0.0189	0.0978	−0.0301	−0.0205	0.0246	−0.0156	0.0621	−0.0528	−0.0042	−0.0788	0.0049	2000	−0.0911
2001	0.0355	−0.0912	−0.0634	0.0777	0.0067	−0.0243	−0.0098	−0.0626	−0.0808	0.0191	0.0767	0.0088	2001	−0.1188
2002	−0.0146	−0.0193	0.0376	−0.0606	−0.0074	−0.0712	−0.0780	0.0066	−0.1087	0.0880	0.0589	−0.0588	2002	−0.2210

*Compound annual return

Table B–2

Large Company Stocks: Income Returns

from January 1926 to December 1970

Year	Jan	Feb	Mar	Apr	May	Jun	Jul	Aug	Sep	Oct	Nov	Dec	Year	Jan–Dec*
1926	0.0016	0.0055	0.0016	0.0026	0.0102	0.0025	0.0024	0.0078	0.0023	0.0030	0.0123	0.0030	1926	0.0541
1927	0.0015	0.0061	0.0022	0.0029	0.0085	0.0027	0.0020	0.0070	0.0018	0.0029	0.0105	0.0029	1927	0.0571
1928	0.0011	0.0051	0.0017	0.0021	0.0071	0.0020	0.0016	0.0062	0.0019	0.0023	0.0092	0.0021	1928	0.0481
1929	0.0012	0.0039	0.0012	0.0016	0.0066	0.0016	0.0014	0.0048	0.0013	0.0020	0.0091	0.0029	1929	0.0398
1930	0.0014	0.0044	0.0013	0.0016	0.0068	0.0020	0.0020	0.0066	0.0019	0.0032	0.0130	0.0036	1930	0.0457
1931	0.0013	0.0050	0.0017	0.0024	0.0093	0.0031	0.0020	0.0087	0.0022	0.0051	0.0180	0.0053	1931	0.0535
1932	0.0012	0.0063	0.0024	0.0027	0.0137	0.0067	0.0045	0.0115	0.0024	0.0037	0.0172	0.0046	1932	0.0616
1933	0.0015	0.0072	0.0018	0.0034	0.0096	0.0021	0.0018	0.0060	0.0018	0.0031	0.0100	0.0030	1933	0.0639
1934	0.0010	0.0045	0.0009	0.0019	0.0076	0.0021	0.0020	0.0069	0.0022	0.0033	0.0114	0.0031	1934	0.0446
1935	0.0011	0.0055	0.0023	0.0024	0.0086	0.0021	0.0020	0.0063	0.0018	0.0026	0.0080	0.0023	1935	0.0495
1936	0.0015	0.0056	0.0014	0.0020	0.0087	0.0028	0.0020	0.0063	0.0019	0.0025	0.0093	0.0029	1936	0.0536
1937	0.0012	0.0045	0.0017	0.0022	0.0079	0.0025	0.0019	0.0071	0.0019	0.0036	0.0146	0.0045	1937	0.0466
1938	0.0019	0.0065	0.0018	0.0035	0.0113	0.0032	0.0017	0.0048	0.0017	0.0016	0.0061	0.0024	1938	0.0483
1939	0.0015	0.0065	0.0016	0.0027	0.0110	0.0026	0.0018	0.0066	0.0027	0.0023	0.0094	0.0033	1939	0.0469
1940	0.0016	0.0066	0.0025	0.0024	0.0107	0.0043	0.0030	0.0087	0.0028	0.0028	0.0108	0.0038	1940	0.0536
1941	0.0019	0.0089	0.0030	0.0040	0.0140	0.0043	0.0030	0.0096	0.0029	0.0029	0.0137	0.0044	1941	0.0671
1942	0.0023	0.0091	0.0023	0.0037	0.0157	0.0037	0.0024	0.0093	0.0023	0.0034	0.0117	0.0032	1942	0.0679
1943	0.0020	0.0076	0.0018	0.0026	0.0104	0.0025	0.0016	0.0068	0.0025	0.0025	0.0101	0.0027	1943	0.0624
1944	0.0017	0.0068	0.0025	0.0025	0.0101	0.0032	0.0015	0.0071	0.0023	0.0023	0.0094	0.0023	1944	0.0548
1945	0.0015	0.0067	0.0021	0.0022	0.0081	0.0027	0.0020	0.0061	0.0019	0.0019	0.0072	0.0017	1945	0.0497
1946	0.0017	0.0054	0.0017	0.0017	0.0064	0.0021	0.0016	0.0056	0.0018	0.0020	0.0088	0.0027	1946	0.0409
1947	0.0020	0.0070	0.0019	0.0026	0.0103	0.0028	0.0020	0.0076	0.0026	0.0026	0.0110	0.0027	1947	0.0549
1948	0.0020	0.0082	0.0021	0.0027	0.0097	0.0024	0.0024	0.0082	0.0025	0.0032	0.0121	0.0041	1948	0.0608
1949	0.0026	0.0099	0.0027	0.0033	0.0115	0.0035	0.0028	0.0100	0.0026	0.0045	0.0162	0.0050	1949	0.0750
1950	0.0024	0.0100	0.0029	0.0035	0.0116	0.0032	0.0034	0.0118	0.0033	0.0051	0.0179	0.0051	1950	0.0877
1951	0.0025	0.0092	0.0028	0.0028	0.0107	0.0033	0.0024	0.0085	0.0021	0.0034	0.0122	0.0035	1951	0.0691
1952	0.0025	0.0083	0.0026	0.0029	0.0111	0.0029	0.0020	0.0075	0.0020	0.0029	0.0106	0.0027	1952	0.0593
1953	0.0023	0.0076	0.0023	0.0028	0.0110	0.0029	0.0021	0.0077	0.0021	0.0030	0.0114	0.0032	1953	0.0546
1954	0.0024	0.0084	0.0023	0.0026	0.0088	0.0024	0.0017	0.0065	0.0020	0.0028	0.0101	0.0026	1954	0.0621
1955	0.0017	0.0063	0.0019	0.0019	0.0068	0.0018	0.0015	0.0053	0.0016	0.0021	0.0078	0.0022	1955	0.0456
1956	0.0018	0.0066	0.0018	0.0017	0.0064	0.0018	0.0015	0.0053	0.0015	0.0015	0.0059	0.0018	1956	0.0383
1957	0.0017	0.0063	0.0018	0.0018	0.0068	0.0017	0.0017	0.0056	0.0018	0.0019	0.0071	0.0019	1957	0.0384
1958	0.0017	0.0065	0.0020	0.0019	0.0062	0.0018	0.0018	0.0057	0.0017	0.0016	0.0060	0.0015	1958	0.0438
1959	0.0014	0.0051	0.0014	0.0014	0.0050	0.0014	0.0014	0.0048	0.0013	0.0016	0.0054	0.0015	1959	0.0331
1960	0.0015	0.0056	0.0016	0.0014	0.0057	0.0016	0.0014	0.0056	0.0014	0.0017	0.0062	0.0016	1960	0.0326
1961	0.0014	0.0050	0.0014	0.0012	0.0047	0.0014	0.0014	0.0046	0.0013	0.0015	0.0054	0.0014	1961	0.0348
1962	0.0013	0.0046	0.0013	0.0013	0.0049	0.0015	0.0016	0.0055	0.0017	0.0020	0.0071	0.0018	1962	0.0298
1963	0.0014	0.0050	0.0016	0.0015	0.0050	0.0014	0.0013	0.0048	0.0014	0.0017	0.0059	0.0018	1963	0.0361
1964	0.0013	0.0048	0.0013	0.0014	0.0048	0.0014	0.0012	0.0044	0.0013	0.0015	0.0057	0.0017	1964	0.0333
1965	0.0013	0.0046	0.0013	0.0014	0.0047	0.0014	0.0013	0.0047	0.0014	0.0016	0.0056	0.0016	1965	0.0321
1966	0.0013	0.0047	0.0013	0.0015	0.0049	0.0015	0.0014	0.0053	0.0017	0.0018	0.0064	0.0017	1966	0.0311
1967	0.0016	0.0052	0.0015	0.0014	0.0048	0.0015	0.0014	0.0047	0.0014	0.0014	0.0054	0.0015	1967	0.0364
1968	0.0013	0.0051	0.0016	0.0014	0.0049	0.0014	0.0013	0.0049	0.0014	0.0015	0.0051	0.0014	1968	0.0318
1969	0.0013	0.0048	0.0014	0.0014	0.0048	0.0014	0.0014	0.0053	0.0015	0.0016	0.0056	0.0016	1969	0.0304
1970	0.0015	0.0059	0.0016	0.0016	0.0063	0.0018	0.0019	0.0064	0.0017	0.0017	0.0061	0.0016	1970	0.0341

*Compound annual return

Table B–2 (continued)

Large Company Stocks: Income Returns

from January 1971 to December 2002

Year	Jan	Feb	Mar	Apr	May	Jun	Jul	Aug	Sep	Oct	Nov	Dec	Year	Jan–Dec*
1971	0.0014	0.0050	0.0014	0.0014	0.0048	0.0014	0.0014	0.0051	0.0014	0.0014	0.0052	0.0015	1971	0.0333
1972	0.0013	0.0046	0.0013	0.0013	0.0046	0.0013	0.0013	0.0047	0.0013	0.0014	0.0048	0.0013	1972	0.0309
1973	0.0012	0.0042	0.0013	0.0013	0.0050	0.0014	0.0014	0.0049	0.0014	0.0016	0.0056	0.0018	1973	0.0286
1974	0.0015	0.0055	0.0016	0.0017	0.0063	0.0018	0.0019	0.0074	0.0024	0.0027	0.0084	0.0024	1974	0.0369
1975	0.0023	0.0075	0.0020	0.0020	0.0068	0.0019	0.0018	0.0066	0.0018	0.0020	0.0066	0.0019	1975	0.0537
1976	0.0016	0.0056	0.0019	0.0011	0.0071	0.0018	0.0012	0.0065	0.0020	0.0017	0.0069	0.0015	1976	0.0438
1977	0.0016	0.0065	0.0021	0.0012	0.0086	0.0021	0.0011	0.0078	0.0025	0.0019	0.0100	0.0020	1977	0.0431
1978	0.0019	0.0086	0.0027	0.0016	0.0094	0.0023	0.0020	0.0081	0.0024	0.0025	0.0093	0.0023	1978	0.0533
1979	0.0024	0.0081	0.0024	0.0020	0.0095	0.0023	0.0022	0.0080	0.0025	0.0030	0.0088	0.0024	1979	0.0571
1980	0.0034	0.0075	0.0031	0.0018	0.0096	0.0026	0.0026	0.0073	0.0029	0.0026	0.0072	0.0024	1980	0.0573
1981	0.0019	0.0075	0.0020	0.0022	0.0079	0.0021	0.0032	0.0066	0.0036	0.0036	0.0075	0.0036	1981	0.0489
1982	0.0012	0.0093	0.0042	0.0014	0.0104	0.0029	0.0015	0.0107	0.0034	0.0022	0.0077	0.0021	1982	0.0550
1983	0.0017	0.0070	0.0034	0.0009	0.0071	0.0030	0.0017	0.0057	0.0034	0.0018	0.0059	0.0027	1983	0.0500
1984	0.0027	0.0061	0.0036	0.0014	0.0060	0.0046	0.0022	0.0062	0.0037	0.0027	0.0050	0.0029	1984	0.0456
1985	0.0027	0.0051	0.0047	0.0014	0.0074	0.0038	0.0022	0.0059	0.0026	0.0022	0.0065	0.0016	1985	0.0510
1986	0.0020	0.0046	0.0026	0.0017	0.0047	0.0025	0.0018	0.0036	0.0032	0.0009	0.0041	0.0019	1986	0.0374
1987	0.0025	0.0044	0.0008	0.0027	0.0043	0.0020	0.0016	0.0035	0.0022	0.0024	0.0034	0.0009	1987	0.0364
1988	0.0023	0.0052	0.0031	0.0014	0.0046	0.0031	0.0014	0.0055	0.0027	0.0013	0.0047	0.0034	1988	0.0417
1989	0.0012	0.0040	0.0028	0.0015	0.0051	0.0025	0.0014	0.0038	0.0026	0.0019	0.0043	0.0022	1989	0.0385
1990	0.0017	0.0044	0.0020	0.0022	0.0055	0.0019	0.0020	0.0040	0.0020	0.0030	0.0045	0.0026	1990	0.0336
1991	0.0027	0.0043	0.0016	0.0025	0.0042	0.0022	0.0019	0.0039	0.0027	0.0015	0.0035	0.0027	1991	0.0382
1992	0.0013	0.0032	0.0022	0.0012	0.0044	0.0028	0.0009	0.0038	0.0024	0.0015	0.0034	0.0030	1992	0.0303
1993	0.0003	0.0030	0.0028	0.0009	0.0043	0.0025	0.0006	0.0037	0.0026	0.0009	0.0035	0.0022	1993	0.0283
1994	0.0010	0.0030	0.0022	0.0015	0.0039	0.0021	0.0016	0.0031	0.0028	0.0020	0.0028	0.0023	1994	0.0282
1995	0.0017	0.0027	0.0023	0.0011	0.0032	0.0022	0.0015	0.0030	0.0018	0.0015	0.0030	0.0011	1995	0.0291
1996	0.0018	0.0027	0.0017	0.0013	0.0029	0.0018	0.0012	0.0024	0.0020	0.0013	0.0025	0.0019	1996	0.0254
1997	0.0008	0.0022	0.0010	0.0013	0.0028	0.0011	0.0013	0.0018	0.0016	0.0011	0.0017	0.0014	1997	0.0211
1998	0.0009	0.0017	0.0013	0.0010	0.0016	0.0012	0.0010	0.0012	0.0017	0.0010	0.0015	0.0012	1998	0.0168
1999	0.0008	0.0012	0.0012	0.0008	0.0014	0.0011	0.0008	0.0013	0.0011	0.0007	0.0013	0.0011	1999	0.0136
2000	0.0007	0.0012	0.0011	0.0007	0.0014	0.0007	0.0007	0.0014	0.0007	0.0007	0.0012	0.0008	2000	0.0110
2001	0.0008	0.0011	0.0009	0.0009	0.0016	0.0007	0.0009	0.0015	0.0010	0.0010	0.0015	0.0012	2001	0.0118
2002	0.0010	0.0015	0.0009	0.0008	0.0017	0.0012	0.0011	0.0017	0.0013	0.0016	0.0018	0.0015	2002	0.0139

*Compound annual return

Table B–3

Large Company Stocks: Capital Appreciation Returns

from January 1926 to December 1970

Year	Jan	Feb	Mar	Apr	May	Jun	Jul	Aug	Sep	Oct	Nov	Dec	Year	Jan–Dec*
1926	−0.0016	−0.0440	−0.0591	0.0227	0.0077	0.0432	0.0455	0.0171	0.0229	−0.0313	0.0223	0.0166	1926	0.0572
1927	−0.0208	0.0477	0.0065	0.0172	0.0522	−0.0094	0.0650	0.0445	0.0432	−0.0531	0.0616	0.0250	1927	0.3091
1928	−0.0051	−0.0176	0.1083	0.0324	0.0127	−0.0405	0.0125	0.0741	0.0240	0.0145	0.1199	0.0029	1928	0.3788
1929	0.0571	−0.0058	−0.0023	0.0161	−0.0428	0.1124	0.0456	0.0980	−0.0489	−0.1993	−0.1337	0.0253	1929	−0.1191
1930	0.0625	0.0215	0.0799	−0.0095	−0.0165	−0.1646	0.0367	0.0075	−0.1301	−0.0888	−0.0218	−0.0742	1930	−0.2848
1931	0.0489	0.1144	−0.0692	−0.0959	−0.1372	0.1390	−0.0742	0.0095	−0.2994	0.0844	−0.0978	−0.1453	1931	−0.4707
1932	−0.0283	0.0507	−0.1182	−0.2025	−0.2333	−0.0089	0.3770	0.3754	−0.0369	−0.1386	−0.0589	0.0519	1932	−0.1515
1933	0.0073	−0.1844	0.0336	0.4222	0.1587	0.1317	−0.0880	0.1146	−0.1136	−0.0885	0.1027	0.0223	1933	0.4659
1934	0.1059	−0.0367	−0.0009	−0.0270	−0.0813	0.0208	−0.1152	0.0541	−0.0055	−0.0319	0.0829	−0.0042	1934	−0.0594
1935	−0.0421	−0.0396	−0.0309	0.0956	0.0323	0.0679	0.0831	0.0217	0.0239	0.0751	0.0393	0.0371	1935	0.4137
1936	0.0655	0.0168	0.0254	−0.0771	0.0458	0.0306	0.0681	0.0088	0.0013	0.0750	0.0041	−0.0058	1936	0.2792
1937	0.0378	0.0146	−0.0094	−0.0831	−0.0103	−0.0529	0.1026	−0.0554	−0.1421	−0.1017	−0.1011	−0.0504	1937	−0.3859
1938	0.0133	0.0608	−0.2504	0.1412	−0.0443	0.2470	0.0727	−0.0274	0.0149	0.0760	−0.0334	0.0377	1938	0.2521
1939	−0.0689	0.0325	−0.1354	−0.0055	0.0623	−0.0638	0.1087	−0.0714	0.1646	−0.0146	−0.0491	0.0238	1939	−0.0545
1940	−0.0352	0.0066	0.0099	−0.0049	−0.2395	0.0766	0.0311	0.0262	0.0095	0.0394	−0.0424	−0.0028	1940	−0.1529
1941	−0.0482	−0.0149	0.0040	−0.0653	0.0043	0.0535	0.0548	−0.0087	−0.0097	−0.0686	−0.0421	−0.0451	1941	−0.1786
1942	0.0138	−0.0250	−0.0675	−0.0437	0.0640	0.0184	0.0313	0.0070	0.0267	0.0644	−0.0138	0.0517	1942	0.1243
1943	0.0716	0.0506	0.0527	0.0009	0.0449	0.0198	−0.0543	0.0103	0.0237	−0.0132	−0.0755	0.0590	1943	0.1945
1944	0.0154	−0.0025	0.0169	−0.0125	0.0404	0.0510	−0.0208	0.0087	−0.0031	0.0000	0.0039	0.0351	1944	0.1380
1945	0.0143	0.0616	−0.0462	0.0880	0.0115	−0.0033	−0.0201	0.0580	0.0419	0.0303	0.0324	0.0099	1945	0.3072
1946	0.0697	−0.0695	0.0463	0.0376	0.0224	−0.0391	−0.0255	−0.0729	−0.1015	−0.0080	−0.0115	0.0429	1946	−0.1187
1947	0.0235	−0.0147	−0.0169	−0.0389	−0.0089	0.0526	0.0362	−0.0279	−0.0137	0.0212	−0.0285	0.0207	1947	0.0000
1948	−0.0399	−0.0470	0.0771	0.0265	0.0782	0.0030	−0.0532	0.0076	−0.0301	0.0678	−0.1082	0.0305	1948	−0.0065
1949	0.0013	−0.0394	0.0301	−0.0212	−0.0373	−0.0021	0.0621	0.0120	0.0237	0.0295	0.0012	0.0436	1949	0.1026
1950	0.0173	0.0100	0.0041	0.0451	0.0393	−0.0580	0.0085	0.0325	0.0559	0.0041	−0.0010	0.0461	1950	0.2178
1951	0.0612	0.0065	−0.0183	0.0481	−0.0406	−0.0260	0.0687	0.0393	−0.0009	−0.0138	−0.0026	0.0389	1951	0.1646
1952	0.0156	−0.0365	0.0477	−0.0431	0.0232	0.0461	0.0176	−0.0146	−0.0196	−0.0008	0.0465	0.0355	1952	0.1178
1953	−0.0072	−0.0182	−0.0236	−0.0265	−0.0032	−0.0163	0.0253	−0.0578	0.0013	0.0510	0.0090	0.0020	1953	−0.0662
1954	0.0512	0.0027	0.0302	0.0490	0.0329	0.0007	0.0572	−0.0340	0.0831	−0.0195	0.0808	0.0508	1954	0.4502
1955	0.0181	0.0035	−0.0049	0.0377	−0.0013	0.0823	0.0607	−0.0078	0.0113	−0.0305	0.0749	−0.0007	1955	0.2640
1956	−0.0365	0.0347	0.0693	−0.0021	−0.0657	0.0392	0.0515	−0.0381	−0.0455	0.0051	−0.0110	0.0353	1956	0.0262
1957	−0.0418	−0.0326	0.0196	0.0370	0.0369	−0.0013	0.0114	−0.0561	−0.0619	−0.0321	0.0161	−0.0415	1957	−0.1431
1958	0.0428	−0.0206	0.0309	0.0318	0.0150	0.0261	0.0431	0.0119	0.0484	0.0254	0.0224	0.0520	1958	0.3806
1959	0.0038	−0.0002	0.0005	0.0388	0.0189	−0.0036	0.0349	−0.0150	−0.0456	0.0113	0.0132	0.0276	1959	0.0848
1960	−0.0715	0.0092	−0.0139	−0.0175	0.0269	0.0195	−0.0248	0.0261	−0.0604	−0.0024	0.0403	0.0463	1960	−0.0297
1961	0.0632	0.0269	0.0255	0.0038	0.0191	−0.0288	0.0328	0.0196	−0.0197	0.0283	0.0393	0.0032	1961	0.2313
1962	−0.0379	0.0163	−0.0059	−0.0620	−0.0860	−0.0818	0.0636	0.0153	−0.0482	0.0044	0.1016	0.0135	1962	−0.1181
1963	0.0491	−0.0289	0.0355	0.0485	0.0143	−0.0202	−0.0035	0.0487	−0.0110	0.0322	−0.0105	0.0244	1963	0.1889
1964	0.0269	0.0099	0.0152	0.0061	0.0115	0.0164	0.0182	−0.0162	0.0287	0.0081	−0.0052	0.0039	1964	0.1297
1965	0.0332	−0.0015	−0.0145	0.0342	−0.0077	−0.0486	0.0134	0.0225	0.0320	0.0273	−0.0088	0.0090	1965	0.0906
1966	0.0049	−0.0179	−0.0218	0.0205	−0.0541	−0.0161	−0.0135	−0.0778	−0.0070	0.0475	0.0031	−0.0015	1966	−0.1309
1967	0.0782	0.0020	0.0394	0.0422	−0.0524	0.0175	0.0453	−0.0117	0.0328	−0.0291	0.0011	0.0263	1967	0.2009
1968	−0.0438	−0.0312	0.0094	0.0819	0.0112	0.0091	−0.0185	0.0115	0.0385	0.0072	0.0480	−0.0416	1968	0.0766
1969	−0.0082	−0.0474	0.0344	0.0215	−0.0022	−0.0556	−0.0602	0.0401	−0.0250	0.0442	−0.0353	−0.0193	1969	−0.1142
1970	−0.0759	0.0527	0.0015	−0.0905	−0.0610	−0.0500	0.0733	0.0445	0.0330	−0.0114	0.0474	0.0568	1970	0.0016

*Compound annual return

Table B–3 (continued)

Large Company Stocks: Capital Appreciation Returns

from January 1971 to December 2002

Year	Jan	Feb	Mar	Apr	May	Jun	Jul	Aug	Sep	Oct	Nov	Dec	Year	Jan–Dec*
1971	0.0405	0.0091	0.0368	0.0363	−0.0416	0.0007	−0.0413	0.0361	−0.0070	−0.0418	−0.0025	0.0862	1971	0.1079
1972	0.0181	0.0253	0.0059	0.0044	0.0173	−0.0218	0.0023	0.0345	−0.0049	0.0093	0.0456	0.0118	1972	0.1563
1973	−0.0171	−0.0375	−0.0014	−0.0408	−0.0189	−0.0066	0.0380	−0.0367	0.0401	−0.0013	−0.1139	0.0166	1973	−0.1737
1974	−0.0100	−0.0036	−0.0233	−0.0391	−0.0336	−0.0147	−0.0778	−0.0903	−0.1193	0.1630	−0.0532	−0.0202	1974	−0.2972
1975	0.1228	0.0599	0.0217	0.0473	0.0441	0.0443	−0.0677	−0.0211	−0.0346	0.0616	0.0247	−0.0115	1975	0.3155
1976	0.1183	−0.0114	0.0307	−0.0110	−0.0144	0.0409	−0.0081	−0.0051	0.0226	−0.0222	−0.0078	0.0525	1976	0.1915
1977	−0.0505	−0.0217	−0.0140	0.0002	−0.0236	0.0454	−0.0162	−0.0210	−0.0025	−0.0434	0.0270	0.0028	1977	−0.1150
1978	−0.0615	−0.0248	0.0249	0.0854	0.0042	−0.0176	0.0539	0.0259	−0.0073	−0.0916	0.0166	0.0149	1978	0.0106
1979	0.0397	−0.0365	0.0551	0.0017	−0.0263	0.0387	0.0088	0.0531	0.0000	−0.0686	0.0426	0.0168	1979	0.1231
1980	0.0576	−0.0044	−0.1018	0.0411	0.0466	0.0270	0.0650	0.0058	0.0252	0.0160	0.1023	−0.0339	1980	0.2577
1981	−0.0457	0.0133	0.0360	−0.0235	−0.0017	−0.0101	−0.0025	−0.0620	−0.0538	0.0492	0.0366	−0.0301	1981	−0.0972
1982	−0.0175	−0.0605	−0.0102	0.0400	−0.0392	−0.0203	−0.0230	0.1160	0.0076	0.1104	0.0361	0.0152	1982	0.1476
1983	0.0331	0.0190	0.0331	0.0749	−0.0123	0.0352	−0.0330	0.0113	0.0102	−0.0152	0.0174	−0.0088	1983	0.1727
1984	−0.0092	−0.0389	0.0135	0.0055	−0.0594	0.0175	−0.0165	0.1063	−0.0035	−0.0001	−0.0151	0.0224	1984	0.0139
1985	0.0741	0.0086	−0.0029	−0.0046	0.0541	0.0121	−0.0048	−0.0120	−0.0347	0.0425	0.0651	0.0451	1985	0.2634
1986	0.0024	0.0715	0.0528	−0.0141	0.0502	0.0141	−0.0587	0.0712	−0.0854	0.0547	0.0215	−0.0283	1986	0.1463
1987	0.1318	0.0369	0.0264	−0.0115	0.0060	0.0479	0.0482	0.0350	−0.0242	−0.2176	−0.0853	0.0729	1987	0.0203
1988	0.0404	0.0418	−0.0333	0.0094	0.0032	0.0433	−0.0054	−0.0386	0.0397	0.0260	−0.0189	0.0147	1988	0.1241
1989	0.0711	−0.0289	0.0208	0.0501	0.0351	−0.0079	0.0884	0.0155	−0.0065	−0.0252	0.0165	0.0214	1989	0.2726
1990	−0.0688	0.0085	0.0243	−0.0269	0.0920	−0.0089	−0.0052	−0.0943	−0.0512	−0.0067	0.0599	0.0248	1990	−0.0656
1991	0.0415	0.0673	0.0222	0.0003	0.0386	−0.0479	0.0449	0.0196	−0.0191	0.0119	−0.0439	0.1116	1991	0.2631
1992	−0.0199	0.0096	−0.0218	0.0279	0.0010	−0.0174	0.0394	−0.0240	0.0091	0.0021	0.0303	0.0101	1992	0.0446
1993	0.0070	0.0105	0.0187	−0.0254	0.0227	0.0008	−0.0053	0.0344	−0.0100	0.0194	−0.0129	0.0101	1993	0.0706
1994	0.0325	−0.0300	−0.0457	0.0115	0.0124	−0.0268	0.0315	0.0376	−0.0269	0.0209	−0.0395	0.0123	1994	−0.0154
1995	0.0243	0.0361	0.0273	0.0280	0.0363	0.0213	0.0318	−0.0003	0.0401	−0.0050	0.0410	0.0174	1995	0.3411
1996	0.0326	0.0069	0.0079	0.0134	0.0229	0.0023	−0.0457	0.0188	0.0542	0.0261	0.0734	−0.0215	1996	0.2026
1997	0.0613	0.0059	−0.0426	0.0584	0.0586	0.0435	0.0781	−0.0574	0.0532	−0.0345	0.0446	0.0157	1997	0.3101
1998	0.0102	0.0704	0.0499	0.0091	−0.0188	0.0394	−0.0116	−0.1458	0.0624	0.0803	0.0591	0.0564	1998	0.2667
1999	0.0410	−0.0323	0.0388	0.0379	−0.0250	0.0544	−0.0320	−0.0063	−0.0286	0.0625	0.0191	0.0578	1999	0.1953
2000	−0.0509	−0.0201	0.0967	−0.0308	−0.0219	0.0239	−0.0163	0.0607	−0.0535	−0.0049	−0.0801	0.0041	2000	−0.1014
2001	0.0346	−0.0923	−0.0642	0.0768	0.0051	−0.0250	−0.0108	−0.0641	−0.0817	0.0181	0.0752	0.0076	2001	−0.1304
2002	−0.0156	−0.0208	0.0367	−0.0614	−0.0091	−0.0725	−0.0790	0.0049	−0.1100	0.0865	0.0571	−0.0603	2002	−0.2337

*Compound annual return

Table B–4

Ibbotson Small Company Stocks: Total Returns

from January 1926 to December 1970

Year	Jan	Feb	Mar	Apr	May	Jun	Jul	Aug	Sep	Oct	Nov	Dec	Year	Jan–Dec*
1926	0.0699	−0.0639	−0.1073	0.0179	−0.0066	0.0378	0.0112	0.0256	−0.0001	−0.0227	0.0207	0.0332	1926	0.0028
1927	0.0296	0.0547	−0.0548	0.0573	0.0734	−0.0303	0.0516	−0.0178	0.0047	−0.0659	0.0808	0.0316	1927	0.2210
1928	0.0482	−0.0236	0.0531	0.0910	0.0438	−0.0842	0.0059	0.0442	0.0890	0.0276	0.1147	−0.0513	1928	0.3969
1929	0.0035	−0.0026	−0.0200	0.0306	−0.1336	0.0533	0.0114	−0.0164	−0.0922	−0.2768	−0.1500	−0.0501	1929	−0.5136
1930	0.1293	0.0643	0.1007	−0.0698	−0.0542	−0.2168	0.0301	−0.0166	−0.1459	−0.1097	−0.0028	−0.1166	1930	−0.3815
1931	0.2103	0.2566	−0.0708	−0.2164	−0.1379	0.1819	−0.0557	−0.0763	−0.3246	0.0770	−0.1008	−0.2195	1931	−0.4975
1932	0.1019	0.0291	−0.1311	−0.2220	−0.1193	0.0033	0.3523	0.7346	−0.1320	−0.1775	−0.1227	−0.0492	1932	−0.0539
1933	−0.0083	−0.1278	0.1118	0.5038	0.6339	0.2617	−0.0550	0.0924	−0.1595	−0.1236	0.0654	0.0055	1933	1.4287
1934	0.3891	0.0166	−0.0012	0.0240	−0.1275	−0.0024	−0.2259	0.1546	−0.0167	0.0097	0.0948	0.0172	1934	0.2422
1935	−0.0328	−0.0592	−0.1189	0.0791	−0.0024	0.0305	0.0855	0.0545	0.0357	0.0994	0.1412	0.0598	1935	0.4019
1936	0.3009	0.0602	0.0066	−0.1795	0.0272	−0.0231	0.0873	0.0210	0.0542	0.0635	0.1400	0.0160	1936	0.6480
1937	0.1267	0.0658	0.0120	−0.1679	−0.0408	−0.1183	0.1235	−0.0736	−0.2539	−0.1093	−0.1453	−0.1694	1937	−0.5801
1938	0.0534	0.0343	−0.3600	0.2776	−0.0849	0.3498	0.1499	−0.1001	−0.0157	0.2136	−0.0689	0.0487	1938	0.3280
1939	−0.0848	0.0107	−0.2466	0.0142	0.1088	−0.1042	0.2535	−0.1590	0.5145	−0.0397	−0.1053	0.0422	1939	0.0035
1940	0.0009	0.0821	0.0632	0.0654	−0.3674	0.1051	0.0231	0.0255	0.0213	0.0545	0.0245	−0.0447	1940	−0.0516
1941	0.0025	−0.0288	0.0319	−0.0669	0.0044	0.0753	0.2165	−0.0060	−0.0469	−0.0672	−0.0495	−0.1204	1941	−0.0900
1942	0.1894	−0.0073	−0.0709	−0.0353	−0.0032	0.0336	0.0737	0.0325	0.0912	0.1087	−0.0511	0.0413	1942	0.4451
1943	0.2132	0.1931	0.1445	0.0933	0.1156	−0.0083	−0.1083	−0.0002	0.0428	0.0123	−0.1113	0.1241	1943	0.8837
1944	0.0641	0.0295	0.0749	−0.0532	0.0740	0.1384	−0.0299	0.0318	−0.0020	−0.0108	0.0499	0.0869	1944	0.5372
1945	0.0482	0.1009	−0.0861	0.1157	0.0500	0.0855	−0.0556	0.0557	0.0679	0.0701	0.1172	0.0171	1945	0.7361
1946	0.1562	−0.0637	0.0273	0.0696	0.0591	−0.0462	−0.0530	−0.0849	−0.1603	−0.0118	−0.0141	0.0373	1946	−0.1163
1947	0.0421	−0.0041	−0.0336	−0.1031	−0.0534	0.0552	0.0789	−0.0037	0.0115	0.0282	−0.0303	0.0359	1947	0.0092
1948	−0.0154	−0.0783	0.0986	0.0368	0.1059	0.0048	−0.0578	0.0006	−0.0526	0.0647	−0.1116	0.0088	1948	−0.0211
1949	0.0182	−0.0481	0.0629	−0.0336	−0.0564	−0.0096	0.0671	0.0256	0.0489	0.0472	0.0016	0.0690	1949	0.1975
1950	0.0492	0.0221	−0.0037	0.0411	0.0255	−0.0777	0.0591	0.0530	0.0521	−0.0059	0.0322	0.0953	1950	0.3875
1951	0.0830	0.0061	−0.0477	0.0367	−0.0331	−0.0529	0.0373	0.0605	0.0215	−0.0222	−0.0083	0.0044	1951	0.0780
1952	0.0191	−0.0300	0.0175	−0.0519	0.0032	0.0272	0.0112	−0.0006	−0.0161	−0.0103	0.0485	0.0160	1952	0.0303
1953	0.0409	0.0269	−0.0067	−0.0287	0.0141	−0.0486	0.0152	−0.0628	−0.0262	0.0292	0.0126	−0.0266	1953	−0.0649
1954	0.0756	0.0094	0.0183	0.0140	0.0451	0.0086	0.0808	0.0014	0.0410	0.0068	0.0779	0.1112	1954	0.6058
1955	0.0201	0.0479	0.0085	0.0150	0.0078	0.0293	0.0064	−0.0028	0.0109	−0.0170	0.0468	0.0163	1955	0.2044
1956	−0.0047	0.0278	0.0431	0.0047	−0.0398	0.0056	0.0283	−0.0134	−0.0260	0.0104	0.0053	0.0038	1956	0.0428
1957	0.0236	−0.0200	0.0167	0.0248	0.0075	0.0073	−0.0060	−0.0386	−0.0452	−0.0832	0.0113	−0.0481	1957	−0.1457
1958	0.1105	−0.0170	0.0471	0.0376	0.0387	0.0324	0.0492	0.0428	0.0518	0.0407	0.0496	0.0313	1958	0.6489
1959	0.0575	0.0295	0.0027	0.0117	0.0014	−0.0042	0.0327	−0.0088	−0.0431	0.0227	0.0222	0.0322	1959	0.1640
1960	−0.0306	0.0050	−0.0315	−0.0187	0.0204	0.0340	−0.0189	0.0525	−0.0738	−0.0401	0.0437	0.0332	1960	−0.0329
1961	0.0915	0.0589	0.0619	0.0127	0.0427	−0.0543	0.0031	0.0130	−0.0339	0.0262	0.0613	0.0079	1961	0.3209
1962	0.0136	0.0187	0.0057	−0.0777	−0.1009	−0.0785	0.0763	0.0289	−0.0659	−0.0373	0.1248	−0.0089	1962	−0.1190
1963	0.0906	0.0034	0.0149	0.0312	0.0436	−0.0118	0.0033	0.0517	−0.0163	0.0236	−0.0106	−0.0048	1963	0.2357
1964	0.0274	0.0365	0.0219	0.0093	0.0157	0.0163	0.0398	−0.0029	0.0402	0.0205	0.0011	−0.0112	1964	0.2352
1965	0.0529	0.0390	0.0238	0.0509	−0.0078	−0.0901	0.0449	0.0595	0.0347	0.0572	0.0371	0.0622	1965	0.4175
1966	0.0756	0.0311	−0.0192	0.0343	−0.0961	−0.0012	−0.0012	−0.1080	−0.0164	−0.0107	0.0491	0.0065	1966	−0.0701
1967	0.1838	0.0450	0.0615	0.0271	−0.0085	0.1017	0.0951	0.0020	0.0565	−0.0311	0.0117	0.0965	1967	0.8357
1968	0.0154	−0.0709	−0.0109	0.1461	0.0999	0.0030	−0.0345	0.0367	0.0599	0.0030	0.0764	0.0062	1968	0.3597
1969	−0.0166	−0.0990	0.0396	0.0395	0.0173	−0.1165	−0.1070	0.0732	−0.0261	0.0610	−0.0557	−0.0687	1969	−0.2505
1970	−0.0608	0.0387	−0.0285	−0.1728	−0.1031	−0.0929	0.0554	0.0949	0.1086	−0.0706	0.0137	0.0726	1970	−0.1743

*Compound annual return

Table B–4 (continued)

Ibbotson Small Company Stocks: Total Returns

from January 1971 to December 2002

Year	Jan	Feb	Mar	Apr	May	Jun	Jul	Aug	Sep	Oct	Nov	Dec	Year	Jan–Dec*
1971	0.1592	0.0317	0.0564	0.0247	−0.0605	−0.0319	−0.0563	0.0583	−0.0226	−0.0551	−0.0373	0.1144	1971	0.1650
1972	0.1130	0.0296	−0.0143	0.0129	−0.0191	−0.0305	−0.0413	0.0186	−0.0349	−0.0175	0.0592	−0.0214	1972	0.0443
1973	−0.0432	−0.0799	−0.0208	−0.0621	−0.0811	−0.0290	0.1194	−0.0445	0.1064	0.0084	−0.1962	−0.0014	1973	−0.3090
1974	0.1326	−0.0085	−0.0074	−0.0464	−0.0793	−0.0147	−0.0219	−0.0681	−0.0653	0.1063	−0.0438	−0.0788	1974	−0.1995
1975	0.2767	0.0285	0.0618	0.0531	0.0663	0.0750	−0.0254	−0.0574	−0.0182	−0.0050	0.0320	−0.0197	1975	0.5282
1976	0.2684	0.1390	−0.0015	−0.0359	−0.0361	0.0459	0.0045	−0.0290	0.0104	−0.0209	0.0404	0.1180	1976	0.5738
1977	0.0450	−0.0039	0.0131	0.0228	−0.0028	0.0772	0.0030	−0.0107	0.0092	−0.0330	0.1086	0.0081	1977	0.2538
1978	−0.0189	0.0347	0.1032	0.0788	0.0820	−0.0189	0.0684	0.0939	−0.0032	−0.2427	0.0732	0.0168	1978	0.2346
1979	0.1321	−0.0282	0.1120	0.0387	0.0035	0.0472	0.0171	0.0756	−0.0344	−0.1154	0.0858	0.0588	1979	0.4346
1980	0.0836	−0.0284	−0.1778	0.0694	0.0750	0.0452	0.1323	0.0604	0.0418	0.0333	0.0766	−0.0338	1980	0.3988
1981	0.0207	0.0094	0.0943	0.0657	0.0422	0.0076	−0.0316	−0.0684	−0.0733	0.0742	0.0276	−0.0220	1981	0.1388
1982	−0.0196	−0.0296	−0.0086	0.0383	−0.0248	−0.0159	−0.0015	0.0698	0.0327	0.1305	0.0779	0.0132	1982	0.2801
1983	0.0628	0.0712	0.0525	0.0767	0.0870	0.0348	−0.0088	−0.0197	0.0133	−0.0568	0.0516	−0.0145	1983	0.3967
1984	−0.0008	−0.0645	0.0174	−0.0085	−0.0521	0.0300	−0.0420	0.0998	0.0027	−0.0217	−0.0336	0.0150	1984	−0.0667
1985	0.1059	0.0272	−0.0214	−0.0174	0.0276	0.0106	0.0260	−0.0072	−0.0544	0.0261	0.0620	0.0470	1985	0.2466
1986	0.0112	0.0719	0.0477	0.0064	0.0360	0.0026	−0.0710	0.0218	−0.0559	0.0346	−0.0031	−0.0262	1986	0.0685
1987	0.0943	0.0809	0.0233	−0.0313	−0.0039	0.0266	0.0364	0.0287	−0.0081	−0.2919	−0.0397	0.0520	1987	−0.0930
1988	0.0556	0.0760	0.0408	0.0209	−0.0179	0.0612	−0.0025	−0.0246	0.0227	−0.0123	−0.0437	0.0394	1988	0.2287
1989	0.0404	0.0083	0.0358	0.0279	0.0362	−0.0201	0.0407	0.0122	0.0000	−0.0604	−0.0051	−0.0134	1989	0.1018
1990	−0.0764	0.0187	0.0368	−0.0266	0.0561	0.0144	−0.0382	−0.1296	−0.0829	−0.0572	0.0450	0.0194	1990	−0.2156
1991	0.0841	0.1113	0.0680	0.0034	0.0334	−0.0485	0.0407	0.0261	0.0032	0.0317	−0.0276	0.0601	1991	0.4463
1992	0.1128	0.0452	−0.0249	−0.0403	−0.0014	−0.0519	0.0370	−0.0228	0.0131	0.0259	0.0885	0.0441	1992	0.2335
1993	0.0543	−0.0180	0.0289	−0.0306	0.0342	−0.0038	0.0166	0.0339	0.0316	0.0471	−0.0175	0.0194	1993	0.2098
1994	0.0618	−0.0023	−0.0446	0.0060	−0.0012	−0.0262	0.0184	0.0337	0.0105	0.0115	−0.0326	0.0002	1994	0.0311
1995	0.0283	0.0252	0.0145	0.0352	0.0298	0.0568	0.0645	0.0358	0.0195	−0.0487	0.0192	0.0239	1995	0.3446
1996	0.0028	0.0369	0.0228	0.0848	0.0749	−0.0582	−0.0943	0.0476	0.0291	−0.0175	0.0288	0.0204	1996	0.1762
1997	0.0420	−0.0206	−0.0490	−0.0276	0.1022	0.0498	0.0605	0.0509	0.0844	−0.0386	−0.0155	−0.0171	1997	0.2278
1998	−0.0059	0.0649	0.0481	0.0168	−0.0497	−0.0206	−0.0671	−0.2010	0.0369	0.0356	0.0758	0.0252	1998	−0.0731
1999	0.0279	−0.0687	−0.0379	0.0949	0.0387	0.0568	0.0092	−0.0191	−0.0221	−0.0087	0.0971	0.1137	1999	0.2979
2000	0.0595	0.2358	−0.0751	−0.1251	−0.0808	0.1368	−0.0322	0.0925	−0.0217	−0.0706	−0.1110	0.0189	2000	−0.0359
2001	0.1380	−0.0702	−0.0480	0.0731	0.0960	0.0359	−0.0254	−0.0295	−0.1278	0.0645	0.0674	0.0672	2001	0.2277
2002	0.0110	−0.0277	0.0884	0.0243	−0.0273	−0.0356	−0.1448	−0.0057	−0.0674	0.0257	0.0836	−0.0429	2002	−0.1328

*Compound annual return

Table B–5

Long–Term Corporate Bonds: Total Returns

from January 1926 to December 1970

Year	Jan	Feb	Mar	Apr	May	Jun	Jul	Aug	Sep	Oct	Nov	Dec	Year	Jan–Dec*
1926	0.0072	0.0045	0.0084	0.0097	0.0044	0.0004	0.0057	0.0044	0.0057	0.0097	0.0057	0.0056	1926	0.0737
1927	0.0056	0.0069	0.0083	0.0055	−0.0011	0.0043	0.0003	0.0083	0.0149	0.0055	0.0068	0.0068	1927	0.0744
1928	0.0027	0.0068	0.0041	0.0014	−0.0078	−0.0024	−0.0010	0.0083	0.0030	0.0083	−0.0036	0.0084	1928	0.0284
1929	0.0043	0.0030	−0.0087	0.0019	0.0045	−0.0046	0.0020	0.0020	0.0034	0.0073	−0.0018	0.0192	1929	0.0327
1930	0.0059	0.0072	0.0138	0.0084	0.0057	0.0110	0.0056	0.0136	0.0108	0.0054	−0.0012	−0.0090	1930	0.0798
1931	0.0203	0.0068	0.0094	0.0067	0.0134	0.0052	0.0052	0.0012	−0.0014	−0.0363	−0.0189	−0.0286	1931	−0.0185
1932	−0.0052	−0.0238	0.0356	−0.0176	0.0107	−0.0009	0.0043	0.0436	0.0301	0.0074	0.0073	0.0139	1932	0.1082
1933	0.0547	−0.0523	0.0047	−0.0095	0.0588	0.0190	0.0161	0.0093	−0.0014	0.0040	−0.0248	0.0257	1933	0.1038
1934	0.0257	0.0146	0.0187	0.0104	0.0090	0.0158	0.0047	0.0047	−0.0061	0.0102	0.0129	0.0101	1934	0.1384
1935	0.0211	0.0141	0.0043	0.0112	0.0042	0.0112	0.0111	−0.0042	0.0000	0.0042	0.0069	0.0083	1935	0.0961
1936	0.0082	0.0054	0.0082	0.0026	0.0040	0.0082	0.0011	0.0067	0.0067	0.0025	0.0109	0.0010	1936	0.0674
1937	0.0024	−0.0046	−0.0114	0.0068	0.0040	0.0053	0.0039	−0.0017	0.0025	0.0067	0.0067	0.0067	1937	0.0275
1938	0.0038	0.0010	−0.0087	0.0138	0.0010	0.0095	0.0066	−0.0019	0.0109	0.0080	0.0037	0.0122	1938	0.0613
1939	0.0022	0.0064	0.0022	0.0064	0.0049	0.0035	−0.0007	−0.0392	0.0151	0.0237	0.0079	0.0078	1939	0.0397
1940	0.0049	0.0021	0.0049	−0.0092	−0.0021	0.0121	0.0021	0.0007	0.0092	0.0049	0.0063	−0.0023	1940	0.0339
1941	0.0006	0.0006	−0.0022	0.0078	0.0049	0.0063	0.0063	0.0034	0.0048	0.0034	−0.0094	0.0006	1941	0.0273
1942	0.0006	−0.0008	0.0063	0.0006	0.0020	0.0034	0.0020	0.0035	0.0020	0.0006	0.0006	0.0049	1942	0.0260
1943	0.0049	0.0006	0.0020	0.0049	0.0048	0.0048	0.0019	0.0019	0.0005	−0.0009	−0.0023	0.0049	1943	0.0283
1944	0.0020	0.0034	0.0048	0.0034	0.0005	0.0020	0.0034	0.0034	0.0019	0.0019	0.0048	0.0149	1944	0.0473
1945	0.0076	0.0046	0.0018	0.0018	−0.0011	0.0032	−0.0011	0.0004	0.0032	0.0032	0.0032	0.0133	1945	0.0408
1946	0.0128	0.0034	0.0034	−0.0043	0.0019	0.0019	−0.0012	−0.0088	−0.0026	0.0020	−0.0025	0.0113	1946	0.0172
1947	0.0005	0.0005	0.0067	0.0020	0.0020	0.0004	0.0020	−0.0071	−0.0131	−0.0099	−0.0098	0.0024	1947	−0.0234
1948	0.0024	0.0039	0.0115	0.0038	0.0008	−0.0083	−0.0052	0.0055	0.0024	0.0024	0.0085	0.0131	1948	0.0414
1949	0.0038	0.0038	0.0007	0.0023	0.0038	0.0084	0.0099	0.0037	0.0021	0.0067	0.0021	−0.0145	1949	0.0331
1950	0.0037	0.0007	0.0022	−0.0008	−0.0008	0.0023	0.0069	0.0038	−0.0039	−0.0008	0.0054	0.0023	1950	0.0212
1951	0.0019	−0.0044	−0.0237	−0.0009	−0.0015	−0.0093	0.0205	0.0114	−0.0057	−0.0145	−0.0061	0.0058	1951	−0.0269
1952	0.0199	−0.0085	0.0076	−0.0004	0.0031	0.0016	0.0016	0.0063	−0.0018	0.0039	0.0108	−0.0091	1952	0.0352
1953	−0.0080	−0.0040	−0.0033	−0.0248	−0.0030	0.0109	0.0177	−0.0085	0.0253	0.0227	−0.0073	0.0172	1953	0.0341
1954	0.0124	0.0198	0.0039	−0.0034	−0.0042	0.0063	0.0040	0.0018	0.0040	0.0040	0.0025	0.0017	1954	0.0539
1955	−0.0097	−0.0063	0.0092	−0.0001	−0.0018	0.0029	−0.0041	−0.0038	0.0076	0.0078	−0.0030	0.0063	1955	0.0048
1956	0.0104	0.0026	−0.0146	−0.0115	0.0052	−0.0018	−0.0093	−0.0208	0.0012	−0.0105	−0.0126	−0.0082	1956	−0.0681
1957	0.0197	0.0093	0.0050	−0.0066	−0.0075	−0.0322	−0.0110	−0.0009	0.0095	0.0023	0.0311	0.0685	1957	0.0871
1958	0.0099	−0.0008	−0.0046	0.0163	0.0031	−0.0038	−0.0153	−0.0320	−0.0096	0.0107	0.0105	−0.0058	1958	−0.0222
1959	−0.0028	0.0126	−0.0083	−0.0172	−0.0114	0.0044	0.0089	−0.0068	−0.0088	0.0165	0.0135	−0.0096	1959	−0.0097
1960	0.0107	0.0128	0.0191	−0.0022	−0.0021	0.0141	0.0257	0.0117	−0.0063	0.0008	−0.0070	0.0104	1960	0.0907
1961	0.0148	0.0210	−0.0029	−0.0116	0.0049	−0.0080	0.0040	−0.0018	0.0144	0.0127	0.0028	−0.0026	1961	0.0482
1962	0.0080	0.0052	0.0151	0.0142	0.0000	−0.0026	−0.0015	0.0143	0.0089	0.0068	0.0062	0.0023	1962	0.0795
1963	0.0059	0.0023	0.0026	−0.0051	0.0048	0.0043	0.0028	0.0035	−0.0023	0.0049	0.0015	−0.0034	1963	0.0219
1964	0.0087	0.0054	−0.0062	0.0040	0.0057	0.0048	0.0052	0.0037	0.0021	0.0050	−0.0004	0.0088	1964	0.0477
1965	0.0081	0.0009	0.0012	0.0021	−0.0008	0.0003	0.0019	−0.0006	−0.0015	0.0046	−0.0057	−0.0149	1965	−0.0046
1966	0.0022	−0.0113	−0.0059	0.0013	−0.0026	0.0030	−0.0098	−0.0259	0.0078	0.0261	−0.0020	0.0201	1966	0.0020
1967	0.0450	−0.0201	0.0117	−0.0071	−0.0254	−0.0223	0.0041	−0.0007	0.0094	−0.0281	−0.0272	0.0127	1967	−0.0495
1968	0.0361	0.0037	−0.0197	0.0048	0.0032	0.0122	0.0341	0.0206	−0.0053	−0.0160	−0.0226	−0.0233	1968	0.0257
1969	0.0139	−0.0160	−0.0200	0.0335	−0.0227	0.0035	0.0005	−0.0020	−0.0244	0.0127	−0.0471	−0.0134	1969	−0.0809
1970	0.0141	0.0401	−0.0045	−0.0250	−0.0163	0.0001	0.0556	0.0100	0.0139	−0.0096	0.0584	0.0372	1970	0.1837

*Compound annual return

Table B–5 (continued)
Long–Term Corporate Bonds: Total Returns

from January 1971 to December 2002

Year	Jan	Feb	Mar	Apr	May	Jun	Jul	Aug	Sep	Oct	Nov	Dec	Year	Jan–Dec*
1971	0.0532	−0.0366	0.0258	−0.0236	−0.0161	0.0107	−0.0025	0.0554	−0.0102	0.0282	0.0029	0.0223	1971	0.1101
1972	−0.0033	0.0107	0.0024	0.0035	0.0163	−0.0068	0.0030	0.0072	0.0031	0.0101	0.0249	−0.0004	1972	0.0726
1973	−0.0054	0.0023	0.0045	0.0061	−0.0039	−0.0056	−0.0476	0.0356	0.0356	−0.0066	0.0078	−0.0089	1973	0.0114
1974	−0.0053	0.0009	−0.0307	−0.0341	0.0105	−0.0285	−0.0211	−0.0268	0.0174	0.0885	0.0117	−0.0075	1974	−0.0306
1975	0.0596	0.0137	−0.0247	−0.0052	0.0106	0.0304	−0.0030	−0.0175	−0.0126	0.0553	−0.0088	0.0442	1975	0.1464
1976	0.0188	0.0061	0.0167	−0.0015	−0.0103	0.0150	0.0149	0.0231	0.0167	0.0070	0.0319	0.0347	1976	0.1865
1977	−0.0303	−0.0020	0.0094	0.0100	0.0106	0.0175	−0.0005	0.0136	−0.0022	−0.0038	0.0061	−0.0105	1977	0.0171
1978	−0.0089	0.0051	0.0042	−0.0023	−0.0108	0.0023	0.0101	0.0257	−0.0048	−0.0205	0.0134	−0.0133	1978	−0.0007
1979	0.0184	−0.0128	0.0106	−0.0052	0.0228	0.0269	−0.0031	0.0006	−0.0179	−0.0890	0.0222	−0.0108	1979	−0.0418
1980	−0.0645	−0.0665	−0.0062	0.1376	0.0560	0.0341	−0.0429	−0.0445	−0.0237	−0.0159	0.0017	0.0248	1980	−0.0276
1981	−0.0130	−0.0269	0.0311	−0.0769	0.0595	0.0023	−0.0372	−0.0345	−0.0199	0.0521	0.1267	−0.0580	1981	−0.0124
1982	−0.0129	0.0312	0.0306	0.0338	0.0245	−0.0468	0.0540	0.0837	0.0623	0.0759	0.0201	0.0108	1982	0.4256
1983	−0.0094	0.0428	0.0072	0.0548	−0.0324	−0.0046	−0.0455	0.0051	0.0392	−0.0025	0.0142	−0.0033	1983	0.0626
1984	0.0270	−0.0172	−0.0235	−0.0073	−0.0483	0.0199	0.0586	0.0307	0.0314	0.0572	0.0212	0.0128	1984	0.1686
1985	0.0325	−0.0373	0.0179	0.0296	0.0820	0.0083	−0.0121	0.0260	0.0071	0.0329	0.0370	0.0469	1985	0.3009
1986	0.0045	0.0752	0.0256	0.0016	−0.0164	0.0218	0.0031	0.0275	−0.0114	0.0189	0.0233	0.0117	1986	0.1985
1987	0.0216	0.0058	−0.0087	−0.0502	−0.0052	0.0155	−0.0119	−0.0075	−0.0422	0.0507	0.0125	0.0212	1987	−0.0027
1988	0.0517	0.0138	−0.0188	−0.0149	−0.0057	0.0379	−0.0111	0.0054	0.0326	0.0273	−0.0169	0.0039	1988	0.1070
1989	0.0202	−0.0129	0.0064	0.0213	0.0379	0.0395	0.0178	−0.0163	0.0040	0.0276	0.0070	0.0006	1989	0.1623
1990	−0.0191	−0.0012	−0.0011	−0.0191	0.0385	0.0216	0.0102	−0.0292	0.0091	0.0132	0.0285	0.0167	1990	0.0678
1991	0.0150	0.0121	0.0108	0.0138	0.0039	−0.0018	0.0167	0.0275	0.0271	0.0043	0.0106	0.0436	1991	0.1989
1992	−0.0173	0.0096	−0.0073	0.0016	0.0254	0.0156	0.0308	0.0090	0.0099	−0.0156	0.0069	0.0228	1992	0.0939
1993	0.0250	0.0256	0.0025	0.0052	0.0020	0.0293	0.0100	0.0287	0.0043	0.0051	−0.0188	0.0067	1993	0.1319
1994	0.0202	−0.0286	−0.0383	−0.0097	−0.0062	−0.0081	0.0309	−0.0031	−0.0265	−0.0050	0.0018	0.0157	1994	−0.0576
1995	0.0256	0.0289	0.0095	0.0175	0.0631	0.0079	−0.0101	0.0214	0.0153	0.0185	0.0242	0.0228	1995	0.2720
1996	0.0014	−0.0373	−0.0130	−0.0160	0.0005	0.0172	0.0010	−0.0070	0.0259	0.0361	0.0263	−0.0186	1996	0.0140
1997	−0.0028	0.0028	−0.0221	0.0184	0.0128	0.0187	0.0528	−0.0240	0.0226	0.0191	0.0101	0.0163	1997	0.1295
1998	0.0137	−0.0007	0.0038	0.0053	0.0167	0.0115	−0.0056	0.0089	0.0413	−0.0190	0.0270	0.0010	1998	0.1076
1999	0.0123	−0.0401	0.0002	−0.0024	−0.0176	−0.0160	−0.0113	−0.0026	0.0093	0.0047	−0.0024	−0.0102	1999	−0.0745
2000	−0.0021	0.0092	0.0169	−0.0115	−0.0161	0.0326	0.0179	0.0135	0.0046	0.0045	0.0263	0.0270	2000	0.1287
2001	0.0359	0.0127	−0.0029	−0.0128	0.0132	0.0055	0.0361	0.0156	−0.0152	0.0437	−0.0188	−0.0090	2001	0.1065
2002	0.0175	0.0130	−0.0295	0.0253	0.0113	0.0073	0.0094	0.0452	0.0330	−0.0240	0.0103	0.0361	2002	0.1633

*Compound annual return

Table B–6

Long–Term Government Bonds: Total Returns

from January 1926 to December 1970

Year	Jan	Feb	Mar	Apr	May	Jun	Jul	Aug	Sep	Oct	Nov	Dec	Year	Jan–Dec*
1926	0.0138	0.0063	0.0041	0.0076	0.0014	0.0038	0.0004	0.0000	0.0038	0.0102	0.0160	0.0078	1926	0.0777
1927	0.0075	0.0088	0.0253	-0.0005	0.0109	-0.0069	0.0050	0.0076	0.0018	0.0099	0.0097	0.0072	1927	0.0893
1928	-0.0036	0.0061	0.0045	-0.0004	-0.0077	0.0041	-0.0217	0.0076	-0.0041	0.0158	0.0003	0.0004	1928	0.0010
1929	-0.0090	-0.0157	-0.0144	0.0275	-0.0162	0.0110	0.0000	-0.0034	0.0027	0.0382	0.0236	-0.0089	1929	0.0342
1930	-0.0057	0.0129	0.0083	-0.0016	0.0139	0.0051	0.0034	0.0013	0.0074	0.0035	0.0042	-0.0070	1930	0.0466
1931	-0.0121	0.0085	0.0104	0.0086	0.0145	0.0004	-0.0042	0.0012	-0.0281	-0.0330	0.0027	-0.0220	1931	-0.0531
1932	0.0034	0.0413	-0.0018	0.0604	-0.0188	0.0065	0.0481	0.0003	0.0057	-0.0017	0.0032	0.0131	1932	0.1684
1933	0.0148	-0.0258	0.0097	-0.0032	0.0303	0.0050	-0.0017	0.0044	0.0023	-0.0091	-0.0149	-0.0113	1933	-0.0007
1934	0.0257	0.0081	0.0197	0.0126	0.0131	0.0067	0.0040	-0.0118	-0.0146	0.0182	0.0037	0.0112	1934	0.1003
1935	0.0182	0.0092	0.0041	0.0079	-0.0057	0.0092	0.0046	-0.0133	0.0009	0.0061	0.0010	0.0070	1935	0.0498
1936	0.0055	0.0081	0.0106	0.0035	0.0040	0.0021	0.0060	0.0111	-0.0031	0.0006	0.0205	0.0038	1936	0.0752
1937	-0.0013	0.0086	-0.0411	0.0039	0.0053	-0.0018	0.0138	-0.0104	0.0045	0.0042	0.0096	0.0082	1937	0.0023
1938	0.0057	0.0052	-0.0037	0.0210	0.0044	0.0004	0.0043	0.0000	0.0022	0.0087	-0.0022	0.0080	1938	0.0553
1939	0.0059	0.0080	0.0125	0.0118	0.0171	-0.0027	0.0113	-0.0201	-0.0545	0.0410	0.0162	0.0145	1939	0.0594
1940	-0.0017	0.0027	0.0177	-0.0035	-0.0299	0.0258	0.0052	0.0028	0.0110	0.0031	0.0205	0.0067	1940	0.0609
1941	-0.0201	0.0020	0.0096	0.0129	0.0027	0.0066	0.0022	0.0018	-0.0012	0.0140	-0.0029	-0.0177	1941	0.0093
1942	0.0069	0.0011	0.0092	-0.0029	0.0075	0.0003	0.0018	0.0038	0.0003	0.0024	-0.0035	0.0049	1942	0.0322
1943	0.0033	-0.0005	0.0009	0.0048	0.0050	0.0018	-0.0001	0.0021	0.0011	0.0005	0.0000	0.0018	1943	0.0208
1944	0.0021	0.0032	0.0021	0.0013	0.0028	0.0008	0.0036	0.0027	0.0014	0.0012	0.0024	0.0042	1944	0.0281
1945	0.0127	0.0077	0.0021	0.0160	0.0056	0.0169	-0.0086	0.0026	0.0054	0.0104	0.0125	0.0194	1945	0.1073
1946	0.0025	0.0032	0.0010	-0.0135	-0.0012	0.0070	-0.0040	-0.0111	-0.0009	0.0074	-0.0054	0.0145	1946	-0.0010
1947	-0.0006	0.0021	0.0020	-0.0037	0.0033	0.0010	0.0063	0.0081	-0.0044	-0.0037	-0.0174	-0.0192	1947	-0.0262
1948	0.0020	0.0046	0.0034	0.0045	0.0141	-0.0084	-0.0021	0.0001	0.0014	0.0007	0.0076	0.0056	1948	0.0340
1949	0.0082	0.0049	0.0074	0.0011	0.0019	0.0167	0.0033	0.0111	-0.0011	0.0019	0.0021	0.0052	1949	0.0645
1950	-0.0061	0.0021	0.0008	0.0030	0.0033	-0.0025	0.0055	0.0014	-0.0072	-0.0048	0.0035	0.0016	1950	0.0006
1951	0.0058	-0.0074	-0.0157	-0.0063	-0.0069	-0.0062	0.0138	0.0099	-0.0080	0.0010	-0.0136	-0.0061	1951	-0.0393
1952	0.0028	0.0014	0.0111	0.0171	-0.0033	0.0003	-0.0020	-0.0070	-0.0130	0.0148	-0.0015	-0.0086	1952	0.0116
1953	0.0012	-0.0087	-0.0088	-0.0105	-0.0148	0.0223	0.0039	-0.0008	0.0299	0.0074	-0.0049	0.0206	1953	0.0364
1954	0.0089	0.0240	0.0058	0.0104	-0.0087	0.0163	0.0134	-0.0036	-0.0010	0.0006	-0.0025	0.0064	1954	0.0719
1955	-0.0241	-0.0078	0.0087	0.0001	0.0073	-0.0076	-0.0102	0.0004	0.0073	0.0144	-0.0045	0.0037	1955	-0.0129
1956	0.0083	-0.0002	-0.0149	-0.0113	0.0225	0.0027	-0.0209	-0.0187	0.0050	-0.0054	-0.0057	-0.0179	1956	-0.0559
1957	0.0346	0.0025	-0.0024	-0.0222	-0.0023	-0.0180	-0.0041	0.0002	0.0076	-0.0050	0.0533	0.0307	1957	0.0746
1958	-0.0084	0.0100	0.0102	0.0186	0.0001	-0.0160	-0.0278	-0.0435	-0.0117	0.0138	0.0120	-0.0181	1958	-0.0609
1959	-0.0080	0.0117	0.0017	-0.0117	-0.0005	0.0010	0.0060	-0.0041	-0.0057	0.0150	-0.0119	-0.0159	1959	-0.0226
1960	0.0112	0.0204	0.0282	-0.0170	0.0152	0.0173	0.0368	-0.0067	0.0075	-0.0028	-0.0066	0.0279	1960	0.1378
1961	-0.0107	0.0200	-0.0037	0.0115	-0.0046	-0.0075	0.0035	-0.0038	0.0129	0.0071	-0.0020	-0.0125	1961	0.0097
1962	-0.0014	0.0103	0.0253	0.0082	0.0046	-0.0076	-0.0109	0.0187	0.0061	0.0084	0.0021	0.0035	1962	0.0689
1963	-0.0001	0.0008	0.0009	-0.0012	0.0023	0.0019	0.0031	0.0021	0.0004	-0.0026	0.0051	-0.0006	1963	0.0121
1964	-0.0014	-0.0011	0.0037	0.0047	0.0050	0.0069	0.0008	0.0020	0.0050	0.0043	0.0017	0.0030	1964	0.0351
1965	0.0040	0.0014	0.0054	0.0036	0.0018	0.0047	0.0022	-0.0013	-0.0034	0.0027	-0.0062	-0.0078	1965	0.0071
1966	-0.0104	-0.0250	0.0296	-0.0063	-0.0059	-0.0016	-0.0037	-0.0206	0.0332	0.0228	-0.0148	0.0413	1966	0.0365
1967	0.0154	-0.0221	0.0198	-0.0291	-0.0039	-0.0312	0.0068	-0.0084	-0.0004	-0.0400	-0.0196	0.0192	1967	-0.0918
1968	0.0328	-0.0033	-0.0212	0.0227	0.0043	0.0230	0.0289	-0.0003	-0.0102	-0.0132	-0.0269	-0.0363	1968	-0.0026
1969	-0.0206	0.0042	0.0010	0.0427	-0.0490	0.0214	0.0079	-0.0069	-0.0531	0.0365	-0.0243	-0.0068	1969	-0.0507
1970	-0.0021	0.0587	-0.0068	-0.0413	-0.0468	0.0486	0.0319	-0.0019	0.0228	-0.0109	0.0791	-0.0084	1970	0.1211

*Compound annual return

Table B–6 (continued)

Long–Term Government Bonds: Total Returns

from January 1971 to December 2002

Year	Jan	Feb	Mar	Apr	May	Jun	Jul	Aug	Sep	Oct	Nov	Dec	Year	Jan–Dec*
1971	0.0506	−0.0163	0.0526	−0.0283	−0.0006	−0.0159	0.0030	0.0471	0.0204	0.0167	−0.0047	0.0044	1971	0.1323
1972	−0.0063	0.0088	−0.0082	0.0027	0.0270	−0.0065	0.0216	0.0029	−0.0083	0.0234	0.0226	−0.0229	1972	0.0569
1973	−0.0321	0.0014	0.0082	0.0046	−0.0105	−0.0021	−0.0433	0.0391	0.0318	0.0215	−0.0183	−0.0082	1973	−0.0111
1974	−0.0083	−0.0024	−0.0292	−0.0253	0.0123	0.0045	−0.0029	−0.0232	0.0247	0.0489	0.0295	0.0171	1974	0.0435
1975	0.0225	0.0131	−0.0267	−0.0182	0.0212	0.0292	−0.0087	−0.0068	−0.0098	0.0475	−0.0109	0.0390	1975	0.0920
1976	0.0090	0.0062	0.0166	0.0018	−0.0158	0.0208	0.0078	0.0211	0.0145	0.0084	0.0339	0.0327	1976	0.1675
1977	−0.0388	−0.0049	0.0091	0.0071	0.0125	0.0164	−0.0070	0.0198	−0.0029	−0.0093	0.0093	−0.0168	1977	−0.0069
1978	−0.0080	0.0004	−0.0021	−0.0005	−0.0058	−0.0062	0.0143	0.0218	−0.0106	−0.0200	0.0189	−0.0130	1978	−0.0118
1979	0.0191	−0.0135	0.0129	−0.0112	0.0261	0.0311	−0.0085	−0.0035	−0.0122	−0.0841	0.0311	0.0057	1979	−0.0123
1980	−0.0741	−0.0467	−0.0315	0.1523	0.0419	0.0359	−0.0476	−0.0432	−0.0262	−0.0263	0.0100	0.0352	1980	−0.0395
1981	−0.0115	−0.0435	0.0384	−0.0518	0.0622	−0.0179	−0.0353	−0.0386	−0.0145	0.0829	0.1410	−0.0713	1981	0.0186
1982	0.0046	0.0182	0.0231	0.0373	0.0034	−0.0223	0.0501	0.0781	0.0618	0.0634	−0.0002	0.0312	1982	0.4036
1983	−0.0309	0.0492	−0.0094	0.0350	−0.0386	0.0039	−0.0486	0.0020	0.0505	−0.0132	0.0183	−0.0059	1983	0.0065
1984	0.0244	−0.0178	−0.0156	−0.0105	−0.0516	0.0150	0.0693	0.0266	0.0342	0.0561	0.0118	0.0091	1984	0.1548
1985	0.0364	−0.0493	0.0307	0.0242	0.0896	0.0142	−0.0180	0.0259	−0.0021	0.0338	0.0401	0.0541	1985	0.3097
1986	−0.0025	0.1145	0.0770	−0.0080	−0.0505	0.0613	−0.0108	0.0499	−0.0500	0.0289	0.0267	−0.0018	1986	0.2453
1987	0.0161	0.0202	−0.0223	−0.0473	−0.0105	0.0098	−0.0178	−0.0165	−0.0369	0.0623	0.0037	0.0165	1987	−0.0271
1988	0.0666	0.0052	−0.0307	−0.0160	−0.0102	0.0368	−0.0170	0.0058	0.0345	0.0308	−0.0196	0.0110	1988	0.0967
1989	0.0203	−0.0179	0.0122	0.0159	0.0401	0.0550	0.0238	−0.0259	0.0019	0.0379	0.0078	−0.0006	1989	0.1811
1990	−0.0343	−0.0025	−0.0044	−0.0202	0.0415	0.0230	0.0107	−0.0419	0.0117	0.0215	0.0402	0.0187	1990	0.0618
1991	0.0130	0.0030	0.0038	0.0140	0.0000	−0.0063	0.0157	0.0340	0.0303	0.0054	0.0082	0.0581	1991	0.1930
1992	−0.0324	0.0051	−0.0094	0.0016	0.0243	0.0200	0.0398	0.0067	0.0185	−0.0198	0.0010	0.0246	1992	0.0805
1993	0.0280	0.0354	0.0021	0.0072	0.0047	0.0449	0.0191	0.0434	0.0005	0.0096	−0.0259	0.0020	1993	0.1824
1994	0.0257	−0.0450	−0.0395	−0.0150	−0.0082	−0.0100	0.0363	−0.0086	−0.0331	−0.0025	0.0066	0.0161	1994	−0.0777
1995	0.0273	0.0287	0.0091	0.0169	0.0790	0.0139	−0.0168	0.0236	0.0175	0.0294	0.0249	0.0272	1995	0.3167
1996	−0.0011	−0.0483	−0.0210	−0.0165	−0.0054	0.0203	0.0018	−0.0139	0.0290	0.0404	0.0351	−0.0256	1996	−0.0093
1997	−0.0079	0.0005	−0.0252	0.0255	0.0097	0.0195	0.0626	−0.0317	0.0316	0.0341	0.0148	0.0184	1997	0.1585
1998	0.0200	−0.0072	0.0025	0.0026	0.0182	0.0228	−0.0040	0.0465	0.0395	−0.0218	0.0097	−0.0032	1998	0.1306
1999	0.0121	−0.0520	−0.0008	0.0021	−0.0185	−0.0078	−0.0077	−0.0053	0.0084	−0.0012	−0.0061	−0.0155	1999	−0.0896
2000	0.0228	0.0264	0.0367	−0.0076	−0.0054	0.0244	0.0173	0.0240	−0.0157	0.0187	0.0319	0.0243	2000	0.2148
2001	0.0005	0.0191	−0.0074	−0.0313	0.0037	0.0085	0.0376	0.0206	0.0081	0.0464	−0.0471	−0.0183	2001	0.0370
2002	0.0138	0.0115	−0.0436	0.0410	0.0015	0.0187	0.0303	0.0464	0.0417	−0.0294	−0.0122	0.0507	2002	0.1784

*Compound annual return

Table B–7

Long–Term Government Bonds: Income Returns

from January 1926 to December 1970

Year	Jan	Feb	Mar	Apr	May	Jun	Jul	Aug	Sep	Oct	Nov	Dec	Year	Jan–Dec*
1926	0.0031	0.0028	0.0032	0.0030	0.0028	0.0033	0.0031	0.0031	0.0030	0.0030	0.0031	0.0030	1926	0.0373
1927	0.0030	0.0027	0.0029	0.0027	0.0028	0.0027	0.0027	0.0029	0.0027	0.0028	0.0027	0.0027	1927	0.0341
1928	0.0027	0.0025	0.0027	0.0026	0.0027	0.0027	0.0027	0.0029	0.0027	0.0030	0.0027	0.0029	1928	0.0322
1929	0.0029	0.0027	0.0028	0.0034	0.0030	0.0029	0.0032	0.0030	0.0032	0.0031	0.0026	0.0031	1929	0.0347
1930	0.0029	0.0026	0.0029	0.0027	0.0027	0.0029	0.0028	0.0026	0.0029	0.0027	0.0026	0.0028	1930	0.0332
1931	0.0028	0.0026	0.0029	0.0027	0.0026	0.0028	0.0027	0.0027	0.0027	0.0029	0.0031	0.0032	1931	0.0333
1932	0.0032	0.0032	0.0031	0.0030	0.0028	0.0028	0.0028	0.0028	0.0026	0.0027	0.0026	0.0027	1932	0.0369
1933	0.0027	0.0023	0.0027	0.0025	0.0028	0.0025	0.0026	0.0026	0.0025	0.0026	0.0025	0.0028	1933	0.0312
1934	0.0029	0.0024	0.0027	0.0025	0.0025	0.0024	0.0024	0.0024	0.0023	0.0027	0.0025	0.0025	1934	0.0318
1935	0.0025	0.0021	0.0022	0.0023	0.0023	0.0022	0.0024	0.0023	0.0023	0.0023	0.0024	0.0024	1935	0.0281
1936	0.0024	0.0023	0.0024	0.0022	0.0022	0.0024	0.0023	0.0023	0.0021	0.0023	0.0022	0.0022	1936	0.0277
1937	0.0021	0.0020	0.0022	0.0023	0.0022	0.0025	0.0024	0.0023	0.0023	0.0023	0.0024	0.0023	1937	0.0266
1938	0.0023	0.0021	0.0023	0.0022	0.0022	0.0021	0.0021	0.0022	0.0021	0.0022	0.0021	0.0022	1938	0.0264
1939	0.0021	0.0019	0.0021	0.0019	0.0020	0.0018	0.0019	0.0018	0.0019	0.0023	0.0020	0.0019	1939	0.0240
1940	0.0020	0.0018	0.0019	0.0018	0.0019	0.0019	0.0020	0.0019	0.0018	0.0018	0.0018	0.0017	1940	0.0223
1941	0.0016	0.0016	0.0018	0.0017	0.0017	0.0016	0.0016	0.0016	0.0016	0.0016	0.0014	0.0016	1941	0.0194
1942	0.0021	0.0019	0.0021	0.0020	0.0019	0.0021	0.0021	0.0021	0.0020	0.0021	0.0020	0.0021	1942	0.0246
1943	0.0020	0.0019	0.0021	0.0020	0.0019	0.0021	0.0021	0.0021	0.0020	0.0020	0.0021	0.0021	1943	0.0244
1944	0.0021	0.0020	0.0021	0.0020	0.0022	0.0020	0.0021	0.0021	0.0020	0.0021	0.0020	0.0020	1944	0.0246
1945	0.0021	0.0018	0.0020	0.0019	0.0019	0.0019	0.0018	0.0019	0.0018	0.0019	0.0018	0.0018	1945	0.0234
1946	0.0017	0.0015	0.0016	0.0017	0.0018	0.0016	0.0019	0.0017	0.0018	0.0019	0.0018	0.0019	1946	0.0204
1947	0.0018	0.0016	0.0018	0.0017	0.0017	0.0019	0.0018	0.0017	0.0018	0.0018	0.0017	0.0021	1947	0.0213
1948	0.0020	0.0019	0.0022	0.0020	0.0018	0.0021	0.0019	0.0021	0.0020	0.0019	0.0021	0.0020	1948	0.0240
1949	0.0020	0.0018	0.0019	0.0018	0.0020	0.0019	0.0017	0.0019	0.0017	0.0018	0.0017	0.0017	1949	0.0225
1950	0.0018	0.0016	0.0018	0.0016	0.0019	0.0017	0.0018	0.0018	0.0017	0.0019	0.0018	0.0018	1950	0.0212
1951	0.0020	0.0017	0.0019	0.0020	0.0021	0.0020	0.0023	0.0021	0.0019	0.0023	0.0021	0.0022	1951	0.0238
1952	0.0023	0.0021	0.0023	0.0022	0.0020	0.0022	0.0022	0.0021	0.0023	0.0023	0.0021	0.0024	1952	0.0266
1953	0.0023	0.0021	0.0025	0.0024	0.0024	0.0027	0.0025	0.0025	0.0025	0.0023	0.0024	0.0024	1953	0.0284
1954	0.0023	0.0022	0.0025	0.0022	0.0020	0.0025	0.0022	0.0023	0.0022	0.0021	0.0023	0.0023	1954	0.0279
1955	0.0022	0.0022	0.0024	0.0022	0.0025	0.0023	0.0023	0.0027	0.0024	0.0025	0.0024	0.0024	1955	0.0275
1956	0.0025	0.0023	0.0023	0.0026	0.0026	0.0023	0.0026	0.0026	0.0025	0.0029	0.0027	0.0028	1956	0.0299
1957	0.0029	0.0025	0.0026	0.0029	0.0029	0.0025	0.0033	0.0030	0.0031	0.0031	0.0029	0.0029	1957	0.0344
1958	0.0027	0.0025	0.0027	0.0026	0.0024	0.0027	0.0027	0.0027	0.0032	0.0032	0.0028	0.0033	1958	0.0327
1959	0.0031	0.0031	0.0035	0.0033	0.0033	0.0036	0.0035	0.0035	0.0034	0.0035	0.0035	0.0036	1959	0.0401
1960	0.0035	0.0037	0.0036	0.0032	0.0037	0.0034	0.0032	0.0034	0.0032	0.0033	0.0032	0.0033	1960	0.0426
1961	0.0033	0.0030	0.0031	0.0031	0.0034	0.0032	0.0033	0.0033	0.0032	0.0034	0.0032	0.0031	1961	0.0383
1962	0.0037	0.0032	0.0033	0.0033	0.0032	0.0030	0.0034	0.0034	0.0030	0.0035	0.0031	0.0032	1962	0.0400
1963	0.0032	0.0029	0.0031	0.0034	0.0033	0.0030	0.0036	0.0033	0.0034	0.0034	0.0032	0.0036	1963	0.0389
1964	0.0035	0.0032	0.0037	0.0035	0.0032	0.0038	0.0035	0.0035	0.0034	0.0034	0.0035	0.0035	1964	0.0415
1965	0.0033	0.0032	0.0038	0.0033	0.0033	0.0038	0.0034	0.0037	0.0035	0.0034	0.0037	0.0037	1965	0.0419
1966	0.0038	0.0034	0.0040	0.0036	0.0041	0.0039	0.0038	0.0043	0.0041	0.0040	0.0038	0.0039	1966	0.0449
1967	0.0040	0.0034	0.0039	0.0035	0.0043	0.0039	0.0043	0.0042	0.0040	0.0045	0.0045	0.0044	1967	0.0459
1968	0.0050	0.0042	0.0043	0.0049	0.0046	0.0042	0.0048	0.0042	0.0044	0.0045	0.0043	0.0049	1968	0.0550
1969	0.0050	0.0046	0.0047	0.0055	0.0047	0.0055	0.0052	0.0048	0.0055	0.0057	0.0049	0.0060	1969	0.0595
1970	0.0056	0.0052	0.0056	0.0054	0.0055	0.0064	0.0059	0.0057	0.0056	0.0055	0.0058	0.0053	1970	0.0674

*Compound annual return

Table B–7 (continued)

Long–Term Government Bonds: Income Returns

from January 1971 to December 2002

Year	Jan	Feb	Mar	Apr	May	Jun	Jul	Aug	Sep	Oct	Nov	Dec	Year	Jan–Dec*
1971	0.0051	0.0046	0.0056	0.0048	0.0047	0.0056	0.0052	0.0055	0.0049	0.0047	0.0051	0.0050	1971	0.0632
1972	0.0050	0.0047	0.0049	0.0048	0.0055	0.0049	0.0051	0.0049	0.0047	0.0052	0.0048	0.0045	1972	0.0587
1973	0.0054	0.0051	0.0056	0.0057	0.0058	0.0055	0.0061	0.0062	0.0055	0.0063	0.0056	0.0060	1973	0.0651
1974	0.0061	0.0055	0.0058	0.0068	0.0068	0.0061	0.0072	0.0065	0.0071	0.0070	0.0062	0.0067	1974	0.0727
1975	0.0068	0.0060	0.0066	0.0067	0.0067	0.0070	0.0068	0.0065	0.0073	0.0072	0.0061	0.0074	1975	0.0799
1976	0.0065	0.0060	0.0071	0.0064	0.0059	0.0073	0.0065	0.0069	0.0064	0.0061	0.0066	0.0063	1976	0.0789
1977	0.0059	0.0057	0.0065	0.0061	0.0067	0.0062	0.0059	0.0067	0.0061	0.0063	0.0063	0.0062	1977	0.0714
1978	0.0069	0.0060	0.0069	0.0063	0.0075	0.0069	0.0073	0.0070	0.0065	0.0073	0.0071	0.0068	1978	0.0790
1979	0.0079	0.0065	0.0074	0.0076	0.0077	0.0071	0.0076	0.0073	0.0068	0.0082	0.0083	0.0083	1979	0.0886
1980	0.0083	0.0084	0.0099	0.0100	0.0087	0.0086	0.0084	0.0081	0.0097	0.0097	0.0091	0.0108	1980	0.0997
1981	0.0094	0.0088	0.0111	0.0101	0.0104	0.0109	0.0109	0.0110	0.0114	0.0117	0.0113	0.0100	1981	0.1155
1982	0.0108	0.0103	0.0124	0.0112	0.0101	0.0120	0.0114	0.0112	0.0100	0.0091	0.0094	0.0093	1982	0.1350
1983	0.0087	0.0081	0.0089	0.0085	0.0091	0.0090	0.0088	0.0103	0.0096	0.0095	0.0094	0.0094	1983	0.1038
1984	0.0103	0.0092	0.0098	0.0104	0.0103	0.0106	0.0116	0.0106	0.0094	0.0108	0.0091	0.0098	1984	0.1174
1985	0.0096	0.0082	0.0094	0.0102	0.0097	0.0080	0.0094	0.0085	0.0088	0.0089	0.0081	0.0086	1985	0.1125
1986	0.0079	0.0073	0.0071	0.0063	0.0062	0.0070	0.0066	0.0063	0.0065	0.0069	0.0059	0.0070	1986	0.0898
1987	0.0064	0.0059	0.0066	0.0065	0.0066	0.0075	0.0073	0.0075	0.0075	0.0079	0.0075	0.0078	1987	0.0792
1988	0.0072	0.0071	0.0072	0.0070	0.0078	0.0076	0.0071	0.0083	0.0076	0.0076	0.0070	0.0075	1988	0.0897
1989	0.0080	0.0069	0.0079	0.0070	0.0080	0.0070	0.0068	0.0066	0.0065	0.0072	0.0064	0.0064	1989	0.0881
1990	0.0073	0.0066	0.0071	0.0075	0.0075	0.0068	0.0074	0.0071	0.0069	0.0081	0.0071	0.0072	1990	0.0819
1991	0.0071	0.0064	0.0064	0.0076	0.0068	0.0063	0.0076	0.0068	0.0068	0.0065	0.0060	0.0068	1991	0.0822
1992	0.0061	0.0059	0.0067	0.0065	0.0061	0.0067	0.0063	0.0060	0.0058	0.0057	0.0061	0.0063	1992	0.0726
1993	0.0059	0.0055	0.0063	0.0057	0.0052	0.0062	0.0054	0.0056	0.0050	0.0049	0.0053	0.0055	1993	0.0717
1994	0.0055	0.0049	0.0058	0.0057	0.0063	0.0061	0.0060	0.0066	0.0061	0.0066	0.0064	0.0066	1994	0.0659
1995	0.0070	0.0059	0.0064	0.0058	0.0065	0.0054	0.0056	0.0057	0.0052	0.0057	0.0051	0.0049	1995	0.0760
1996	0.0054	0.0048	0.0052	0.0059	0.0058	0.0054	0.0062	0.0057	0.0060	0.0058	0.0052	0.0056	1996	0.0618
1997	0.0056	0.0051	0.0059	0.0059	0.0059	0.0057	0.0058	0.0049	0.0058	0.0054	0.0047	0.0054	1997	0.0664
1998	0.0048	0.0044	0.0052	0.0049	0.0048	0.0052	0.0049	0.0048	0.0044	0.0042	0.0045	0.0045	1998	0.0583
1999	0.0042	0.0040	0.0053	0.0048	0.0045	0.0055	0.0053	0.0053	0.0052	0.0050	0.0056	0.0055	1999	0.0557
2000	0.0057	0.0051	0.0054	0.0047	0.0056	0.0052	0.0052	0.0050	0.0046	0.0053	0.0048	0.0045	2000	0.0650
2001	0.0049	0.0042	0.0045	0.0047	0.0050	0.0047	0.0052	0.0046	0.0041	0.0048	0.0041	0.0046	2001	0.0553
2002	0.0048	0.0043	0.0043	0.0054	0.0049	0.0044	0.0051	0.0044	0.0042	0.0040	0.0040	0.0045	2002	0.0559

*Compound annual return

Table B-8

Long-Term Government Bonds: Capital Appreciation Returns

from January 1926 to December 1970

Year	Jan	Feb	Mar	Apr	May	Jun	Jul	Aug	Sep	Oct	Nov	Dec	Year	Jan–Dec*
1926	0.0106	0.0035	0.0009	0.0046	-0.0014	0.0005	-0.0027	-0.0031	0.0007	0.0072	0.0129	0.0048	1926	0.0391
1927	0.0045	0.0061	0.0224	-0.0032	0.0081	-0.0096	0.0022	0.0047	-0.0009	0.0071	0.0071	0.0045	1927	0.0540
1928	-0.0063	0.0036	0.0019	-0.0029	-0.0104	0.0015	-0.0245	0.0047	-0.0067	0.0128	-0.0024	-0.0024	1928	-0.0312
1929	-0.0119	-0.0183	-0.0171	0.0242	-0.0192	0.0081	-0.0032	-0.0064	-0.0004	0.0351	0.0211	-0.0120	1929	-0.0020
1930	-0.0086	0.0102	0.0055	-0.0043	0.0113	0.0022	0.0007	-0.0013	0.0045	0.0008	0.0017	-0.0098	1930	0.0128
1931	-0.0149	0.0059	0.0076	0.0059	0.0119	-0.0024	-0.0069	-0.0015	-0.0307	-0.0360	-0.0004	-0.0252	1931	-0.0846
1932	0.0002	0.0382	-0.0049	0.0574	-0.0216	0.0037	0.0453	-0.0025	0.0031	-0.0044	0.0006	0.0104	1932	0.1294
1933	0.0122	-0.0282	0.0070	-0.0057	0.0274	0.0025	-0.0043	0.0018	-0.0002	-0.0117	-0.0174	-0.0140	1933	-0.0314
1934	0.0228	0.0057	0.0170	0.0101	0.0106	0.0043	0.0016	-0.0143	-0.0169	0.0155	0.0013	0.0087	1934	0.0676
1935	0.0157	0.0070	0.0019	0.0056	-0.0079	0.0070	0.0022	-0.0156	-0.0014	0.0038	-0.0014	0.0047	1935	0.0214
1936	0.0031	0.0059	0.0083	0.0013	0.0019	-0.0003	0.0037	0.0088	-0.0053	-0.0017	0.0183	0.0017	1936	0.0464
1937	-0.0034	0.0067	-0.0433	0.0016	0.0031	-0.0043	0.0114	-0.0128	0.0022	0.0019	0.0072	0.0059	1937	-0.0248
1938	0.0034	0.0031	-0.0059	0.0187	0.0022	-0.0016	0.0022	-0.0022	0.0001	0.0065	-0.0043	0.0059	1938	0.0283
1939	0.0038	0.0061	0.0105	0.0099	0.0151	-0.0045	0.0095	-0.0219	-0.0564	0.0386	0.0142	0.0125	1939	0.0348
1940	-0.0037	0.0009	0.0158	-0.0053	-0.0318	0.0239	0.0032	0.0009	0.0092	0.0013	0.0187	0.0050	1940	0.0377
1941	-0.0217	0.0004	0.0078	0.0112	0.0011	0.0050	0.0005	0.0002	-0.0028	0.0124	-0.0044	-0.0194	1941	-0.0101
1942	0.0048	-0.0008	0.0071	-0.0049	0.0056	-0.0018	-0.0003	0.0017	-0.0016	0.0004	-0.0055	0.0028	1942	0.0074
1943	0.0013	-0.0024	-0.0012	0.0028	0.0031	-0.0003	-0.0021	0.0000	-0.0009	-0.0015	-0.0021	-0.0003	1943	-0.0037
1944	0.0000	0.0012	0.0000	-0.0006	0.0006	-0.0012	0.0015	0.0006	-0.0006	-0.0009	0.0003	0.0022	1944	0.0032
1945	0.0105	0.0058	0.0001	0.0141	0.0037	0.0150	-0.0104	0.0007	0.0037	0.0085	0.0108	0.0177	1945	0.0827
1946	0.0008	0.0017	-0.0006	-0.0152	-0.0030	0.0054	-0.0058	-0.0129	-0.0028	0.0055	-0.0072	0.0126	1946	-0.0215
1947	-0.0024	0.0005	0.0002	-0.0054	0.0016	-0.0009	0.0044	0.0064	-0.0062	-0.0055	-0.0191	-0.0213	1947	-0.0470
1948	0.0000	0.0028	0.0013	0.0025	0.0123	-0.0105	-0.0041	-0.0019	-0.0006	-0.0012	0.0055	0.0036	1948	0.0096
1949	0.0062	0.0031	0.0055	-0.0006	0.0000	0.0148	0.0016	0.0092	-0.0029	0.0001	0.0004	0.0035	1949	0.0415
1950	-0.0080	0.0005	-0.0010	0.0014	0.0014	-0.0042	0.0037	-0.0004	-0.0089	-0.0067	0.0017	-0.0001	1950	-0.0206
1951	0.0038	-0.0091	-0.0176	-0.0083	-0.0090	-0.0082	0.0116	0.0077	-0.0098	-0.0012	-0.0157	-0.0083	1951	-0.0627
1952	0.0005	-0.0007	0.0088	0.0149	-0.0054	-0.0019	-0.0041	-0.0091	-0.0153	0.0124	-0.0036	-0.0110	1952	-0.0148
1953	-0.0011	-0.0108	-0.0113	-0.0129	-0.0171	0.0195	0.0014	-0.0033	0.0275	0.0051	-0.0073	0.0182	1953	0.0067
1954	0.0066	0.0218	0.0034	0.0081	-0.0107	0.0138	0.0113	-0.0059	-0.0031	-0.0015	-0.0048	0.0042	1954	0.0435
1955	-0.0264	-0.0100	0.0063	-0.0022	0.0048	-0.0099	-0.0125	-0.0022	0.0049	0.0119	-0.0069	0.0013	1955	-0.0407
1956	0.0058	-0.0025	-0.0172	-0.0139	0.0199	0.0004	-0.0234	-0.0213	0.0025	-0.0083	-0.0084	-0.0206	1956	-0.0846
1957	0.0317	0.0000	-0.0050	-0.0250	-0.0052	-0.0206	-0.0074	-0.0028	0.0045	-0.0081	0.0504	0.0277	1957	0.0382
1958	-0.0112	0.0075	0.0075	0.0160	-0.0023	-0.0187	-0.0305	-0.0463	-0.0149	0.0106	0.0092	-0.0213	1958	-0.0923
1959	-0.0111	0.0087	-0.0018	-0.0150	-0.0038	-0.0026	0.0025	-0.0076	-0.0091	0.0115	-0.0154	-0.0195	1959	-0.0620
1960	0.0077	0.0167	0.0246	-0.0202	0.0115	0.0139	0.0335	-0.0101	0.0043	-0.0061	-0.0098	0.0247	1960	0.0929
1961	-0.0140	0.0170	-0.0069	0.0085	-0.0080	-0.0106	0.0001	-0.0071	0.0097	0.0037	-0.0052	-0.0156	1961	-0.0286
1962	-0.0051	0.0071	0.0220	0.0049	0.0014	-0.0106	-0.0143	0.0153	0.0031	0.0049	-0.0010	0.0003	1962	0.0278
1963	-0.0033	-0.0022	-0.0022	-0.0046	-0.0010	-0.0011	-0.0005	-0.0011	-0.0029	-0.0060	0.0019	-0.0042	1963	-0.0270
1964	-0.0048	-0.0043	0.0000	0.0012	0.0018	0.0031	-0.0027	-0.0015	0.0015	0.0009	-0.0018	-0.0005	1964	-0.0072
1965	0.0007	-0.0018	0.0016	0.0003	-0.0015	0.0009	-0.0012	-0.0050	-0.0069	-0.0007	-0.0099	-0.0115	1965	-0.0345
1966	-0.0142	-0.0284	0.0256	-0.0099	-0.0100	-0.0054	-0.0074	-0.0249	0.0292	0.0188	-0.0187	0.0374	1966	-0.0106
1967	0.0115	-0.0255	0.0159	-0.0326	-0.0082	-0.0351	0.0026	-0.0126	-0.0045	-0.0445	-0.0241	0.0148	1967	-0.1355
1968	0.0278	-0.0075	-0.0254	0.0178	-0.0003	0.0188	0.0241	-0.0044	-0.0146	-0.0177	-0.0312	-0.0412	1968	-0.0551
1969	-0.0256	-0.0004	-0.0036	0.0371	-0.0537	0.0159	0.0027	-0.0117	-0.0586	0.0309	-0.0293	-0.0129	1969	-0.1083
1970	-0.0077	0.0535	-0.0124	-0.0467	-0.0523	0.0422	0.0260	-0.0076	0.0172	-0.0164	0.0733	-0.0137	1970	0.0484

*Compound annual return

Table B–8 (continued)

Long–Term Government Bonds: Capital Appreciation Returns

from January 1971 to December 2002

Year	Jan	Feb	Mar	Apr	May	Jun	Jul	Aug	Sep	Oct	Nov	Dec	Year	Jan–Dec*
1971	0.0455	−0.0209	0.0470	−0.0331	−0.0053	−0.0214	−0.0022	0.0416	0.0154	0.0120	−0.0098	−0.0006	1971	0.0661
1972	−0.0114	0.0041	−0.0131	−0.0021	0.0215	−0.0113	0.0165	−0.0021	−0.0129	0.0182	0.0178	−0.0275	1972	−0.0035
1973	−0.0375	−0.0037	0.0026	−0.0012	−0.0162	−0.0076	−0.0495	0.0329	0.0263	0.0153	−0.0238	−0.0142	1973	−0.0770
1974	−0.0144	−0.0079	−0.0350	−0.0320	0.0055	−0.0016	−0.0101	−0.0298	0.0176	0.0419	0.0233	0.0105	1974	−0.0345
1975	0.0157	0.0071	−0.0333	−0.0248	0.0145	0.0222	−0.0155	−0.0133	−0.0171	0.0403	−0.0170	0.0316	1975	0.0073
1976	0.0025	0.0001	0.0094	−0.0046	−0.0217	0.0135	0.0013	0.0142	0.0081	0.0023	0.0273	0.0265	1976	0.0807
1977	−0.0447	−0.0106	0.0026	0.0010	0.0058	0.0102	−0.0130	0.0131	−0.0089	−0.0156	0.0031	−0.0230	1977	−0.0786
1978	−0.0149	−0.0056	−0.0090	−0.0068	−0.0133	−0.0132	0.0070	0.0148	−0.0171	−0.0273	0.0117	−0.0198	1978	−0.0905
1979	0.0112	−0.0200	0.0056	−0.0188	0.0184	0.0240	−0.0161	−0.0108	−0.0190	−0.0922	0.0229	−0.0026	1979	−0.0984
1980	−0.0824	−0.0551	−0.0413	0.1424	0.0332	0.0272	−0.0560	−0.0513	−0.0358	−0.0360	0.0009	0.0244	1980	−0.1400
1981	−0.0209	−0.0524	0.0274	−0.0618	0.0518	−0.0288	−0.0462	−0.0496	−0.0259	0.0712	0.1297	−0.0813	1981	−0.1033
1982	−0.0062	0.0079	0.0107	0.0262	−0.0067	−0.0343	0.0387	0.0669	0.0519	0.0543	−0.0097	0.0219	1982	0.2395
1983	−0.0396	0.0410	−0.0183	0.0265	−0.0477	−0.0051	−0.0574	−0.0083	0.0408	−0.0227	0.0089	−0.0152	1983	−0.0982
1984	0.0141	−0.0270	−0.0254	−0.0210	−0.0619	0.0044	0.0577	0.0160	0.0248	0.0453	0.0027	−0.0007	1984	0.0232
1985	0.0268	−0.0575	0.0212	0.0140	0.0798	0.0061	−0.0274	0.0173	−0.0109	0.0248	0.0320	0.0455	1985	0.1784
1986	−0.0105	0.1073	0.0699	−0.0142	−0.0567	0.0543	−0.0173	0.0437	−0.0565	0.0220	0.0208	−0.0087	1986	0.1499
1987	0.0096	0.0143	−0.0289	−0.0538	−0.0171	0.0023	−0.0251	−0.0239	−0.0443	0.0544	−0.0038	0.0088	1987	−0.1069
1988	0.0595	−0.0019	−0.0378	−0.0230	−0.0180	0.0292	−0.0241	−0.0025	0.0269	0.0232	−0.0266	0.0035	1988	0.0036
1989	0.0124	−0.0248	0.0044	0.0088	0.0321	0.0480	0.0170	−0.0325	−0.0046	0.0307	0.0014	−0.0070	1989	0.0862
1990	−0.0416	−0.0090	−0.0115	−0.0277	0.0340	0.0162	0.0033	−0.0490	0.0048	0.0135	0.0331	0.0114	1990	−0.0261
1991	0.0059	−0.0033	−0.0026	0.0065	−0.0068	−0.0126	0.0082	0.0272	0.0236	−0.0011	0.0022	0.0513	1991	0.1010
1992	−0.0385	−0.0008	−0.0161	−0.0049	0.0181	0.0133	0.0334	0.0007	0.0127	−0.0255	−0.0051	0.0183	1992	0.0034
1993	0.0222	0.0299	−0.0042	0.0015	−0.0006	0.0387	0.0138	0.0378	−0.0045	0.0048	−0.0312	−0.0035	1993	0.1071
1994	0.0202	−0.0498	−0.0453	−0.0208	−0.0146	−0.0161	0.0303	−0.0152	−0.0392	−0.0091	0.0002	0.0095	1994	−0.1429
1995	0.0203	0.0227	0.0028	0.0112	0.0725	0.0084	−0.0223	0.0179	0.0122	0.0237	0.0198	0.0223	1995	0.2304
1996	−0.0065	−0.0530	−0.0262	−0.0224	−0.0112	0.0149	−0.0045	−0.0196	0.0230	0.0345	0.0299	−0.0312	1996	−0.0737
1997	−0.0135	−0.0046	−0.0311	0.0196	0.0037	0.0138	0.0567	−0.0367	0.0258	0.0287	0.0101	0.0130	1997	0.0851
1998	0.0152	−0.0116	−0.0028	−0.0023	0.0135	0.0176	−0.0088	0.0416	0.0350	−0.0260	0.0052	−0.0077	1998	0.0689
1999	0.0079	−0.0560	−0.0061	−0.0028	−0.0230	−0.0133	−0.0130	−0.0105	0.0032	−0.0062	−0.0117	−0.0210	1999	−0.1435
2000	0.0171	0.0213	0.0312	−0.0123	−0.0111	0.0192	0.0120	0.0190	−0.0203	0.0135	0.0270	0.0198	2000	0.1436
2001	−0.0044	0.0149	−0.0119	−0.0360	−0.0013	0.0038	0.0324	0.0159	0.0040	0.0416	−0.0512	−0.0229	2001	−0.0189
2002	0.0090	0.0072	−0.0479	0.0355	−0.0034	0.0143	0.0252	0.0420	0.0374	−0.0334	−0.0161	0.0462	2002	0.1169

*Compound annual return

Table B–9

Long–Term Government Bonds: Yields

from January 1926 to December 1970

Year	Jan	Feb	Mar	Apr	May	Jun	Jul	Aug	Sep	Oct	Nov	Dec	Yr–end	Yield
1926	0.0374	0.0372	0.0371	0.0368	0.0369	0.0368	0.0370	0.0373	0.0372	0.0367	0.0358	0.0354	1926	0.0354
1927	0.0351	0.0347	0.0331	0.0333	0.0327	0.0334	0.0333	0.0329	0.0330	0.0325	0.0320	0.0316	1927	0.0316
1928	0.0321	0.0318	0.0317	0.0319	0.0327	0.0326	0.0344	0.0341	0.0346	0.0336	0.0338	0.0340	1928	0.0340
1929	0.0349	0.0363	0.0377	0.0358	0.0373	0.0367	0.0369	0.0375	0.0375	0.0347	0.0331	0.0340	1929	0.0340
1930	0.0347	0.0339	0.0335	0.0338	0.0329	0.0328	0.0327	0.0328	0.0324	0.0324	0.0322	0.0330	1930	0.0330
1931	0.0343	0.0338	0.0332	0.0327	0.0317	0.0319	0.0325	0.0326	0.0353	0.0385	0.0385	0.0407	1931	0.0407
1932	0.0390	0.0367	0.0370	0.0336	0.0349	0.0347	0.0320	0.0321	0.0319	0.0322	0.0322	0.0315	1932	0.0315
1933	0.0308	0.0325	0.0321	0.0325	0.0308	0.0306	0.0309	0.0308	0.0308	0.0315	0.0327	0.0336	1933	0.0336
1934	0.0321	0.0317	0.0307	0.0300	0.0292	0.0289	0.0288	0.0299	0.0310	0.0300	0.0299	0.0293	1934	0.0293
1935	0.0281	0.0275	0.0274	0.0269	0.0276	0.0270	0.0268	0.0281	0.0282	0.0279	0.0280	0.0276	1935	0.0276
1936	0.0285	0.0281	0.0275	0.0274	0.0273	0.0273	0.0271	0.0264	0.0268	0.0269	0.0257	0.0255	1936	0.0255
1937	0.0258	0.0253	0.0285	0.0284	0.0282	0.0285	0.0277	0.0286	0.0284	0.0283	0.0278	0.0273	1937	0.0273
1938	0.0271	0.0268	0.0273	0.0259	0.0257	0.0259	0.0257	0.0259	0.0259	0.0254	0.0257	0.0252	1938	0.0252
1939	0.0249	0.0245	0.0237	0.0229	0.0217	0.0221	0.0213	0.0231	0.0278	0.0247	0.0236	0.0226	1939	0.0226
1940	0.0229	0.0228	0.0215	0.0220	0.0246	0.0227	0.0224	0.0223	0.0215	0.0214	0.0199	0.0194	1940	0.0194
1941	0.0213	0.0213	0.0206	0.0196	0.0195	0.0191	0.0191	0.0190	0.0193	0.0182	0.0186	0.0204	1941	0.0204
1942	0.0247	0.0247	0.0244	0.0246	0.0243	0.0244	0.0244	0.0244	0.0244	0.0244	0.0247	0.0246	1942	0.0246
1943	0.0245	0.0246	0.0247	0.0246	0.0244	0.0244	0.0245	0.0245	0.0246	0.0247	0.0248	0.0248	1943	0.0248
1944	0.0248	0.0247	0.0247	0.0248	0.0247	0.0248	0.0247	0.0247	0.0247	0.0247	0.0247	0.0246	1944	0.0246
1945	0.0240	0.0236	0.0236	0.0228	0.0226	0.0217	0.0224	0.0223	0.0221	0.0216	0.0210	0.0199	1945	0.0199
1946	0.0199	0.0198	0.0198	0.0207	0.0209	0.0206	0.0209	0.0217	0.0219	0.0216	0.0220	0.0212	1946	0.0212
1947	0.0214	0.0214	0.0213	0.0217	0.0216	0.0216	0.0214	0.0210	0.0213	0.0217	0.0229	0.0243	1947	0.0243
1948	0.0243	0.0241	0.0241	0.0239	0.0231	0.0238	0.0241	0.0242	0.0242	0.0243	0.0239	0.0237	1948	0.0237
1949	0.0233	0.0231	0.0227	0.0227	0.0227	0.0217	0.0216	0.0210	0.0212	0.0212	0.0212	0.0209	1949	0.0209
1950	0.0215	0.0214	0.0215	0.0214	0.0213	0.0216	0.0214	0.0214	0.0220	0.0225	0.0224	0.0224	1950	0.0224
1951	0.0221	0.0228	0.0241	0.0248	0.0254	0.0259	0.0252	0.0246	0.0253	0.0254	0.0264	0.0269	1951	0.0269
1952	0.0268	0.0269	0.0263	0.0254	0.0257	0.0259	0.0261	0.0267	0.0277	0.0269	0.0272	0.0279	1952	0.0279
1953	0.0279	0.0287	0.0294	0.0303	0.0314	0.0301	0.0301	0.0303	0.0284	0.0281	0.0286	0.0274	1953	0.0274
1954	0.0291	0.0279	0.0278	0.0273	0.0279	0.0272	0.0266	0.0269	0.0271	0.0271	0.0274	0.0272	1954	0.0272
1955	0.0286	0.0292	0.0288	0.0290	0.0287	0.0293	0.0300	0.0301	0.0298	0.0292	0.0295	0.0295	1955	0.0295
1956	0.0292	0.0293	0.0303	0.0311	0.0299	0.0299	0.0313	0.0325	0.0324	0.0329	0.0333	0.0345	1956	0.0345
1957	0.0328	0.0328	0.0331	0.0345	0.0348	0.0361	0.0365	0.0367	0.0364	0.0369	0.0340	0.0323	1957	0.0323
1958	0.0330	0.0325	0.0321	0.0311	0.0313	0.0324	0.0343	0.0371	0.0380	0.0374	0.0368	0.0382	1958	0.0382
1959	0.0408	0.0402	0.0403	0.0414	0.0417	0.0419	0.0417	0.0423	0.0429	0.0421	0.0432	0.0447	1959	0.0447
1960	0.0441	0.0429	0.0411	0.0426	0.0417	0.0407	0.0382	0.0390	0.0387	0.0391	0.0399	0.0380	1960	0.0380
1961	0.0404	0.0392	0.0397	0.0391	0.0397	0.0404	0.0404	0.0410	0.0403	0.0400	0.0404	0.0415	1961	0.0415
1962	0.0419	0.0414	0.0398	0.0394	0.0393	0.0401	0.0412	0.0401	0.0398	0.0395	0.0396	0.0395	1962	0.0395
1963	0.0398	0.0400	0.0401	0.0405	0.0406	0.0407	0.0407	0.0408	0.0410	0.0415	0.0414	0.0417	1963	0.0417
1964	0.0421	0.0424	0.0424	0.0423	0.0422	0.0419	0.0421	0.0423	0.0421	0.0421	0.0422	0.0423	1964	0.0423
1965	0.0422	0.0424	0.0422	0.0422	0.0423	0.0423	0.0424	0.0428	0.0433	0.0433	0.0441	0.0450	1965	0.0450
1966	0.0457	0.0477	0.0460	0.0467	0.0473	0.0477	0.0482	0.0499	0.0480	0.0467	0.0480	0.0455	1966	0.0455
1967	0.0448	0.0465	0.0455	0.0477	0.0482	0.0507	0.0505	0.0514	0.0517	0.0549	0.0567	0.0556	1967	0.0556
1968	0.0536	0.0542	0.0560	0.0547	0.0547	0.0534	0.0517	0.0520	0.0531	0.0543	0.0566	0.0598	1968	0.0598
1969	0.0617	0.0618	0.0620	0.0593	0.0635	0.0623	0.0621	0.0630	0.0677	0.0653	0.0676	0.0687	1969	0.0687
1970	0.0693	0.0651	0.0661	0.0699	0.0743	0.0709	0.0687	0.0694	0.0680	0.0693	0.0637	0.0648	1970	0.0648

Table B–9 (continued)

Long–Term Government Bonds: Yields

from January 1971 to December 2002

Year	Jan	Feb	Mar	Apr	May	Jun	Jul	Aug	Sep	Oct	Nov	Dec	Yr–end	Yield
1971	0.0612	0.0629	0.0593	0.0619	0.0624	0.0641	0.0643	0.0610	0.0598	0.0588	0.0596	0.0597	1971	0.0597
1972	0.0606	0.0602	0.0613	0.0615	0.0597	0.0607	0.0593	0.0595	0.0606	0.0591	0.0577	0.0599	1972	0.0599
1973	0.0685	0.0688	0.0686	0.0687	0.0703	0.0710	0.0760	0.0728	0.0703	0.0689	0.0712	0.0726	1973	0.0726
1974	0.0740	0.0748	0.0783	0.0816	0.0810	0.0812	0.0823	0.0855	0.0837	0.0795	0.0771	0.0760	1974	0.0760
1975	0.0796	0.0788	0.0824	0.0852	0.0836	0.0813	0.0829	0.0844	0.0862	0.0819	0.0838	0.0805	1975	0.0805
1976	0.0802	0.0802	0.0792	0.0797	0.0821	0.0807	0.0805	0.0790	0.0781	0.0779	0.0749	0.0721	1976	0.0721
1977	0.0764	0.0775	0.0772	0.0771	0.0765	0.0754	0.0768	0.0754	0.0764	0.0781	0.0777	0.0803	1977	0.0803
1978	0.0816	0.0822	0.0831	0.0838	0.0852	0.0865	0.0858	0.0843	0.0860	0.0889	0.0877	0.0898	1978	0.0898
1979	0.0886	0.0908	0.0902	0.0922	0.0903	0.0877	0.0895	0.0907	0.0927	0.1034	0.1009	0.1012	1979	0.1012
1980	0.1114	0.1186	0.1239	0.1076	0.1037	0.1006	0.1074	0.1140	0.1185	0.1231	0.1230	0.1199	1980	0.1199
1981	0.1211	0.1283	0.1248	0.1332	0.1265	0.1304	0.1370	0.1445	0.1482	0.1384	0.1220	0.1334	1981	0.1334
1982	0.1415	0.1402	0.1387	0.1348	0.1358	0.1412	0.1352	0.1254	0.1183	0.1112	0.1125	0.1095	1982	0.1095
1983	0.1113	0.1060	0.1083	0.1051	0.1112	0.1119	0.1198	0.1210	0.1157	0.1188	0.1176	0.1197	1983	0.1197
1984	0.1180	0.1217	0.1253	0.1284	0.1381	0.1374	0.1293	0.1270	0.1235	0.1173	0.1169	0.1170	1984	0.1170
1985	0.1127	0.1209	0.1181	0.1162	0.1062	0.1055	0.1091	0.1068	0.1082	0.1051	0.1011	0.0956	1985	0.0956
1986	0.0958	0.0841	0.0766	0.0782	0.0848	0.0790	0.0809	0.0763	0.0827	0.0803	0.0779	0.0789	1986	0.0789
1987	0.0778	0.0763	0.0795	0.0859	0.0880	0.0877	0.0907	0.0936	0.0992	0.0926	0.0931	0.0920	1987	0.0920
1988	0.0852	0.0854	0.0901	0.0929	0.0952	0.0917	0.0947	0.0950	0.0917	0.0889	0.0923	0.0918	1988	0.0918
1989	0.0903	0.0935	0.0929	0.0918	0.0878	0.0821	0.0801	0.0841	0.0847	0.0810	0.0808	0.0816	1989	0.0816
1990	0.0865	0.0876	0.0889	0.0924	0.0883	0.0864	0.0860	0.0920	0.0914	0.0898	0.0858	0.0844	1990	0.0844
1991	0.0837	0.0841	0.0844	0.0837	0.0845	0.0860	0.0850	0.0818	0.0790	0.0791	0.0789	0.0730	1991	0.0730
1992	0.0776	0.0777	0.0797	0.0803	0.0781	0.0765	0.0726	0.0725	0.0710	0.0741	0.0748	0.0726	1992	0.0726
1993	0.0725	0.0698	0.0702	0.0701	0.0701	0.0668	0.0656	0.0623	0.0627	0.0623	0.0651	0.0654	1993	0.0654
1994	0.0637	0.0682	0.0725	0.0745	0.0759	0.0774	0.0746	0.0761	0.0800	0.0809	0.0808	0.0799	1994	0.0799
1995	0.0780	0.0758	0.0755	0.0745	0.0677	0.0670	0.0691	0.0674	0.0663	0.0641	0.0623	0.0603	1995	0.0603
1996	0.0609	0.0659	0.0684	0.0706	0.0717	0.0703	0.0707	0.0726	0.0704	0.0671	0.0643	0.0673	1996	0.0673
1997	0.0689	0.0694	0.0723	0.0705	0.0701	0.0688	0.0637	0.0672	0.0649	0.0623	0.0614	0.0602	1997	0.0602
1998	0.0589	0.0599	0.0602	0.0604	0.0592	0.0576	0.0584	0.0547	0.0517	0.0540	0.0535	0.0542	1998	0.0542
1999	0.0536	0.0587	0.0592	0.0594	0.0615	0.0627	0.0639	0.0649	0.0646	0.0651	0.0662	0.0682	1999	0.0682
2000	0.0666	0.0646	0.0618	0.0630	0.0640	0.0622	0.0611	0.0594	0.0612	0.0600	0.0576	0.0558	2000	0.0558
2001	0.0562	0.0549	0.0559	0.0593	0.0594	0.0590	0.0561	0.0546	0.0542	0.0506	0.0553	0.0575	2001	0.0575
2002	0.0569	0.0563	0.0604	0.0575	0.0578	0.0566	0.0544	0.0510	0.0480	0.0508	0.0521	0.0484	2002	0.0484

Table B–10

Intermediate–Term Government Bonds: Total Returns

from January 1926 to December 1970

Year	Jan	Feb	Mar	Apr	May	Jun	Jul	Aug	Sep	Oct	Nov	Dec	Year	Jan–Dec*
1926	0.0068	0.0032	0.0041	0.0090	0.0008	0.0027	0.0013	0.0009	0.0050	0.0054	0.0045	0.0089	1926	0.0538
1927	0.0057	0.0038	0.0038	0.0016	0.0020	0.0029	0.0043	0.0056	0.0060	−0.0034	0.0083	0.0037	1927	0.0452
1928	0.0046	−0.0004	0.0010	−0.0003	−0.0006	0.0017	−0.0089	0.0050	0.0028	0.0032	0.0019	−0.0007	1928	0.0092
1929	−0.0029	−0.0018	0.0005	0.0089	−0.0061	0.0107	0.0066	0.0052	−0.0014	0.0168	0.0180	0.0044	1929	0.0601
1930	−0.0041	0.0094	0.0161	−0.0071	0.0061	0.0142	0.0054	0.0022	0.0063	0.0076	0.0070	0.0024	1930	0.0672
1931	−0.0071	0.0099	0.0052	0.0083	0.0119	−0.0214	0.0016	0.0017	−0.0113	−0.0105	0.0049	−0.0159	1931	−0.0232
1932	−0.0032	0.0128	0.0078	0.0194	−0.0090	0.0108	0.0120	0.0124	0.0027	0.0045	0.0031	0.0118	1932	0.0881
1933	−0.0016	−0.0001	0.0099	0.0057	0.0199	0.0008	−0.0006	0.0073	0.0026	−0.0025	0.0027	−0.0253	1933	0.0183
1934	0.0130	0.0052	0.0189	0.0182	0.0120	0.0091	0.0024	0.0092	−0.0138	0.0190	0.0046	0.0125	1934	0.0900
1935	0.0114	0.0105	0.0125	0.0107	−0.0035	0.0113	0.0037	−0.0071	−0.0057	0.0109	0.0014	0.0120	1935	0.0701
1936	−0.0003	0.0069	0.0031	0.0024	0.0038	0.0012	0.0022	0.0050	0.0010	0.0025	0.0081	−0.0057	1936	0.0306
1937	−0.0031	0.0007	−0.0164	0.0047	0.0080	−0.0012	0.0059	−0.0043	0.0081	0.0032	0.0042	0.0062	1937	0.0156
1938	0.0085	0.0052	−0.0012	0.0230	0.0023	0.0075	0.0010	0.0015	−0.0013	0.0093	−0.0001	0.0052	1938	0.0623
1939	0.0029	0.0082	0.0081	0.0038	0.0095	0.0002	0.0040	−0.0147	−0.0262	0.0315	0.0074	0.0108	1939	0.0452
1940	−0.0014	0.0035	0.0088	0.0002	−0.0214	0.0187	0.0003	0.0043	0.0047	0.0036	0.0056	0.0028	1940	0.0296
1941	0.0001	−0.0047	0.0069	0.0033	0.0012	0.0056	0.0000	0.0011	0.0000	0.0023	−0.0092	−0.0016	1941	0.0050
1942	0.0074	0.0015	0.0023	0.0022	0.0016	0.0013	0.0000	0.0017	−0.0023	0.0017	0.0017	0.0000	1942	0.0194
1943	0.0039	0.0013	0.0021	0.0024	0.0057	0.0033	0.0021	0.0002	0.0014	0.0017	0.0015	0.0021	1943	0.0281
1944	0.0011	0.0016	0.0019	0.0028	0.0005	0.0007	0.0029	0.0024	0.0011	0.0011	0.0009	0.0010	1944	0.0180
1945	0.0052	0.0038	0.0004	0.0014	0.0012	0.0019	0.0000	0.0016	0.0017	0.0016	0.0010	0.0021	1945	0.0222
1946	0.0039	0.0048	−0.0038	−0.0020	0.0006	0.0033	−0.0010	0.0004	−0.0011	0.0026	−0.0008	0.0032	1946	0.0100
1947	0.0023	0.0006	0.0024	−0.0013	0.0008	0.0008	0.0006	0.0026	0.0000	−0.0023	0.0006	0.0021	1947	0.0091
1948	0.0015	0.0018	0.0018	0.0019	0.0053	−0.0008	−0.0002	−0.0004	0.0010	0.0013	0.0021	0.0032	1948	0.0185
1949	0.0028	0.0011	0.0025	0.0015	0.0023	0.0050	0.0020	0.0031	0.0008	0.0006	0.0002	0.0012	1949	0.0232
1950	−0.0005	0.0008	0.0000	0.0008	0.0020	0.0003	0.0020	−0.0007	−0.0004	0.0001	0.0018	0.0008	1950	0.0070
1951	0.0022	0.0007	−0.0127	0.0057	−0.0040	0.0050	0.0058	0.0036	−0.0057	0.0016	0.0032	−0.0016	1951	0.0036
1952	0.0038	−0.0020	0.0067	0.0054	0.0019	−0.0035	−0.0034	−0.0024	0.0019	0.0066	−0.0006	0.0019	1952	0.0163
1953	−0.0002	0.0003	−0.0017	−0.0096	−0.0117	0.0155	0.0056	−0.0008	0.0194	0.0038	0.0014	0.0103	1953	0.0323
1954	0.0065	0.0100	0.0027	0.0043	−0.0073	0.0125	−0.0005	0.0011	−0.0020	−0.0009	−0.0001	0.0005	1954	0.0268
1955	−0.0032	−0.0052	0.0024	0.0004	0.0001	−0.0036	−0.0071	0.0007	0.0082	0.0072	−0.0053	−0.0011	1955	−0.0065
1956	0.0105	0.0003	−0.0100	−0.0001	0.0112	0.0003	−0.0095	−0.0103	0.0092	−0.0019	−0.0047	0.0011	1956	−0.0042
1957	0.0237	−0.0012	0.0018	−0.0101	−0.0017	−0.0106	−0.0015	0.0109	0.0002	0.0043	0.0396	0.0215	1957	0.0784
1958	0.0034	0.0139	0.0053	0.0052	0.0060	−0.0068	−0.0091	−0.0356	−0.0017	0.0002	0.0132	−0.0061	1958	−0.0129
1959	−0.0013	0.0107	−0.0037	−0.0052	−0.0001	−0.0077	0.0034	−0.0078	0.0020	0.0174	−0.0092	−0.0020	1959	−0.0039
1960	0.0154	0.0072	0.0292	−0.0064	0.0031	0.0217	0.0267	−0.0004	0.0029	0.0016	−0.0094	0.0210	1960	0.1176
1961	−0.0059	0.0090	0.0037	0.0054	−0.0028	−0.0025	0.0007	0.0019	0.0079	0.0014	−0.0019	0.0018	1961	0.0185
1962	−0.0045	0.0155	0.0089	0.0025	0.0049	−0.0028	−0.0012	0.0125	0.0021	0.0051	0.0060	0.0056	1962	0.0556
1963	−0.0029	0.0017	0.0027	0.0030	0.0014	0.0014	0.0003	0.0019	0.0014	0.0011	0.0040	0.0003	1963	0.0164
1964	0.0033	0.0012	0.0016	0.0033	0.0081	0.0036	0.0027	0.0027	0.0045	0.0032	−0.0004	0.0058	1964	0.0404
1965	0.0042	0.0018	0.0043	0.0026	0.0035	0.0049	0.0017	0.0019	−0.0005	0.0000	0.0007	−0.0149	1965	0.0102
1966	0.0003	−0.0083	0.0187	−0.0019	0.0011	−0.0024	−0.0025	−0.0125	0.0216	0.0075	0.0027	0.0223	1966	0.0469
1967	0.0118	−0.0013	0.0183	−0.0089	0.0044	−0.0227	0.0133	−0.0036	0.0007	−0.0049	0.0028	0.0007	1967	0.0101
1968	0.0145	0.0040	−0.0026	−0.0016	0.0064	0.0167	0.0176	0.0021	0.0055	0.0009	−0.0013	−0.0173	1968	0.0454
1969	0.0086	−0.0013	0.0097	0.0079	−0.0082	−0.0084	0.0082	−0.0018	−0.0300	0.0333	−0.0047	−0.0193	1969	−0.0074
1970	0.0030	0.0439	0.0087	−0.0207	0.0110	0.0061	0.0152	0.0116	0.0196	0.0095	0.0451	0.0054	1970	0.1686

*Compound annual return

Table B–10 (continued)

Intermediate–Term Government Bonds: Total Returns

from January 1971 to December 2002

Year	Jan	Feb	Mar	Apr	May	Jun	Jul	Aug	Sep	Oct	Nov	Dec	Year	Jan–Dec*
1971	0.0168	0.0224	0.0186	−0.0327	0.0011	−0.0187	0.0027	0.0350	0.0026	0.0220	0.0052	0.0110	1971	0.0872
1972	0.0106	0.0014	0.0015	0.0014	0.0016	0.0045	0.0015	0.0015	0.0014	0.0016	0.0045	0.0192	1972	0.0516
1973	−0.0006	−0.0075	0.0046	0.0064	0.0057	−0.0006	−0.0276	0.0254	0.0250	0.0050	0.0064	0.0040	1973	0.0461
1974	0.0009	0.0035	−0.0212	−0.0152	0.0130	−0.0087	0.0007	−0.0012	0.0319	0.0109	0.0236	0.0185	1974	0.0569
1975	0.0053	0.0148	−0.0059	−0.0186	0.0260	0.0027	−0.0030	−0.0009	0.0010	0.0366	−0.0010	0.0198	1975	0.0783
1976	0.0057	0.0084	0.0075	0.0116	−0.0145	0.0159	0.0119	0.0189	0.0076	0.0147	0.0321	0.0026	1976	0.1287
1977	−0.0190	0.0048	0.0055	0.0051	0.0056	0.0102	0.0001	0.0008	0.0015	−0.0060	0.0079	−0.0023	1977	0.0141
1978	0.0013	0.0017	0.0037	0.0024	−0.0002	−0.0021	0.0098	0.0079	0.0057	−0.0112	0.0092	0.0063	1978	0.0349
1979	0.0055	−0.0059	0.0112	0.0033	0.0193	0.0205	−0.0011	−0.0091	0.0006	−0.0468	0.0363	0.0087	1979	0.0409
1980	−0.0135	−0.0641	0.0143	0.1198	0.0490	−0.0077	−0.0106	−0.0387	−0.0038	−0.0152	0.0029	0.0171	1980	0.0391
1981	0.0032	−0.0235	0.0263	−0.0216	0.0245	0.0060	−0.0270	−0.0178	0.0164	0.0611	0.0624	−0.0142	1981	0.0945
1982	0.0050	0.0148	0.0042	0.0299	0.0146	−0.0135	0.0464	0.0469	0.0325	0.0531	0.0080	0.0185	1982	0.2910
1983	0.0007	0.0252	−0.0049	0.0259	−0.0122	0.0016	−0.0198	0.0081	0.0315	0.0019	0.0103	0.0047	1983	0.0741
1984	0.0177	−0.0064	−0.0035	−0.0003	−0.0250	0.0099	0.0393	0.0101	0.0202	0.0383	0.0192	0.0143	1984	0.1402
1985	0.0206	−0.0179	0.0166	0.0264	0.0485	0.0108	−0.0045	0.0148	0.0113	0.0162	0.0195	0.0257	1985	0.2033
1986	0.0082	0.0275	0.0338	0.0081	−0.0215	0.0276	0.0157	0.0266	−0.0110	0.0162	0.0113	0.0007	1986	0.1514
1987	0.0107	0.0059	−0.0031	−0.0244	−0.0038	0.0122	0.0025	−0.0038	−0.0141	0.0299	0.0083	0.0093	1987	0.0290
1988	0.0316	0.0123	−0.0086	−0.0044	−0.0049	0.0181	−0.0047	−0.0009	0.0196	0.0148	−0.0115	−0.0010	1988	0.0610
1989	0.0121	−0.0051	0.0049	0.0220	0.0212	0.0324	0.0235	−0.0246	0.0069	0.0237	0.0084	0.0012	1989	0.1329
1990	−0.0104	0.0007	0.0002	−0.0077	0.0261	0.0151	0.0174	−0.0092	0.0094	0.0171	0.0193	0.0161	1990	0.0973
1991	0.0107	0.0048	0.0023	0.0117	0.0059	−0.0023	0.0129	0.0247	0.0216	0.0134	0.0128	0.0265	1991	0.1546
1992	−0.0195	0.0022	−0.0079	0.0098	0.0222	0.0177	0.0242	0.0150	0.0194	−0.0182	−0.0084	0.0146	1992	0.0719
1993	0.0270	0.0243	0.0043	0.0088	−0.0009	0.0201	0.0005	0.0223	0.0056	0.0018	−0.0093	0.0032	1993	0.1124
1994	0.0138	−0.0258	−0.0257	−0.0105	−0.0002	−0.0028	0.0169	0.0026	−0.0158	−0.0023	−0.0070	0.0053	1994	−0.0514
1995	0.0182	0.0234	0.0063	0.0143	0.0369	0.0079	−0.0016	0.0086	0.0064	0.0121	0.0149	0.0095	1995	0.1680
1996	0.0006	−0.0138	−0.0118	−0.0050	−0.0032	0.0117	0.0025	−0.0005	0.0155	0.0183	0.0149	−0.0078	1996	0.0210
1997	0.0025	0.0002	−0.0114	0.0148	0.0079	0.0102	0.0264	−0.0098	0.0151	0.0150	−0.0001	0.0106	1997	0.0838
1998	0.0180	−0.0039	0.0026	0.0061	0.0070	0.0079	0.0027	0.0271	0.0330	0.0041	−0.0098	0.0037	1998	0.1021
1999	0.0055	−0.0262	0.0086	0.0021	−0.0147	0.0032	−0.0003	0.0013	0.0097	−0.0008	−0.0008	−0.0048	1999	−0.0177
2000	−0.0053	0.0078	0.0203	−0.0043	0.0052	0.0191	0.0072	0.0134	0.0096	0.0079	0.0174	0.0214	2000	0.1259
2001	0.0098	0.0105	0.0076	−0.0114	−0.0007	0.0066	0.0247	0.0095	0.0253	0.0180	−0.0171	−0.0082	2001	0.0762
2002	0.0036	0.0108	−0.0242	0.0239	0.0118	0.0169	0.0272	0.0167	0.0288	−0.0024	−0.0169	0.0279	2002	0.1293

*Compound annual return

Table B–11

Intermediate–Term Government Bonds: Income Returns

from January 1926 to December 1970

Year	Jan	Feb	Mar	Apr	May	Jun	Jul	Aug	Sep	Oct	Nov	Dec	Year	Jan–Dec*
1926	0.0032	0.0032	0.0032	0.0031	0.0031	0.0031	0.0032	0.0032	0.0032	0.0031	0.0031	0.0030	1926	0.0378
1927	0.0029	0.0029	0.0029	0.0029	0.0029	0.0029	0.0029	0.0029	0.0028	0.0029	0.0028	0.0028	1927	0.0349
1928	0.0028	0.0028	0.0029	0.0029	0.0030	0.0030	0.0032	0.0032	0.0032	0.0032	0.0032	0.0033	1928	0.0364
1929	0.0034	0.0035	0.0036	0.0035	0.0037	0.0035	0.0035	0.0034	0.0035	0.0033	0.0030	0.0030	1929	0.0407
1930	0.0031	0.0030	0.0028	0.0030	0.0029	0.0027	0.0026	0.0026	0.0026	0.0025	0.0024	0.0024	1930	0.0330
1931	0.0026	0.0025	0.0024	0.0023	0.0021	0.0026	0.0026	0.0026	0.0028	0.0031	0.0031	0.0034	1931	0.0316
1932	0.0035	0.0034	0.0033	0.0030	0.0032	0.0031	0.0029	0.0027	0.0027	0.0027	0.0027	0.0025	1932	0.0363
1933	0.0026	0.0026	0.0025	0.0025	0.0021	0.0022	0.0022	0.0021	0.0021	0.0022	0.0022	0.0027	1933	0.0283
1934	0.0030	0.0024	0.0027	0.0024	0.0023	0.0021	0.0021	0.0021	0.0021	0.0026	0.0022	0.0023	1934	0.0293
1935	0.0021	0.0018	0.0018	0.0017	0.0016	0.0015	0.0015	0.0014	0.0015	0.0016	0.0015	0.0016	1935	0.0202
1936	0.0014	0.0013	0.0013	0.0012	0.0012	0.0013	0.0012	0.0012	0.0011	0.0011	0.0011	0.0010	1936	0.0144
1937	0.0010	0.0010	0.0012	0.0015	0.0013	0.0014	0.0014	0.0013	0.0014	0.0012	0.0012	0.0011	1937	0.0148
1938	0.0018	0.0016	0.0017	0.0017	0.0015	0.0014	0.0013	0.0014	0.0013	0.0014	0.0013	0.0013	1938	0.0182
1939	0.0013	0.0011	0.0012	0.0010	0.0011	0.0009	0.0009	0.0009	0.0011	0.0015	0.0010	0.0009	1939	0.0131
1940	0.0009	0.0008	0.0008	0.0007	0.0007	0.0010	0.0008	0.0008	0.0007	0.0007	0.0006	0.0005	1940	0.0090
1941	0.0006	0.0006	0.0008	0.0006	0.0006	0.0006	0.0005	0.0005	0.0005	0.0005	0.0004	0.0007	1941	0.0067
1942	0.0008	0.0006	0.0007	0.0006	0.0006	0.0006	0.0006	0.0006	0.0006	0.0006	0.0006	0.0006	1942	0.0076
1943	0.0014	0.0013	0.0014	0.0013	0.0013	0.0013	0.0013	0.0012	0.0012	0.0012	0.0012	0.0012	1943	0.0156
1944	0.0013	0.0012	0.0013	0.0012	0.0013	0.0012	0.0012	0.0012	0.0011	0.0012	0.0011	0.0011	1944	0.0144
1945	0.0012	0.0010	0.0010	0.0010	0.0010	0.0010	0.0010	0.0010	0.0009	0.0010	0.0009	0.0009	1945	0.0119
1946	0.0009	0.0008	0.0007	0.0009	0.0009	0.0009	0.0009	0.0009	0.0010	0.0010	0.0009	0.0010	1946	0.0108
1947	0.0010	0.0009	0.0010	0.0009	0.0010	0.0011	0.0010	0.0010	0.0010	0.0010	0.0010	0.0012	1947	0.0121
1948	0.0013	0.0012	0.0014	0.0013	0.0012	0.0013	0.0012	0.0013	0.0013	0.0013	0.0014	0.0013	1948	0.0156
1949	0.0013	0.0012	0.0013	0.0012	0.0013	0.0012	0.0010	0.0011	0.0010	0.0010	0.0010	0.0010	1949	0.0136
1950	0.0011	0.0010	0.0011	0.0010	0.0012	0.0011	0.0012	0.0011	0.0011	0.0013	0.0013	0.0013	1950	0.0139
1951	0.0016	0.0014	0.0015	0.0018	0.0017	0.0017	0.0018	0.0017	0.0015	0.0019	0.0017	0.0018	1951	0.0198
1952	0.0018	0.0017	0.0019	0.0017	0.0016	0.0017	0.0018	0.0018	0.0021	0.0020	0.0017	0.0021	1952	0.0219
1953	0.0019	0.0018	0.0021	0.0021	0.0022	0.0027	0.0024	0.0023	0.0023	0.0020	0.0020	0.0020	1953	0.0255
1954	0.0016	0.0014	0.0014	0.0013	0.0011	0.0016	0.0011	0.0012	0.0011	0.0012	0.0014	0.0014	1954	0.0160
1955	0.0018	0.0017	0.0020	0.0019	0.0021	0.0020	0.0020	0.0025	0.0023	0.0023	0.0021	0.0022	1955	0.0245
1956	0.0025	0.0021	0.0022	0.0026	0.0026	0.0023	0.0025	0.0027	0.0026	0.0030	0.0028	0.0030	1956	0.0305
1957	0.0030	0.0025	0.0026	0.0029	0.0030	0.0027	0.0036	0.0032	0.0032	0.0033	0.0031	0.0028	1957	0.0359
1958	0.0024	0.0021	0.0022	0.0021	0.0019	0.0021	0.0021	0.0022	0.0032	0.0032	0.0029	0.0032	1958	0.0293
1959	0.0031	0.0030	0.0033	0.0032	0.0033	0.0037	0.0038	0.0037	0.0039	0.0039	0.0038	0.0041	1959	0.0418
1960	0.0039	0.0039	0.0039	0.0032	0.0037	0.0035	0.0031	0.0030	0.0028	0.0029	0.0028	0.0031	1960	0.0415
1961	0.0030	0.0028	0.0029	0.0027	0.0030	0.0029	0.0031	0.0031	0.0030	0.0032	0.0030	0.0030	1961	0.0354
1962	0.0035	0.0031	0.0031	0.0031	0.0031	0.0029	0.0033	0.0032	0.0028	0.0033	0.0029	0.0030	1962	0.0373
1963	0.0030	0.0028	0.0029	0.0032	0.0031	0.0029	0.0034	0.0031	0.0033	0.0033	0.0031	0.0034	1963	0.0371
1964	0.0034	0.0030	0.0035	0.0033	0.0031	0.0036	0.0034	0.0033	0.0033	0.0033	0.0034	0.0034	1964	0.0400
1965	0.0033	0.0031	0.0037	0.0033	0.0033	0.0037	0.0034	0.0036	0.0034	0.0034	0.0038	0.0037	1965	0.0415
1966	0.0040	0.0036	0.0043	0.0038	0.0042	0.0040	0.0040	0.0047	0.0046	0.0044	0.0042	0.0042	1966	0.0493
1967	0.0041	0.0035	0.0039	0.0033	0.0042	0.0038	0.0045	0.0042	0.0041	0.0047	0.0046	0.0044	1967	0.0488
1968	0.0051	0.0043	0.0043	0.0049	0.0048	0.0043	0.0049	0.0042	0.0044	0.0044	0.0041	0.0047	1968	0.0549
1969	0.0054	0.0048	0.0049	0.0057	0.0050	0.0058	0.0059	0.0054	0.0061	0.0067	0.0056	0.0068	1969	0.0665
1970	0.0066	0.0061	0.0063	0.0059	0.0062	0.0067	0.0065	0.0062	0.0060	0.0057	0.0058	0.0050	1970	0.0749

*Compound annual return

Table B–11 (continued)

Intermediate–Term Government Bonds: Income Returns

from January 1971 to December 2002

Year	Jan	Feb	Mar	Apr	May	Jun	Jul	Aug	Sep	Oct	Nov	Dec	Year	Jan–Dec*
1971	0.0047	0.0043	0.0047	0.0040	0.0044	0.0053	0.0053	0.0056	0.0048	0.0046	0.0047	0.0046	1971	0.0575
1972	0.0048	0.0044	0.0046	0.0044	0.0052	0.0048	0.0049	0.0050	0.0047	0.0053	0.0051	0.0049	1972	0.0575
1973	0.0056	0.0048	0.0054	0.0056	0.0056	0.0053	0.0059	0.0064	0.0055	0.0060	0.0055	0.0056	1973	0.0658
1974	0.0057	0.0051	0.0054	0.0065	0.0067	0.0059	0.0073	0.0067	0.0072	0.0067	0.0061	0.0064	1974	0.0724
1975	0.0061	0.0055	0.0059	0.0060	0.0063	0.0063	0.0063	0.0061	0.0069	0.0068	0.0055	0.0067	1975	0.0735
1976	0.0060	0.0055	0.0066	0.0059	0.0054	0.0069	0.0060	0.0062	0.0056	0.0054	0.0058	0.0050	1976	0.0710
1977	0.0051	0.0050	0.0056	0.0053	0.0058	0.0055	0.0052	0.0059	0.0056	0.0059	0.0059	0.0059	1977	0.0649
1978	0.0066	0.0057	0.0066	0.0060	0.0071	0.0066	0.0070	0.0068	0.0065	0.0072	0.0072	0.0069	1978	0.0783
1979	0.0079	0.0066	0.0075	0.0077	0.0077	0.0070	0.0074	0.0073	0.0070	0.0084	0.0089	0.0086	1979	0.0904
1980	0.0086	0.0083	0.0107	0.0103	0.0081	0.0075	0.0079	0.0076	0.0097	0.0094	0.0096	0.0111	1980	0.1055
1981	0.0101	0.0095	0.0117	0.0106	0.0110	0.0118	0.0116	0.0120	0.0130	0.0129	0.0121	0.0108	1981	0.1297
1982	0.0107	0.0102	0.0122	0.0112	0.0101	0.0118	0.0113	0.0109	0.0097	0.0089	0.0087	0.0085	1982	0.1281
1983	0.0084	0.0079	0.0084	0.0081	0.0086	0.0085	0.0082	0.0103	0.0094	0.0092	0.0091	0.0091	1983	0.1035
1984	0.0096	0.0088	0.0095	0.0101	0.0104	0.0105	0.0113	0.0105	0.0095	0.0110	0.0093	0.0093	1984	0.1168
1985	0.0090	0.0081	0.0089	0.0097	0.0090	0.0073	0.0083	0.0081	0.0082	0.0081	0.0074	0.0078	1985	0.1029
1986	0.0071	0.0066	0.0068	0.0060	0.0060	0.0068	0.0062	0.0057	0.0058	0.0060	0.0052	0.0060	1986	0.0772
1987	0.0055	0.0052	0.0060	0.0058	0.0062	0.0071	0.0066	0.0068	0.0068	0.0073	0.0070	0.0070	1987	0.0747
1988	0.0065	0.0066	0.0064	0.0063	0.0072	0.0070	0.0064	0.0077	0.0072	0.0071	0.0067	0.0071	1988	0.0824
1989	0.0077	0.0066	0.0078	0.0071	0.0080	0.0070	0.0067	0.0061	0.0065	0.0071	0.0063	0.0060	1989	0.0846
1990	0.0071	0.0064	0.0069	0.0071	0.0075	0.0067	0.0072	0.0068	0.0065	0.0074	0.0067	0.0067	1990	0.0815
1991	0.0064	0.0059	0.0059	0.0070	0.0065	0.0059	0.0069	0.0062	0.0061	0.0058	0.0052	0.0056	1991	0.0743
1992	0.0052	0.0052	0.0060	0.0058	0.0056	0.0058	0.0053	0.0050	0.0047	0.0044	0.0050	0.0053	1992	0.0627
1993	0.0049	0.0045	0.0049	0.0045	0.0041	0.0050	0.0041	0.0044	0.0041	0.0038	0.0042	0.0043	1993	0.0553
1994	0.0045	0.0039	0.0048	0.0049	0.0058	0.0055	0.0055	0.0060	0.0055	0.0060	0.0061	0.0063	1994	0.0607
1995	0.0067	0.0056	0.0060	0.0054	0.0062	0.0050	0.0051	0.0051	0.0047	0.0052	0.0047	0.0043	1995	0.0669
1996	0.0046	0.0041	0.0045	0.0053	0.0054	0.0050	0.0058	0.0052	0.0056	0.0053	0.0047	0.0050	1996	0.0582
1997	0.0052	0.0047	0.0054	0.0055	0.0055	0.0053	0.0054	0.0046	0.0054	0.0050	0.0043	0.0052	1997	0.0614
1998	0.0046	0.0041	0.0049	0.0046	0.0045	0.0049	0.0047	0.0046	0.0041	0.0035	0.0036	0.0039	1998	0.0529
1999	0.0037	0.0035	0.0048	0.0043	0.0041	0.0052	0.0049	0.0049	0.0048	0.0046	0.0052	0.0052	1999	0.0530
2000	0.0054	0.0052	0.0056	0.0048	0.0059	0.0054	0.0053	0.0051	0.0047	0.0051	0.0047	0.0043	2000	0.0619
2001	0.0032	0.0026	0.0027	0.0033	0.0042	0.0040	0.0044	0.0039	0.0034	0.0035	0.0030	0.0035	2001	0.0427
2002	0.0038	0.0034	0.0034	0.0045	0.0039	0.0034	0.0037	0.0029	0.0027	0.0022	0.0022	0.0028	2002	0.0398

*Compound annual return

Table B-12

Intermediate-Term Government Bonds: Capital Appreciation Returns

from January 1926 to December 1970

Year	Jan	Feb	Mar	Apr	May	Jun	Jul	Aug	Sep	Oct	Nov	Dec	Year	Jan-Dec*
1926	0.0036	0.0000	0.0009	0.0059	-0.0023	-0.0004	-0.0018	-0.0023	0.0018	0.0023	0.0014	0.0059	1926	0.0151
1927	0.0027	0.0009	0.0009	-0.0014	-0.0009	0.0000	0.0014	0.0027	0.0032	-0.0064	0.0055	0.0009	1927	0.0096
1928	0.0018	-0.0032	-0.0018	-0.0032	-0.0036	-0.0014	-0.0122	0.0018	-0.0004	0.0000	-0.0014	-0.0041	1928	-0.0273
1929	-0.0063	-0.0054	-0.0031	0.0054	-0.0098	0.0072	0.0031	0.0018	-0.0049	0.0135	0.0150	0.0014	1929	0.0177
1930	-0.0072	0.0064	0.0133	-0.0100	0.0032	0.0115	0.0028	-0.0005	0.0037	0.0051	0.0046	0.0000	1930	0.0330
1931	-0.0097	0.0074	0.0028	0.0060	0.0098	-0.0240	-0.0009	-0.0009	-0.0142	-0.0136	0.0018	-0.0193	1931	-0.0540
1932	-0.0067	0.0094	0.0045	0.0164	-0.0122	0.0077	0.0091	0.0096	0.0000	0.0018	0.0005	0.0092	1932	0.0502
1933	-0.0041	-0.0028	0.0074	0.0032	0.0178	-0.0014	-0.0028	0.0051	0.0005	-0.0047	0.0005	-0.0280	1933	-0.0099
1934	0.0100	0.0028	0.0162	0.0158	0.0097	0.0070	-0.0044	-0.0113	-0.0160	0.0164	0.0024	0.0102	1934	0.0597
1935	0.0093	0.0088	0.0107	0.0090	-0.0050	0.0098	0.0022	-0.0086	-0.0072	0.0093	-0.0002	0.0105	1935	0.0494
1936	-0.0017	0.0056	0.0018	0.0012	0.0026	-0.0001	0.0010	0.0038	-0.0001	0.0014	0.0070	-0.0067	1936	0.0160
1937	-0.0041	-0.0003	-0.0176	0.0032	0.0067	-0.0027	0.0045	-0.0056	0.0068	0.0020	0.0030	0.0051	1937	0.0005
1938	0.0067	0.0036	-0.0030	0.0214	0.0008	0.0061	-0.0003	0.0000	-0.0026	0.0079	-0.0014	0.0039	1938	0.0437
1939	0.0016	0.0071	0.0069	0.0028	0.0084	-0.0007	0.0030	-0.0155	-0.0273	0.0300	0.0063	0.0098	1939	0.0318
1940	-0.0023	0.0027	0.0080	-0.0005	-0.0221	0.0177	-0.0005	0.0035	0.0040	0.0030	0.0050	0.0023	1940	0.0204
1941	-0.0006	-0.0052	0.0061	0.0027	0.0006	0.0051	-0.0004	0.0006	-0.0004	0.0018	-0.0096	-0.0023	1941	-0.0017
1942	0.0066	0.0009	0.0016	0.0016	0.0010	0.0006	-0.0006	0.0011	-0.0029	0.0011	0.0011	-0.0006	1942	0.0117
1943	0.0025	0.0001	0.0007	0.0010	0.0044	0.0020	0.0008	-0.0010	0.0002	0.0005	0.0002	0.0008	1943	0.0123
1944	-0.0002	0.0004	0.0007	0.0016	-0.0008	-0.0005	0.0016	0.0012	0.0000	-0.0001	-0.0003	-0.0001	1944	0.0035
1945	0.0040	0.0028	-0.0005	0.0005	0.0002	0.0009	-0.0010	0.0006	0.0008	0.0006	0.0001	0.0012	1945	0.0102
1946	0.0030	0.0040	-0.0045	-0.0028	-0.0003	0.0024	-0.0019	-0.0005	-0.0020	0.0015	-0.0018	0.0022	1946	-0.0008
1947	0.0012	-0.0003	0.0014	-0.0022	-0.0002	-0.0003	-0.0004	0.0016	-0.0010	-0.0033	-0.0004	0.0008	1947	-0.0030
1948	0.0002	0.0006	0.0003	0.0006	0.0042	-0.0021	-0.0014	-0.0018	-0.0003	0.0000	0.0006	0.0019	1948	0.0027
1949	0.0015	0.0000	0.0012	0.0003	0.0010	0.0038	0.0010	0.0019	-0.0002	-0.0004	-0.0008	0.0002	1949	0.0095
1950	-0.0016	-0.0002	-0.0011	-0.0003	0.0007	-0.0008	0.0009	-0.0019	-0.0015	-0.0012	0.0005	-0.0004	1950	-0.0069
1951	0.0006	-0.0007	-0.0142	0.0040	-0.0058	0.0033	0.0040	0.0019	-0.0072	-0.0003	0.0015	-0.0033	1951	-0.0163
1952	0.0019	-0.0037	0.0048	0.0037	0.0004	-0.0052	-0.0052	-0.0042	-0.0002	0.0046	-0.0023	-0.0002	1952	-0.0057
1953	-0.0022	-0.0016	-0.0038	-0.0117	-0.0138	0.0129	0.0032	-0.0031	0.0171	0.0018	-0.0006	0.0083	1953	0.0061
1954	0.0049	0.0086	0.0013	0.0031	-0.0084	0.0109	-0.0016	-0.0001	-0.0032	-0.0021	-0.0015	-0.0010	1954	0.0108
1955	-0.0050	-0.0070	0.0004	-0.0014	-0.0019	-0.0057	-0.0091	-0.0018	0.0059	0.0050	-0.0074	-0.0033	1955	-0.0310
1956	0.0080	-0.0018	-0.0122	-0.0027	0.0086	-0.0020	-0.0120	-0.0130	0.0066	-0.0049	-0.0075	-0.0019	1956	-0.0345
1957	0.0207	-0.0037	-0.0009	-0.0130	-0.0047	-0.0133	-0.0051	0.0077	-0.0030	0.0010	0.0365	0.0188	1957	0.0405
1958	0.0010	0.0117	0.0031	0.0031	0.0041	-0.0088	-0.0112	-0.0378	-0.0048	-0.0029	0.0103	-0.0093	1958	-0.0417
1959	-0.0045	0.0078	-0.0070	-0.0084	-0.0033	-0.0113	-0.0004	-0.0116	-0.0019	0.0134	-0.0130	-0.0060	1959	-0.0456
1960	0.0115	0.0032	0.0253	-0.0096	-0.0006	0.0182	0.0236	-0.0034	0.0001	-0.0012	-0.0122	0.0180	1960	0.0742
1961	-0.0089	0.0063	0.0008	0.0026	-0.0058	-0.0054	-0.0024	-0.0012	0.0049	-0.0018	-0.0049	-0.0012	1961	-0.0172
1962	-0.0080	0.0124	0.0058	-0.0006	0.0018	-0.0056	-0.0045	0.0092	-0.0007	0.0018	0.0031	0.0026	1962	0.0173
1963	-0.0059	-0.0011	-0.0002	-0.0002	-0.0017	-0.0015	-0.0030	-0.0012	-0.0019	-0.0022	0.0008	-0.0032	1963	-0.0210
1964	-0.0001	-0.0019	-0.0019	0.0000	0.0049	0.0000	-0.0006	-0.0006	0.0012	0.0000	-0.0037	0.0024	1964	-0.0003
1965	0.0009	-0.0013	0.0006	-0.0007	0.0002	0.0012	-0.0016	-0.0017	-0.0039	-0.0033	-0.0031	-0.0186	1965	-0.0310
1966	-0.0037	-0.0120	0.0145	-0.0056	-0.0032	-0.0064	-0.0065	-0.0171	0.0170	0.0031	-0.0015	0.0180	1966	-0.0041
1967	0.0077	-0.0048	0.0144	-0.0122	0.0002	-0.0265	0.0089	-0.0078	-0.0035	-0.0095	-0.0018	-0.0038	1967	-0.0385
1968	0.0095	-0.0003	-0.0069	-0.0065	0.0015	0.0123	0.0128	-0.0021	0.0011	-0.0034	-0.0054	-0.0220	1968	-0.0099
1969	0.0032	-0.0061	0.0048	0.0021	-0.0131	-0.0142	0.0024	-0.0072	-0.0361	0.0266	-0.0103	-0.0260	1969	-0.0727
1970	-0.0035	0.0378	0.0024	-0.0266	0.0049	-0.0006	0.0087	0.0054	0.0136	0.0037	0.0393	0.0005	1970	0.0871

*Compound annual return

Table B–12 (continued)

Intermediate–Term Government Bonds: Capital Appreciation Returns

from January 1971 to December 2002

Year	Jan	Feb	Mar	Apr	May	Jun	Jul	Aug	Sep	Oct	Nov	Dec	Year	Jan–Dec*
1971	0.0121	0.0181	0.0139	−0.0367	−0.0034	−0.0240	−0.0027	0.0294	−0.0022	0.0173	0.0005	0.0064	1971	0.0272
1972	0.0058	−0.0030	−0.0031	−0.0030	−0.0035	−0.0003	−0.0034	−0.0035	−0.0033	−0.0037	−0.0006	0.0143	1972	−0.0075
1973	−0.0062	−0.0123	−0.0008	0.0007	0.0001	−0.0059	−0.0336	0.0190	0.0195	−0.0010	0.0009	−0.0016	1973	−0.0219
1974	−0.0048	−0.0016	−0.0266	−0.0217	0.0063	−0.0147	−0.0066	−0.0078	0.0247	0.0043	0.0175	0.0120	1974	−0.0199
1975	−0.0008	0.0092	−0.0119	−0.0246	0.0197	−0.0035	−0.0093	−0.0070	−0.0059	0.0298	−0.0065	0.0131	1975	0.0012
1976	−0.0003	0.0028	0.0010	0.0057	−0.0200	0.0090	0.0059	0.0127	0.0019	0.0093	0.0264	−0.0024	1976	0.0525
1977	−0.0241	−0.0002	−0.0001	−0.0001	−0.0002	0.0048	−0.0051	−0.0052	−0.0041	−0.0118	0.0019	−0.0082	1977	−0.0515
1978	−0.0053	−0.0041	−0.0029	−0.0036	−0.0073	−0.0087	0.0028	0.0010	−0.0008	−0.0184	0.0020	−0.0005	1978	−0.0449
1979	−0.0024	−0.0125	0.0038	−0.0044	0.0116	0.0135	−0.0086	−0.0163	−0.0065	−0.0553	0.0274	0.0001	1979	−0.0507
1980	−0.0221	−0.0724	0.0036	0.1095	0.0409	−0.0152	−0.0185	−0.0463	−0.0135	−0.0246	−0.0067	0.0060	1980	−0.0681
1981	−0.0069	−0.0331	0.0146	−0.0322	0.0135	−0.0058	−0.0386	−0.0298	0.0034	0.0482	0.0502	−0.0250	1981	−0.0455
1982	−0.0057	0.0046	−0.0080	0.0186	0.0045	−0.0253	0.0351	0.0359	0.0228	0.0442	−0.0007	0.0100	1982	0.1423
1983	−0.0076	0.0173	−0.0133	0.0177	−0.0208	−0.0069	−0.0280	−0.0022	0.0220	−0.0073	0.0012	−0.0043	1983	−0.0330
1984	0.0081	−0.0153	−0.0129	−0.0104	−0.0353	−0.0007	0.0280	−0.0005	0.0106	0.0274	0.0099	0.0050	1984	0.0122
1985	0.0116	−0.0260	0.0077	0.0167	0.0395	0.0035	−0.0129	0.0067	0.0031	0.0081	0.0121	0.0178	1985	0.0901
1986	0.0011	0.0210	0.0270	0.0021	−0.0274	0.0208	0.0095	0.0209	−0.0168	0.0102	0.0061	−0.0053	1986	0.0699
1987	0.0051	0.0007	−0.0091	−0.0302	−0.0100	0.0051	−0.0040	−0.0105	−0.0209	0.0226	0.0013	0.0023	1987	−0.0475
1988	0.0251	0.0057	−0.0151	−0.0107	−0.0121	0.0111	−0.0111	−0.0086	0.0124	0.0077	−0.0182	−0.0081	1988	−0.0226
1989	0.0044	−0.0117	−0.0029	0.0149	0.0132	0.0254	0.0168	−0.0307	0.0004	0.0166	0.0021	−0.0048	1989	0.0434
1990	−0.0176	−0.0057	−0.0067	−0.0148	0.0186	0.0084	0.0102	−0.0160	0.0030	0.0096	0.0126	0.0095	1990	0.0102
1991	0.0042	−0.0011	−0.0036	0.0046	−0.0006	−0.0081	0.0060	0.0184	0.0155	0.0077	0.0076	0.0209	1991	0.0736
1992	−0.0247	−0.0030	−0.0139	0.0039	0.0166	0.0118	0.0189	0.0100	0.0147	−0.0226	−0.0134	0.0093	1992	0.0064
1993	0.0221	0.0198	−0.0006	0.0043	−0.0051	0.0152	−0.0036	0.0179	0.0015	−0.0020	−0.0135	−0.0011	1993	0.0556
1994	0.0093	−0.0297	−0.0306	−0.0154	−0.0060	−0.0084	0.0115	−0.0034	−0.0213	−0.0084	−0.0131	−0.0010	1994	−0.1114
1995	0.0115	0.0178	0.0003	0.0090	0.0307	0.0030	−0.0066	0.0035	0.0017	0.0069	0.0102	0.0052	1995	0.0966
1996	−0.0040	−0.0178	−0.0164	−0.0103	−0.0086	0.0067	−0.0033	−0.0057	0.0100	0.0129	0.0102	−0.0128	1996	−0.0390
1997	−0.0027	−0.0045	−0.0168	0.0093	0.0024	0.0048	0.0210	−0.0143	0.0098	0.0100	−0.0045	0.0054	1997	0.0194
1998	0.0134	−0.0080	−0.0024	0.0015	0.0025	0.0030	−0.0020	0.0225	0.0289	0.0006	−0.0134	−0.0002	1998	0.0466
1999	0.0018	−0.0297	0.0038	−0.0023	−0.0188	−0.0020	−0.0052	−0.0035	0.0049	−0.0054	−0.0060	−0.0100	1999	−0.0706
2000	−0.0107	0.0026	0.0147	−0.0091	−0.0007	0.0138	0.0019	0.0083	0.0049	0.0028	0.0127	0.0171	2000	0.0594
2001	0.0066	0.0079	0.0049	−0.0146	−0.0049	0.0025	0.0203	0.0056	0.0219	0.0145	−0.0201	−0.0117	2001	0.0323
2002	−0.0003	0.0073	−0.0276	0.0193	0.0079	0.0135	0.0234	0.0138	0.0261	−0.0046	−0.0191	0.0251	2002	0.0865

*Compound annual return

Table B–13

Intermediate–Term Government Bonds: Yields

from January 1926 to December 1970

Year	Jan	Feb	Mar	Apr	May	Jun	Jul	Aug	Sep	Oct	Nov	Dec	Yr–end	Yield
1926	0.0386	0.0386	0.0384	0.0371	0.0376	0.0377	0.0381	0.0386	0.0382	0.0377	0.0374	0.0361	1926	0.0361
1927	0.0355	0.0353	0.0351	0.0354	0.0356	0.0356	0.0353	0.0347	0.0340	0.0354	0.0342	0.0340	1927	0.0340
1928	0.0336	0.0343	0.0347	0.0354	0.0362	0.0365	0.0392	0.0388	0.0389	0.0389	0.0392	0.0401	1928	0.0401
1929	0.0415	0.0427	0.0434	0.0422	0.0444	0.0428	0.0421	0.0417	0.0428	0.0398	0.0365	0.0362	1929	0.0362
1930	0.0378	0.0364	0.0335	0.0357	0.0350	0.0325	0.0319	0.0320	0.0312	0.0301	0.0291	0.0291	1930	0.0291
1931	0.0312	0.0296	0.0290	0.0277	0.0256	0.0308	0.0310	0.0312	0.0343	0.0373	0.0369	0.0412	1931	0.0412
1932	0.0427	0.0406	0.0396	0.0360	0.0387	0.0370	0.0350	0.0329	0.0329	0.0325	0.0324	0.0304	1932	0.0304
1933	0.0313	0.0319	0.0303	0.0296	0.0258	0.0261	0.0267	0.0256	0.0255	0.0265	0.0264	0.0325	1933	0.0325
1934	0.0325	0.0321	0.0296	0.0272	0.0257	0.0246	0.0253	0.0271	0.0298	0.0271	0.0267	0.0249	1934	0.0249
1935	0.0233	0.0218	0.0199	0.0184	0.0193	0.0175	0.0171	0.0187	0.0201	0.0183	0.0183	0.0163	1935	0.0163
1936	0.0166	0.0155	0.0151	0.0149	0.0143	0.0143	0.0141	0.0133	0.0133	0.0130	0.0114	0.0129	1936	0.0129
1937	0.0134	0.0135	0.0184	0.0175	0.0156	0.0164	0.0151	0.0168	0.0147	0.0141	0.0131	0.0114	1937	0.0114
1938	0.0205	0.0200	0.0204	0.0174	0.0173	0.0164	0.0164	0.0164	0.0168	0.0156	0.0158	0.0152	1938	0.0152
1939	0.0149	0.0138	0.0127	0.0122	0.0108	0.0110	0.0105	0.0131	0.0180	0.0127	0.0116	0.0098	1939	0.0098
1940	0.0103	0.0098	0.0083	0.0084	0.0127	0.0092	0.0093	0.0086	0.0078	0.0072	0.0061	0.0057	1940	0.0057
1941	0.0077	0.0089	0.0075	0.0069	0.0067	0.0055	0.0056	0.0055	0.0056	0.0051	0.0076	0.0082	1941	0.0082
1942	0.0083	0.0081	0.0077	0.0074	0.0071	0.0070	0.0071	0.0069	0.0076	0.0073	0.0070	0.0072	1942	0.0072
1943	0.0166	0.0166	0.0164	0.0162	0.0153	0.0149	0.0147	0.0149	0.0149	0.0147	0.0147	0.0145	1943	0.0145
1944	0.0150	0.0150	0.0148	0.0143	0.0146	0.0147	0.0142	0.0139	0.0139	0.0139	0.0140	0.0140	1944	0.0140
1945	0.0127	0.0118	0.0120	0.0118	0.0117	0.0114	0.0118	0.0115	0.0112	0.0109	0.0109	0.0103	1945	0.0103
1946	0.0099	0.0087	0.0101	0.0111	0.0112	0.0103	0.0110	0.0112	0.0120	0.0114	0.0121	0.0112	1946	0.0112
1947	0.0116	0.0117	0.0112	0.0120	0.0121	0.0122	0.0124	0.0117	0.0121	0.0136	0.0138	0.0134	1947	0.0134
1948	0.0160	0.0158	0.0157	0.0155	0.0142	0.0149	0.0154	0.0160	0.0161	0.0161	0.0158	0.0151	1948	0.0151
1949	0.0153	0.0153	0.0148	0.0147	0.0144	0.0129	0.0125	0.0117	0.0118	0.0120	0.0124	0.0123	1949	0.0123
1950	0.0131	0.0132	0.0137	0.0138	0.0134	0.0139	0.0134	0.0145	0.0154	0.0162	0.0159	0.0162	1950	0.0162
1951	0.0179	0.0180	0.0211	0.0202	0.0215	0.0208	0.0199	0.0194	0.0212	0.0212	0.0209	0.0217	1951	0.0217
1952	0.0212	0.0222	0.0209	0.0199	0.0198	0.0213	0.0228	0.0241	0.0242	0.0227	0.0235	0.0235	1952	0.0235
1953	0.0242	0.0245	0.0253	0.0277	0.0307	0.0279	0.0272	0.0279	0.0241	0.0237	0.0238	0.0218	1953	0.0218
1954	0.0187	0.0157	0.0153	0.0142	0.0173	0.0131	0.0138	0.0138	0.0152	0.0161	0.0168	0.0172	1954	0.0172
1955	0.0227	0.0240	0.0240	0.0242	0.0246	0.0257	0.0276	0.0280	0.0267	0.0257	0.0273	0.0280	1955	0.0280
1956	0.0271	0.0275	0.0300	0.0305	0.0287	0.0292	0.0317	0.0346	0.0331	0.0342	0.0359	0.0363	1956	0.0363
1957	0.0326	0.0333	0.0334	0.0357	0.0366	0.0390	0.0399	0.0385	0.0390	0.0388	0.0320	0.0284	1957	0.0284
1958	0.0282	0.0259	0.0253	0.0246	0.0238	0.0250	0.0281	0.0365	0.0376	0.0382	0.0359	0.0381	1958	0.0381
1959	0.0395	0.0378	0.0393	0.0413	0.0420	0.0447	0.0448	0.0477	0.0482	0.0448	0.0482	0.0498	1959	0.0498
1960	0.0471	0.0464	0.0409	0.0431	0.0432	0.0390	0.0334	0.0343	0.0343	0.0346	0.0377	0.0331	1960	0.0331
1961	0.0363	0.0350	0.0348	0.0342	0.0355	0.0368	0.0373	0.0376	0.0365	0.0369	0.0381	0.0384	1961	0.0384
1962	0.0402	0.0377	0.0366	0.0367	0.0363	0.0375	0.0384	0.0365	0.0366	0.0362	0.0355	0.0350	1962	0.0350
1963	0.0368	0.0370	0.0370	0.0371	0.0374	0.0378	0.0385	0.0388	0.0392	0.0398	0.0396	0.0404	1963	0.0404
1964	0.0402	0.0407	0.0411	0.0411	0.0399	0.0399	0.0401	0.0402	0.0399	0.0399	0.0409	0.0403	1964	0.0403
1965	0.0413	0.0416	0.0414	0.0416	0.0415	0.0413	0.0416	0.0420	0.0429	0.0437	0.0444	0.0490	1965	0.0490
1966	0.0482	0.0507	0.0477	0.0489	0.0496	0.0510	0.0525	0.0565	0.0526	0.0519	0.0522	0.0479	1966	0.0479
1967	0.0459	0.0470	0.0437	0.0466	0.0465	0.0530	0.0508	0.0528	0.0537	0.0562	0.0566	0.0577	1967	0.0577
1968	0.0548	0.0549	0.0563	0.0577	0.0574	0.0547	0.0518	0.0523	0.0520	0.0528	0.0541	0.0596	1968	0.0596
1969	0.0637	0.0651	0.0640	0.0636	0.0666	0.0699	0.0693	0.0711	0.0799	0.0735	0.0761	0.0829	1969	0.0829
1970	0.0820	0.0730	0.0724	0.0790	0.0778	0.0780	0.0757	0.0743	0.0707	0.0697	0.0591	0.0590	1970	0.0590

Table B–13 (continued)

Intermediate–Term Government Bonds: Yields

from January 1971 to December 2002

Year	Jan	Feb	Mar	Apr	May	Jun	Jul	Aug	Sep	Oct	Nov	Dec	Yr–end	Yield
1971	0.0570	0.0526	0.0493	0.0585	0.0593	0.0656	0.0663	0.0585	0.0591	0.0545	0.0543	0.0525	1971	0.0525
1972	0.0556	0.0563	0.0570	0.0577	0.0586	0.0587	0.0595	0.0604	0.0613	0.0623	0.0625	0.0585	1972	0.0585
1973	0.0641	0.0671	0.0673	0.0671	0.0671	0.0686	0.0776	0.0725	0.0674	0.0677	0.0674	0.0679	1973	0.0679
1974	0.0687	0.0691	0.0751	0.0801	0.0786	0.0822	0.0838	0.0857	0.0797	0.0787	0.0743	0.0712	1974	0.0712
1975	0.0730	0.0709	0.0737	0.0798	0.0749	0.0758	0.0782	0.0800	0.0815	0.0736	0.0754	0.0719	1975	0.0719
1976	0.0743	0.0736	0.0733	0.0719	0.0771	0.0747	0.0732	0.0697	0.0692	0.0667	0.0594	0.0600	1976	0.0600
1977	0.0673	0.0673	0.0673	0.0674	0.0674	0.0662	0.0675	0.0689	0.0700	0.0733	0.0727	0.0751	1977	0.0751
1978	0.0773	0.0784	0.0791	0.0800	0.0820	0.0843	0.0836	0.0833	0.0835	0.0887	0.0882	0.0883	1978	0.0883
1979	0.0895	0.0928	0.0918	0.0929	0.0899	0.0864	0.0887	0.0933	0.0951	0.1112	0.1033	0.1033	1979	0.1033
1980	0.1093	0.1294	0.1285	0.1009	0.0903	0.0944	0.0996	0.1133	0.1171	0.1244	0.1264	0.1245	1980	0.1245
1981	0.1275	0.1371	0.1328	0.1427	0.1385	0.1404	0.1533	0.1636	0.1625	0.1472	0.1311	0.1396	1981	0.1396
1982	0.1397	0.1385	0.1406	0.1355	0.1343	0.1417	0.1315	0.1209	0.1144	0.1018	0.1020	0.0990	1982	0.0990
1983	0.1057	0.1010	0.1048	0.0997	0.1059	0.1080	0.1168	0.1175	0.1108	0.1131	0.1127	0.1141	1983	0.1141
1984	0.1137	0.1181	0.1219	0.1251	0.1363	0.1365	0.1274	0.1276	0.1242	0.1154	0.1121	0.1104	1984	0.1104
1985	0.1081	0.1152	0.1131	0.1084	0.0974	0.0963	0.1002	0.0982	0.0973	0.0949	0.0911	0.0855	1985	0.0855
1986	0.0870	0.0815	0.0743	0.0737	0.0816	0.0756	0.0728	0.0668	0.0718	0.0687	0.0669	0.0685	1986	0.0685
1987	0.0685	0.0683	0.0708	0.0793	0.0821	0.0806	0.0818	0.0849	0.0912	0.0844	0.0840	0.0832	1987	0.0832
1988	0.0782	0.0768	0.0807	0.0836	0.0870	0.0839	0.0871	0.0895	0.0859	0.0837	0.0892	0.0917	1988	0.0917
1989	0.0896	0.0927	0.0934	0.0895	0.0860	0.0791	0.0745	0.0834	0.0833	0.0786	0.0779	0.0794	1989	0.0794
1990	0.0842	0.0855	0.0871	0.0907	0.0864	0.0843	0.0819	0.0859	0.0851	0.0826	0.0795	0.0770	1990	0.0770
1991	0.0772	0.0774	0.0783	0.0772	0.0773	0.0793	0.0778	0.0732	0.0693	0.0673	0.0653	0.0597	1991	0.0597
1992	0.0683	0.0690	0.0720	0.0711	0.0674	0.0647	0.0604	0.0581	0.0547	0.0601	0.0634	0.0611	1992	0.0611
1993	0.0588	0.0547	0.0549	0.0540	0.0551	0.0517	0.0526	0.0486	0.0483	0.0488	0.0519	0.0522	1993	0.0522
1994	0.0515	0.0575	0.0638	0.0670	0.0682	0.0699	0.0675	0.0683	0.0730	0.0749	0.0778	0.0780	1994	0.0780
1995	0.0754	0.0708	0.0707	0.0685	0.0606	0.0598	0.0616	0.0606	0.0601	0.0582	0.0553	0.0538	1995	0.0538
1996	0.0528	0.0573	0.0614	0.0640	0.0663	0.0645	0.0654	0.0670	0.0643	0.0607	0.0578	0.0616	1996	0.0616
1997	0.0629	0.0639	0.0677	0.0656	0.0650	0.0639	0.0589	0.0624	0.0601	0.0576	0.0587	0.0573	1997	0.0573
1998	0.0545	0.0562	0.0567	0.0564	0.0558	0.0551	0.0556	0.0503	0.0435	0.0434	0.0467	0.0468	1998	0.0468
1999	0.0467	0.0535	0.0526	0.0532	0.0576	0.0581	0.0593	0.0602	0.0590	0.0604	0.0619	0.0645	1999	0.0645
2000	0.0675	0.0669	0.0636	0.0657	0.0658	0.0626	0.0621	0.0601	0.0589	0.0582	0.0551	0.0507	2000	0.0507
2001	0.0499	0.0482	0.0471	0.0504	0.0515	0.0510	0.0464	0.0450	0.0399	0.0365	0.0413	0.0442	2001	0.0442
2002	0.0459	0.0442	0.0504	0.0461	0.0443	0.0412	0.0358	0.0325	0.0265	0.0276	0.0323	0.0261	2002	0.0261

Table B–14

U.S. Treasury Bills: Total Returns

from January 1926 to December 1970

Year	Jan	Feb	Mar	Apr	May	Jun	Jul	Aug	Sep	Oct	Nov	Dec	Year	Jan–Dec*
1926	0.0034	0.0027	0.0030	0.0034	0.0001	0.0035	0.0022	0.0025	0.0023	0.0032	0.0031	0.0028	1926	0.0327
1927	0.0025	0.0026	0.0030	0.0025	0.0030	0.0026	0.0030	0.0028	0.0021	0.0025	0.0021	0.0022	1927	0.0312
1928	0.0025	0.0033	0.0029	0.0022	0.0032	0.0031	0.0032	0.0032	0.0027	0.0041	0.0038	0.0006	1928	0.0356
1929	0.0034	0.0036	0.0034	0.0036	0.0044	0.0052	0.0033	0.0040	0.0035	0.0046	0.0037	0.0037	1929	0.0475
1930	0.0014	0.0030	0.0035	0.0021	0.0026	0.0027	0.0020	0.0009	0.0022	0.0009	0.0013	0.0014	1930	0.0241
1931	0.0015	0.0004	0.0013	0.0008	0.0009	0.0008	0.0006	0.0003	0.0003	0.0010	0.0017	0.0012	1931	0.0107
1932	0.0023	0.0023	0.0016	0.0011	0.0006	0.0002	0.0003	0.0003	0.0003	0.0002	0.0002	0.0001	1932	0.0096
1933	0.0001	−0.0003	0.0004	0.0010	0.0004	0.0002	0.0002	0.0003	0.0002	0.0001	0.0002	0.0002	1933	0.0030
1934	0.0005	0.0002	0.0002	0.0001	0.0001	0.0001	0.0001	0.0001	0.0001	0.0001	0.0001	0.0001	1934	0.0016
1935	0.0001	0.0002	0.0001	0.0001	0.0001	0.0001	0.0001	0.0001	0.0001	0.0001	0.0002	0.0001	1935	0.0017
1936	0.0001	0.0001	0.0002	0.0002	0.0002	0.0003	0.0001	0.0002	0.0001	0.0002	0.0001	0.0000	1936	0.0018
1937	0.0001	0.0002	0.0001	0.0003	0.0006	0.0003	0.0003	0.0002	0.0004	0.0002	0.0002	0.0000	1937	0.0031
1938	0.0000	0.0000	−0.0001	0.0001	0.0000	0.0000	−0.0001	0.0000	0.0002	0.0001	−0.0006	0.0000	1938	−0.0002
1939	−0.0001	0.0001	−0.0001	0.0000	0.0001	0.0001	0.0000	−0.0001	0.0001	0.0000	0.0000	0.0000	1939	0.0002
1940	0.0000	0.0000	0.0000	0.0000	−0.0002	0.0000	0.0001	−0.0001	0.0000	0.0000	0.0000	0.0000	1940	0.0000
1941	−0.0001	−0.0001	0.0001	−0.0001	0.0000	0.0000	0.0003	0.0001	0.0001	0.0000	0.0000	0.0001	1941	0.0006
1942	0.0002	0.0001	0.0001	0.0001	0.0003	0.0002	0.0003	0.0003	0.0003	0.0003	0.0003	0.0003	1942	0.0027
1943	0.0003	0.0003	0.0003	0.0003	0.0003	0.0003	0.0003	0.0003	0.0003	0.0003	0.0003	0.0003	1943	0.0035
1944	0.0003	0.0003	0.0002	0.0003	0.0003	0.0003	0.0003	0.0003	0.0002	0.0003	0.0003	0.0002	1944	0.0033
1945	0.0003	0.0002	0.0002	0.0003	0.0003	0.0002	0.0003	0.0003	0.0003	0.0003	0.0002	0.0003	1945	0.0033
1946	0.0003	0.0003	0.0003	0.0003	0.0003	0.0003	0.0003	0.0003	0.0003	0.0003	0.0003	0.0003	1946	0.0035
1947	0.0003	0.0003	0.0003	0.0003	0.0003	0.0003	0.0003	0.0003	0.0006	0.0006	0.0006	0.0008	1947	0.0050
1948	0.0007	0.0007	0.0009	0.0008	0.0008	0.0009	0.0008	0.0009	0.0004	0.0004	0.0004	0.0004	1948	0.0081
1949	0.0010	0.0009	0.0010	0.0009	0.0010	0.0010	0.0009	0.0009	0.0009	0.0009	0.0008	0.0009	1949	0.0110
1950	0.0009	0.0009	0.0010	0.0009	0.0010	0.0010	0.0010	0.0010	0.0010	0.0012	0.0011	0.0011	1950	0.0120
1951	0.0013	0.0010	0.0011	0.0013	0.0012	0.0012	0.0013	0.0013	0.0012	0.0016	0.0011	0.0012	1951	0.0149
1952	0.0015	0.0012	0.0011	0.0012	0.0013	0.0015	0.0015	0.0015	0.0016	0.0014	0.0010	0.0016	1952	0.0166
1953	0.0016	0.0014	0.0018	0.0016	0.0017	0.0018	0.0015	0.0017	0.0016	0.0013	0.0008	0.0013	1953	0.0182
1954	0.0011	0.0007	0.0008	0.0009	0.0005	0.0006	0.0005	0.0005	0.0009	0.0007	0.0006	0.0008	1954	0.0086
1955	0.0008	0.0009	0.0010	0.0010	0.0014	0.0010	0.0010	0.0016	0.0016	0.0018	0.0017	0.0018	1955	0.0157
1956	0.0022	0.0019	0.0015	0.0019	0.0023	0.0020	0.0022	0.0017	0.0018	0.0025	0.0020	0.0024	1956	0.0246
1957	0.0027	0.0024	0.0023	0.0025	0.0026	0.0024	0.0030	0.0025	0.0026	0.0029	0.0028	0.0024	1957	0.0314
1958	0.0028	0.0012	0.0009	0.0008	0.0011	0.0003	0.0007	0.0004	0.0019	0.0018	0.0011	0.0022	1958	0.0154
1959	0.0021	0.0019	0.0022	0.0020	0.0022	0.0025	0.0025	0.0019	0.0031	0.0030	0.0026	0.0034	1959	0.0295
1960	0.0033	0.0029	0.0035	0.0019	0.0027	0.0024	0.0013	0.0017	0.0016	0.0022	0.0013	0.0016	1960	0.0266
1961	0.0019	0.0014	0.0020	0.0017	0.0018	0.0020	0.0018	0.0014	0.0017	0.0019	0.0015	0.0019	1961	0.0213
1962	0.0024	0.0020	0.0020	0.0022	0.0024	0.0020	0.0027	0.0023	0.0021	0.0026	0.0020	0.0023	1962	0.0273
1963	0.0025	0.0023	0.0023	0.0025	0.0024	0.0023	0.0027	0.0025	0.0027	0.0029	0.0027	0.0029	1963	0.0312
1964	0.0030	0.0026	0.0031	0.0029	0.0026	0.0030	0.0030	0.0028	0.0028	0.0029	0.0029	0.0031	1964	0.0354
1965	0.0028	0.0030	0.0036	0.0031	0.0031	0.0035	0.0031	0.0033	0.0031	0.0031	0.0035	0.0033	1965	0.0393
1966	0.0038	0.0035	0.0038	0.0034	0.0041	0.0038	0.0035	0.0041	0.0040	0.0045	0.0040	0.0040	1966	0.0476
1967	0.0043	0.0036	0.0039	0.0032	0.0033	0.0027	0.0032	0.0031	0.0032	0.0039	0.0036	0.0033	1967	0.0421
1968	0.0040	0.0039	0.0038	0.0043	0.0045	0.0043	0.0048	0.0042	0.0043	0.0044	0.0042	0.0043	1968	0.0521
1969	0.0053	0.0046	0.0046	0.0053	0.0048	0.0051	0.0053	0.0050	0.0062	0.0060	0.0052	0.0064	1969	0.0658
1970	0.0060	0.0062	0.0057	0.0050	0.0053	0.0058	0.0052	0.0053	0.0054	0.0046	0.0046	0.0042	1970	0.0652

*Compound annual return

Table B–14 (continued)

U.S. Treasury Bills: Total Returns

from January 1971 to December 2002

Year	Jan	Feb	Mar	Apr	May	Jun	Jul	Aug	Sep	Oct	Nov	Dec	Year	Jan–Dec*
1971	0.0038	0.0033	0.0030	0.0028	0.0029	0.0037	0.0040	0.0047	0.0037	0.0037	0.0037	0.0037	1971	0.0439
1972	0.0029	0.0025	0.0027	0.0029	0.0030	0.0029	0.0031	0.0029	0.0034	0.0040	0.0037	0.0037	1972	0.0384
1973	0.0044	0.0041	0.0046	0.0052	0.0051	0.0051	0.0064	0.0070	0.0068	0.0065	0.0056	0.0064	1973	0.0693
1974	0.0063	0.0058	0.0056	0.0075	0.0075	0.0060	0.0070	0.0060	0.0081	0.0051	0.0054	0.0070	1974	0.0800
1975	0.0058	0.0043	0.0041	0.0044	0.0044	0.0041	0.0048	0.0048	0.0053	0.0056	0.0041	0.0048	1975	0.0580
1976	0.0047	0.0034	0.0040	0.0042	0.0037	0.0043	0.0047	0.0042	0.0044	0.0041	0.0040	0.0040	1976	0.0508
1977	0.0036	0.0035	0.0038	0.0038	0.0037	0.0040	0.0042	0.0044	0.0043	0.0049	0.0050	0.0049	1977	0.0512
1978	0.0049	0.0046	0.0053	0.0054	0.0051	0.0054	0.0056	0.0055	0.0062	0.0068	0.0070	0.0078	1978	0.0718
1979	0.0077	0.0073	0.0081	0.0080	0.0082	0.0081	0.0077	0.0077	0.0083	0.0087	0.0099	0.0095	1979	0.1038
1980	0.0080	0.0089	0.0121	0.0126	0.0081	0.0061	0.0053	0.0064	0.0075	0.0095	0.0096	0.0131	1980	0.1124
1981	0.0104	0.0107	0.0121	0.0108	0.0115	0.0135	0.0124	0.0128	0.0124	0.0121	0.0107	0.0087	1981	0.1471
1982	0.0080	0.0092	0.0098	0.0113	0.0106	0.0096	0.0105	0.0076	0.0051	0.0059	0.0063	0.0067	1982	0.1054
1983	0.0069	0.0062	0.0063	0.0071	0.0069	0.0067	0.0074	0.0076	0.0076	0.0076	0.0070	0.0073	1983	0.0880
1984	0.0076	0.0071	0.0073	0.0081	0.0078	0.0075	0.0082	0.0083	0.0086	0.0100	0.0073	0.0064	1984	0.0985
1985	0.0065	0.0058	0.0062	0.0072	0.0066	0.0055	0.0062	0.0055	0.0060	0.0065	0.0061	0.0065	1985	0.0772
1986	0.0056	0.0053	0.0060	0.0052	0.0049	0.0052	0.0052	0.0046	0.0045	0.0046	0.0039	0.0049	1986	0.0616
1987	0.0042	0.0043	0.0047	0.0044	0.0038	0.0048	0.0046	0.0047	0.0045	0.0060	0.0035	0.0039	1987	0.0547
1988	0.0029	0.0046	0.0044	0.0046	0.0051	0.0049	0.0051	0.0059	0.0062	0.0061	0.0057	0.0063	1988	0.0635
1989	0.0055	0.0061	0.0067	0.0067	0.0079	0.0071	0.0070	0.0074	0.0065	0.0068	0.0069	0.0061	1989	0.0837
1990	0.0057	0.0057	0.0064	0.0069	0.0068	0.0063	0.0068	0.0066	0.0060	0.0068	0.0057	0.0060	1990	0.0781
1991	0.0052	0.0048	0.0044	0.0053	0.0047	0.0042	0.0049	0.0046	0.0046	0.0042	0.0039	0.0038	1991	0.0560
1992	0.0034	0.0028	0.0034	0.0032	0.0028	0.0032	0.0031	0.0026	0.0026	0.0023	0.0023	0.0028	1992	0.0351
1993	0.0023	0.0022	0.0025	0.0024	0.0022	0.0025	0.0024	0.0025	0.0026	0.0022	0.0025	0.0023	1993	0.0290
1994	0.0025	0.0021	0.0027	0.0027	0.0032	0.0031	0.0028	0.0037	0.0037	0.0038	0.0037	0.0044	1994	0.0390
1995	0.0042	0.0040	0.0046	0.0044	0.0054	0.0047	0.0045	0.0047	0.0043	0.0047	0.0042	0.0049	1995	0.0560
1996	0.0043	0.0039	0.0039	0.0046	0.0042	0.0040	0.0045	0.0041	0.0044	0.0042	0.0041	0.0046	1996	0.0521
1997	0.0045	0.0039	0.0043	0.0043	0.0049	0.0037	0.0043	0.0041	0.0044	0.0042	0.0039	0.0048	1997	0.0526
1998	0.0043	0.0039	0.0039	0.0043	0.0040	0.0041	0.0040	0.0043	0.0046	0.0032	0.0031	0.0038	1998	0.0486
1999	0.0035	0.0035	0.0043	0.0037	0.0034	0.0040	0.0038	0.0039	0.0039	0.0039	0.0036	0.0044	1999	0.0468
2000	0.0041	0.0043	0.0047	0.0046	0.0050	0.0040	0.0048	0.0050	0.0051	0.0056	0.0051	0.0050	2000	0.0589
2001	0.0054	0.0038	0.0042	0.0039	0.0032	0.0028	0.0030	0.0031	0.0028	0.0022	0.0017	0.0015	2001	0.0383
2002	0.0014	0.0013	0.0013	0.0015	0.0014	0.0013	0.0015	0.0014	0.0014	0.0014	0.0012	0.0011	2002	0.0165

*Compound annual return

Table B–15

Inflation

from January 1926 to December 1970

Year	Jan	Feb	Mar	Apr	May	Jun	Jul	Aug	Sep	Oct	Nov	Dec	Year	Jan–Dec*
1926	0.0000	−0.0037	−0.0056	0.0094	−0.0056	−0.0075	−0.0094	−0.0057	0.0057	0.0038	0.0038	0.0000	1926	−0.0149
1927	−0.0076	−0.0076	−0.0058	0.0000	0.0077	0.0096	−0.0190	−0.0058	0.0058	0.0058	−0.0019	−0.0019	1927	−0.0208
1928	−0.0019	−0.0097	0.0000	0.0020	0.0058	−0.0078	0.0000	0.0020	0.0078	−0.0019	−0.0019	−0.0039	1928	−0.0097
1929	−0.0019	−0.0020	−0.0039	−0.0039	0.0059	0.0039	0.0098	0.0039	−0.0019	0.0000	−0.0019	−0.0058	1929	0.0020
1930	−0.0039	−0.0039	−0.0059	0.0059	−0.0059	−0.0059	−0.0139	−0.0060	0.0061	−0.0060	−0.0081	−0.0143	1930	−0.0603
1931	−0.0145	−0.0147	−0.0064	−0.0064	−0.0108	−0.0109	−0.0022	−0.0022	−0.0044	−0.0067	−0.0112	−0.0091	1931	−0.0952
1932	−0.0206	−0.0140	−0.0047	−0.0071	−0.0144	−0.0073	0.0000	−0.0123	−0.0050	−0.0075	−0.0050	−0.0101	1932	−0.1030
1933	−0.0153	−0.0155	−0.0079	−0.0027	0.0027	0.0106	0.0289	0.0102	0.0000	0.0000	0.0000	−0.0051	1933	0.0051
1934	0.0051	0.0076	0.0000	−0.0025	0.0025	0.0025	0.0000	0.0025	0.0150	−0.0074	−0.0025	−0.0025	1934	0.0203
1935	0.0149	0.0074	−0.0024	0.0098	−0.0048	−0.0024	−0.0049	0.0000	0.0049	0.0000	0.0049	0.0024	1935	0.0299
1936	0.0000	−0.0048	−0.0049	0.0000	0.0000	0.0098	0.0048	0.0072	0.0024	−0.0024	0.0000	0.0000	1936	0.0121
1937	0.0072	0.0024	0.0071	0.0047	0.0047	0.0023	0.0046	0.0023	0.0092	−0.0046	−0.0069	−0.0023	1937	0.0310
1938	−0.0139	−0.0094	0.0000	0.0047	−0.0047	0.0000	0.0024	−0.0024	0.0000	−0.0047	−0.0024	0.0024	1938	−0.0278
1939	−0.0048	−0.0048	−0.0024	−0.0024	0.0000	0.0000	0.0000	0.0000	0.0193	−0.0047	0.0000	−0.0048	1939	−0.0048
1940	−0.0024	0.0072	−0.0024	0.0000	0.0024	0.0024	−0.0024	−0.0024	0.0024	0.0000	0.0000	0.0048	1940	0.0096
1941	0.0000	0.0000	0.0047	0.0094	0.0070	0.0186	0.0046	0.0091	0.0180	0.0110	0.0087	0.0022	1941	0.0972
1942	0.0130	0.0085	0.0127	0.0063	0.0104	0.0021	0.0041	0.0061	0.0020	0.0101	0.0060	0.0080	1942	0.0929
1943	0.0000	0.0020	0.0158	0.0116	0.0077	−0.0019	−0.0076	−0.0038	0.0039	0.0038	−0.0019	0.0019	1943	0.0316
1944	−0.0019	−0.0019	0.0000	0.0058	0.0038	0.0019	0.0057	0.0038	0.0000	0.0000	0.0000	0.0038	1944	0.0211
1945	0.0000	−0.0019	0.0000	0.0019	0.0075	0.0093	0.0018	0.0000	−0.0037	0.0000	0.0037	0.0037	1945	0.0225
1946	0.0000	−0.0037	0.0074	0.0055	0.0055	0.0109	0.0590	0.0220	0.0116	0.0196	0.0240	0.0078	1946	0.1816
1947	0.0000	−0.0016	0.0218	0.0000	−0.0030	0.0076	0.0091	0.0105	0.0238	0.0000	0.0058	0.0130	1947	0.0901
1948	0.0114	−0.0085	−0.0028	0.0142	0.0070	0.0070	0.0125	0.0041	0.0000	−0.0041	−0.0068	−0.0069	1948	0.0271
1949	−0.0014	−0.0111	0.0028	0.0014	−0.0014	0.0014	−0.0070	0.0028	0.0042	−0.0056	0.0014	−0.0056	1949	−0.0180
1950	−0.0042	−0.0028	0.0043	0.0014	0.0042	0.0056	0.0098	0.0083	0.0069	0.0055	0.0041	0.0135	1950	0.0579
1951	0.0160	0.0118	0.0039	0.0013	0.0039	−0.0013	0.0013	0.0000	0.0064	0.0051	0.0051	0.0038	1951	0.0587
1952	0.0000	−0.0063	0.0000	0.0038	0.0013	0.0025	0.0076	0.0012	−0.0012	0.0012	0.0000	−0.0012	1952	0.0088
1953	−0.0025	−0.0050	0.0025	0.0013	0.0025	0.0038	0.0025	0.0025	0.0012	0.0025	−0.0037	−0.0012	1953	0.0062
1954	0.0025	−0.0012	−0.0012	−0.0025	0.0037	0.0012	0.0000	−0.0012	−0.0025	−0.0025	0.0012	−0.0025	1954	−0.0050
1955	0.0000	0.0000	0.0000	0.0000	0.0000	0.0000	0.0037	−0.0025	0.0037	0.0000	0.0012	−0.0025	1955	0.0037
1956	−0.0012	0.0000	0.0012	0.0012	0.0050	0.0062	0.0074	−0.0012	0.0012	0.0061	0.0000	0.0024	1956	0.0286
1957	0.0012	0.0036	0.0024	0.0036	0.0024	0.0060	0.0047	0.0012	0.0012	0.0000	0.0035	0.0000	1957	0.0302
1958	0.0059	0.0012	0.0070	0.0023	0.0000	0.0012	0.0012	−0.0012	0.0000	0.0000	0.0012	−0.0012	1958	0.0176
1959	0.0012	−0.0012	0.0000	0.0012	0.0012	0.0046	0.0023	−0.0011	0.0034	0.0034	0.0000	0.0000	1959	0.0150
1960	−0.0011	0.0011	0.0000	0.0057	0.0000	0.0023	0.0000	0.0000	0.0011	0.0045	0.0011	0.0000	1960	0.0148
1961	0.0000	0.0000	0.0000	0.0000	0.0000	0.0011	0.0045	−0.0011	0.0022	0.0000	0.0000	0.0000	1961	0.0067
1962	0.0000	0.0022	0.0022	0.0022	0.0000	0.0000	0.0022	0.0000	0.0055	−0.0011	0.0000	−0.0011	1962	0.0122
1963	0.0011	0.0011	0.0011	0.0000	0.0000	0.0044	0.0044	0.0000	0.0000	0.0011	0.0011	0.0022	1963	0.0165
1964	0.0011	−0.0011	0.0011	0.0011	0.0000	0.0022	0.0022	−0.0011	0.0022	0.0011	0.0021	0.0011	1964	0.0119
1965	0.0000	0.0000	0.0011	0.0032	0.0021	0.0053	0.0011	−0.0021	0.0021	0.0011	0.0021	0.0032	1965	0.0192
1966	0.0000	0.0063	0.0031	0.0042	0.0010	0.0031	0.0031	0.0051	0.0020	0.0041	0.0000	0.0010	1966	0.0335
1967	0.0000	0.0010	0.0020	0.0020	0.0030	0.0030	0.0050	0.0030	0.0020	0.0030	0.0030	0.0030	1967	0.0304
1968	0.0039	0.0029	0.0049	0.0029	0.0029	0.0058	0.0048	0.0029	0.0029	0.0057	0.0038	0.0028	1968	0.0472
1969	0.0028	0.0037	0.0084	0.0065	0.0028	0.0064	0.0046	0.0045	0.0045	0.0036	0.0054	0.0062	1969	0.0611
1970	0.0035	0.0053	0.0053	0.0061	0.0043	0.0052	0.0034	0.0017	0.0051	0.0051	0.0034	0.0051	1970	0.0549

*Compound annual return

Table B–15 (continued)

Inflation

from January 1971 to December 2002

Year	Jan	Feb	Mar	Apr	May	Jun	Jul	Aug	Sep	Oct	Nov	Dec	Year	Jan–Dec*
1971	0.0008	0.0017	0.0033	0.0033	0.0050	0.0058	0.0025	0.0025	0.0008	0.0016	0.0016	0.0041	1971	0.0336
1972	0.0008	0.0049	0.0016	0.0024	0.0032	0.0024	0.0040	0.0016	0.0040	0.0032	0.0024	0.0032	1972	0.0341
1973	0.0031	0.0070	0.0093	0.0069	0.0061	0.0068	0.0023	0.0181	0.0030	0.0081	0.0073	0.0065	1973	0.0880
1974	0.0087	0.0129	0.0113	0.0056	0.0111	0.0096	0.0075	0.0128	0.0120	0.0086	0.0085	0.0071	1974	0.1220
1975	0.0045	0.0070	0.0038	0.0051	0.0044	0.0082	0.0106	0.0031	0.0049	0.0061	0.0061	0.0042	1975	0.0701
1976	0.0024	0.0024	0.0024	0.0042	0.0059	0.0053	0.0059	0.0047	0.0041	0.0041	0.0029	0.0029	1976	0.0481
1977	0.0057	0.0103	0.0062	0.0079	0.0056	0.0066	0.0044	0.0038	0.0038	0.0027	0.0049	0.0038	1977	0.0677
1978	0.0054	0.0069	0.0069	0.0090	0.0099	0.0103	0.0072	0.0051	0.0071	0.0080	0.0055	0.0055	1978	0.0903
1979	0.0089	0.0117	0.0097	0.0115	0.0123	0.0093	0.0130	0.0100	0.0104	0.0090	0.0093	0.0105	1979	0.1331
1980	0.0144	0.0137	0.0144	0.0113	0.0099	0.0110	0.0008	0.0065	0.0092	0.0087	0.0091	0.0086	1980	0.1240
1981	0.0081	0.0104	0.0072	0.0064	0.0082	0.0086	0.0114	0.0077	0.0101	0.0021	0.0029	0.0029	1981	0.0894
1982	0.0036	0.0032	−0.0011	0.0042	0.0098	0.0122	0.0055	0.0021	0.0017	0.0027	−0.0017	−0.0041	1982	0.0387
1983	0.0024	0.0003	0.0007	0.0072	0.0054	0.0034	0.0040	0.0033	0.0050	0.0027	0.0017	0.0013	1983	0.0380
1984	0.0056	0.0046	0.0023	0.0049	0.0029	0.0032	0.0032	0.0042	0.0048	0.0025	0.0000	0.0006	1984	0.0395
1985	0.0019	0.0041	0.0044	0.0041	0.0037	0.0031	0.0016	0.0022	0.0031	0.0031	0.0034	0.0025	1985	0.0377
1986	0.0031	−0.0027	−0.0046	−0.0021	0.0031	0.0049	0.0003	0.0018	0.0049	0.0009	0.0009	0.0009	1986	0.0113
1987	0.0060	0.0039	0.0045	0.0054	0.0030	0.0041	0.0021	0.0056	0.0050	0.0026	0.0014	−0.0003	1987	0.0441
1988	0.0026	0.0026	0.0043	0.0052	0.0034	0.0043	0.0042	0.0042	0.0067	0.0033	0.0008	0.0017	1988	0.0442
1989	0.0050	0.0041	0.0058	0.0065	0.0057	0.0024	0.0024	0.0016	0.0032	0.0048	0.0024	0.0016	1989	0.0465
1990	0.0103	0.0047	0.0055	0.0016	0.0023	0.0054	0.0038	0.0092	0.0084	0.0060	0.0022	0.0000	1990	0.0611
1991	0.0060	0.0015	0.0015	0.0015	0.0030	0.0029	0.0015	0.0029	0.0044	0.0015	0.0029	0.0007	1991	0.0306
1992	0.0015	0.0036	0.0051	0.0014	0.0014	0.0036	0.0021	0.0028	0.0028	0.0035	0.0014	−0.0007	1992	0.0290
1993	0.0049	0.0035	0.0035	0.0028	0.0014	0.0014	0.0000	0.0028	0.0021	0.0041	0.0007	0.0000	1993	0.0275
1994	0.0027	0.0034	0.0034	0.0014	0.0007	0.0034	0.0027	0.0040	0.0027	0.0007	0.0013	0.0000	1994	0.0267
1995	0.0040	0.0040	0.0033	0.0033	0.0020	0.0020	0.0000	0.0026	0.0020	0.0033	−0.0007	−0.0007	1995	0.0254
1996	0.0059	0.0032	0.0052	0.0039	0.0019	0.0006	0.0019	0.0019	0.0032	0.0032	0.0019	0.0000	1996	0.0332
1997	0.0032	0.0031	0.0025	0.0013	−0.0006	0.0012	0.0012	0.0019	0.0025	0.0025	−0.0006	−0.0012	1997	0.0170
1998	0.0019	0.0019	0.0019	0.0018	0.0018	0.0012	0.0012	0.0012	0.0012	0.0024	0.0000	−0.0006	1998	0.0161
1999	0.0024	0.0012	0.0030	0.0073	0.0000	0.0000	0.0030	0.0024	0.0048	0.0018	0.0006	0.0000	1999	0.0268
2000	0.0024	0.0059	0.0082	0.0006	0.0006	0.0058	0.0017	0.0012	0.0052	0.0017	0.0006	−0.0006	2000	0.0339
2001	0.0063	0.0040	0.0023	0.0040	0.0045	0.0017	−0.0028	0.0000	0.0045	−0.0034	−0.0017	−0.0039	2001	0.0155
2002	0.0023	0.0040	0.0056	0.0056	0.0000	0.0006	0.0011	0.0033	0.0017	0.0017	0.0000	−0.0022	2002	0.0238

*Compound annual return

Stocks, Bonds, Bills, and Inflation

Valuation Edition

Yields Riskless

Fixed Income

Equity Risk Prem

Size Premia

Appendix C

IbbotsonAssociates

Appendix C
Key Variables in Estimating the Cost of Capital

Key Variables in Estimating the Cost of Capital

Table C-1

Key Variables in Estimating the Cost of Capital

	Value
Yields (Riskless Rates)[1]	
Long-term (20-year) U.S. Treasury Coupon Bond Yield	4.8%
Intermediate-term (5-year) U.S. Treasury Coupon Note Yield	2.6
Short-term (30-day) U.S. Treasury Bill Yield	1.2
Equity Risk Premium[2]	
Long-horizon expected equity risk premium: large company stock total return minus long-term government bond income returns	7.0
Intermediate-horizon expected equity risk premium: large company stock total returns minus intermediate-term government bond income returns	7.4
Short-horizon expected equity risk premium: large company stock total returns minus U.S. Treasury bill total returns	8.4

Size Premium[3]

Decile	Market Capitalization of Smallest Company (in millions)		Market Capitalization of Largest Company (in millions)	Size Premium (Return in Excess of CAPM)
Mid-Cap, 3-5	$1,144.452	-	$5,012.705	0.82%
Low-Cap, 6-8	$314.174	-	$1,143.845	1.52
Micro-Cap, 9-10	$0.501	-	$314.042	3.53
Breakdown of Deciles 1-10				
1-Largest	$11,636.618	-	$293,137.304	−0.32
2	$5,018.316	-	$11,628.735	0.42
3	$2,686.479	-	$5,012.705	0.66
4	$1,691.463	-	$2,680.573	0.95
5	$1,144.452	-	$1,691.210	1.16
6	$791.917	-	$1,143.845	1.48
7	$521.400	-	$791.336	1.35
8	$314.174	-	$521.298	2.06
9	$141.529	-	$314.042	2.56
10-Smallest	$0.501	-	$141.459	5.67
Breakdown of the 10th Decile				
10a	$64.798	-	$141.459	3.98
10b	$0.501	-	$64.767	9.16

[1] As of December 31, 2002. Maturities are approximate.

[2] Expected risk premia for equities are based on the differences of historical arithmetic mean returns from 1926–2002 using the S&P 500 as the market benchmark.

[3] See chapter 7 for complete methodology.

Note: Examples on how these variables can be used are found in Chapters 3 and 4

Stocks, Bonds, Bills, and Inflation
Valuation Edition

Volatility \,vä-lə-'ti-lə-tē\
1: The extent to which an asse
returns fluctuate from period
period.

Glossary

IbbotsonAssociates

Glossary

American Stock Exchange (AMEX)

One of the largest stock exchanges in the U.S. Securities traded on this exchange are generally of small- to medium-sized companies.

Arbitrage Pricing Theory (APT)

A model in which multiple betas and multiple risk premia are used to generate the expected return of a security.

Arithmetic Mean Return

A simple average of a series of returns.

Beta

A measure of a security's sensitivity to the market, that is otherwise known as its systematic risk. The systematic risk of a security is estimated by regressing the security's excess returns against the market portfolio's excess returns. The slope of the regression equation is the beta.

Bid-Ask Spread

Represents the difference between the highest price a prospective buyer is prepared to pay (bid) and the lowest price the seller is willing to take (ask).

Capital Appreciation Return

The component of total return that results from the price change of an asset class over a given period.

Capital Asset Pricing Model (CAPM)

A model in which the cost of capital for any security or portfolio of securities equals the riskless rate plus a risk premium that is proportionate to the amount of systematic risk of the security or portfolio.

Capitalization Weighted

The weight of each stock in a return index or other average is proportionate to its market capitalization (price times number of shares outstanding).

Correlation Coefficient

The degree of association or strength between two variables. A value of +1 indicates a perfectly positive relationship, −1 indicates a perfectly inverse relationship, and 0 indicates no relationship between the variables.

Cost of Capital

The discount rate that should be used to derive the present value of an asset's future cash flows.

Coupon

The periodic interest payment on a bond, usually semi-annual.

Decile

One of 10 portfolios formed by ranking a set of securities by some criteria and dividing them into 10 equally populated subsets. The New York Stock Exchange market capitalization deciles are formed by ranking the stocks traded on the Exchange by their market capitalization.

Discount Rate

The rate used to convert a series of future cash flows to a single present value.

Equity Risk Premium

The additional return an investor expects to compensate for the additional risk associated with investing in equities as opposed to investing in a riskless asset.

Free Cash Flow

Total amount of cash that can be generated by an entity, or the amount of cash that can potentially flow to the stakeholders of a company.

Geometric Mean Return

The compound rate of return. The geometric mean of a return series is a measure of the actual average performance of a portfolio over a given time period.

Histogram

A bar graph in which the frequency of occurrence for each class of data is represented by the relative height of the bars.

Income Return

The component of total return that results from a periodic cash flow, such as dividends or coupon payments.

Index Value

The cumulative value of returns on a dollar amount invested. It is used when measuring investment performance and computing returns over non-calendar periods.

Inflation

The rate of change in consumer prices. The Consumer Price Index for All Urban Consumers (CPI-U), not seasonally adjusted, is used to measure inflation. Prior to January 1978, the CPI (as compared with CPI-U was used. Both inflation measures are constructed by the U.S. Department of Labor, Bureau of Labor Statistics, Washington.

Inflation-Adjusted Returns

Returns in real terms. The inflation-adjusted return of an asset is calculated by geometrically subtracting inflation from the asset's nominal return.

Intermediate-Term Government Bonds

A one-bond portfolio with a maturity near five years. From 1987 to the present the portfolio is constructed with data from *The Wall Street Journal*. The bond used in 2002 is the 6.125-percent issue that matures in August 2007. Returns from 1934–1986 are obtained from the CRSP Government Bond File. Over 1926–1933, few suitable bonds were available. Estimates were obtained from Thomas S. Coleman, Lawrence Fisher, and Roger G. Ibbotson, *Historical U.S. Treasury Yield Curves*.

January Effect

The empirical regularity with which rates of return for small stocks have historically been higher in January than in the other months of the year.

Levered Beta

Measures the systematic risk for the equity shareholders of a company and is therefore commonly referred to as the equity beta. It is measured directly from the company's returns with no adjustment made for debt financing undertaken by the company.

Logarithmic Scale

A scale in which equal percentage changes are represented by equal distances.

Lognormal Distribution

The distribution of a random variable whose natural logarithm is normally distributed. A lognormal distribution is skewed so that a higher proportion of possible returns exceed the expected value versus falling short of the expected value.

Long-Term Corporate Bonds

Salomon Brothers long-term, high-grade corporate bond total return index.

Long-Term Government Bonds

A one-bond portfolio with a maturity near 20 years. From 1977 to the present the portfolio is constructed with data from *The Wall Street Journal*. The bond used in 2002 is the 6.25-percent issue that matures on August 15, 2023. The data from 1926–1976 are obtained from the Government Bond File at the Center for Research in Security Prices (CRSP) at the University of Chicago Graduate School of Business.

Low-Cap Stocks

The portfolio of stocks comprised of the 6th-8th deciles of the New York Stock Exchange.

Market Capitalization

The current market price of a security determined by the most recently recorded trade multiplied by the number of issues outstanding of that security. For equities, market capitalization is computed by taking the share price of a stock times the number of shares outstanding.

Micro-Cap Stocks

The portfolio of stocks comprised of the 9th-10th deciles of the New York Stock Exchange.

Mid-Cap Stocks

The portfolio of stocks comprised of the 3rd-5th deciles of the New York Stock Exchange.

National Association of Securities Dealers Automated Quotation System (NASDAQ)

A computerized system showing current bid and ask prices for stocks traded on the Over-the-Counter market, as well as some New York Stock Exchange listed stocks.

New York Stock Exchange (NYSE)

The largest and oldest stock exchange in the United States, founded in 1792.

Nominal Return

The return on an investment in absolute terms. It measures the total growth of an investment.

R-squared

Measures the "goodness of fit" of the regression line and describes the percentage of variation in the dependent variable that is explained by the independent variable. The R-squared measure may vary from zero to one.

Real Return

The inflation-adjusted return on an investment. It measures the growth of purchasing power. The real return of an investment is calculated by geometrically subtracting inflation from the investment's nominal return.

Reinvestment Return

The return from investing income from a given month into the same asset class in the subsequent months within the year.

Risk

The extent to which an investment is subject to uncertainty. Total risk may be measured by standard deviation. Systematic risk, or market risk, is measured by beta.

Risk Premium

The reward that investors require to accept the uncertain outcomes associated with securities. The size of the risk premium will depend upon the type and extent of the risk.

Riskless Rate of Return

The return on a riskless investment; it is the rate of return an investor can obtain without taking market risk.

Rolling Period

A series of overlapping contiguous periods defined by the frequency of the data under examination. In examining 5-year rolling periods for annual data that starts in 1970, the first rolling period would be 1970-1974, the second rolling period would be 1971-1975, the third rolling period would be 1972-1976, etc.

S&P 500®

Based upon the S&P Composite Index. Data from September 1997 to the present are obtained directly from Standard and Poor's, while data from 1977 to August 1997 are obtained from the American National Bank and Trust Company of Chicago, which modified monthly income numbers provided by Wilshire Associates, Santa Monica, CA. Prior to 1977, the total return for a given month was calculated by summing the capital appreciation return and the income return found in S&P's *Trade and Securities Statistics*. Currently, the S&P Composite includes 500 of the largest stocks (in terms of stock market value) in the United States; prior to March 1957, it consisted of 90 of the largest stocks.

Serial Correlation (Autocorrelation)

The degree to which the return of a given series is related from period to period. A serial correlation near +1 or −1 indicates that returns are predictable from one period to the next; a serial correlation near zero indicates returns are random or unpredictable.

Size Premium

The return on small company stocks in excess of that predicted by the CAPM. It is the additional return that cannot be explained by the betas of small companies.

Standard Deviation

A measure of the dispersion of returns of an asset, or the extent to which returns vary from the arithmetic mean. It represents the volatility or risk of an asset. The greater the degree of dispersion, the greater the risk associated with the asset.

Standard Error

Measures the extent to which each individual observation in a sample differs from the value predicted by the regression.

Systematic Risk

The risk that is unavoidable according to CAPM. It is the risk that is common to all risky securities and cannot be eliminated through diversification. The amount of an asset's systematic risk is measured by its beta.

t-Statistic

Indicates whether the beta coefficient is statistically different than zero at a certain confidence level.

Total Return

A measure of performance of an asset class over a designated time period. It is comprised of income return, reinvestment of income return, and capital appreciation return components.

Treasury Bills

A one-bill portfolio containing, at the beginning of each month, the bill having the shortest maturity not less than one month. *The Wall Street Journal* is used for 1977 to the present; the Center for Research in Security Prices U.S. Government Bond File is the source until 1976.

Unlevered Beta

Also known as the asset beta, it removes a company's financing decision from the beta calculation. In other words, the unlevered beta represents the risk of the firm, not including the risks implicit in the financial structure of the company.

Unsystematic Risk

The portion of total risk specific to an individual security that can be avoided through diversification.

Volatility

The extent to which an asset's returns fluctuate from period to period.

Weighted Average Cost of Capital (WACC)

The discount rate that should be used to derive the present value of a company's future cash flows. It is the average required rate of return of all the company's financing, equity, debt, and preferred stock, weighted in proportion to the company's total invested capital.

Yield

The internal rate of return that equates the bond's price with the stream of cash flows promised to the bondholder. The yield on a stock is the percentage rate of return paid in dividends.

Stocks, Bonds, Bills, and Inflation

Valuation Edition

Index

IbbotsonAssociates

Index

The Cost of Capital Center
A Special Web Site for Valuation Professionals

The Cost of Capital Center at www.ibbotson.com offers domestic and international data available for download, including:

- **Industry Analysis** is available on over 300 industries and contains the same extensive analysis as the Cost of Capital Yearbook including: industry betas, multiples, cost of equity estimates and much more.
  $50 per industry

- **Individual Company** Betas can be purchased from the Beta Book database of more than 5,000 companies.
  $15 per company

- **Individual Tax Rates** are available for over 5,000 companies. **$15** per company

- **International Cost of Capital Report** contains up to six cost of equity estimates for over 145 countries from the perspective of U.S. investors. **$200**

- **Internatinal Cost of Capital Perspectives Report** contains cost of equity estimates for over 145 countries from the perspective of international investors. **$100**

- **The Risk Premia over Time Report** provides equity and size premia over your choice of historical time periods from 1926-2002. **$100**

- **Standard and Poor's Corporate Value Consulting Risk Premium Report** offers analysis on 25 size groups for use with the buildup approach. **$100**

- **Ibbotson's International Equity Risk Premia Report** contains historical equity risk premia for 16 countries. **$100**

- **The Canadian Risk Premia over Time Report** provides equity risk premia over your choice of historical time periods dating back to 1936. **$75**

- **The U.K. Risk Premia over Time Report** provides equity risk premia over your choice of historical time periods dating back to 1919. **$75**

2003 Cost of Capital Yearbook

Providing data on over 300 industries, the Cost of Capital Yearbook is an invaluable reference for anyone performing discounted cash flow analysis. The yearbook contains critical statistics you need to analyze corporations and industries and includes:

- Five separate measures of cost of equity.

- Weighted average cost of capital.

- Detailed statistics for sales, profitability, capitalization, beta, multiples, ratios, equity returns and capital structure.

Published annually, the Cost of Capital Yearbook is updated with data through March 2003. For the most frequent data available, subscribe to the Cost of Capital Yearbook with Cost of Capital Quarterly™ updates.

Cost of Capital Yearbook with 3 Quarterly Updates $995
Cost of Capital Yearbook $395 (Shipped in June)

Ibbotson Beta Book

The Beta Book is an invaluable resource for modeling stock performance and accurately pricing securities. With data on over 5,000 companies, the book provides statistics critical for calculating cost of equity with the CAPM and the Fama-French 3-factor model. Employing the most current methods, the Beta Book contains traditional 60-month levered beta calculations, unlevered betas, and betas adjusted toward peer group averages. Published semi-annually, the First Edition provides data through December 2002 and the Second Edition provides data through June 2003.

2003 First Edition $625 (Shipped in February)
2003 Second Edition $625 (Shipped in August)
Both Editions $1,000

2003 Stocks, Bonds, Bills, and Inflation® Classic Edition Yearbook

Since its publication over twenty-five years ago, thousands of finance and investment professionals have depended on the Stocks, Bonds, Bills, and Inflation (SBBI®) Yearbook for the most authoritative historical data on U.S. asset classes. The data gives a comprehensive, historical view of the performance of capital markets dating back to 1926. Containing total returns and index values for large and small company stocks, long-term corporate bonds, long- and intermediate-term government bonds, Treasury bills and inflation, the SBBI Yearbook is essential for every financial library.

SBBI Classic Edition Yearbook $110

SBBI Report Subscriptions

Receive the most up-to-date data available when you subscribe to our SBBI reports on a monthly, quarterly or semi-annual basis. The SBBI reports contain year-to-date data on a calendar year basis. These reports feature:

- Updated returns and index values available on a monthly basis for six U.S. asset classes plus inflation.

- Inflation-adjusted returns and index values plus other derived series.

- Quarterly updates to the Stocks, Bonds, Bills, and Inflation index graph.

- Market commentary on a semi-annual basis.

- Prompt delivery of time-sensitive market data via fax.

- All report subscriptions include a 2003 Classic Edition Yearbook and can begin at any time throughout the year.

SBBI Classic Edition Yearbook with Monthly Reports* $695
SBBI Classic Edition Yearbook with Quarterly Reports** $280
SBBI Classic Edition Yearbook with Semi-Annual Report*** $160

* Last report ships in December with data through November.
** Last report ships in October with data through September.
*** Report ships in July with data through June.

For more information or to request a product catalog, call 800 758 3557 or visit our web site at **www.ibbotson.com**.

2004 Yearbook ORDER Form

To Order

Call: 800 758 3557
Fax: 312 616 0404
Web: **www.ibbotson.com**
Mail: Ibbotson Associates
225 North Michigan Avenue
Suite 700
Chicago, Illinois 60601-7676
Attn: Order Processing

Item	Price	Quantity	Total
SBBI Valuation Edition 2004 Yearbook (PB120-04)	$110		
	Merchandise Total		
	Add applicable sales tax (IL, NY, TX, AZ, OH, CA, Canada)		
	Shipping and Handling		$12.50
	Special delivery surcharge (see table at left)		
	Total Amount		

code=V3380

For delivery outside the United States and Canada, please add $27.50.

For an extra charge, we can expedite delivery to most U.S. and Canadian destinations.
Overnight delivery add $22.50
Express delivery (2-day) add $12.50

Name

Company

Street Address   Suite/Floor

City   State   Zip

Phone Number

Payment Method

○ Check enclosed, payable to: ○ MasterCard
Ibbotson Associates (in U.S. dollars)
○ American Express   ○ Visa

Card Number

Expiration Date

Signature of Authorized Buyer

IbbotsonAssociates

Key Variables in Estimating the Cost of Capital

	Value
Yields (Riskless Rates)[1]	
Long-term (20-year) U.S. Treasury Coupon Bond Yield	4.8%
Intermediate-term (5-year) U.S. Treasury Coupon Note Yield	2.6
Short-term (30-day) U.S. Treasury Bill Yield	1.2
Equity Risk Premium[2]	
Long-horizon expected equity risk premium: large company stock total return minus long-term government bond income returns	7.0
Intermediate-horizon expected equity risk premium: large company stock total returns minus intermediate-term government bond income returns	7.4
Short-horizon expected equity risk premium: large company stock total returns minus U.S. Treasury bill total returns	8.4

Size Premium[3]

Decile	Market Capitalization of Smallest Company (in millions)		Market Capitalization of Largest Company (in millions)	Size Premium (Return in Excess of CAPM)
Mid-Cap, 3-5	$1,144.452	-	$5,012.705	0.82%
Low-Cap, 6-8	$314.174	-	$1,143.845	1.52
Micro-Cap, 9-10	$0.501	-	$314.042	3.53
Breakdown of Deciles 1-10				
1-Largest	$11,636.618	-	$293,137.304	−0.32
2	$5,018.316	-	$11,628.735	0.42
3	$2,686.479	-	$5,012.705	0.66
4	$1,691.463	-	$2,680.573	0.95
5	$1,144.452	-	$1,691.210	1.16
6	$791.917	-	$1,143.845	1.48
7	$521.400	-	$791.336	1.35
8	$314.174	-	$521.298	2.06
9	$141.529	-	$314.042	2.56
10-Smallest	$0.501	-	$141.459	5.67
Breakdown of the 10th Decile				
10a	$64.798	-	$141.459	3.98
10b	$0.501	-	$64.767	9.16

[1] As of December 31, 2002. Maturities are approximate.

[2] Expected risk premia for equities are based on the differences of historical arithmetic mean returns from 1926–2002 using the S&P 500 as the market benchmark.

[3] See chapter 7 for complete methodology.

Note: Examples on how these variables can be used are found in Chapters 3 and 4